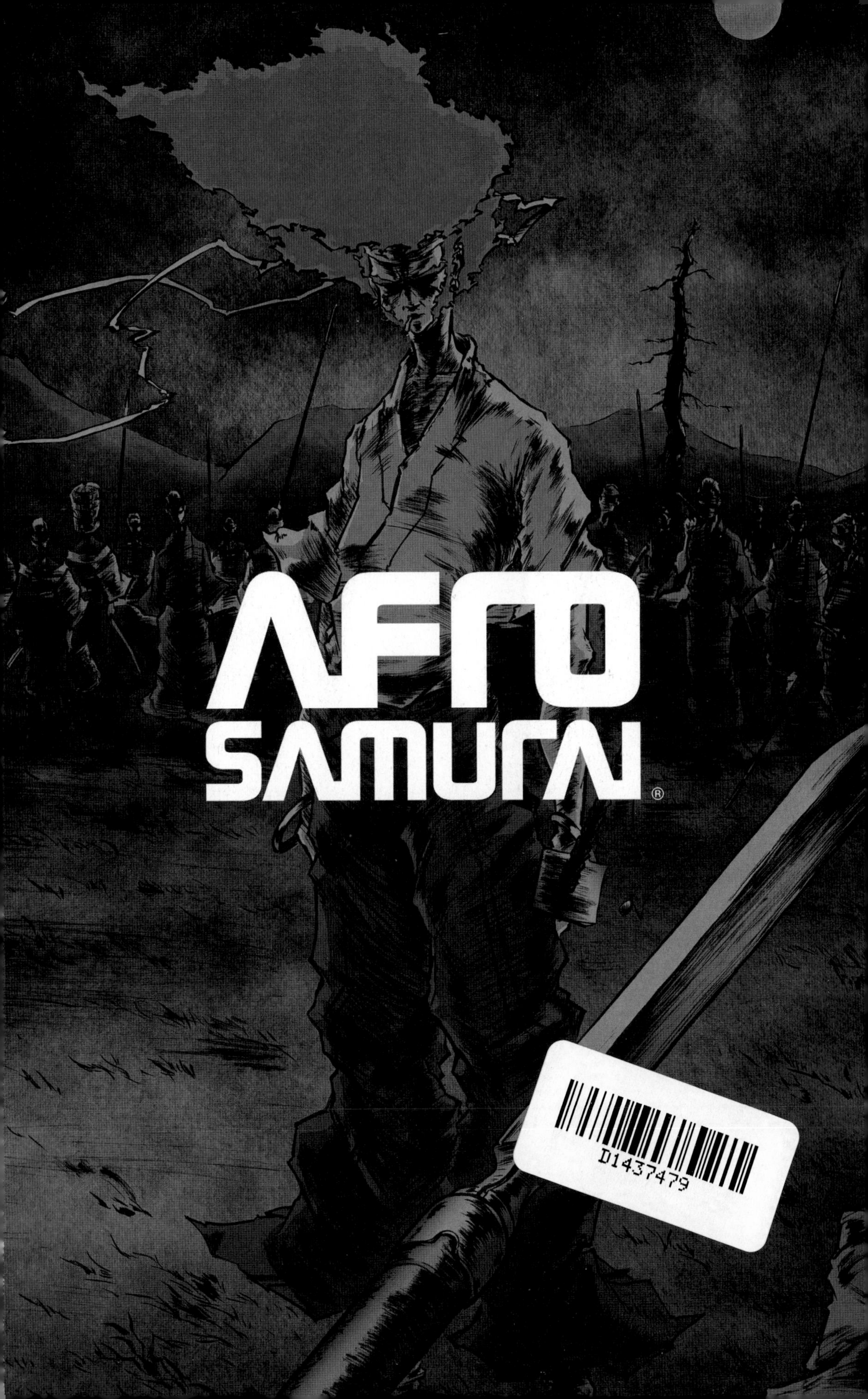
AFRO
SAMURAI®
D1437479

TITAN COMICS

GROUP EDITOR / Jake Devine

DESIGNER / Donna Askem

EDITOR / Phoebe Hedges

EDITORIAL ASSISTANT / Calum Collins

SENIOR CREATIVE EDITOR / David Leach

ART DIRECTOR / Oz Browne

PRODUCTION CONTROLLERS / Caterina Falqui & Kelly Fenlon

PRODUCTION MANAGER / Jackie Flook

SALES & CIRCULATION MANAGER / Steve Tothill

MARKETING COORDINATOR / Lauren Noding

DIGITAL AND MARKETING MANAGER / Jo Teather

PUBLICIST / Will O'Mullane

HEAD OF RIGHTS / Jenny Boyce

ACQUISITIONS EDITOR / Duncan Baizley

PUBLISHING DIRECTORS / Ricky Claydon & John Dziewiatkowski

OPERATIONS DIRECTOR / Leigh Baulch

PUBLISHERS / Vivian Cheung & Nick Landau

Afro Samurai Volume 1
ISBN: 9781787739000
Diamond Edition ISBN: 9781787739932

© 2008 TAKASHI OKAZAKI, GONZO. All rights reserved.
Published by Titan Comics, a division of Titan Publishing
Group, Ltd, 144 Southwark Street, SE1 0UP, London, UK.

Original translation by Greg Moore and Joshua Fialkov. Used
with the permission of Seven Seas Entertainment. Special
thanks to Adam Arnold and Julie Davis.

10 9 8 7 6 5 4 3 2 1

First printed in Spain in August 2022.
A CIP catalogue record for this title is available from the British Library.

www.titan-comics.com

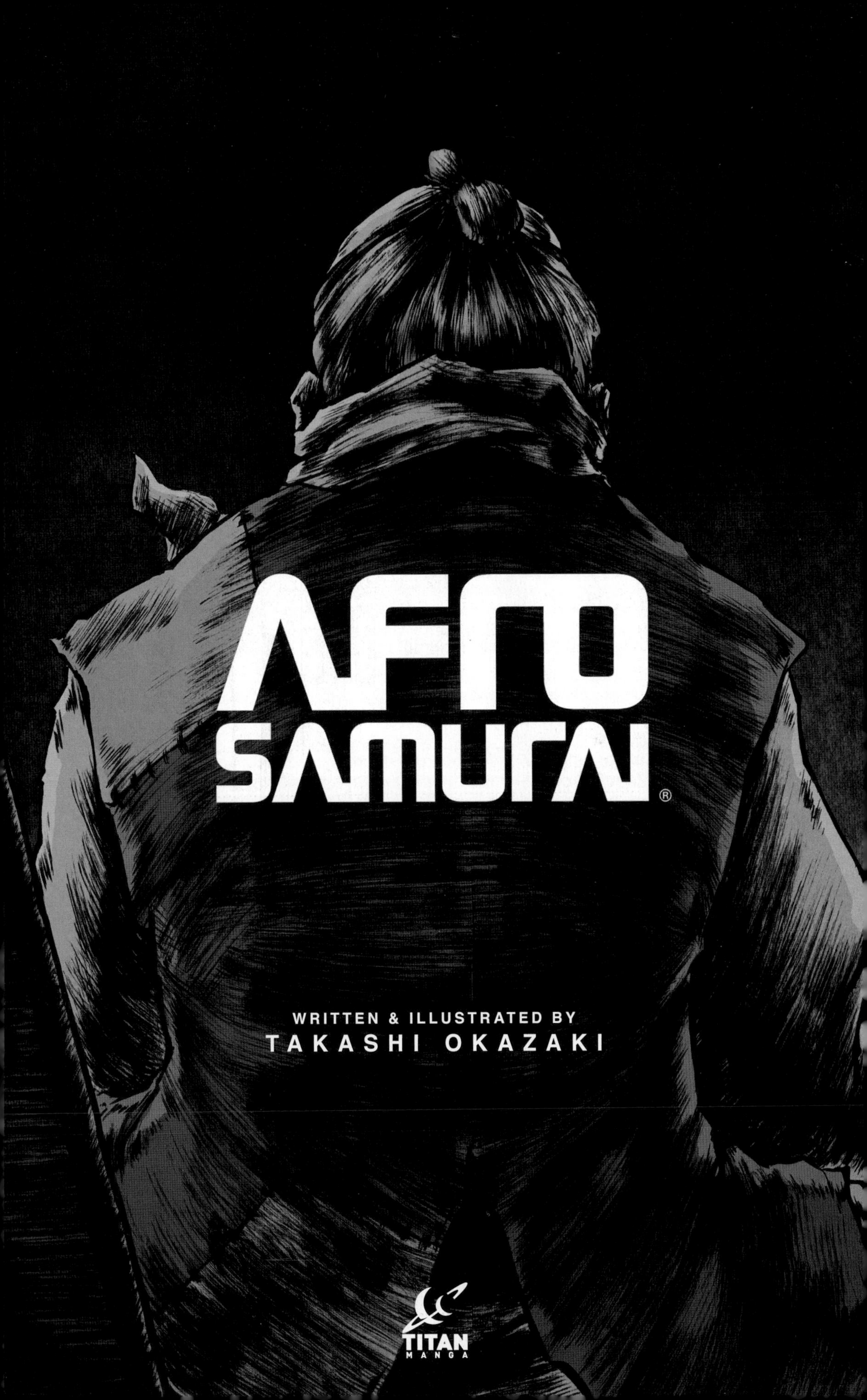

AFRO SAMURAI®

WRITTEN & ILLUSTRATED BY
TAKASHI OKAZAKI

TITAN
MANGA

When I was just starting out as an illustrator, I was frustrated by the lack of opportunities. It was 1998 and I was rolling with other illustrators of the same age who were in a similar situation, so I thought, "Well then, let's just spend our own money and draw what we want to draw!" That's when I started the doujinshi magazine *NOU NOU HAU*. Back then, opportunities to showcase my art on social media or the internet were limited, so I published my work in print at my own expense. We didn't have a lot of money, so we were all having to work part-time as well.

Afro Samurai was born from a doodle I used to draw when I was an art student. At first the characters were more pop and illustrative, but I was really into the US TV show *Soul Train* from the '70s at the time, and Don Cornelius and the Soul Train Gang were really cool, so I thought, "I'll draw a cool Afro!" So, the idea was born from love for that show.

I wanted to create work that was my own, without being bound to any specific influences. Although inspiration came from everywhere – from *Star Wars* to *The Prisoner* – and not just movies and manga, but music in general and especially hip hop.

While drawing *Afro Samurai*, I was listening to J Dilla, Pete Rock, Nas, Gang Star, Black Star, Wu Tang Clan, Marley Marl, A Tribe Called Quest, Slum Village, Public Enemy, DJ Jazzy Jeff, Mad Lib… too many to list here!

Seeing *Do the Right Thing* when I was in high school also had a huge impact on me. It was both a shocking and great movie in many ways, but there were things that most Japanese high-school students didn't understand or appreciate. I liked hip hop before that, but it was this movie that got me interested in its culture and historical background.

Film-makers such as Kenji Misumi, Akira Kurosawa, Alejandro Jodorowsky, and Sergio Leone were big influences, but it was a Panasonic TV commercial from 1988 with George Lucas that strangely made the biggest impression. The end line was "*Always something new*". That became my motto.

The idea of blending a historical setting with futuristic elements came from my childhood love of period dramas, which I always saw as vivid fantasies, rather than just the past being vaguely connected to the present. My thinking was strongly influenced by the art of the samurai in *Wizardry*, *Dungeons & Dragons*, and the *Fighting Fantasy* game books. So, in my mind, the worlds of science fiction and historical drama naturally merged.

And the coolest characters always seemed to be the lone warrior or samurai archetype, and I guess that my favourites – such as Sweetback from *Sweet Sweetback's Baadasssss Song* – all came together in my head to create this ideal Afro character.

I had no idea how iconic he'd become. I just created what I wanted to see! I never thought that something so personal would be enjoyed by so many people, and I feel fortunate that so many have embraced it. "*Always something new*"! I did what I wanted to do for fun without thinking about it.

Afro Samurai is perceived differently in Japan, where it's only known by those familiar with anime and manga, as opposed to overseas, where it sits alongside other major titles. So, I

hope this work has triggered an interest in Japanese culture and helped show that manga and anime are not just for kids, but can be gateways to an incredibly deep and diverse universe that becomes even more interesting the deeper you dig. And as a creator, it is the greatest joy to have work that genuinely depicts something I love accepted by people all over the world. To have Samuel L. Jackson and the RZA's approval is the greatest thrill!

I would also like to thank Titan Comics, as ever since I first drew this manga I've wanted to see it published in a larger format. And now, after many years, my dream has finally come true. It may have been the first full-length book I created but looking back on it now I can be more objectively critical. I think my drawing is better now than it was, but I remember thinking back then, "I don't really understand the logic behind this, but I'll draw it with passion and vigor!" I don't think I'd be able to capture the feeling I had then again, so I'm very happy to have this new book published now.

And 25 years later, drawing Afro is still fun! He was originally my life's work, and the story that is now out in the world again is only a small part of the *Afro Samurai* chronology that I created decades ago, so I want to publish more as soon as possible!

Takashi Okazaki,
Tokyo, 2022

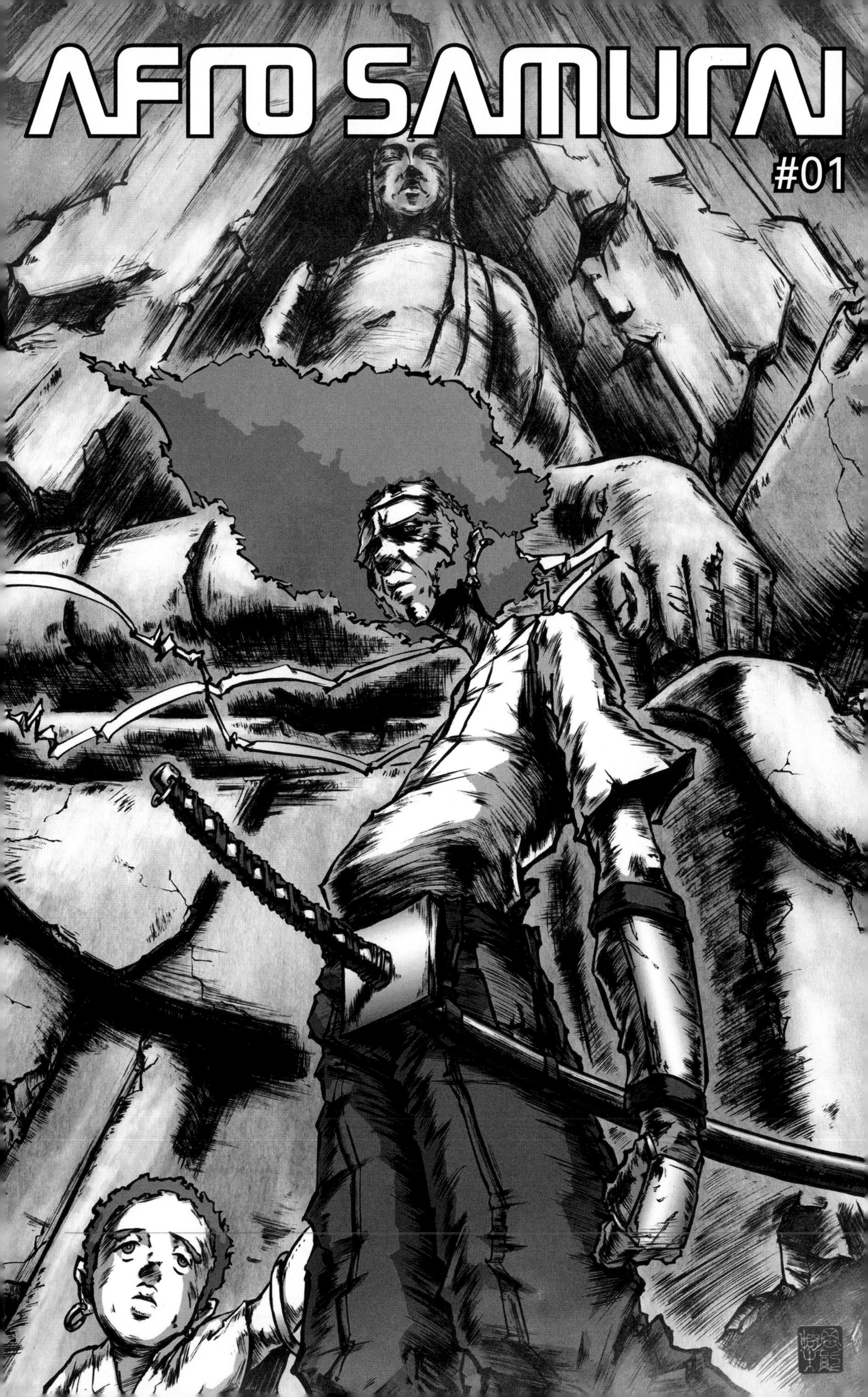
AFRO SAMURAI
#01

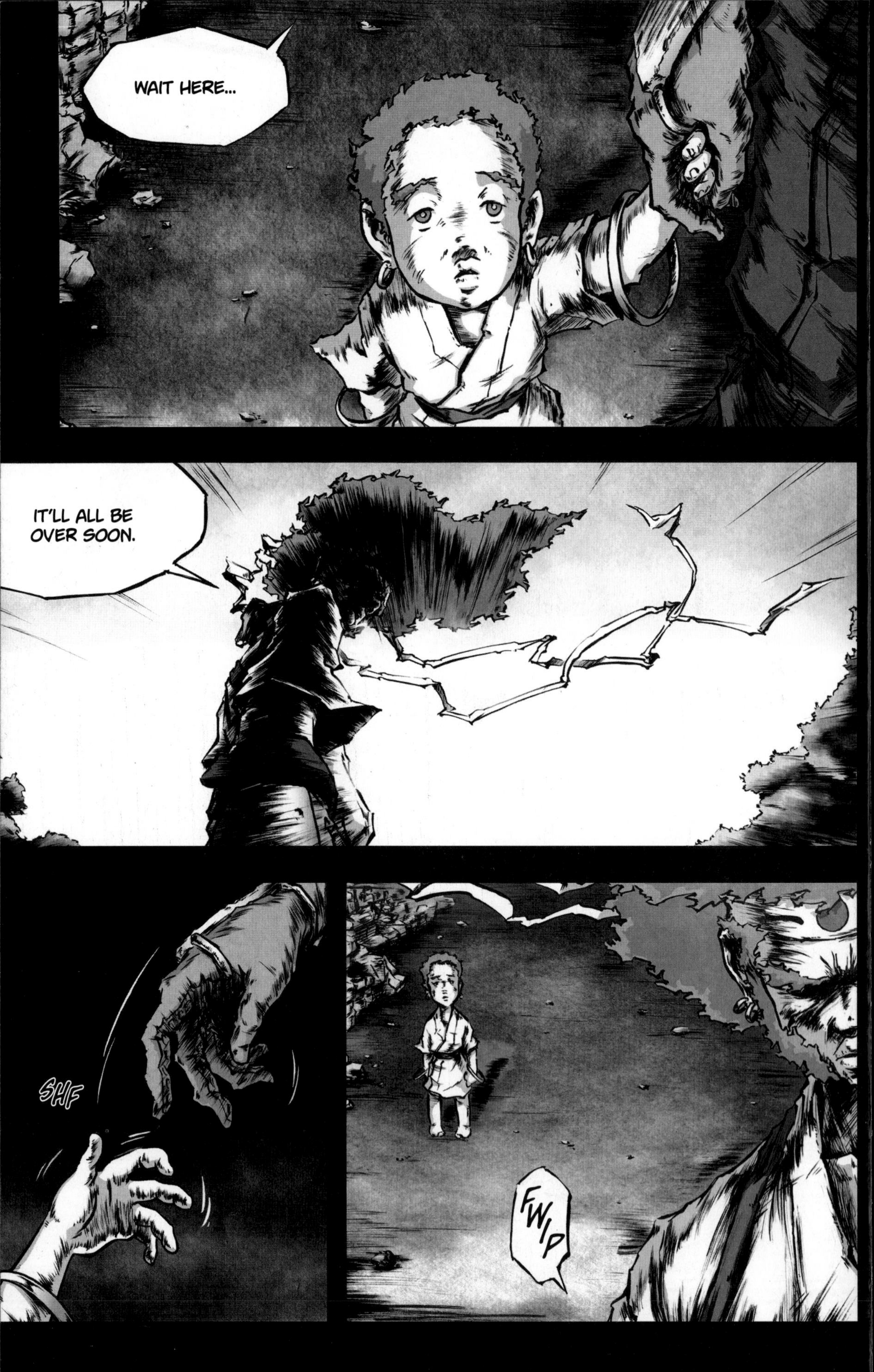
WAIT HERE...
IT'LL ALL BE OVER SOON.
SHF
FWIP

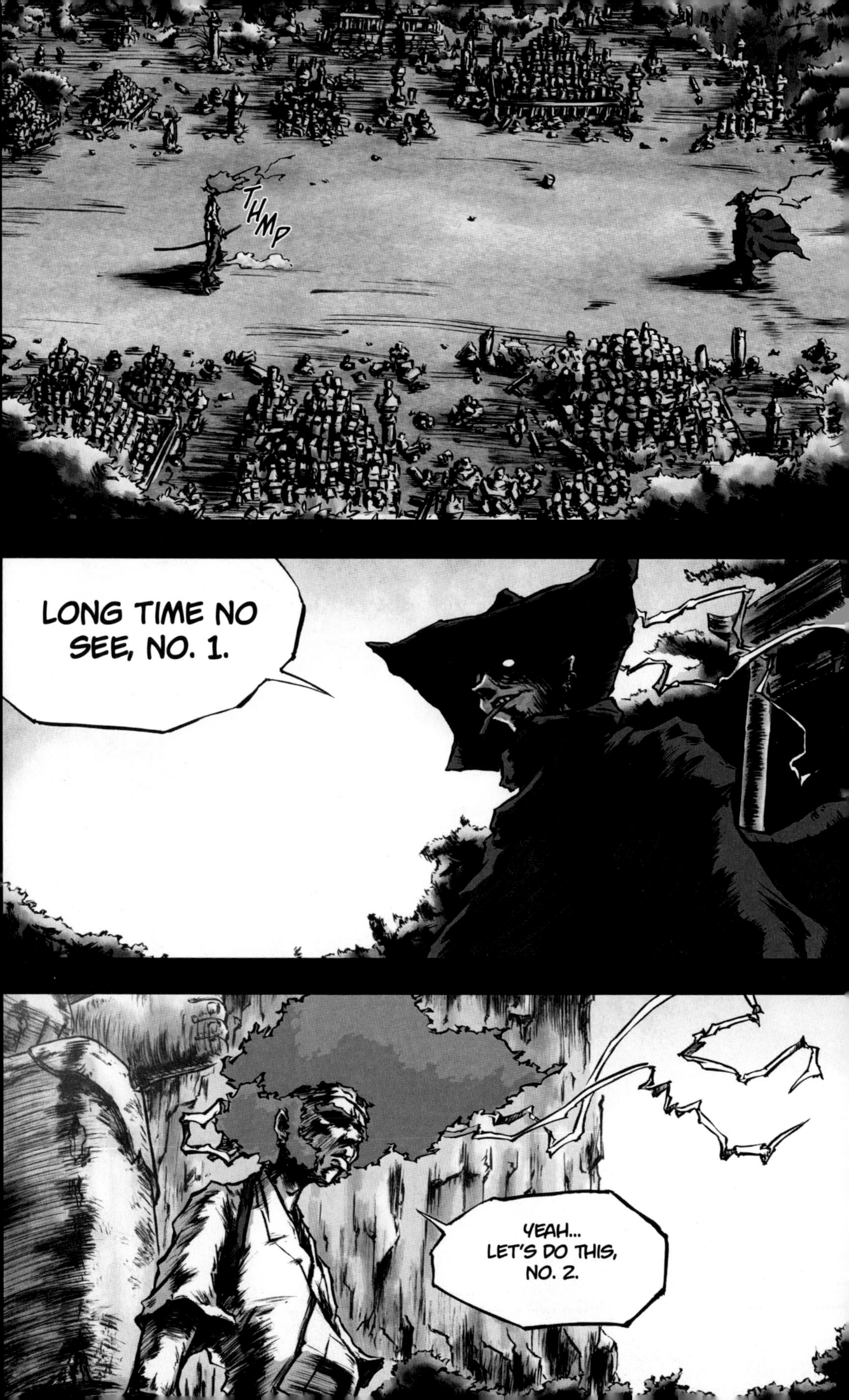
THMP
LONG TIME NO SEE, NO. 1.
YEAH... LET'S DO THIS, NO. 2.

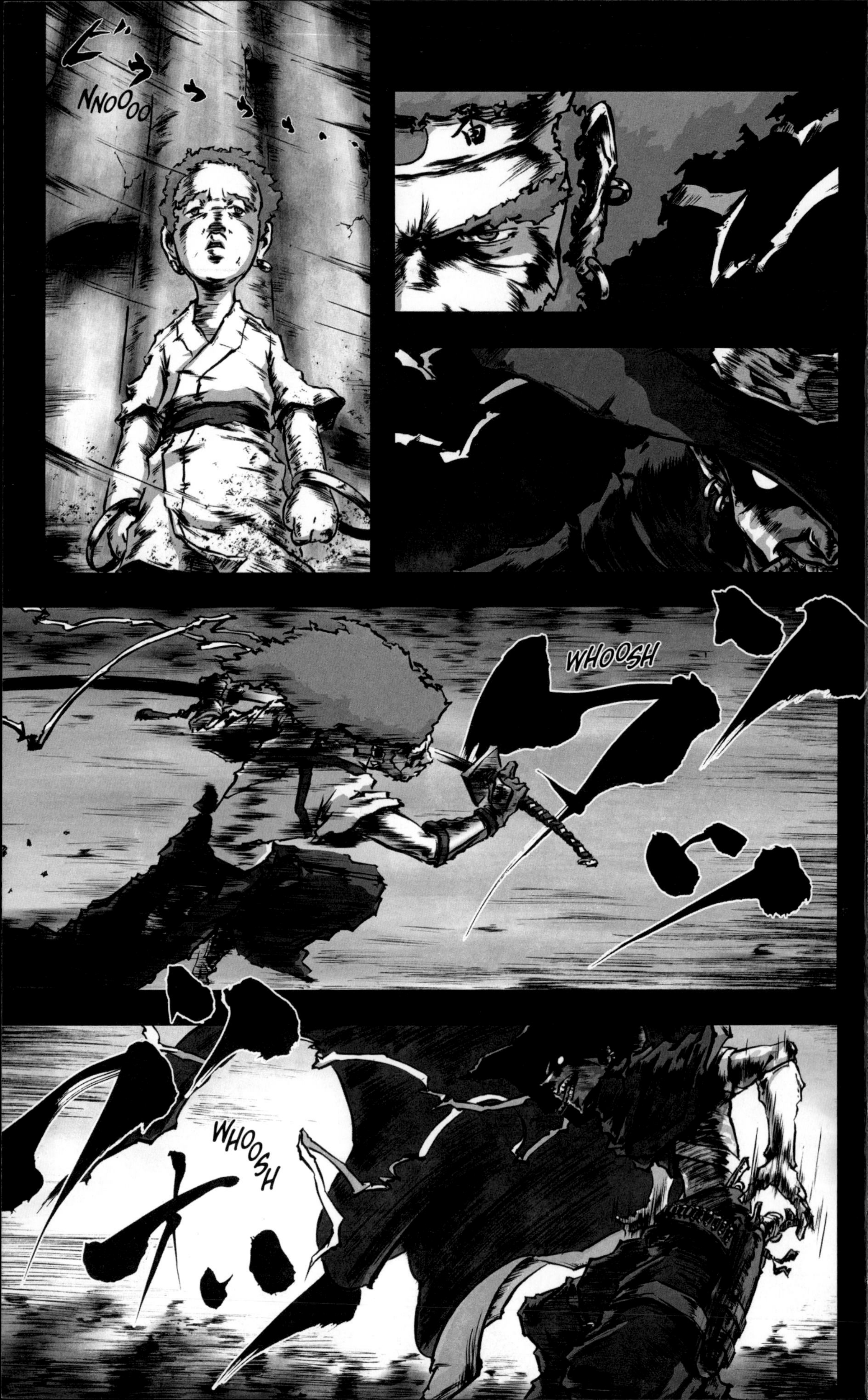
NNOOOO
WHOOSH
WHOOSH

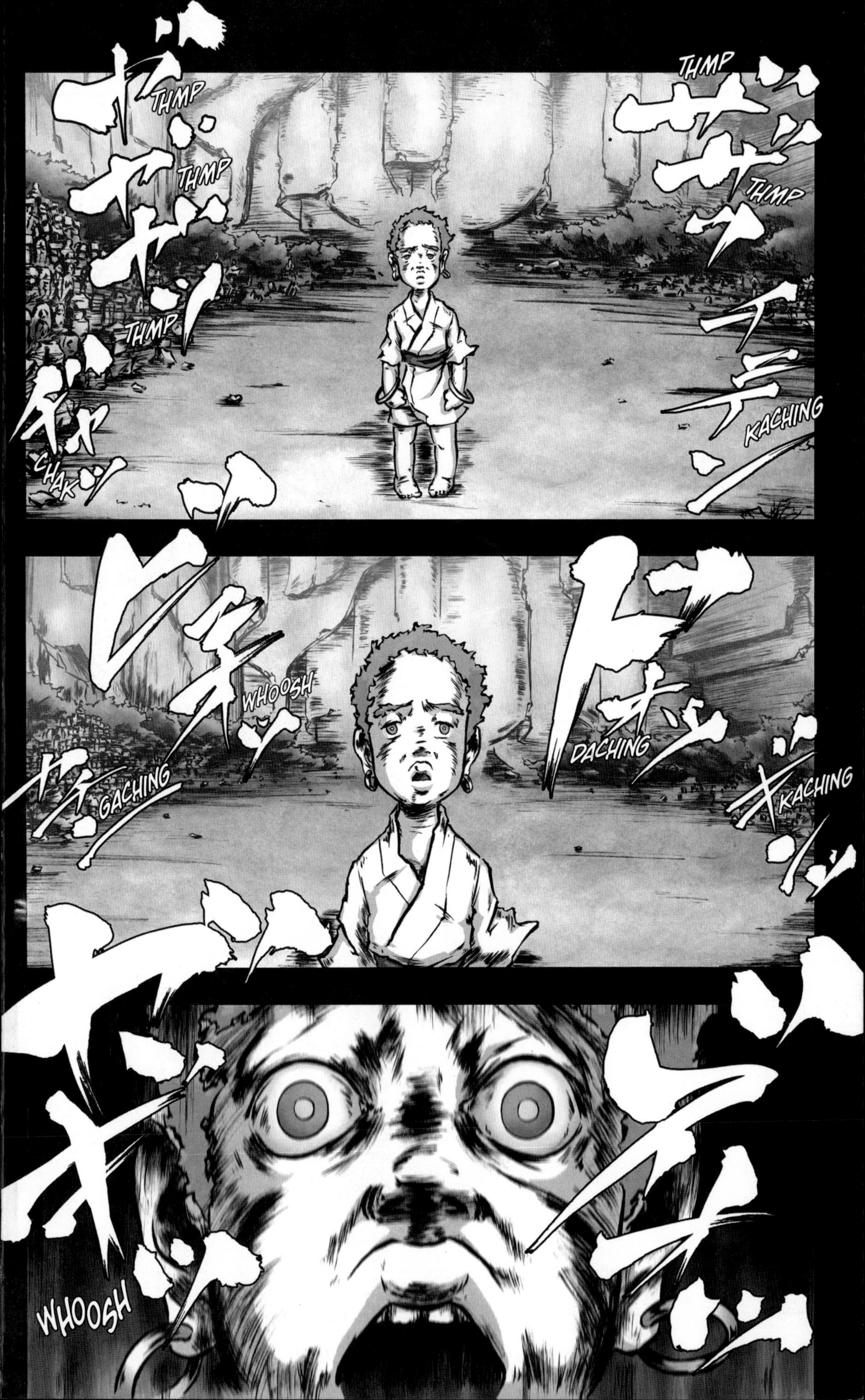
THMP
THMP
THMP
THMP
THMP
KACHING
CHAK
WHOOSH
GACHING
DACHING
KACHING
WHOOSH

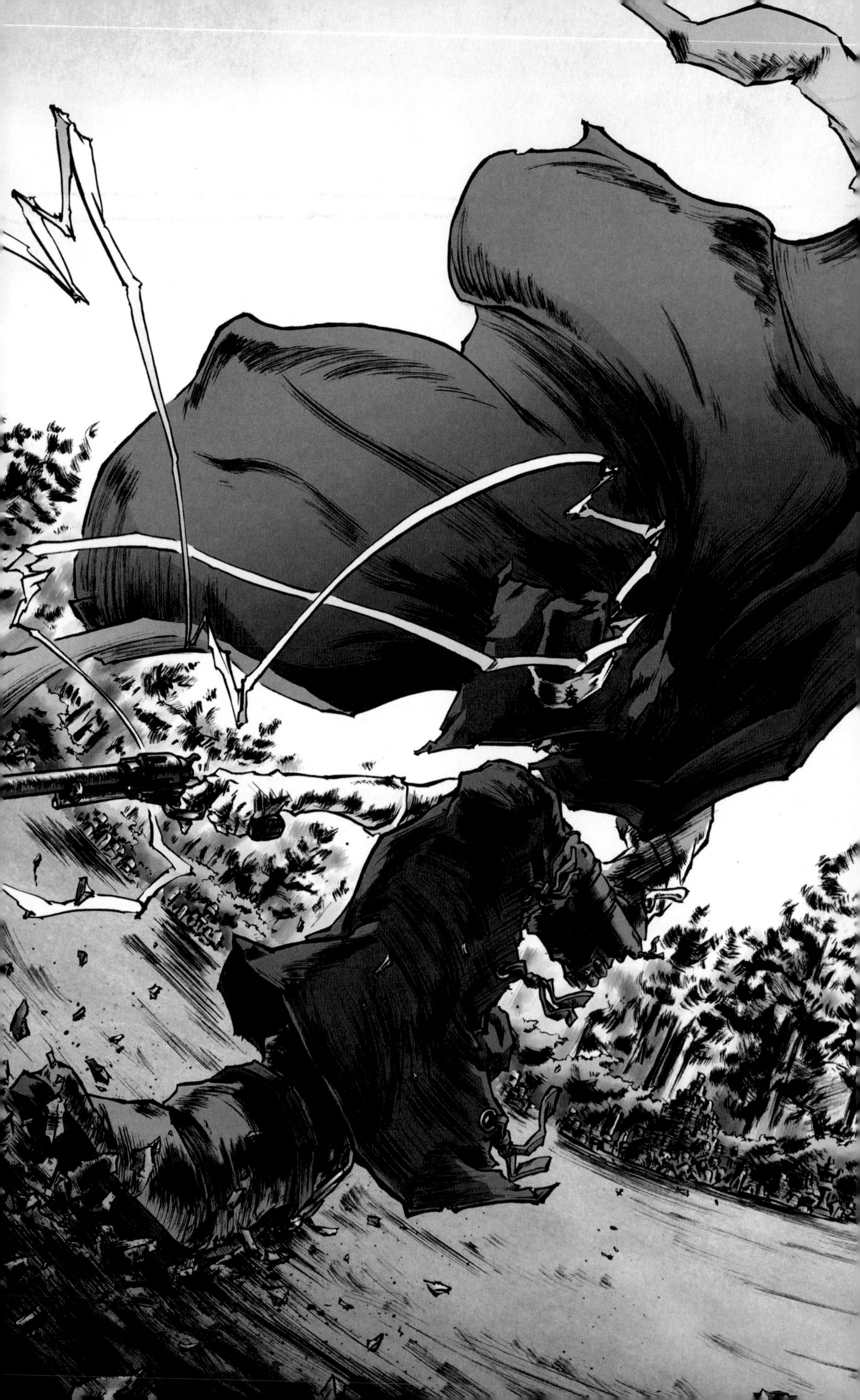

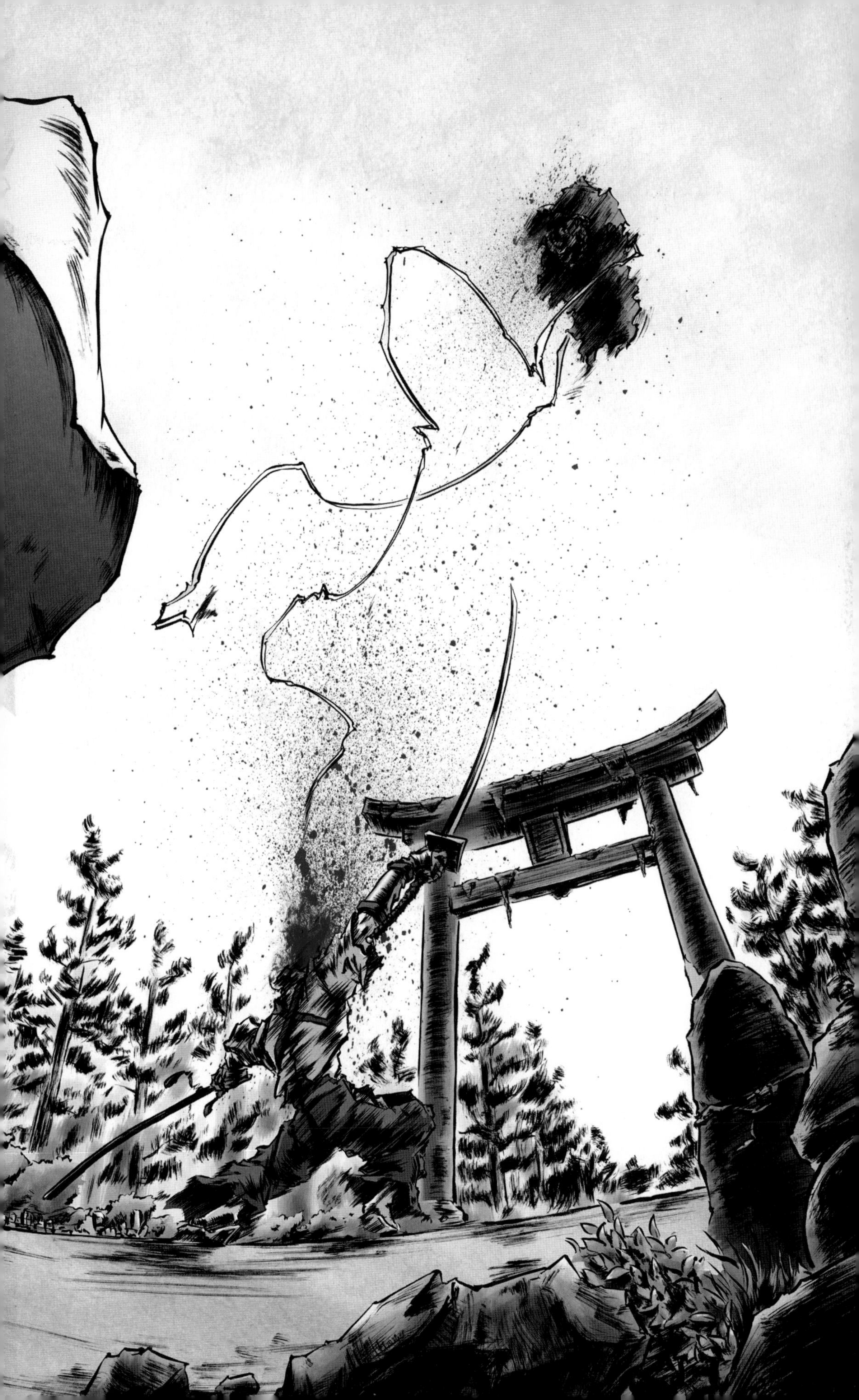

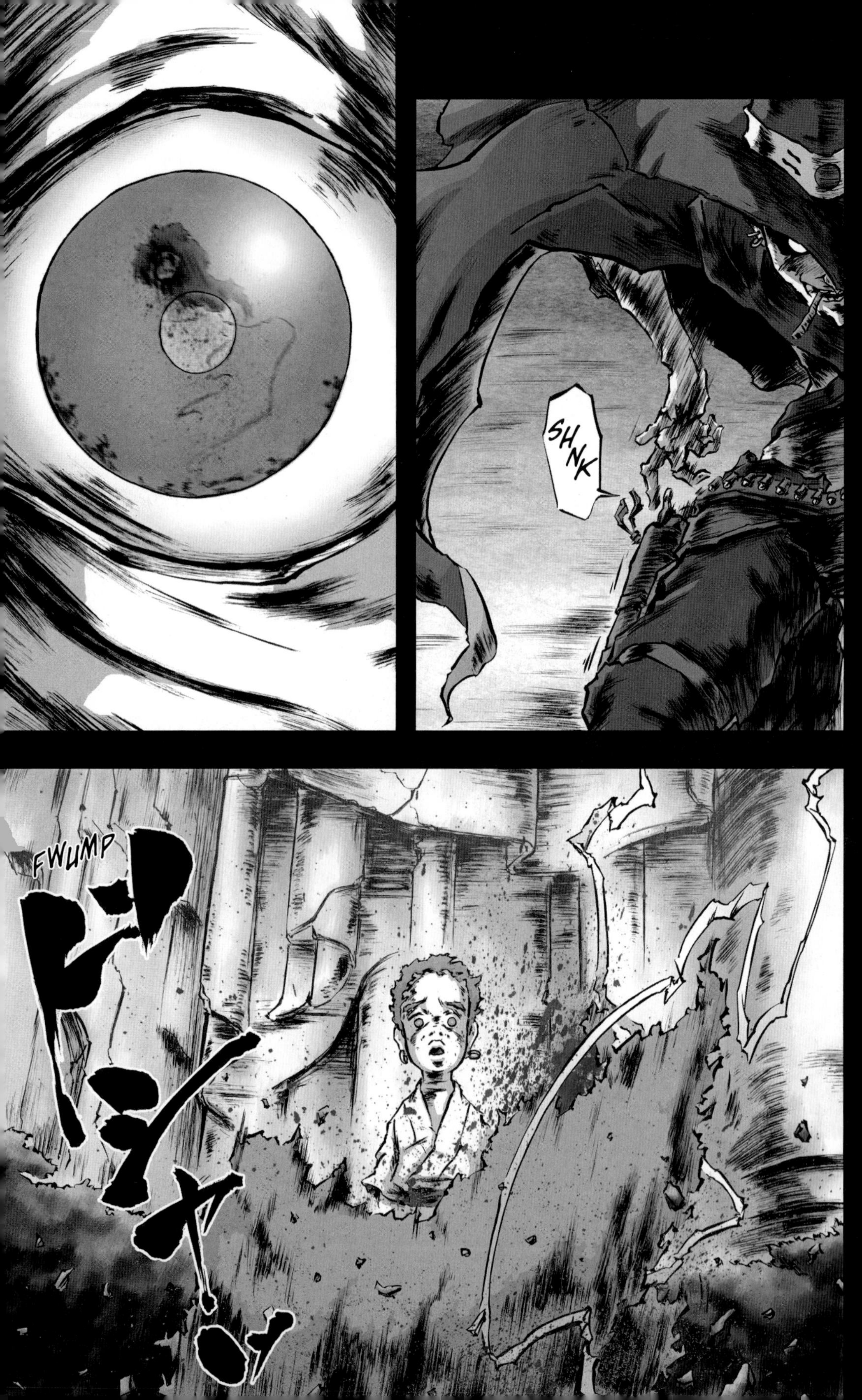
SHNK
FWUMP

THUMP

GANK

HEH HEH HEH! AT LAST, THE POWER OF NO. 1 IS MINE!

THUD

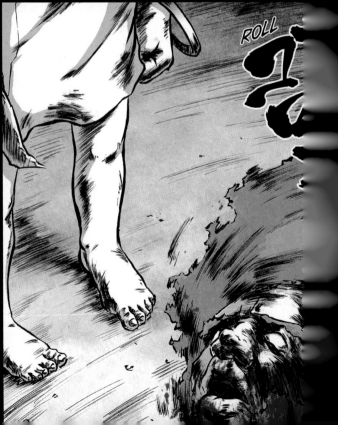

ROLL

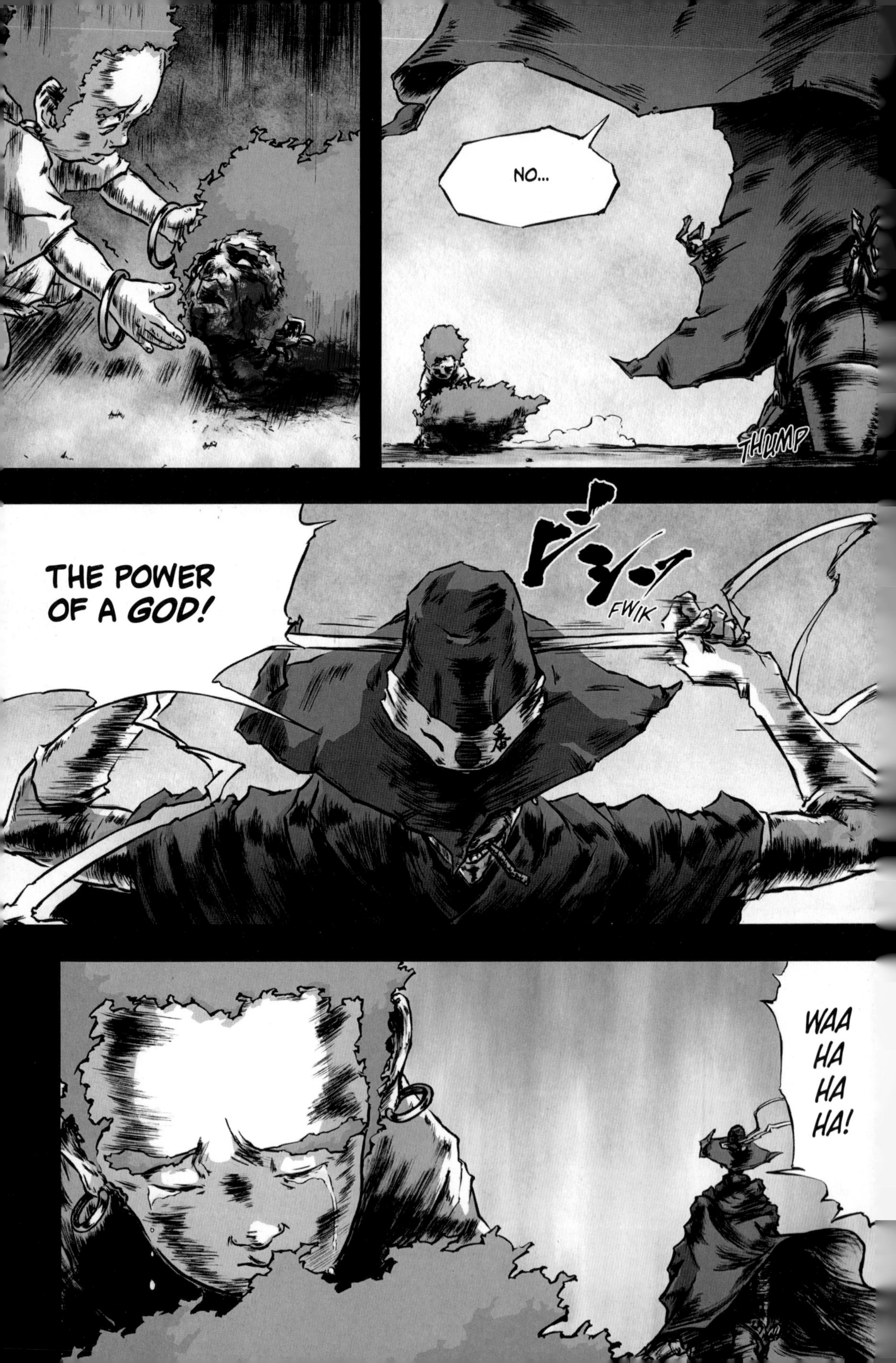
NO...
THUMP
THE POWER OF A GOD!
FWIK
WAA HA HA HA!

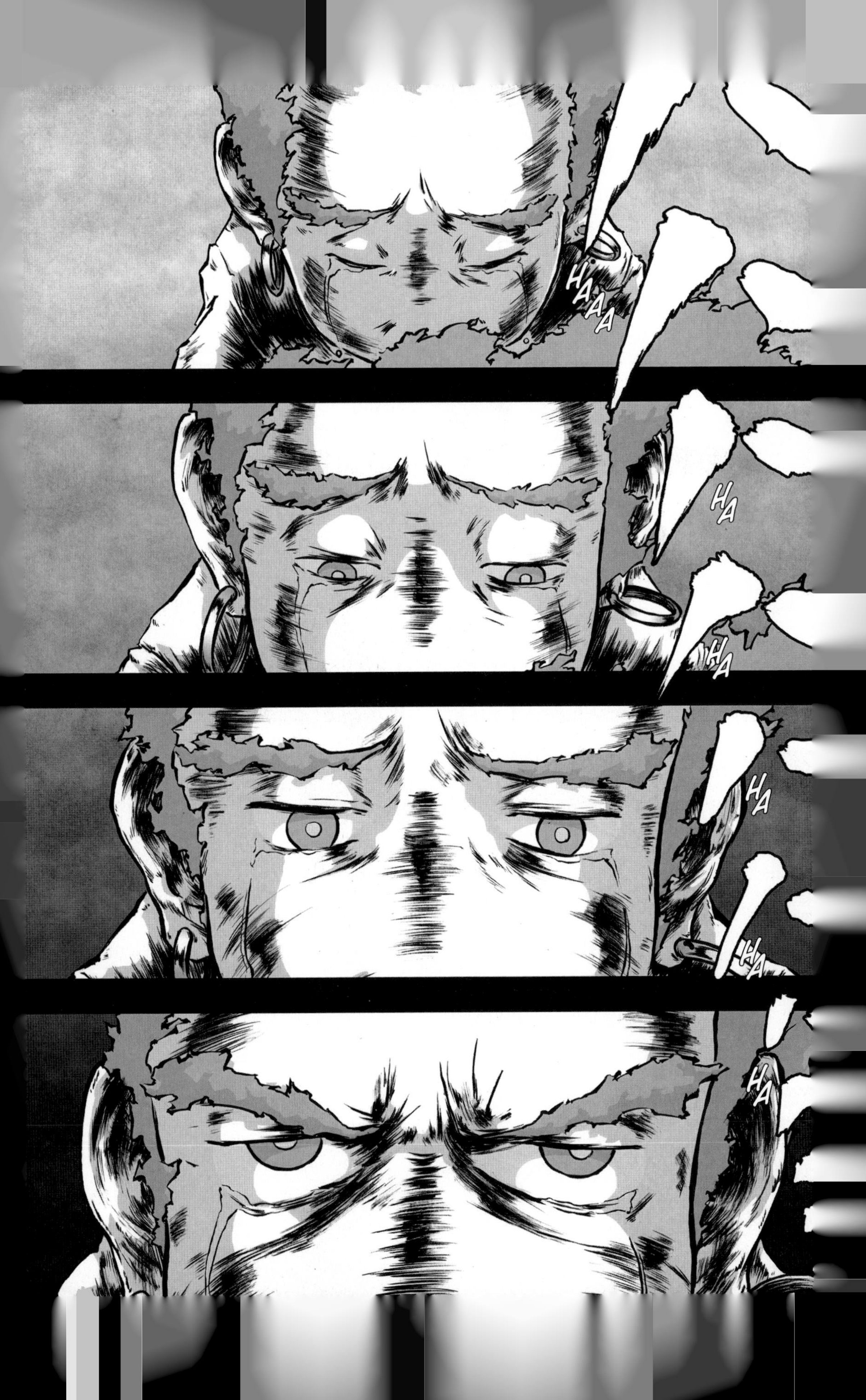
HAAAA
HA
HA
HA
HA
HA

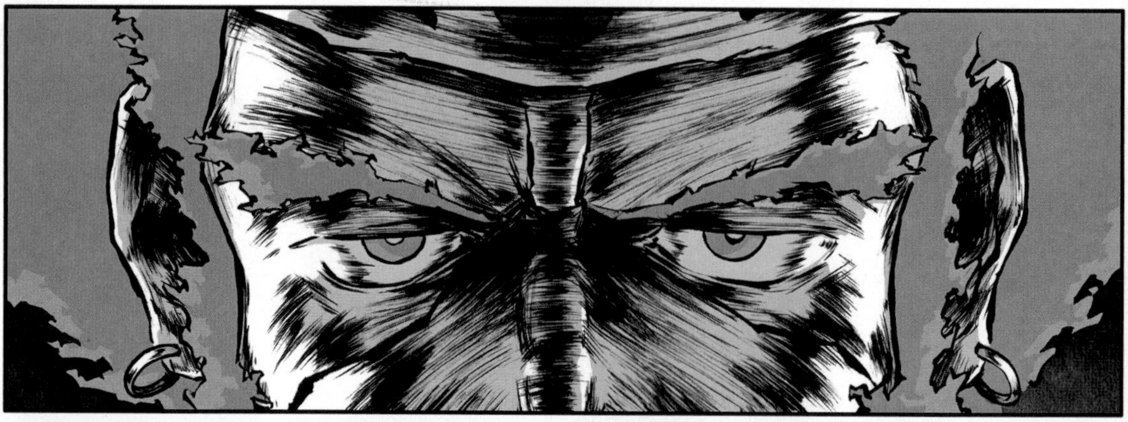
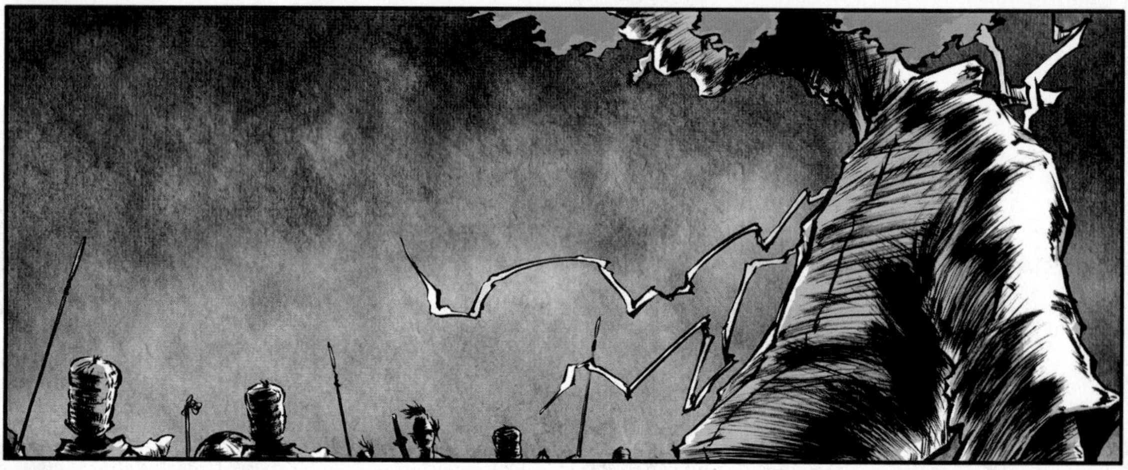
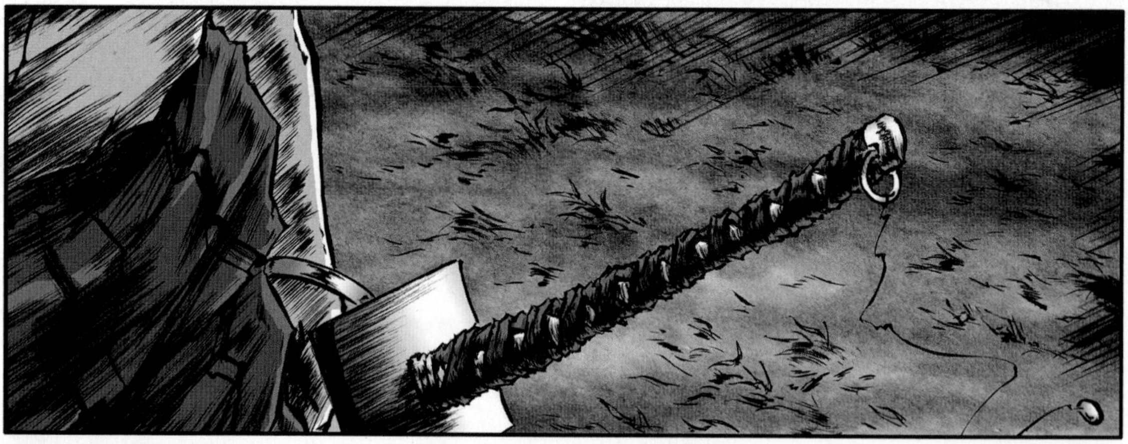
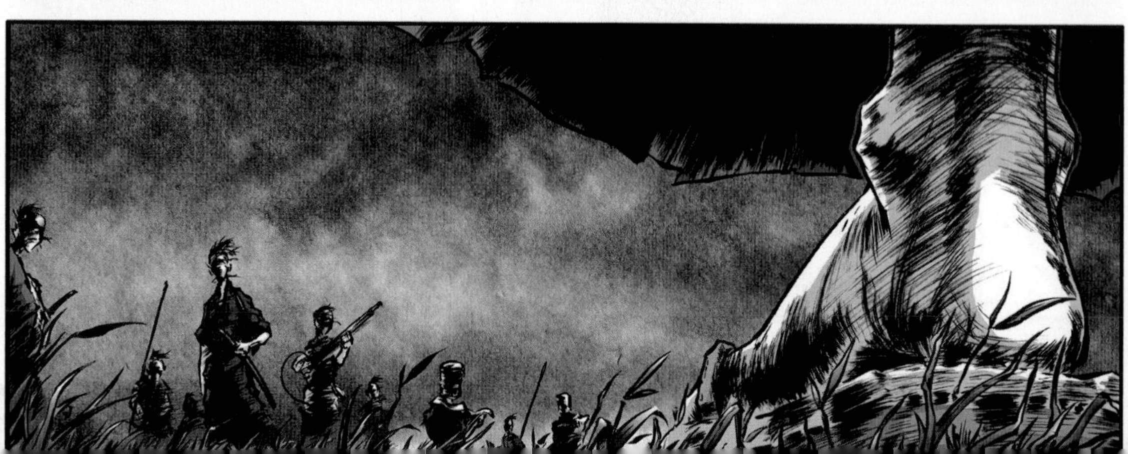

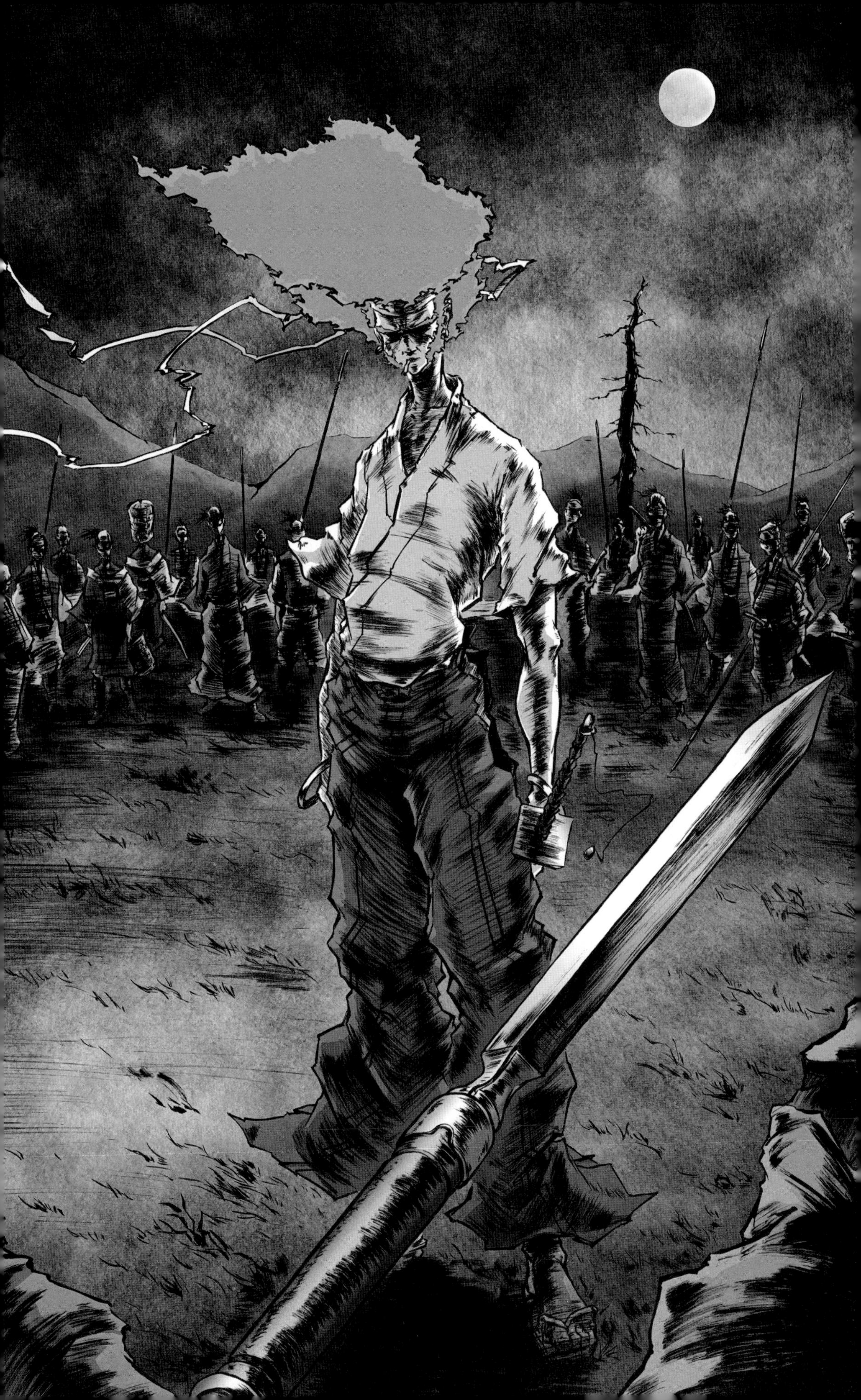

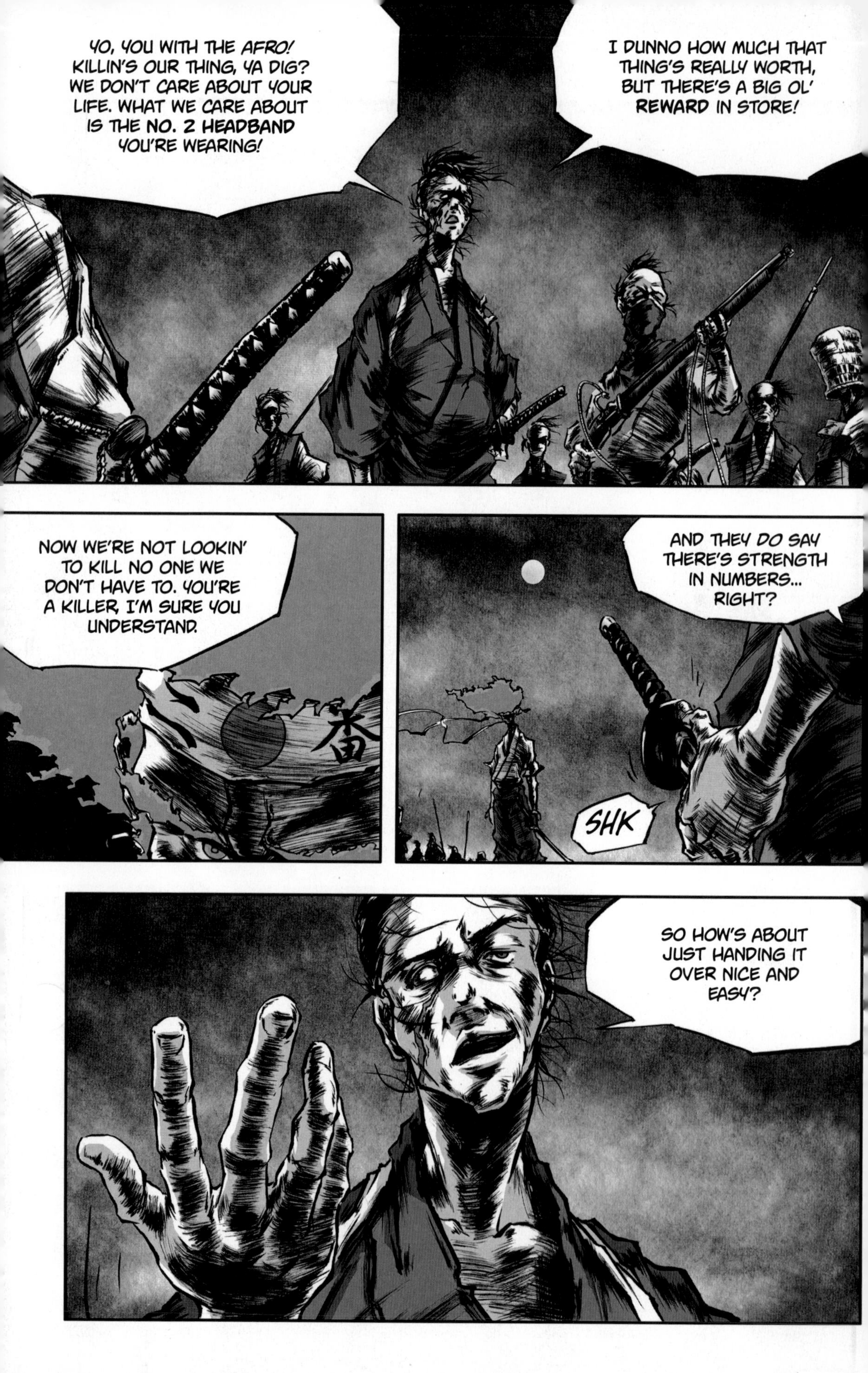
YO, YOU WITH THE AFRO! KILLIN'S OUR THING, YA DIG? WE DON'T CARE ABOUT YOUR LIFE. WHAT WE CARE ABOUT IS THE NO. 2 HEADBAND YOU'RE WEARING!
I DUNNO HOW MUCH THAT THING'S REALLY WORTH, BUT THERE'S A BIG OL' REWARD IN STORE!
NOW WE'RE NOT LOOKIN' TO KILL NO ONE WE DON'T HAVE TO. YOU'RE A KILLER, I'M SURE YOU UNDERSTAND.
番
AND THEY DO SAY THERE'S STRENGTH IN NUMBERS... RIGHT?
SHK
SO HOW'S ABOUT JUST HANDING IT OVER NICE AND EASY?

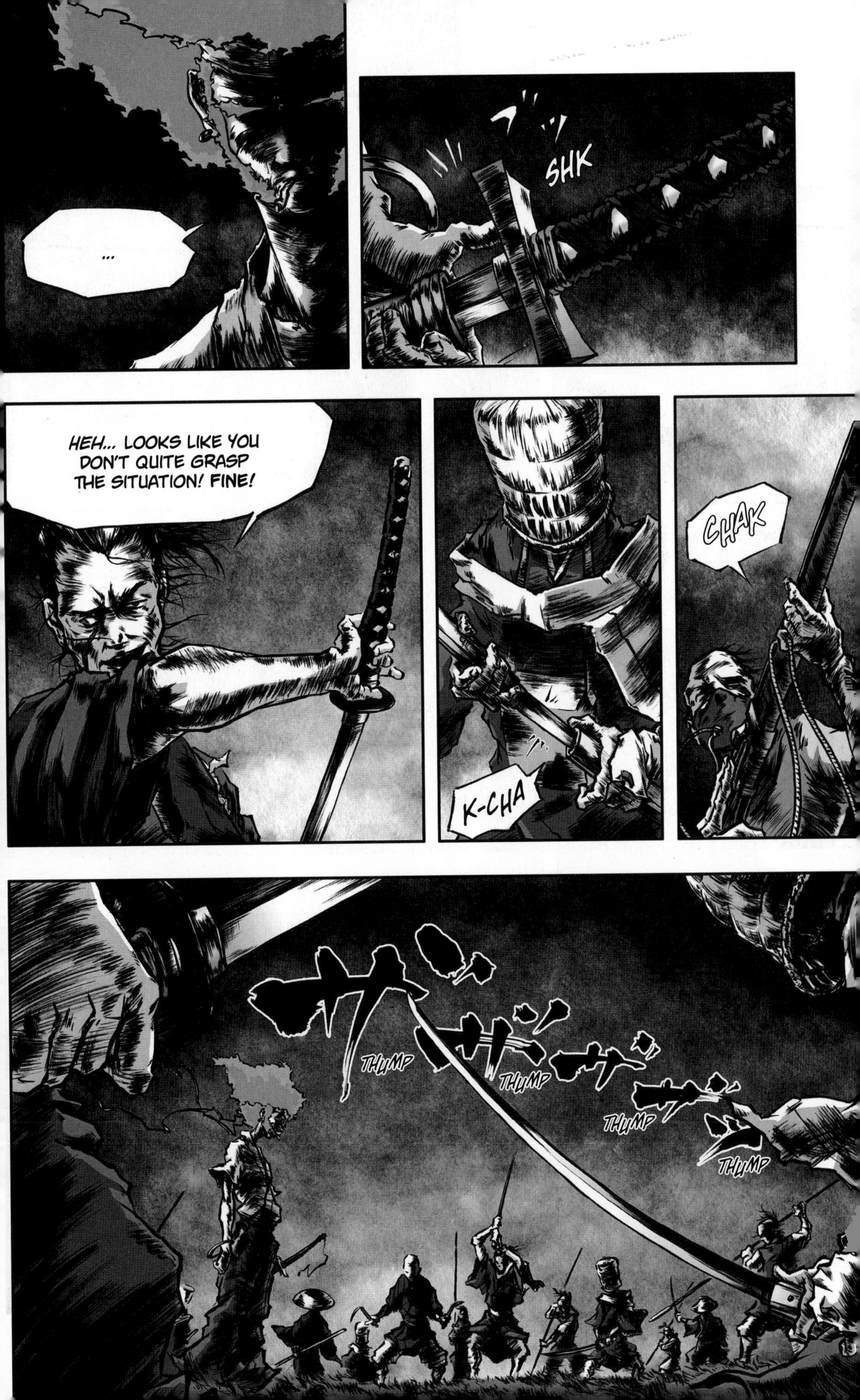
...
SHK
HEH... LOOKS LIKE YOU DON'T QUITE GRASP THE SITUATION! FINE!
K-CHA
CHAK
THUMP
THUMP
THUMP
THUMP

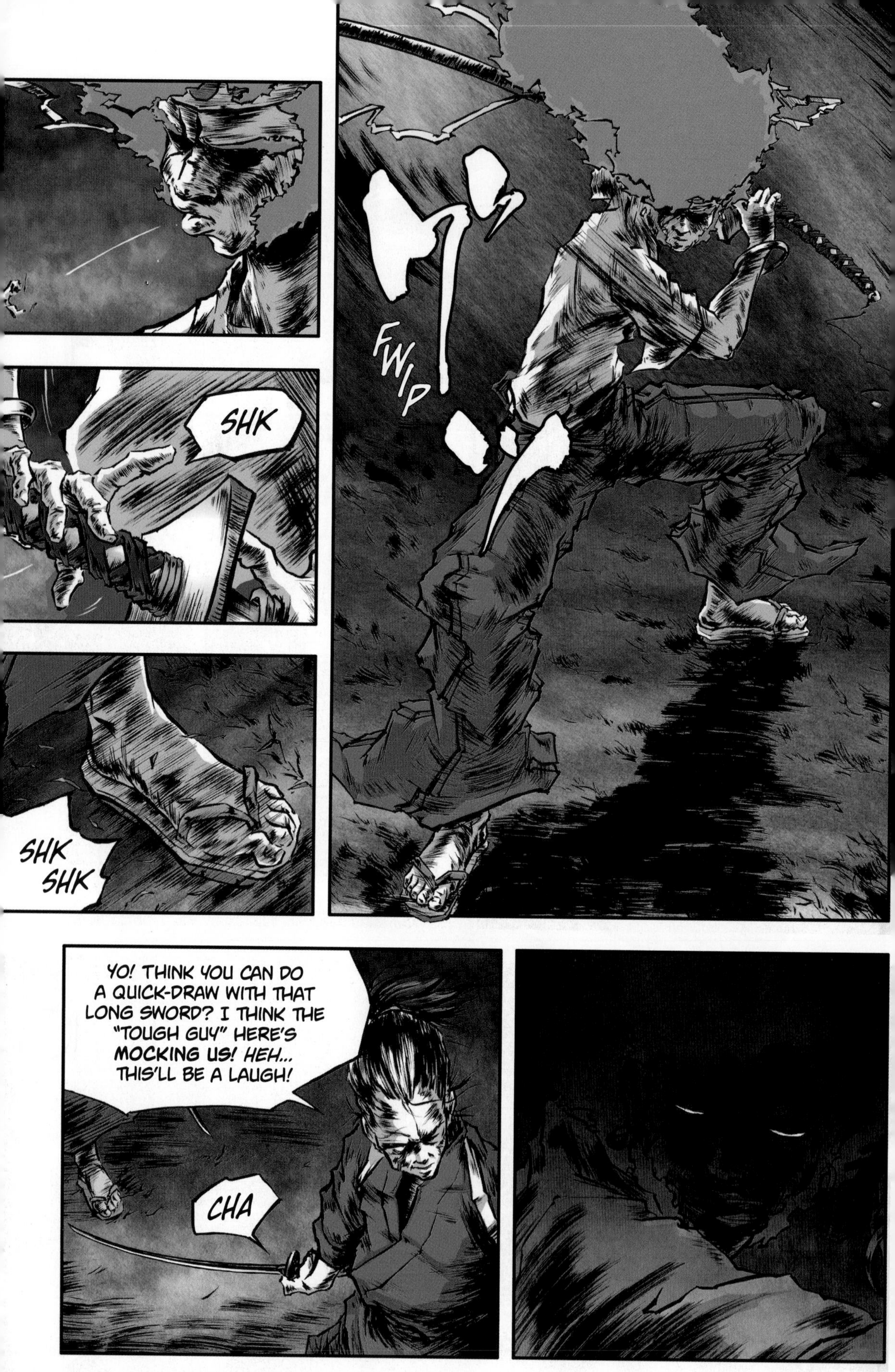
SHK
SHK
SHK
FWIP
YO! THINK YOU CAN DO A QUICK-DRAW WITH THAT LONG SWORD? I THINK THE "TOUGH GUY" HERE'S MOCKING US! HEH... THIS'LL BE A LAUGH!
CHA

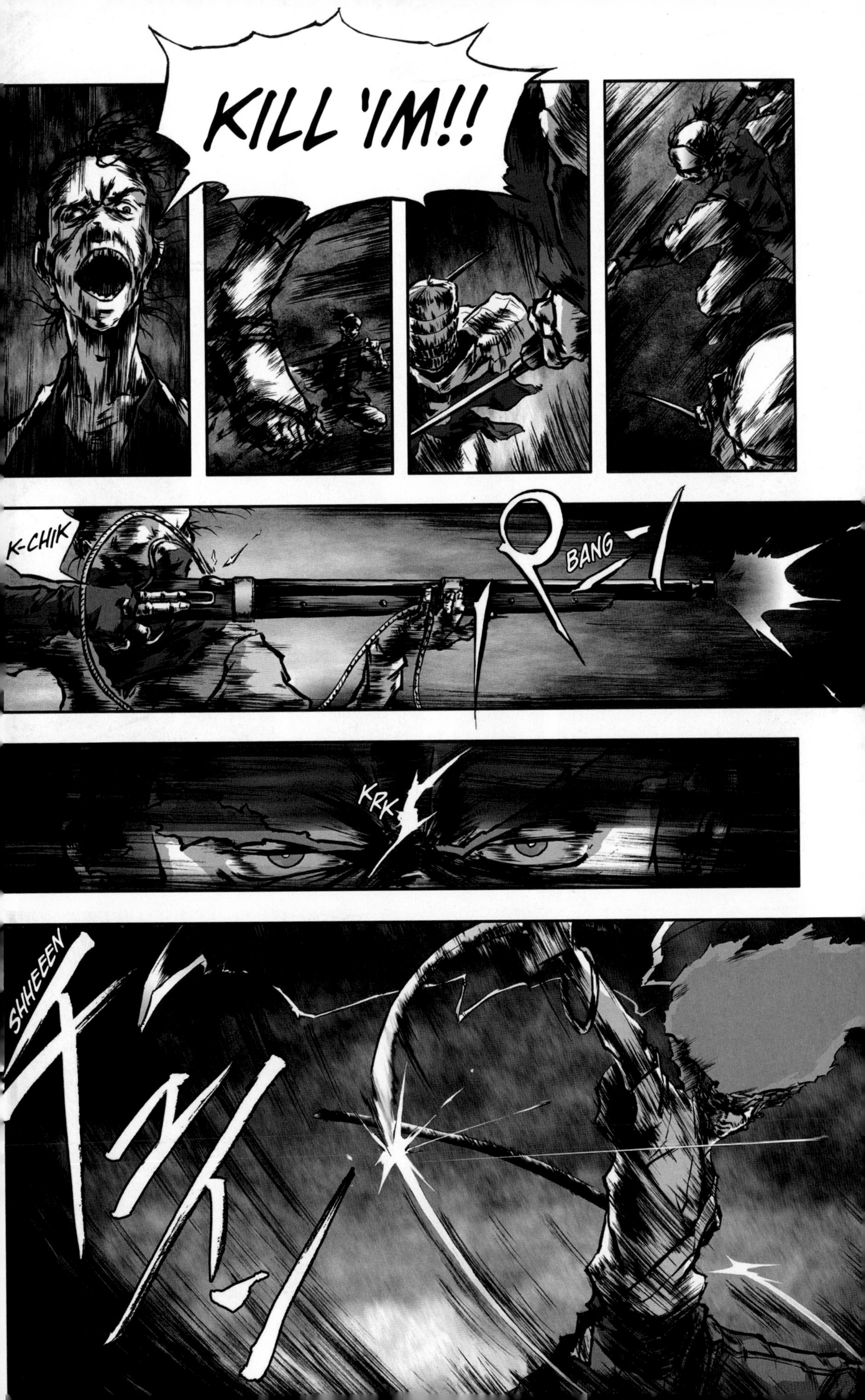
KILL 'IM!!
K-CHIK
BANG
KRK
SHHEEEN

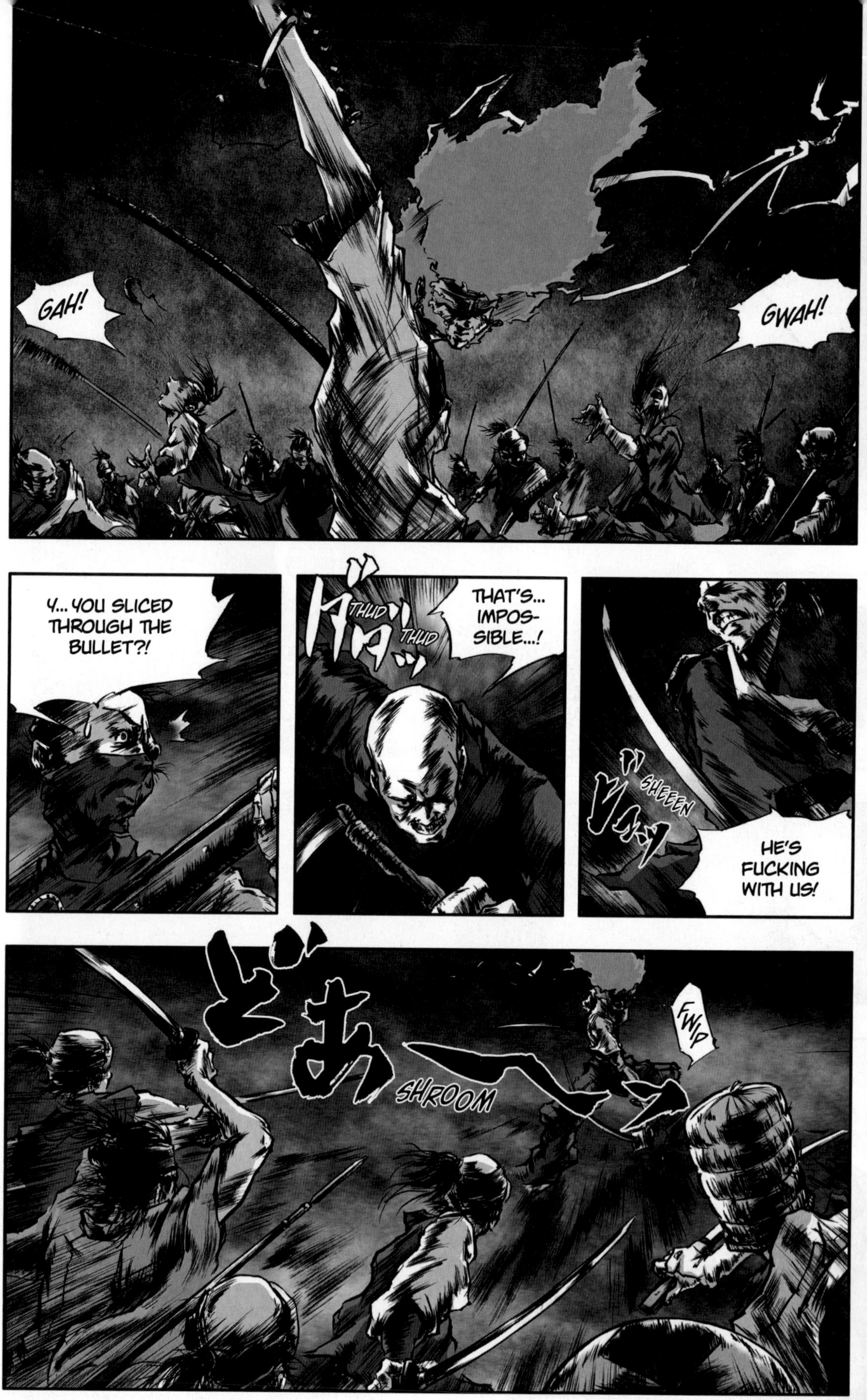
GAH!
GWAH!
Y... YOU SLICED THROUGH THE BULLET?!
THUD
THUD
THAT'S... IMPOS-SIBLE...!
SHEEEN
HE'S FUCKING WITH US!
SHROOM
FWIP

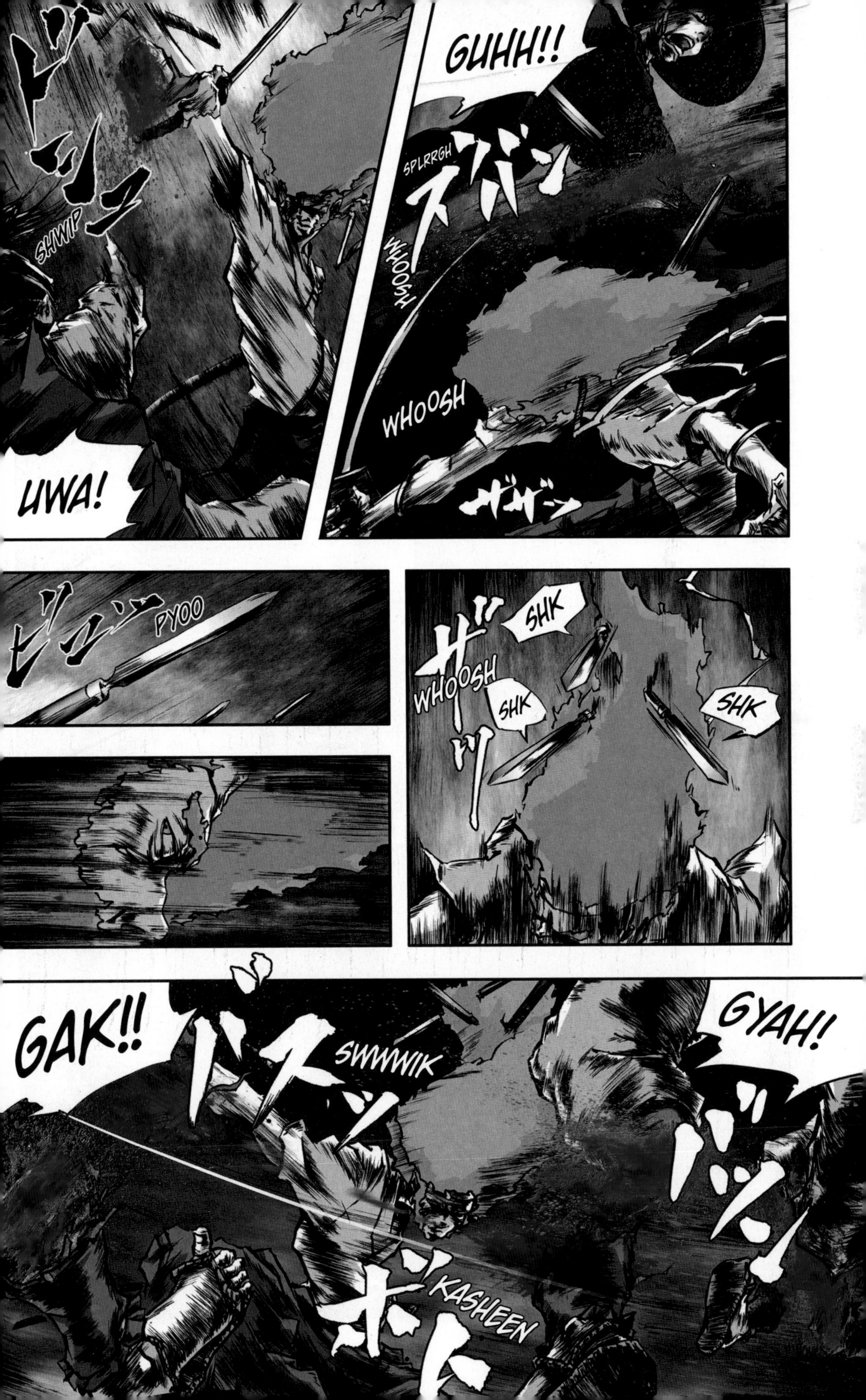
SHWIP
UWA!
GUHH!!
SPLRRGH
WHOOSH
WHOOSH
PYOO
WHOOSH
SHK
SHK
SHK
GAK!!
SWWWIK
GYAH!
KASHEEN

UGAH!

VWEEE VWEEE

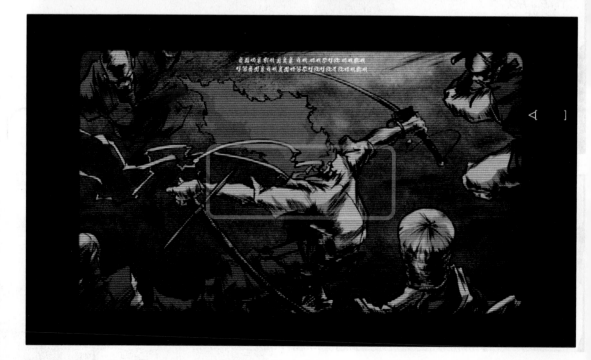

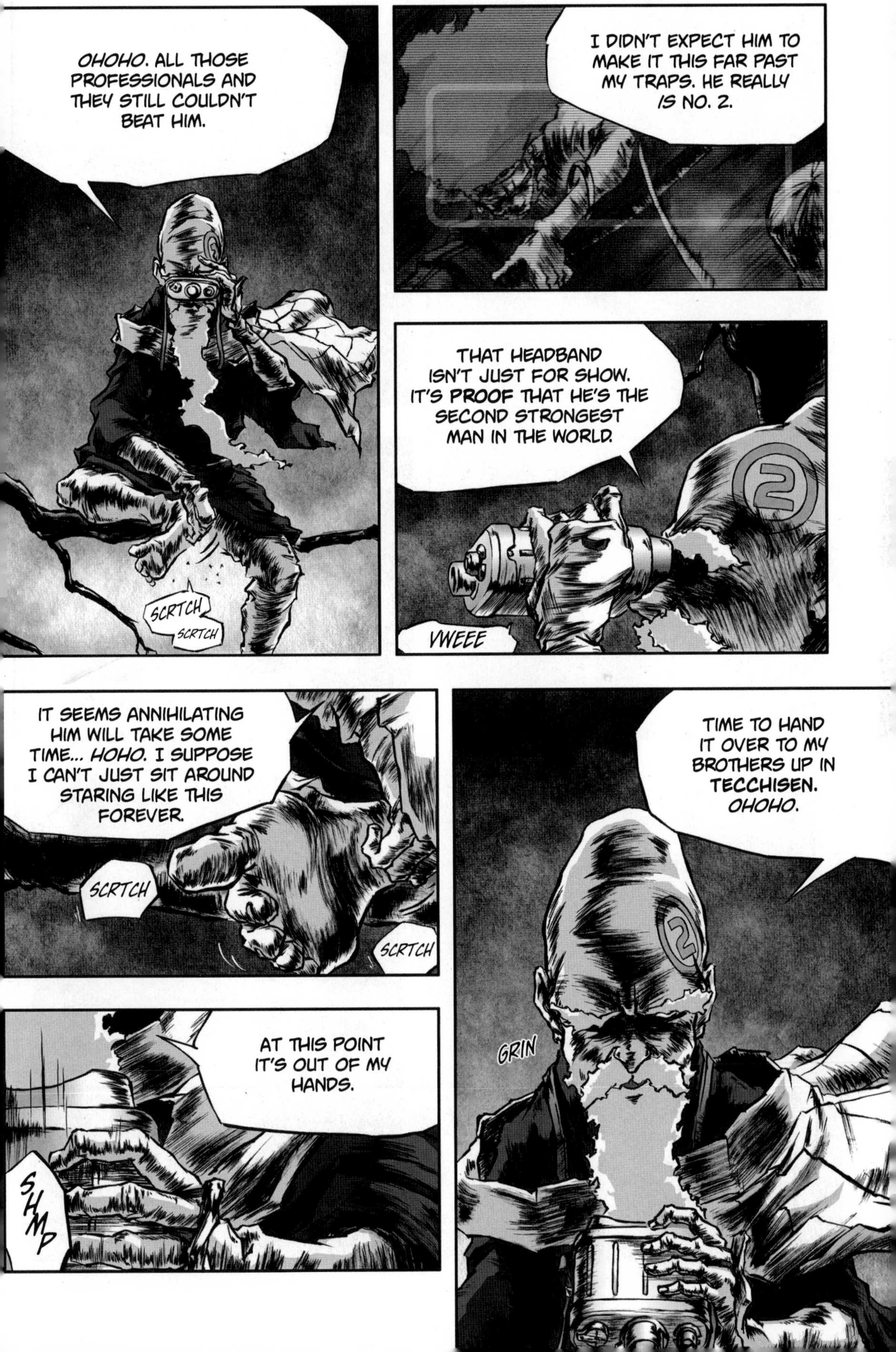
OHOHO. ALL THOSE PROFESSIONALS AND THEY STILL COULDN'T BEAT HIM.
SCRTCH
SCRTCH
I DIDN'T EXPECT HIM TO MAKE IT THIS FAR PAST MY TRAPS. HE REALLY IS NO. 2.
THAT HEADBAND ISN'T JUST FOR SHOW. IT'S PROOF THAT HE'S THE SECOND STRONGEST MAN IN THE WORLD.
VWEEE
IT SEEMS ANNIHILATING HIM WILL TAKE SOME TIME... HOHO. I SUPPOSE I CAN'T JUST SIT AROUND STARING LIKE THIS FOREVER.
SCRTCH
SCRTCH
AT THIS POINT IT'S OUT OF MY HANDS.
SHMP
TIME TO HAND IT OVER TO MY BROTHERS UP IN TECCHISEN. OHOHO.
GRIN

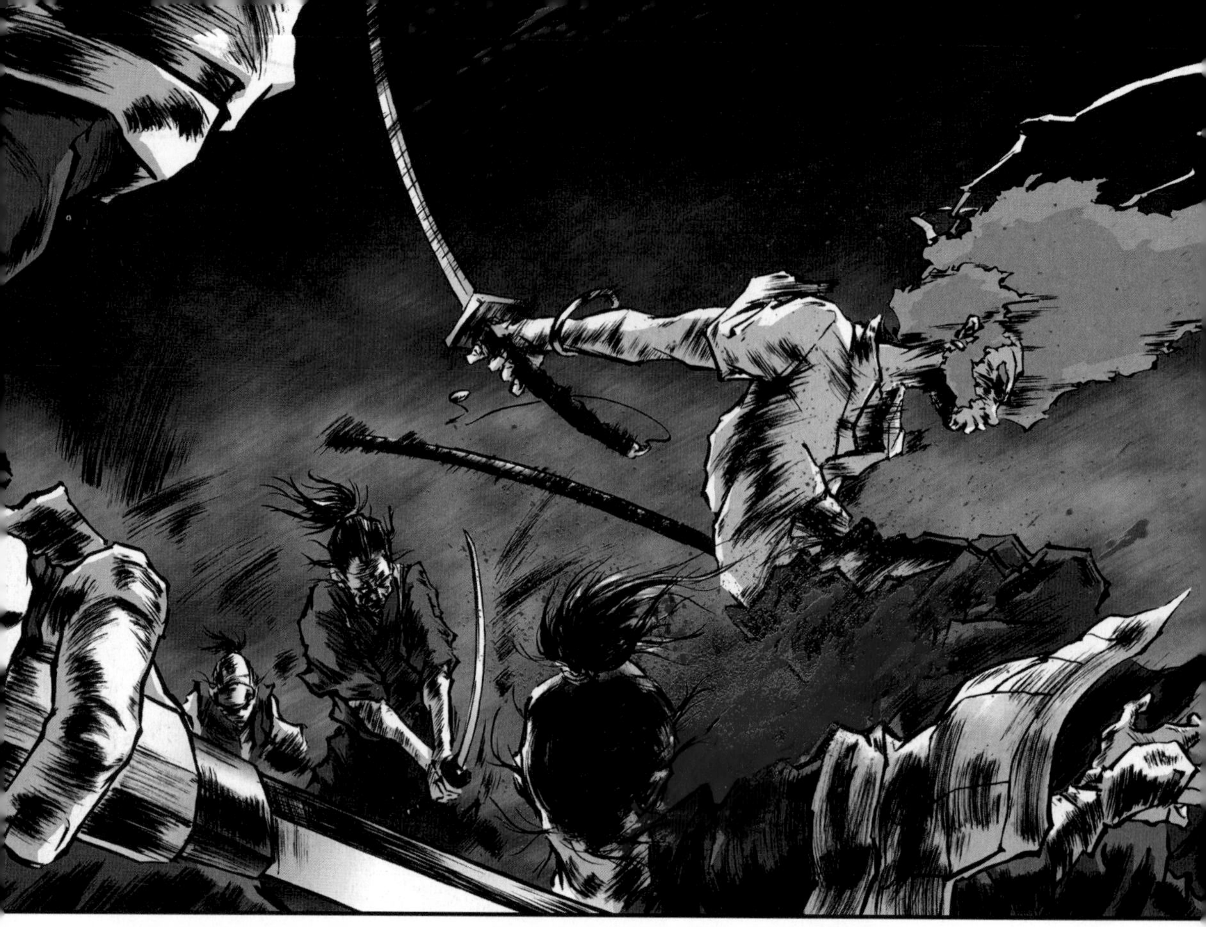

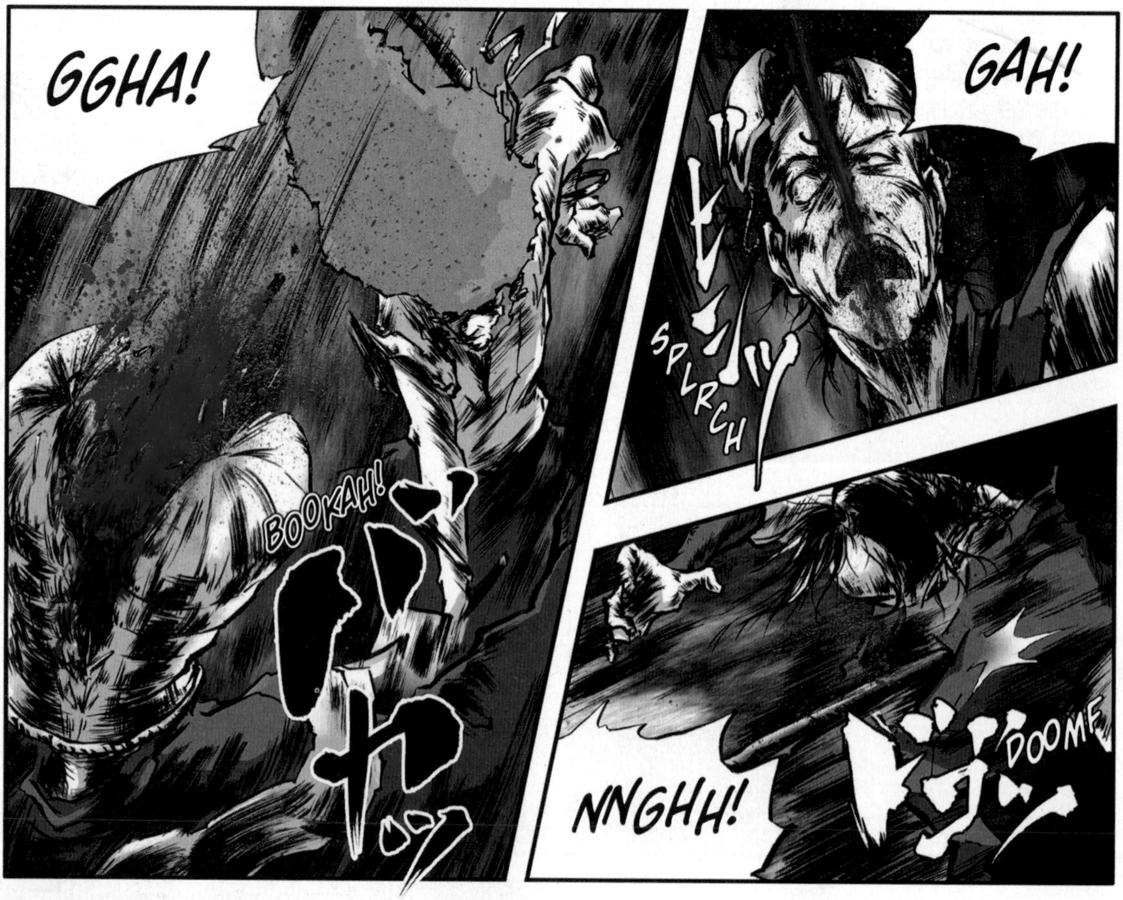
GGHA!
BOOKAH!
GAH!
SPLURCH
NNGHH!
DOOMF

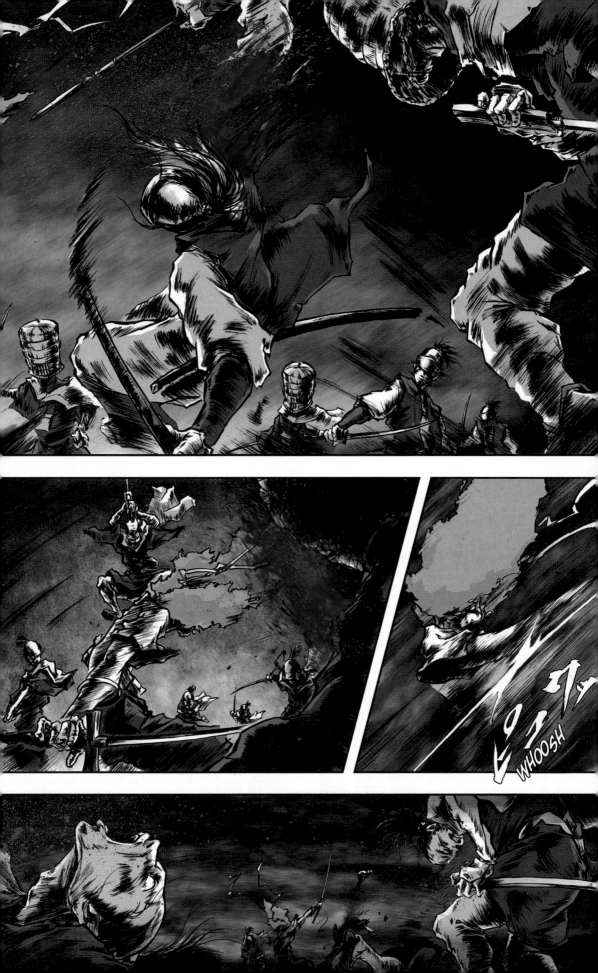

WHOOSH

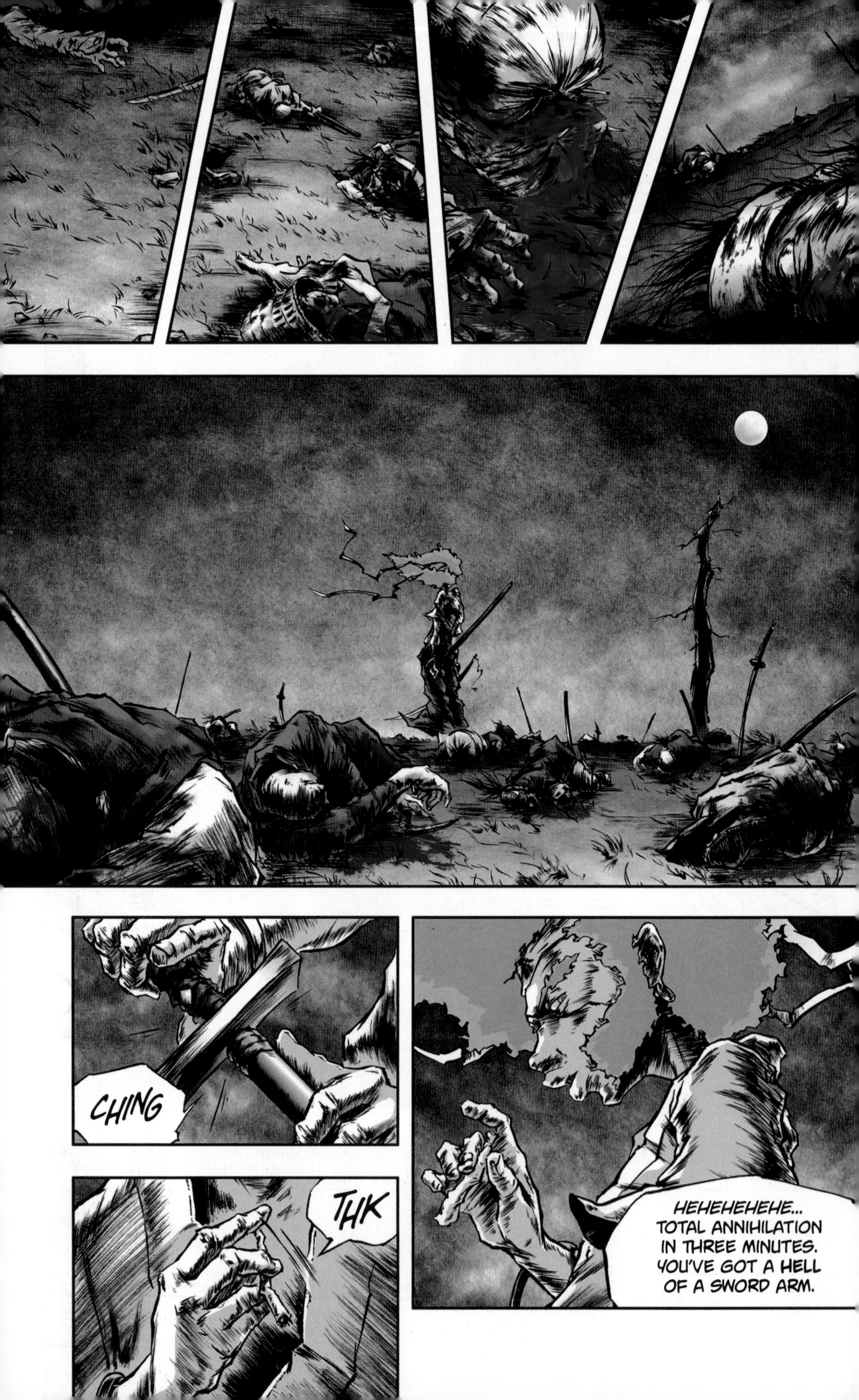
CHING
THK
HEHEHEHEHE... TOTAL ANNIHILATION IN THREE MINUTES. YOU'VE GOT A HELL OF A SWORD ARM.

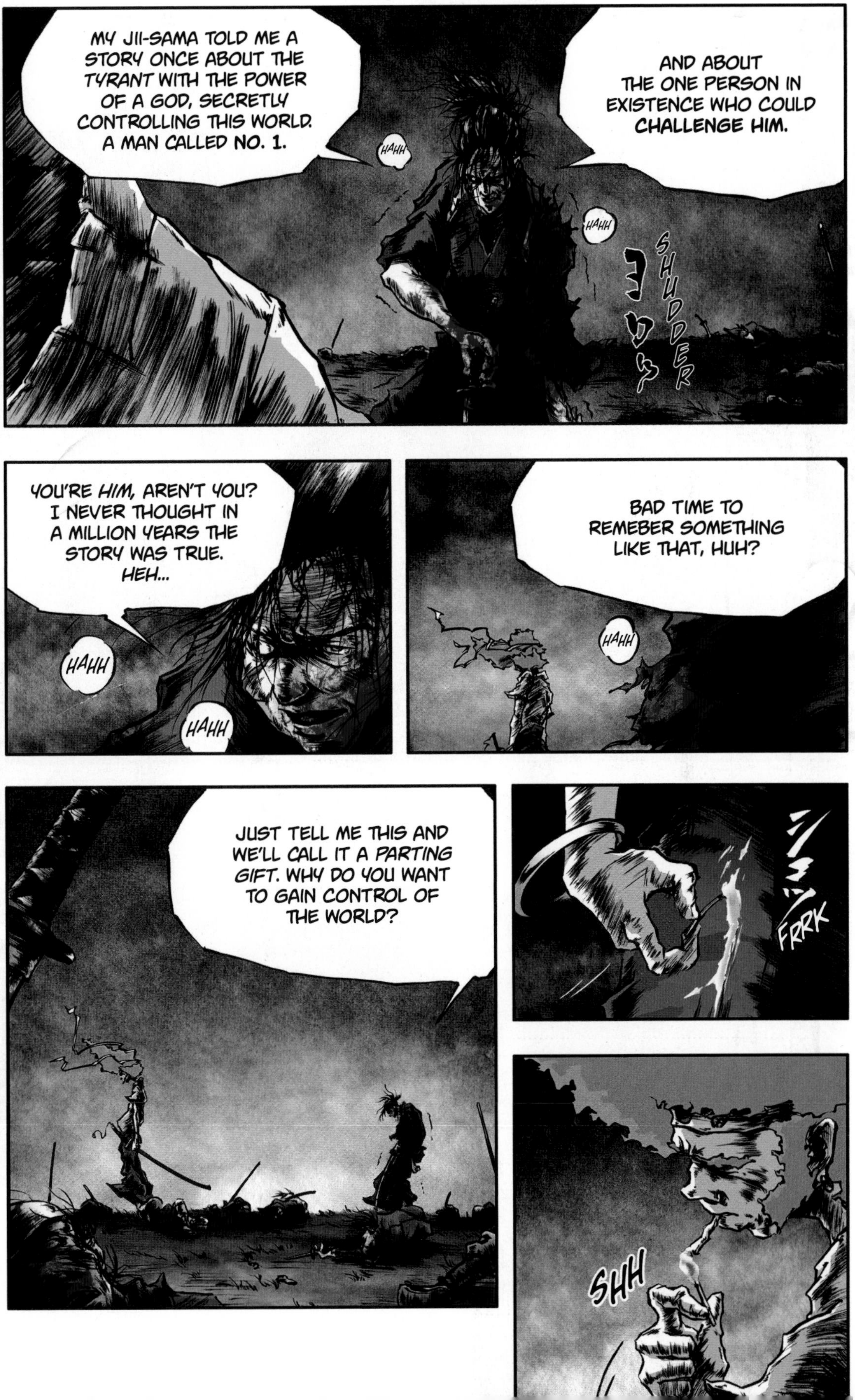
MY JII-SAMA TOLD ME A STORY ONCE ABOUT THE TYRANT WITH THE POWER OF A GOD, SECRETLY CONTROLLING THIS WORLD. A MAN CALLED NO. 1.
HAHH
AND ABOUT THE ONE PERSON IN EXISTENCE WHO COULD CHALLENGE HIM.
HAHH
SHUDDER
YOU'RE HIM, AREN'T YOU? I NEVER THOUGHT IN A MILLION YEARS THE STORY WAS TRUE. HEH...
HAHH
HAHH
BAD TIME TO REMEBER SOMETHING LIKE THAT, HUH?
HAHH
JUST TELL ME THIS AND WE'LL CALL IT A PARTING GIFT. WHY DO YOU WANT TO GAIN CONTROL OF THE WORLD?
FRRK
SHH

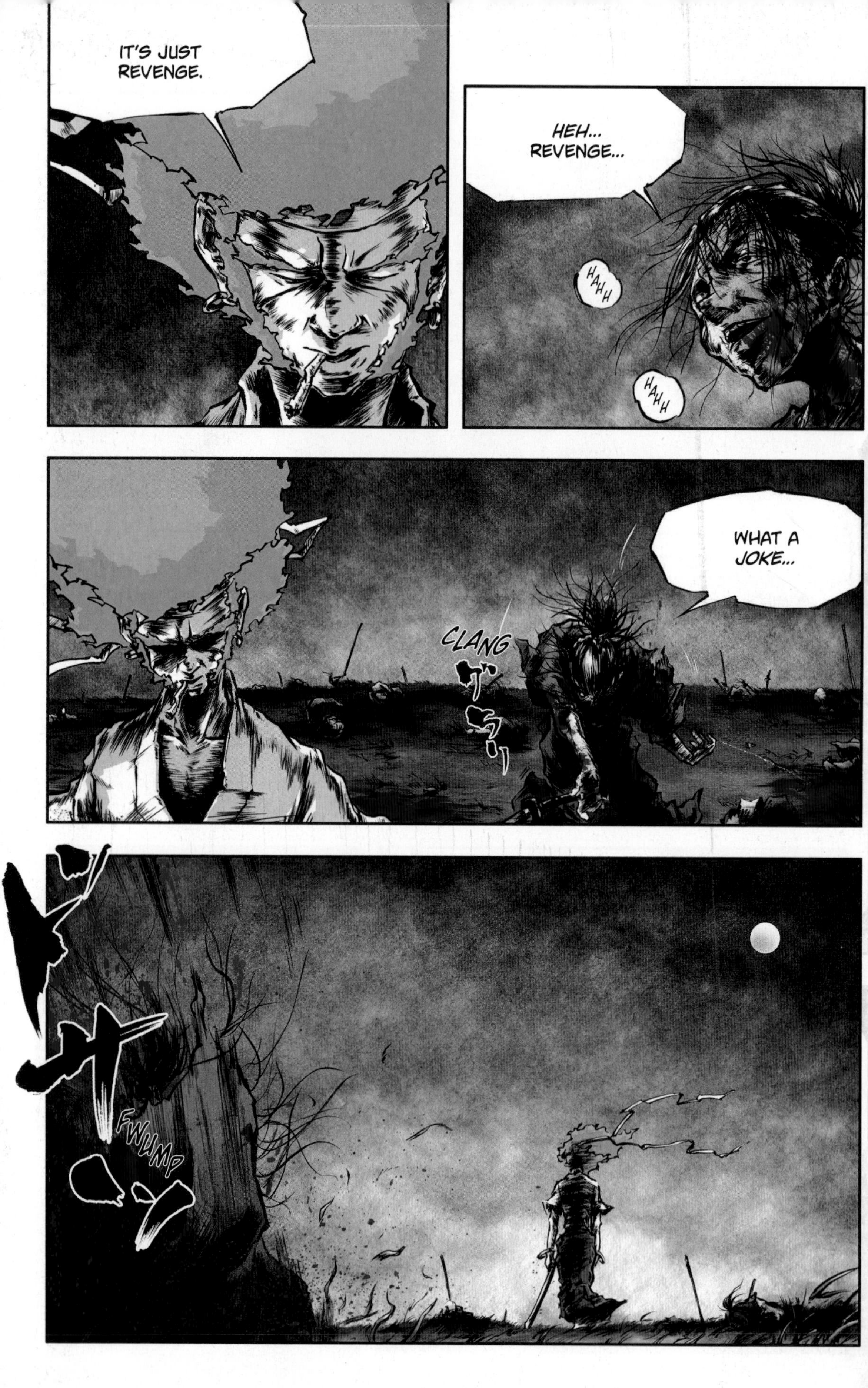
IT'S JUST REVENGE.
HEH... REVENGE...
HAHH
HAHH
CLANG
WHAT A JOKE...
FWUMP

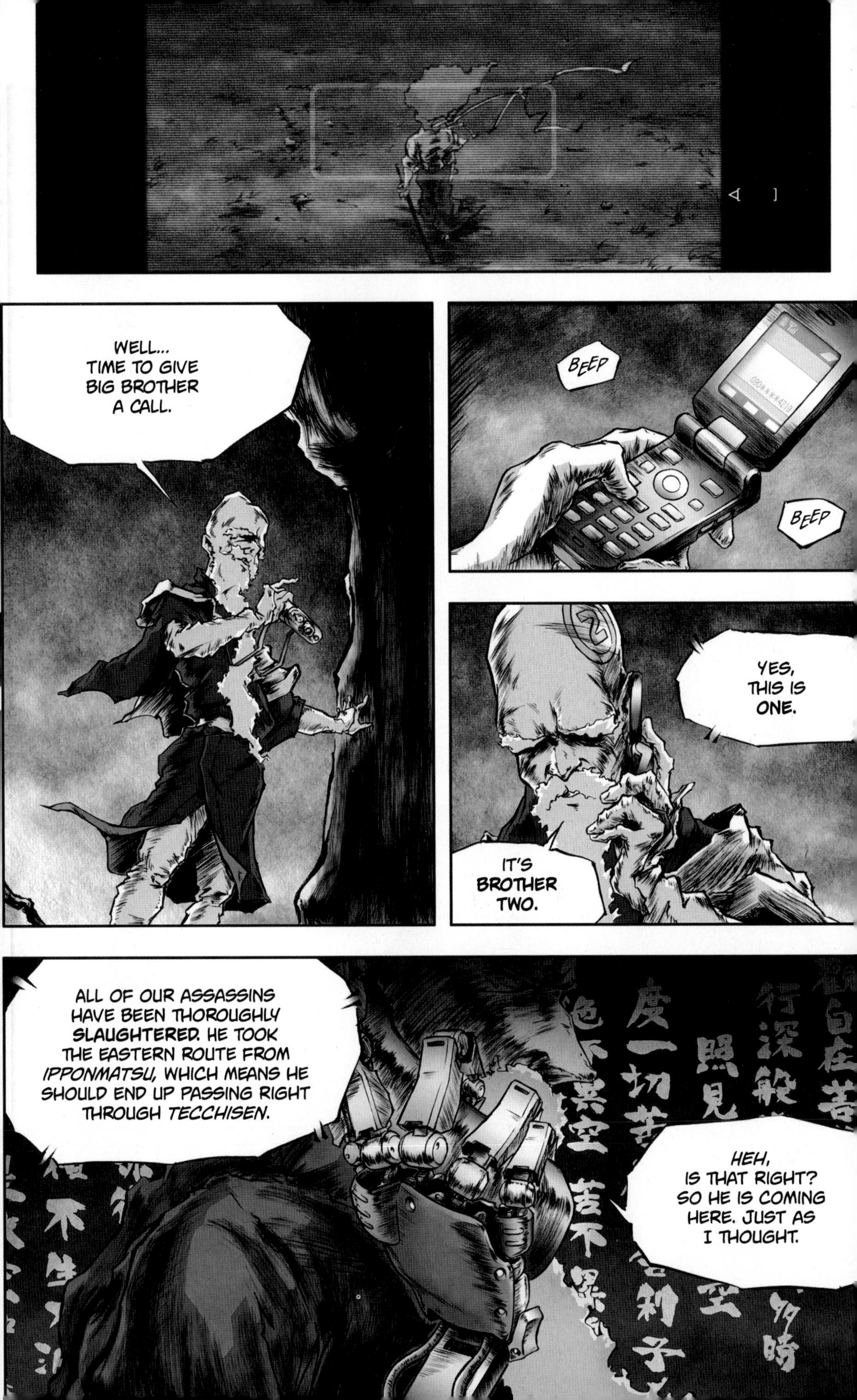
WELL... TIME TO GIVE BIG BROTHER A CALL.
BEEP
BEEP
YES, THIS IS ONE.
IT'S BROTHER TWO.
ALL OF OUR ASSASSINS HAVE BEEN THOROUGHLY SLAUGHTERED. HE TOOK THE EASTERN ROUTE FROM *IPPONMATSU*, WHICH MEANS HE SHOULD END UP PASSING RIGHT THROUGH *TECCHISEN*.
HEH, IS THAT RIGHT? SO HE IS COMING HERE. JUST AS I THOUGHT.

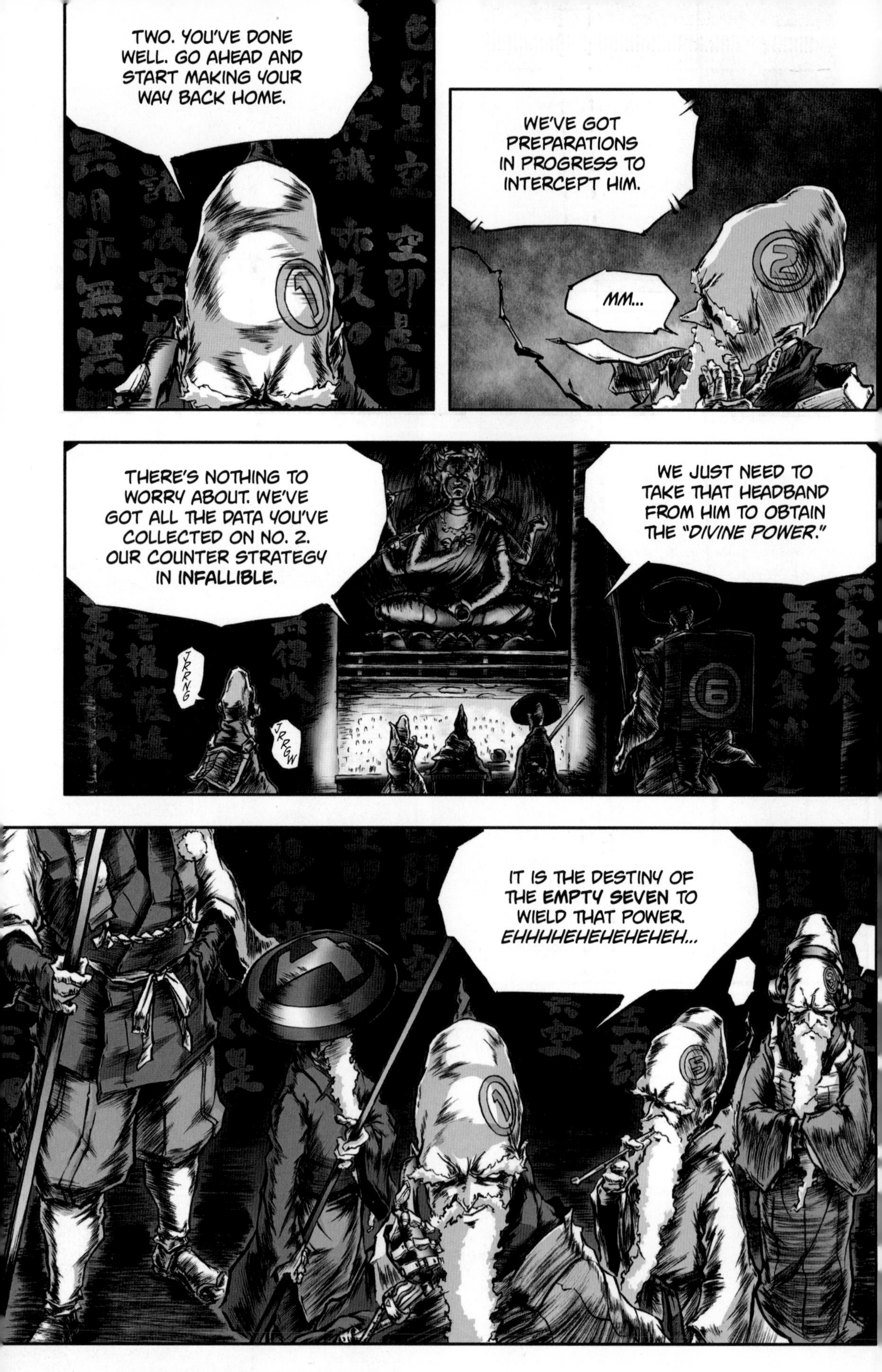
TWO. YOU'VE DONE WELL. GO AHEAD AND START MAKING YOUR WAY BACK HOME.
WE'VE GOT PREPARATIONS IN PROGRESS TO INTERCEPT HIM.
MM...
THERE'S NOTHING TO WORRY ABOUT. WE'VE GOT ALL THE DATA YOU'VE COLLECTED ON NO. 2. OUR COUNTER STRATEGY IN INFALLIBLE.
JRRNG
JRRGW
WE JUST NEED TO TAKE THAT HEADBAND FROM HIM TO OBTAIN THE "DIVINE POWER."
IT IS THE DESTINY OF THE EMPTY SEVEN TO WIELD THAT POWER. EHHHHEHEHEHEHEH...

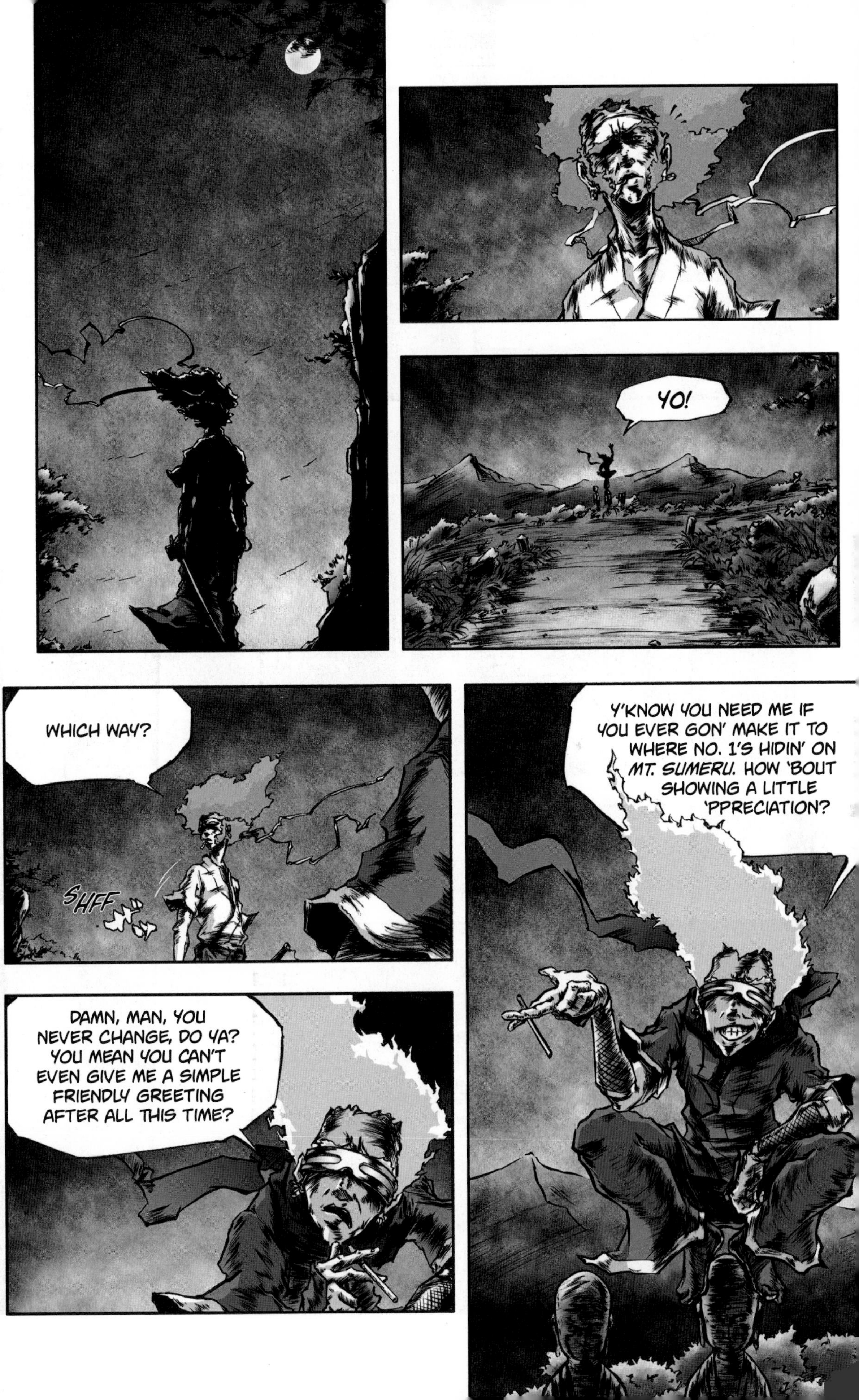
YO!
WHICH WAY?
SHFF
Y'KNOW YOU NEED ME IF YOU EVER GON' MAKE IT TO WHERE NO. 1'S HIDIN' ON MT. SUMERU. HOW 'BOUT SHOWING A LITTLE 'PPRECIATION?
DAMN, MAN, YOU NEVER CHANGE, DO YA? YOU MEAN YOU CAN'T EVEN GIVE ME A SIMPLE FRIENDLY GREETING AFTER ALL THIS TIME?

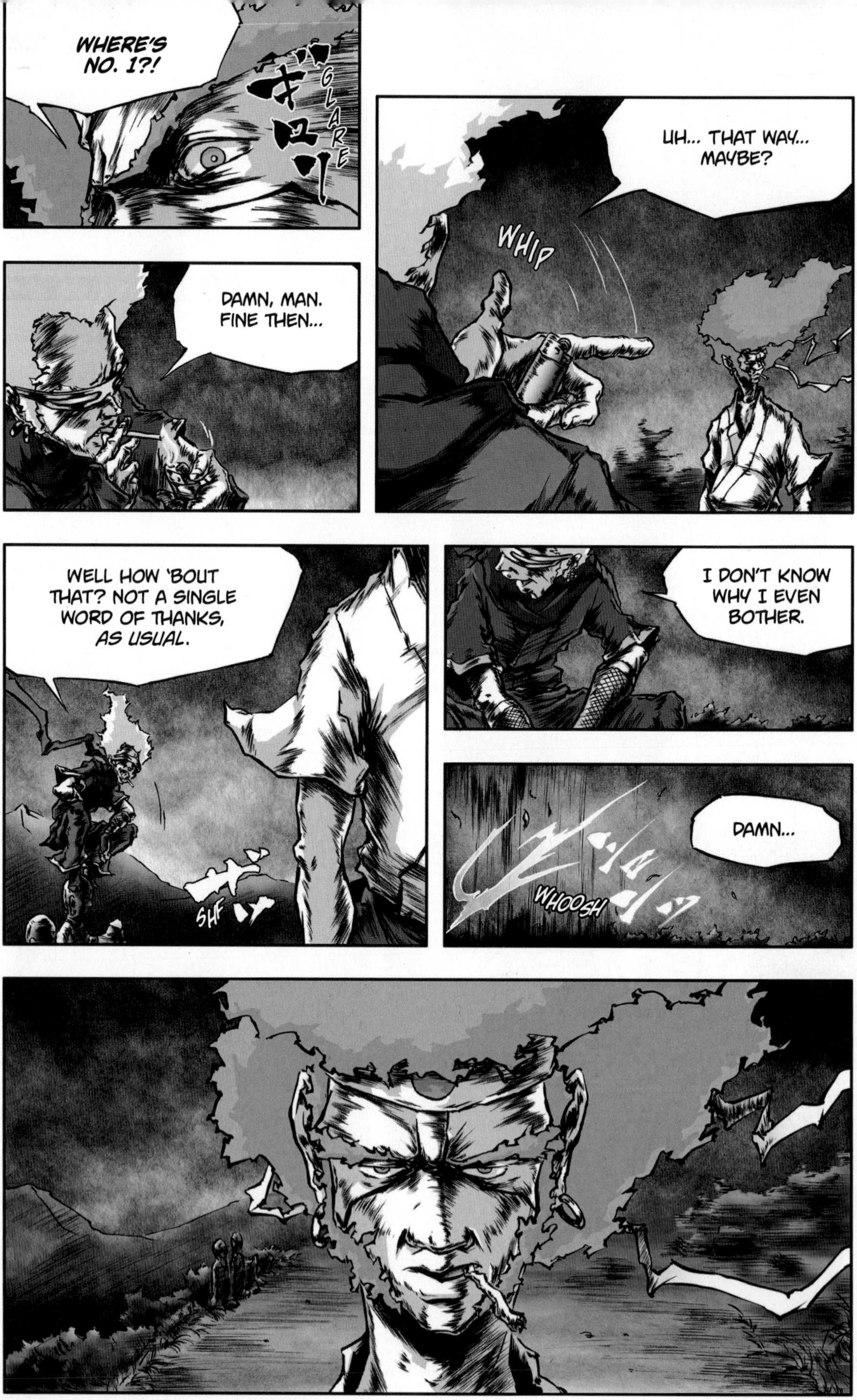
WHERE'S NO. 1?!
GLARE
DAMN, MAN. FINE THEN...
UH... THAT WAY... MAYBE?
WHIP
WELL HOW 'BOUT THAT? NOT A SINGLE WORD OF THANKS, AS USUAL.
SHF
I DON'T KNOW WHY I EVEN BOTHER.
DAMN...
WHOOSH

END OF #01

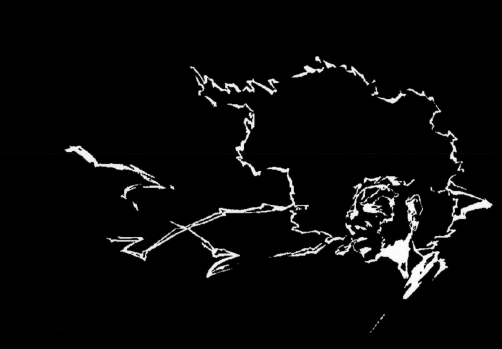

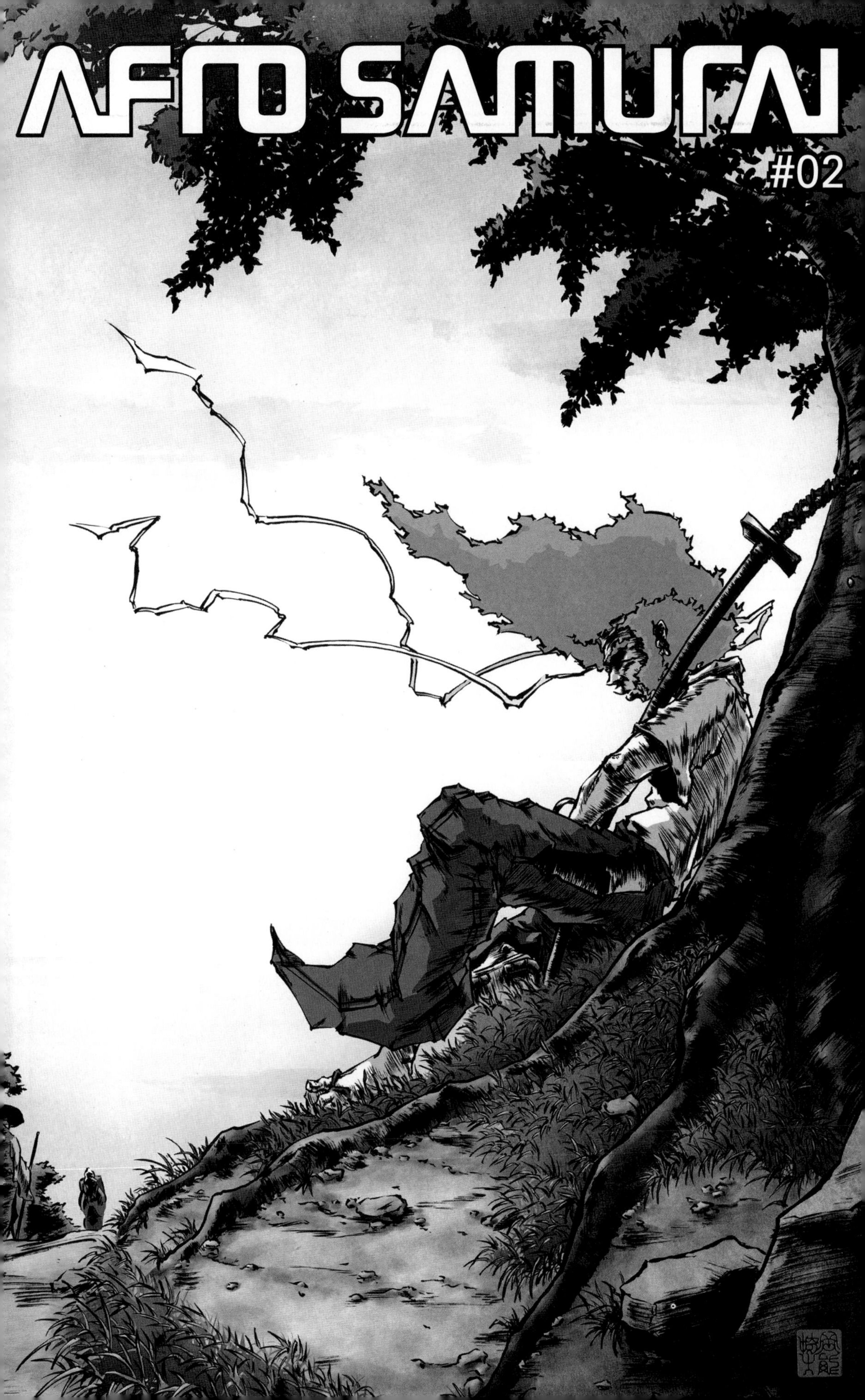
AFRO SAMURAI
#02

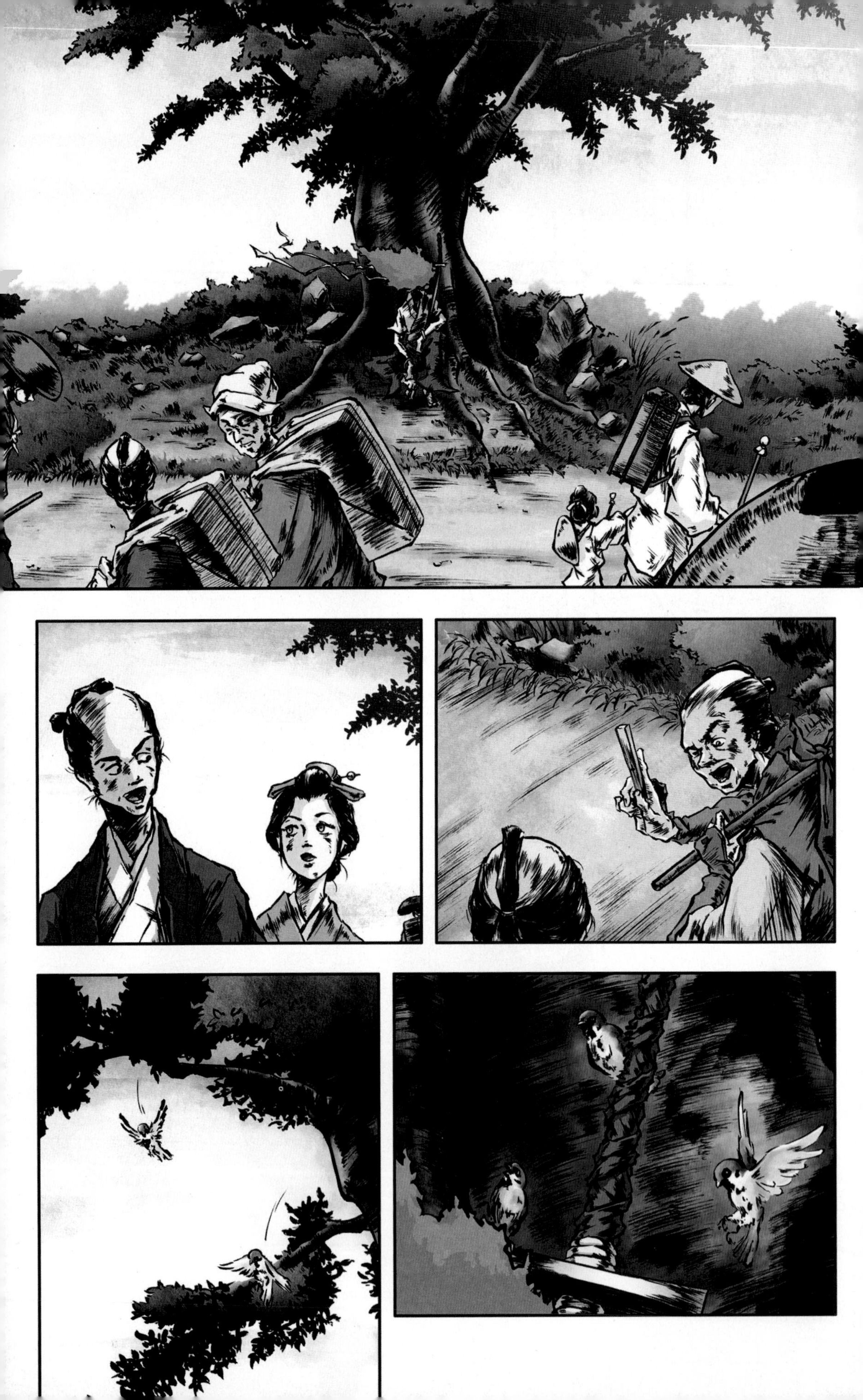

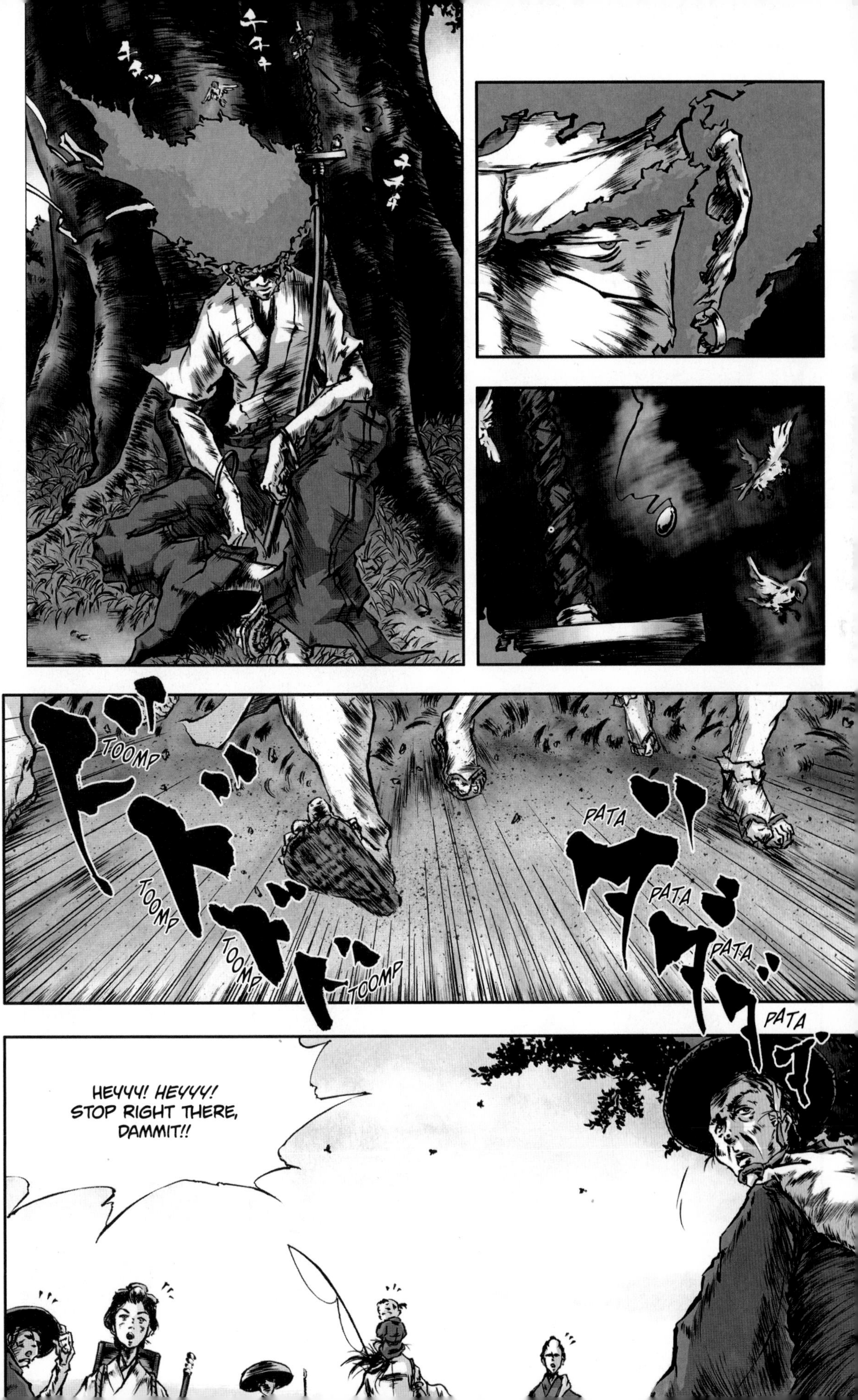
TOOMP
TOOMP
TOOMP
TOOMP
PATA
PATA
PATA
PATA
HEYYY! HEYYY!
STOP RIGHT THERE,
DAMMIT!!

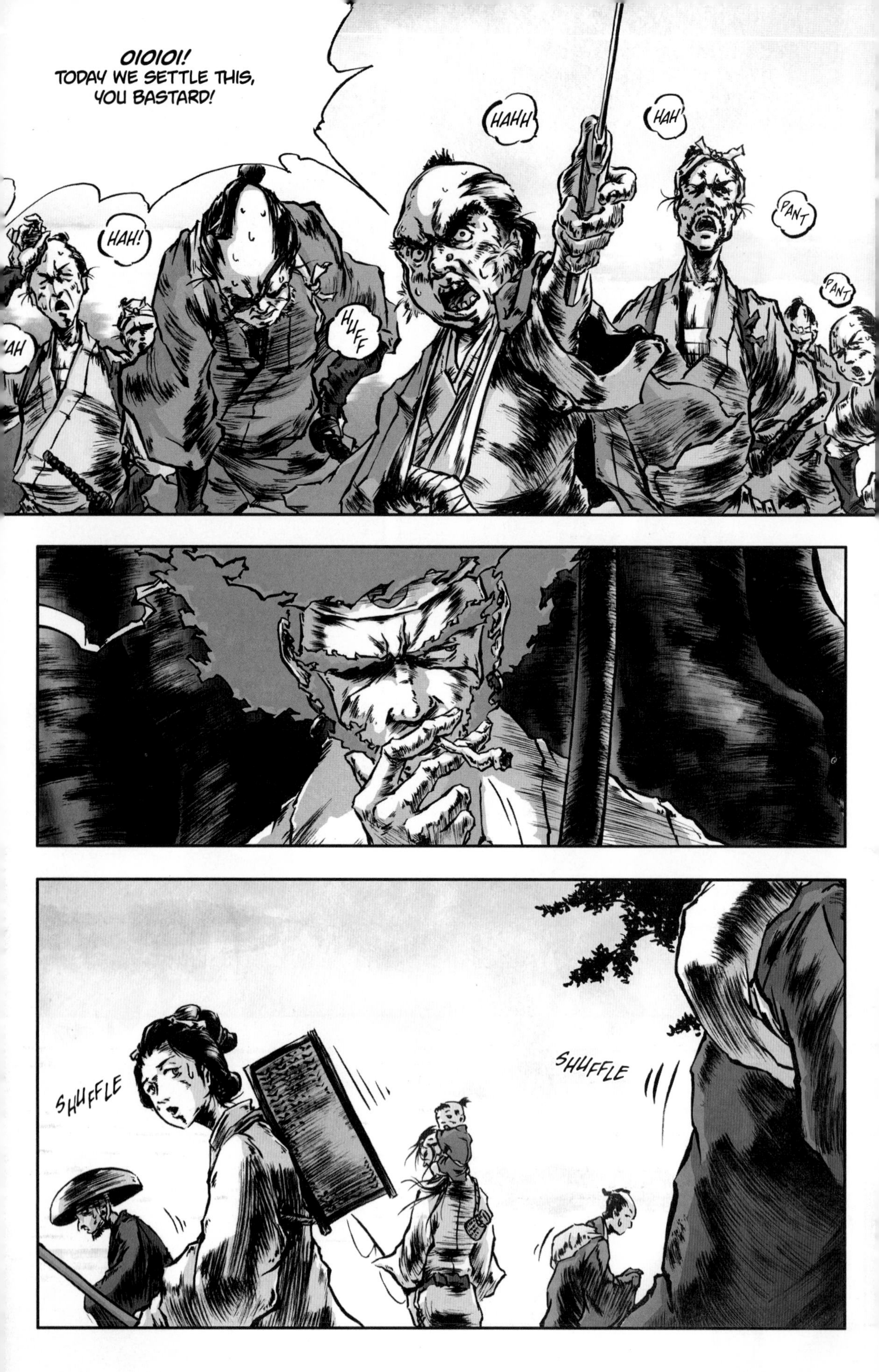
OIOIOI!
TODAY WE SETTLE THIS, YOU BASTARD!
'AH
HAH!
HUFF
HAHH
HAH
PANT
PANT
SHUFFLE
SHUFFLE

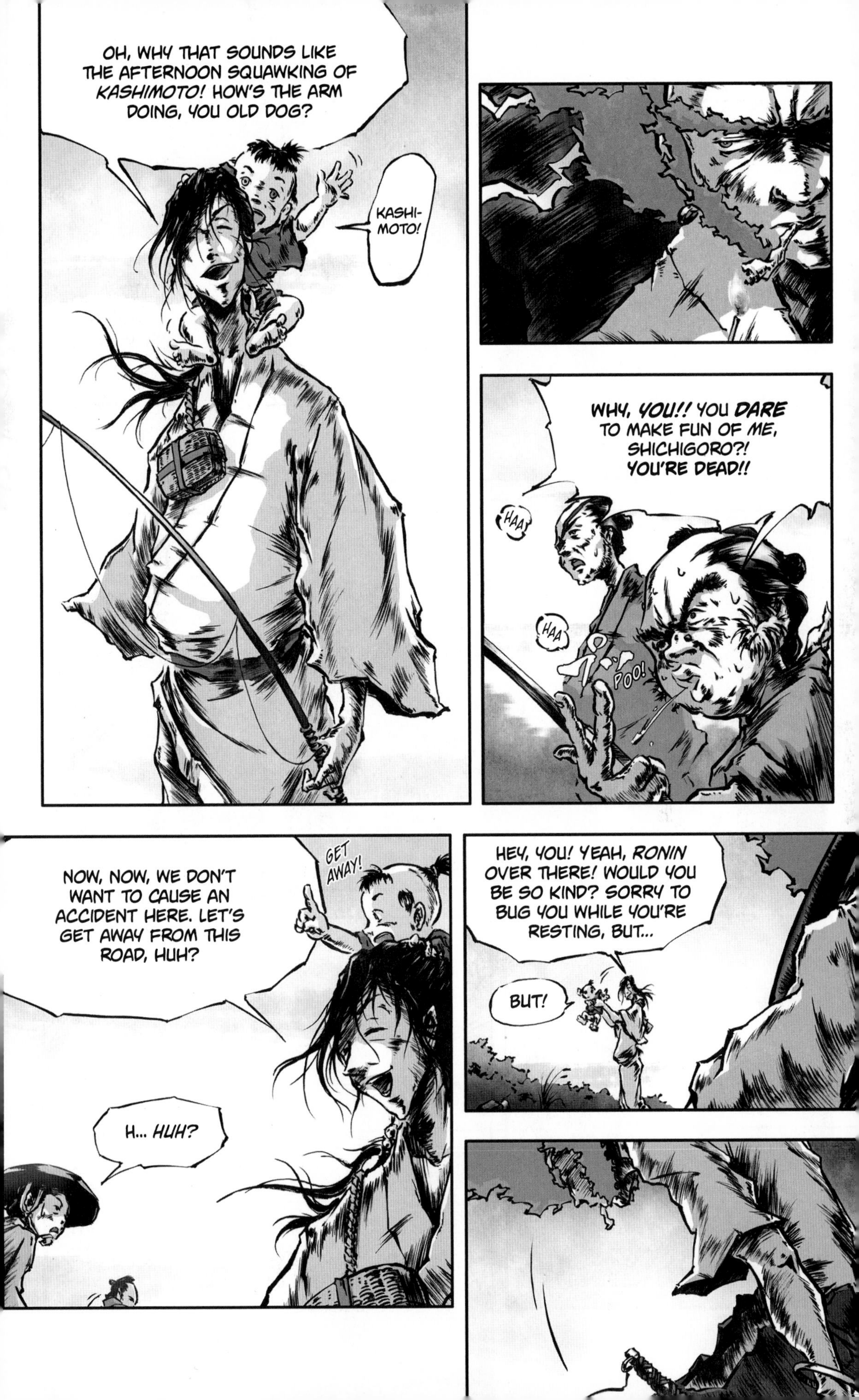
OH, WHY THAT SOUNDS LIKE THE AFTERNOON SQUAWKING OF *KASHIMOTO!* HOW'S THE ARM DOING, YOU OLD DOG?
KASHI-MOTO!
WHY, *YOU!!* YOU **DARE** TO MAKE FUN OF ME, SHICHIGORO?! **YOU'RE DEAD!!**
HAA
HAA
POO!
NOW, NOW, WE DON'T WANT TO CAUSE AN ACCIDENT HERE. LET'S GET AWAY FROM THIS ROAD, HUH?
GET AWAY!
H... *HUH?*
HEY, YOU! YEAH, *RONIN* OVER THERE! WOULD YOU BE SO KIND? SORRY TO BUG YOU WHILE YOU'RE RESTING, BUT...
BUT!

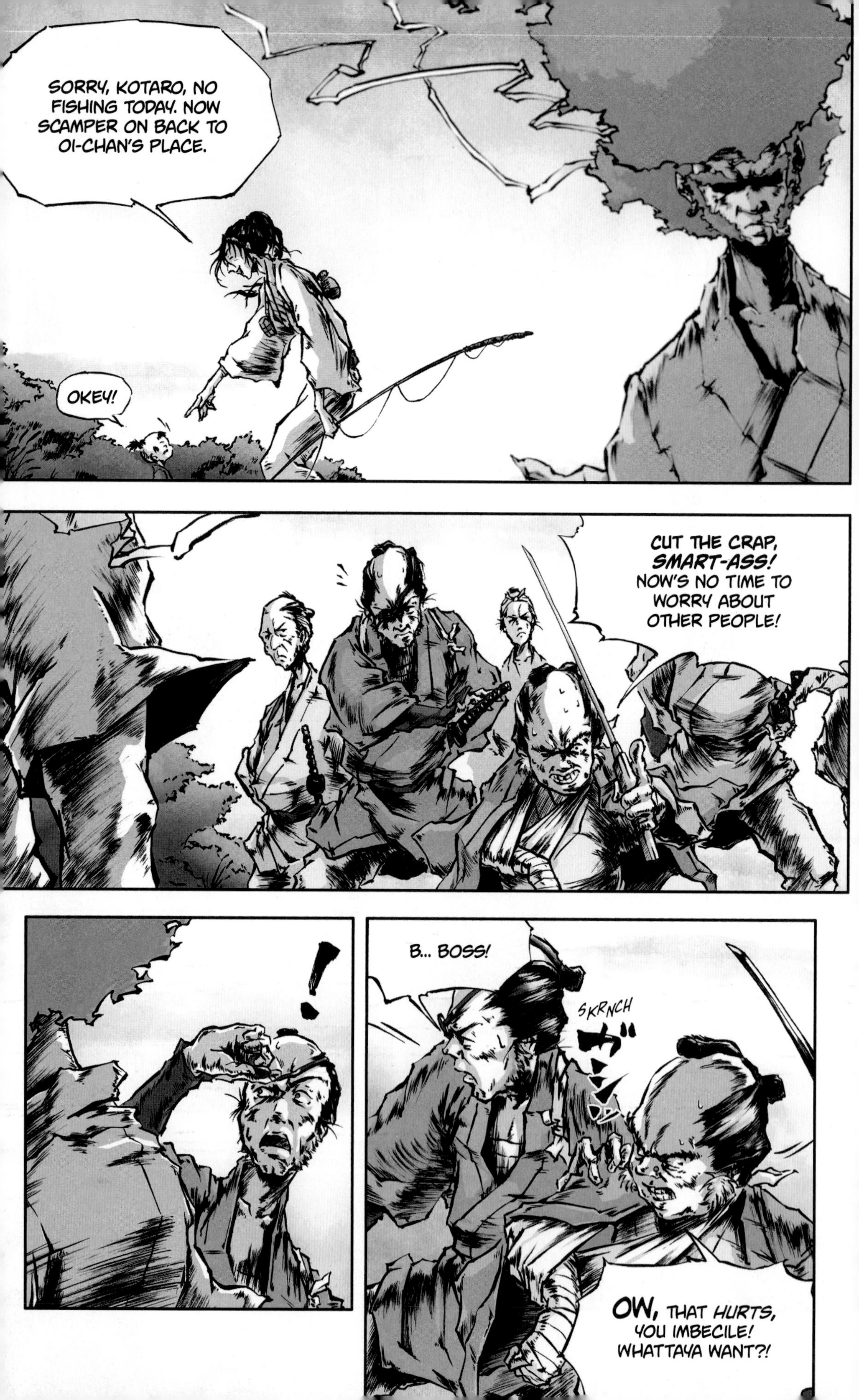
SORRY, KOTARO, NO FISHING TODAY. NOW SCAMPER ON BACK TO OI-CHAN'S PLACE.
OKEY!
CUT THE CRAP, *SMART-ASS!* NOW'S NO TIME TO WORRY ABOUT OTHER PEOPLE!
!
B... BOSS!
SKRNCH
OW, THAT *HURTS*, YOU IMBECILE! WHATTAYA WANT?!

THAT GUY... HE'S--!

RUSTLE

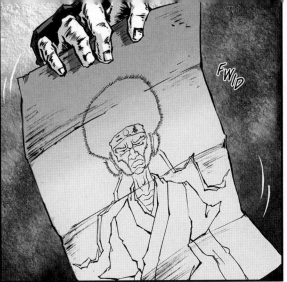

FWID

TH-THAT'S A *RED PAPER!* THIS IS A DIRECT ORDER FOR ARREST FROM THE EMPTY SEVEN, THE BIG GUYS UP IN *TECCHISEN!*

HEH HEH... LOOKS LIKE FATE'S SMILIN' ON US TODAY. MAN, IF WE GET THIS GUY, WE CAN SAY GOODBYE TO ALL THOSE DEBTS.

C'MON, NOW. IF WE'RE GONNA DO THIS THING, LET'S DO IT ALREADY!

SHICHIGORO! I DON'T HAVE TIME FOR YOU ANYMORE!

GO CHASE YOURSELF SOMEWHERE!!

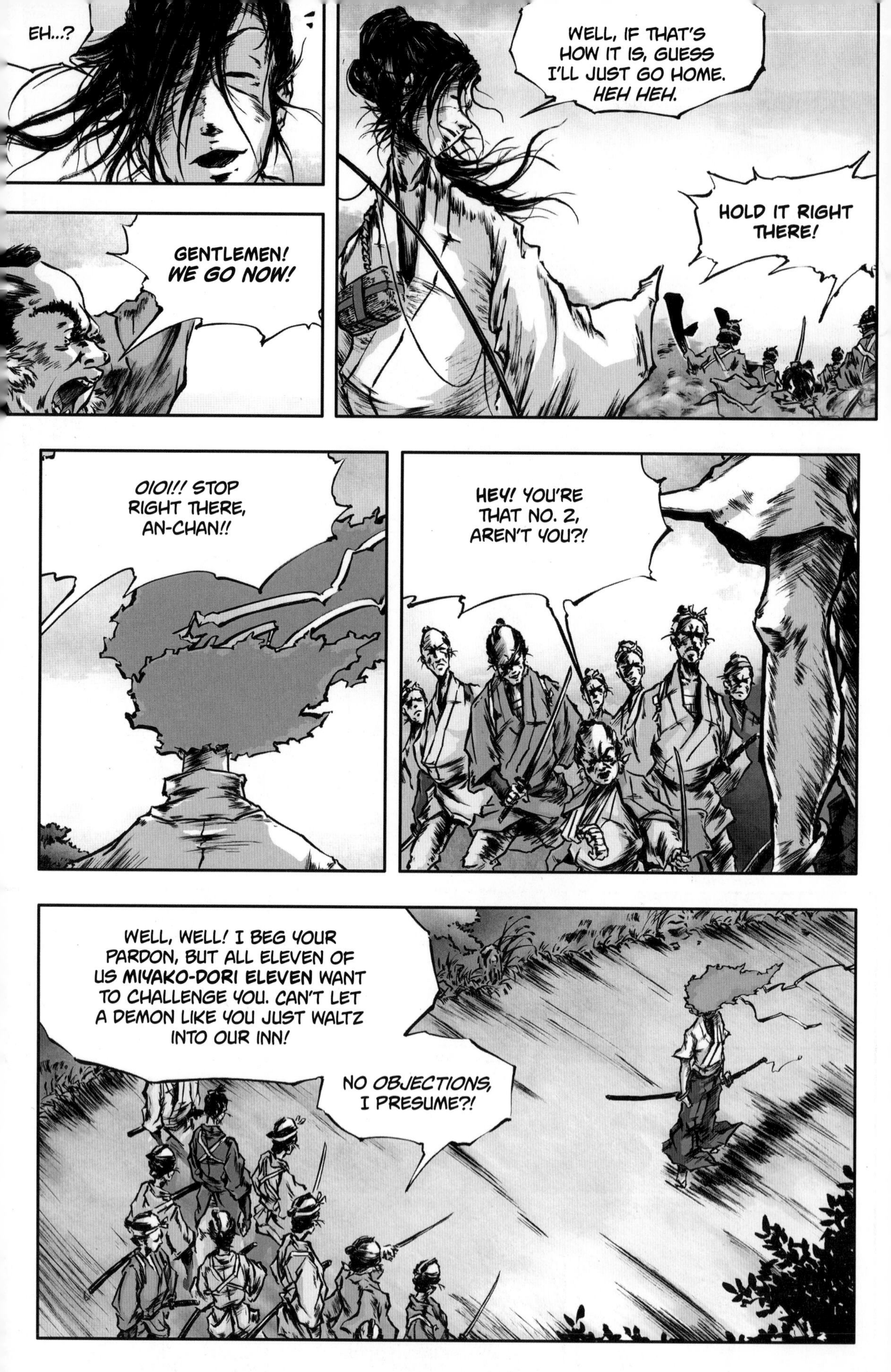
EH...?
GENTLEMEN! WE GO NOW!
WELL, IF THAT'S HOW IT IS, GUESS I'LL JUST GO HOME. HEH HEH.
HOLD IT RIGHT THERE!
OIOI!! STOP RIGHT THERE, AN-CHAN!!
HEY! YOU'RE THAT NO. 2, AREN'T YOU?!
WELL, WELL! I BEG YOUR PARDON, BUT ALL ELEVEN OF US MIYAKO-DORI ELEVEN WANT TO CHALLENGE YOU. CAN'T LET A DEMON LIKE YOU JUST WALTZ INTO OUR INN!
NO OBJECTIONS, I PRESUME?!

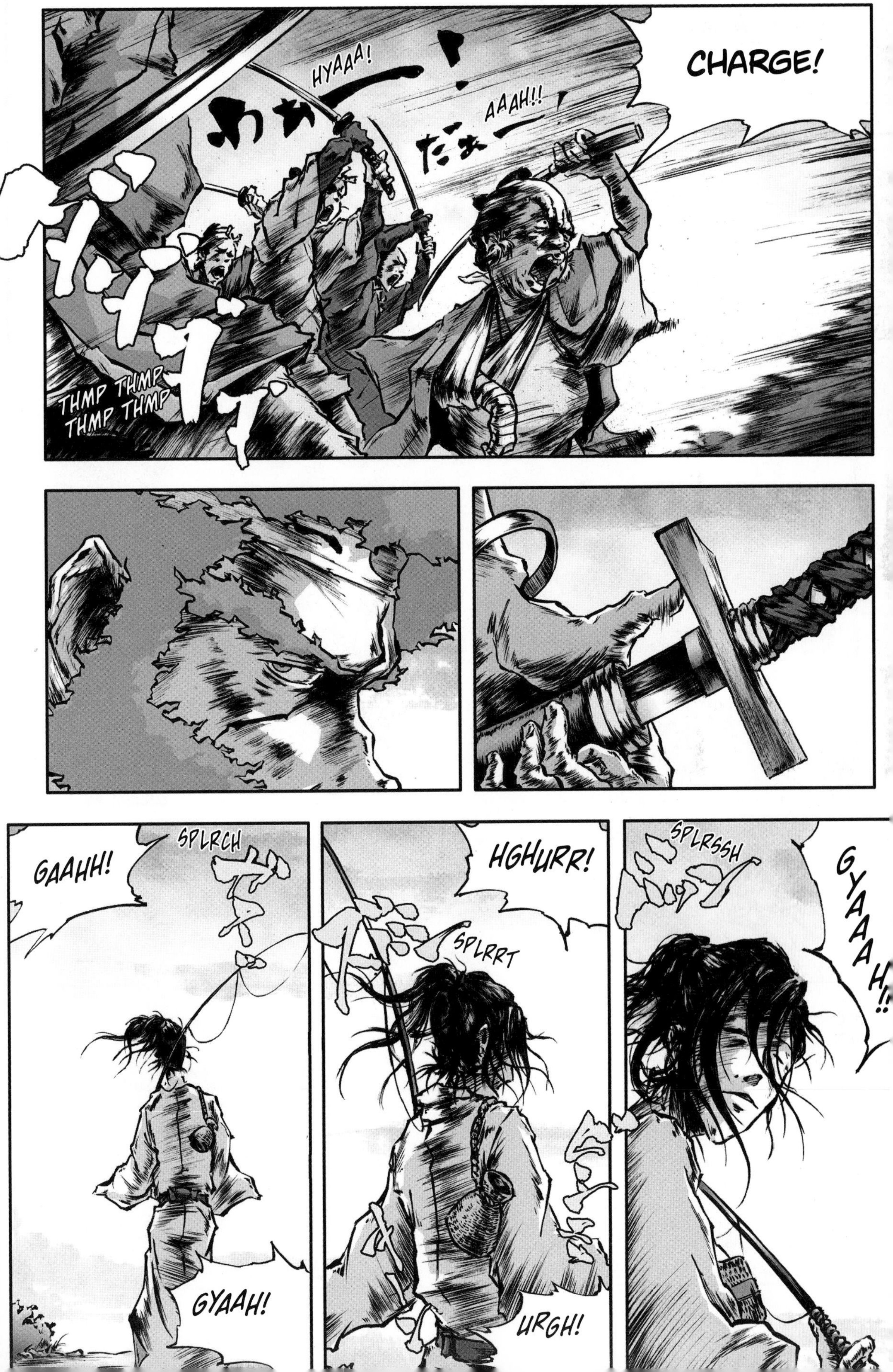
HYAAA!
AAAH!!
CHARGE!
THMP THMP THMP THMP
GAAHH!
SPLRCH
GYAAH!
HGHURR!
SPLRRT
URGH!
SPLRSSH
GYAAAAH!!

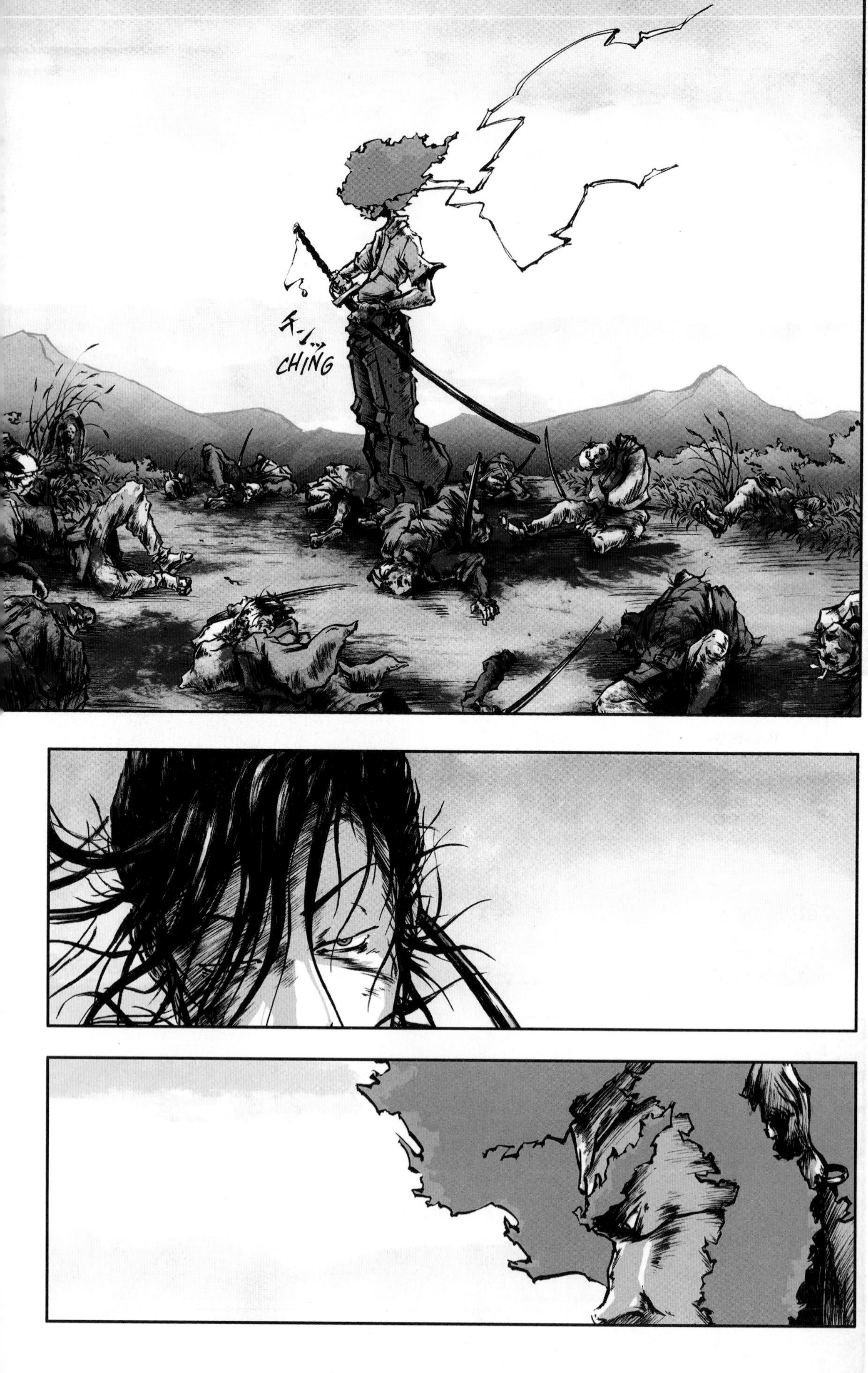
チーンッ
CHING

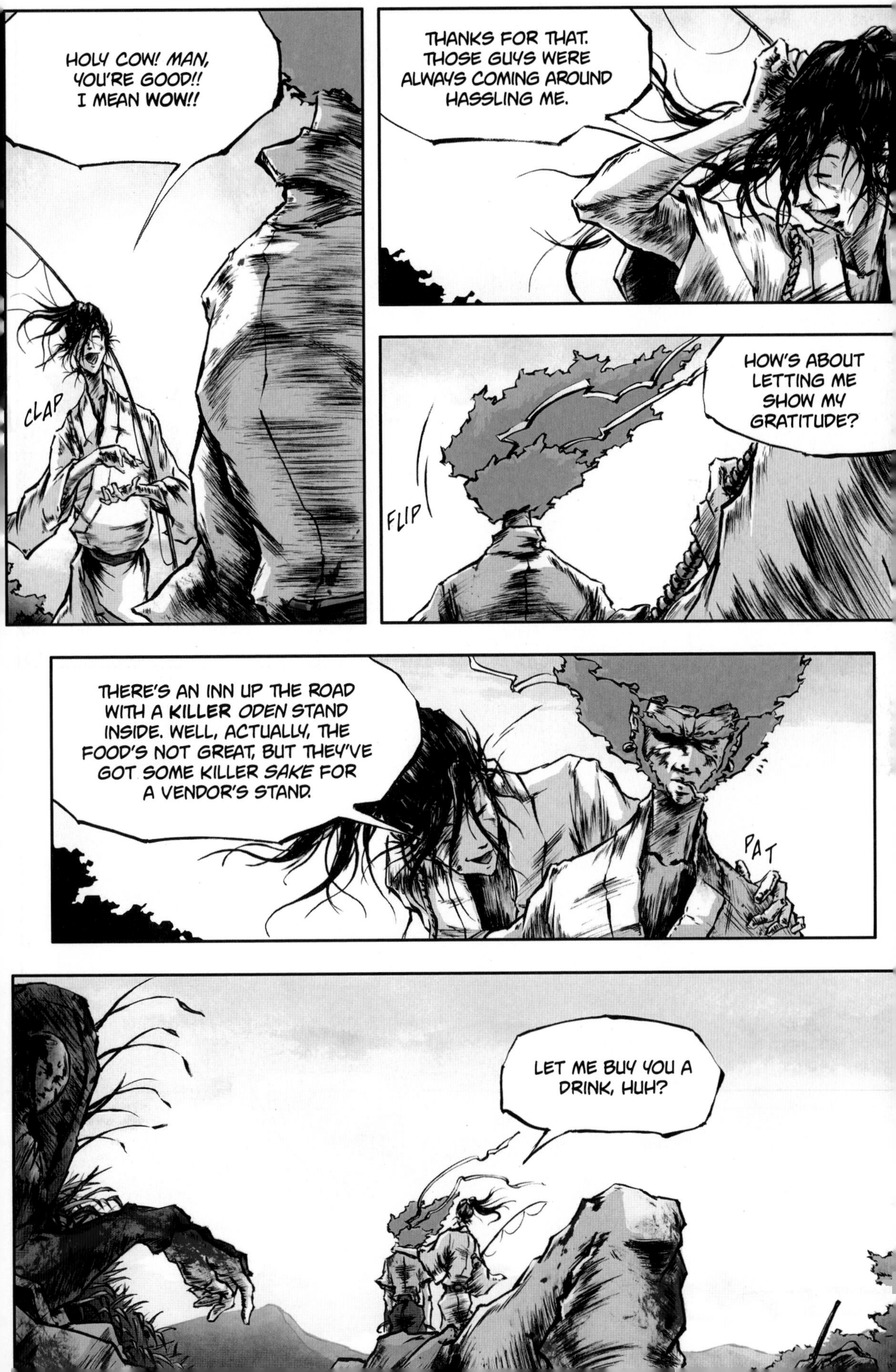
HOLY COW! *MAN,* YOU'RE GOOD!! I MEAN WOW!!
CLAP
THANKS FOR THAT. THOSE GUYS WERE ALWAYS COMING AROUND HASSLING ME.
FLIP
HOW'S ABOUT LETTING ME SHOW MY GRATITUDE?
THERE'S AN INN UP THE ROAD WITH A **KILLER** *ODEN* STAND INSIDE. WELL, ACTUALLY, THE FOOD'S NOT GREAT, BUT THEY'VE GOT SOME KILLER *SAKE* FOR A VENDOR'S STAND.
PAT
LET ME BUY YOU A DRINK, HUH?

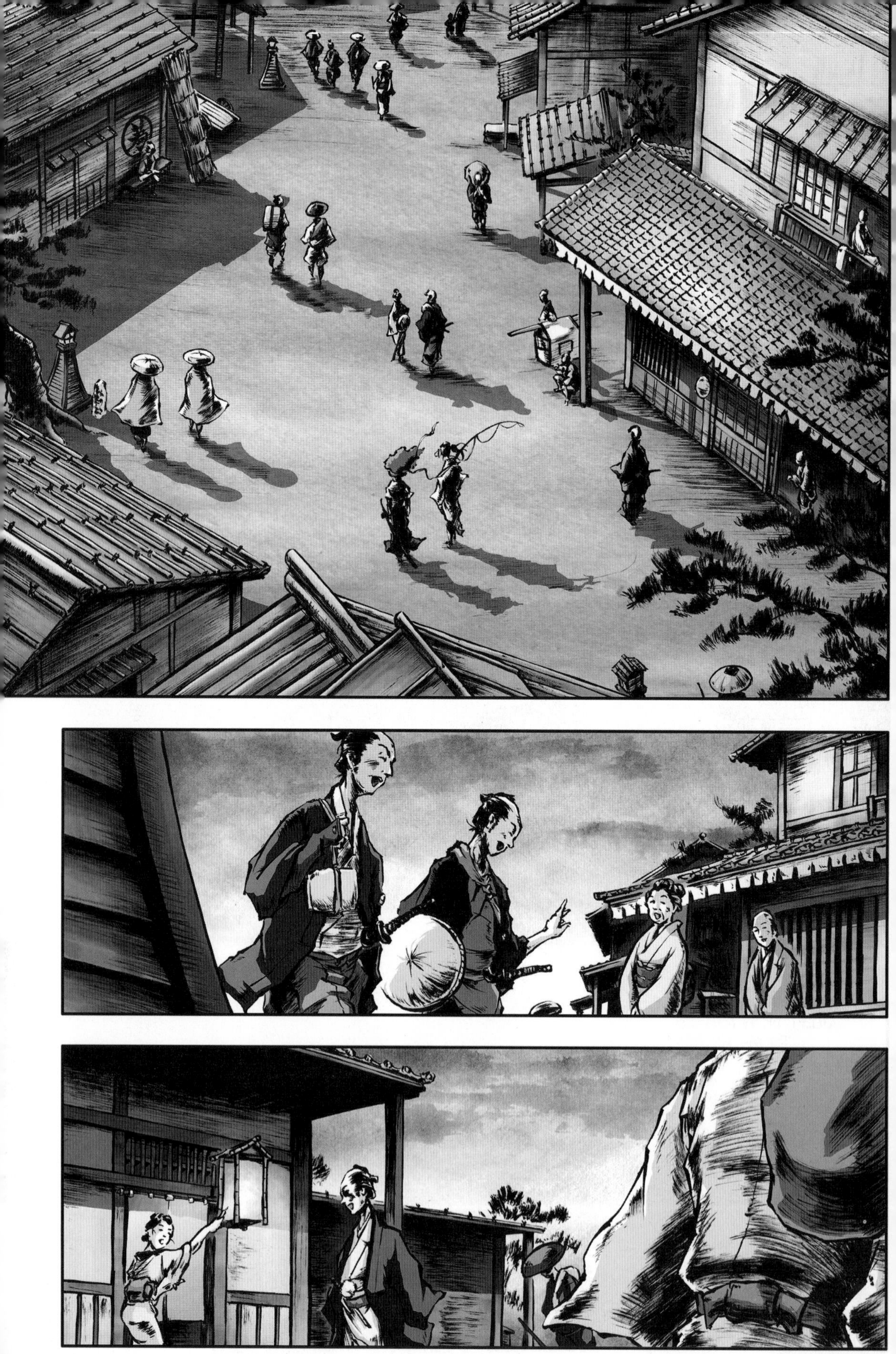

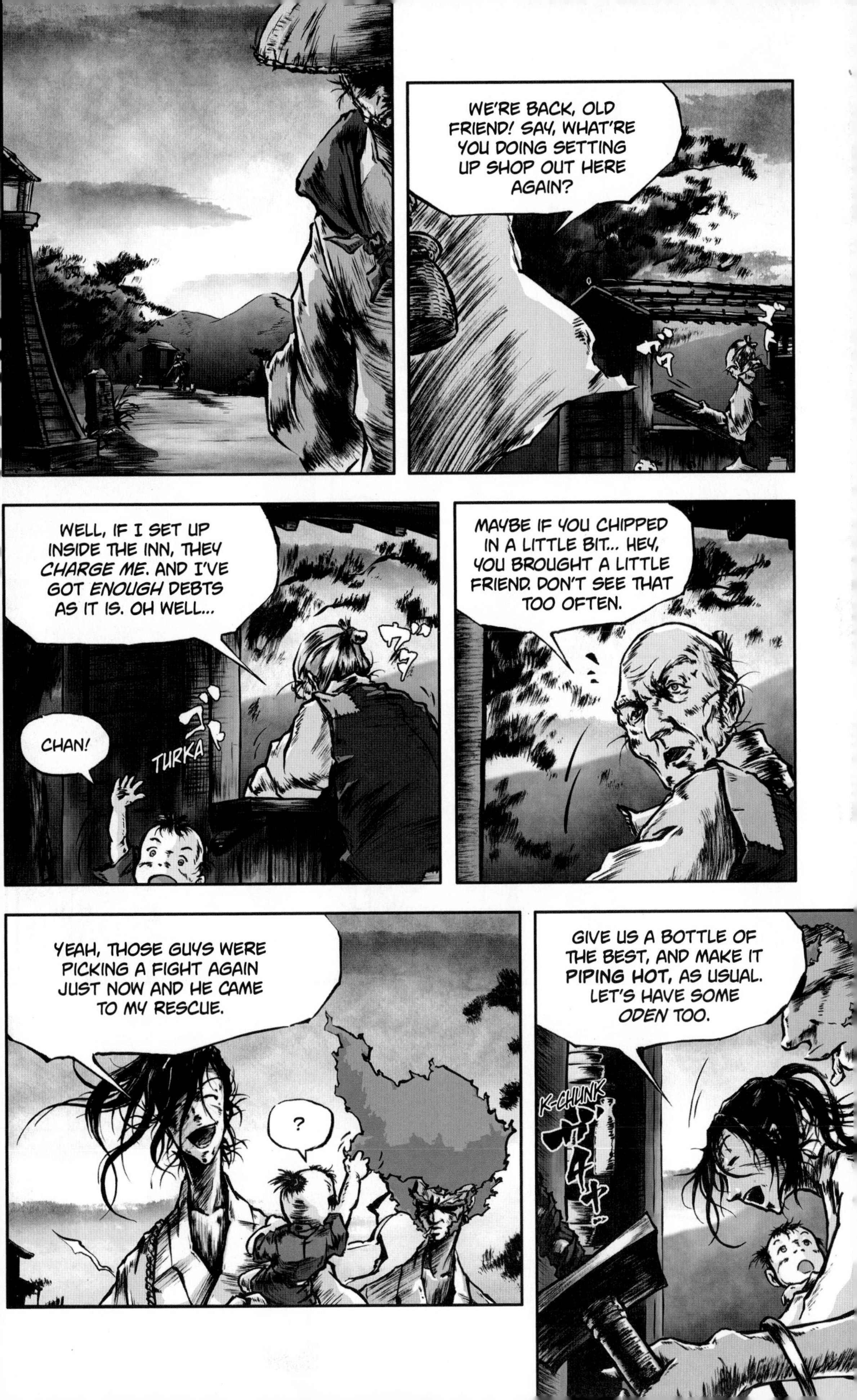
WE'RE BACK, OLD FRIEND! SAY, WHAT'RE YOU DOING SETTING UP SHOP OUT HERE AGAIN?
WELL, IF I SET UP INSIDE THE INN, THEY *CHARGE ME*. AND I'VE GOT *ENOUGH* DEBTS AS IT IS. OH WELL...
CHAN!
TURKA
MAYBE IF YOU CHIPPED IN A LITTLE BIT... HEY, YOU BROUGHT A LITTLE FRIEND. DON'T SEE THAT TOO OFTEN.
YEAH, THOSE GUYS WERE PICKING A FIGHT AGAIN JUST NOW AND HE CAME TO MY RESCUE.
?
GIVE US A BOTTLE OF THE BEST, AND MAKE IT PIPING HOT, AS USUAL. LET'S HAVE SOME *ODEN* TOO.
K-CHUNK

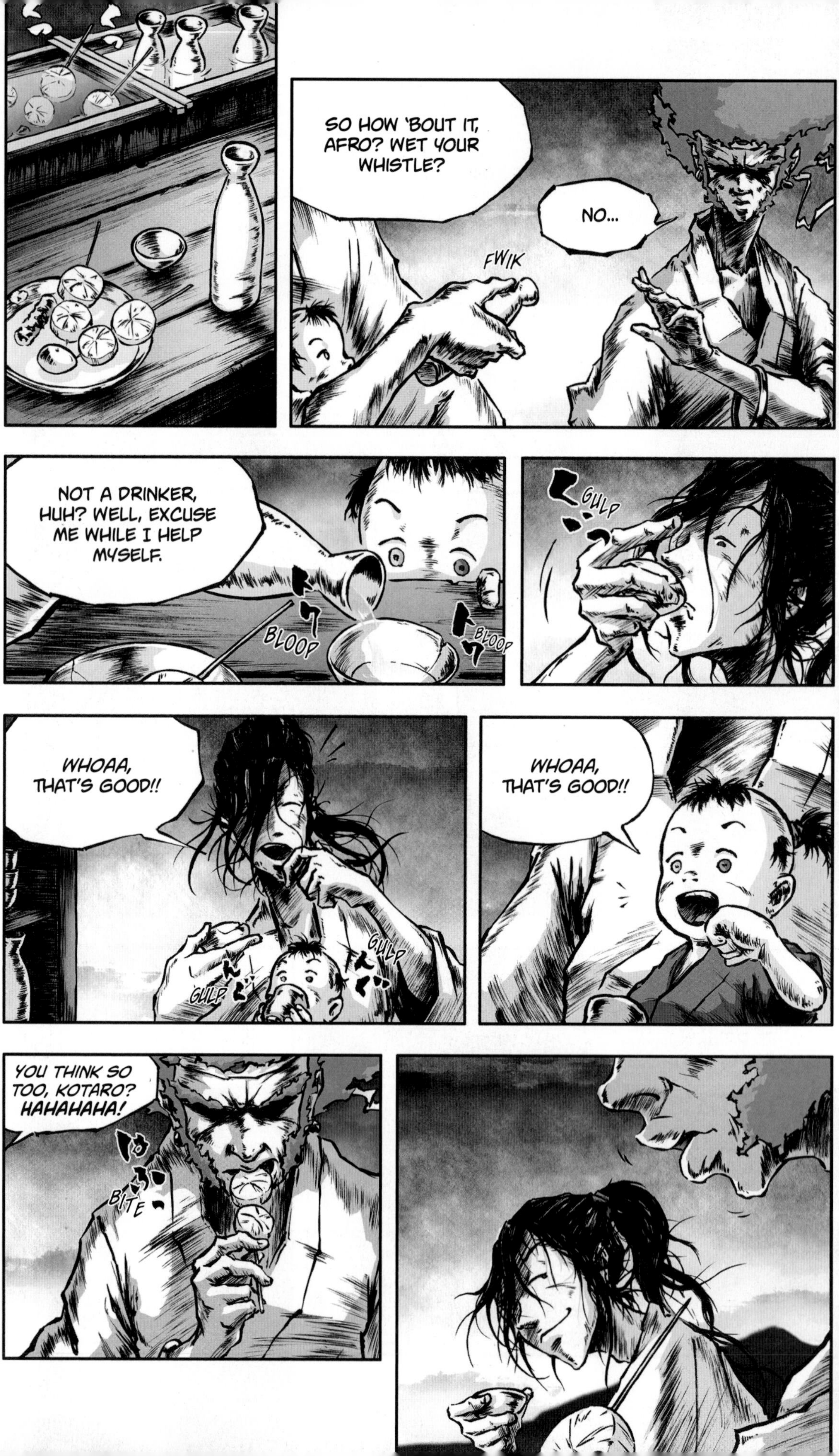
SO HOW 'BOUT IT, AFRO? WET YOUR WHISTLE?
NO...
FWIK
NOT A DRINKER, HUH? WELL, EXCUSE ME WHILE I HELP MYSELF.
BLOOP
BLOOP
GULP
WHOAA, THAT'S GOOD!!
GULP
GULP
WHOAA, THAT'S GOOD!!
YOU THINK SO TOO, KOTARO? HAHAHAHA!
BITE

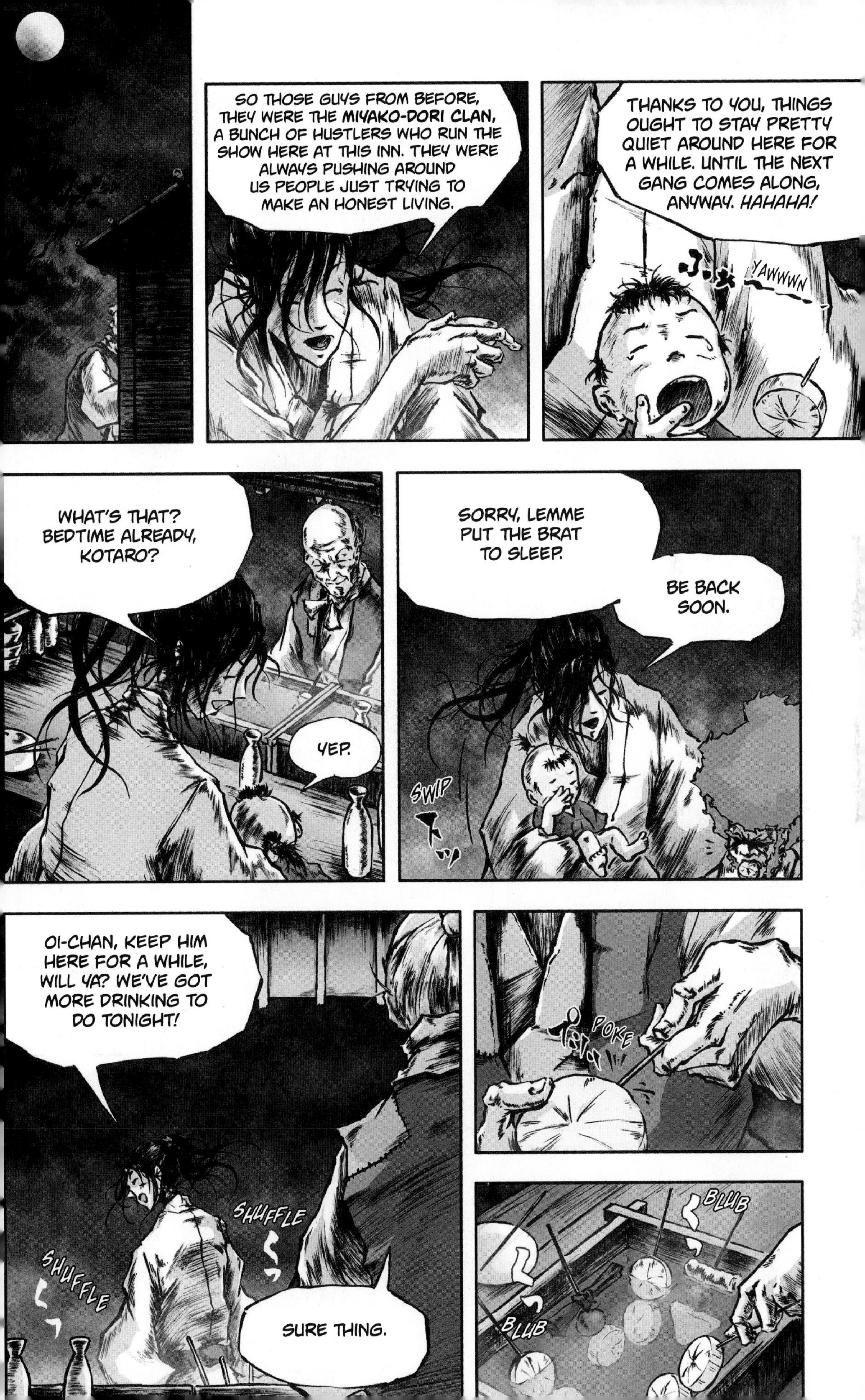
SO THOSE GUYS FROM BEFORE, THEY WERE THE MIYAKO-DORI CLAN, A BUNCH OF HUSTLERS WHO RUN THE SHOW HERE AT THIS INN. THEY WERE ALWAYS PUSHING AROUND US PEOPLE JUST TRYING TO MAKE AN HONEST LIVING.
THANKS TO YOU, THINGS OUGHT TO STAY PRETTY QUIET AROUND HERE FOR A WHILE. UNTIL THE NEXT GANG COMES ALONG, ANYWAY. HAHAHA!
YAWWWN
WHAT'S THAT? BEDTIME ALREADY, KOTARO?
YEP.
SORRY, LEMME PUT THE BRAT TO SLEEP.
BE BACK SOON.
SWIP
OI-CHAN, KEEP HIM HERE FOR A WHILE, WILL YA? WE'VE GOT MORE DRINKING TO DO TONIGHT!
SHUFFLE
SHUFFLE
SURE THING.
POKE
BLUB
BLUB

SO YOU'RE THE FABLED NO. 2...?

MUNCH

NOW, JUST HOLD ON.

RELAX. IF I WANTED TO KILL YOU, I WOULD'VE ALREADY TRIED.

YOU'VE GOT THE FACE OF A GUY WHO'S BEEN MADE A TARGET AT EVERY TURN. LIKE YOU'VE SPENT EVERY DAY SLIPPING THROUGH THE FINGERS OF DEATH.

YOU MUST REALLY BE SOMETHIN' TO MAKE IT THIS FAR.

THE ONES AFTER YOU ARE A NEFARIOUS GROUP. THEY'RE THE KINGPINS LEADING ALL THE ASSASSINS OF THE WORLD.

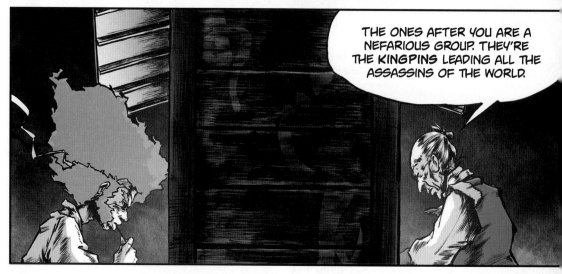

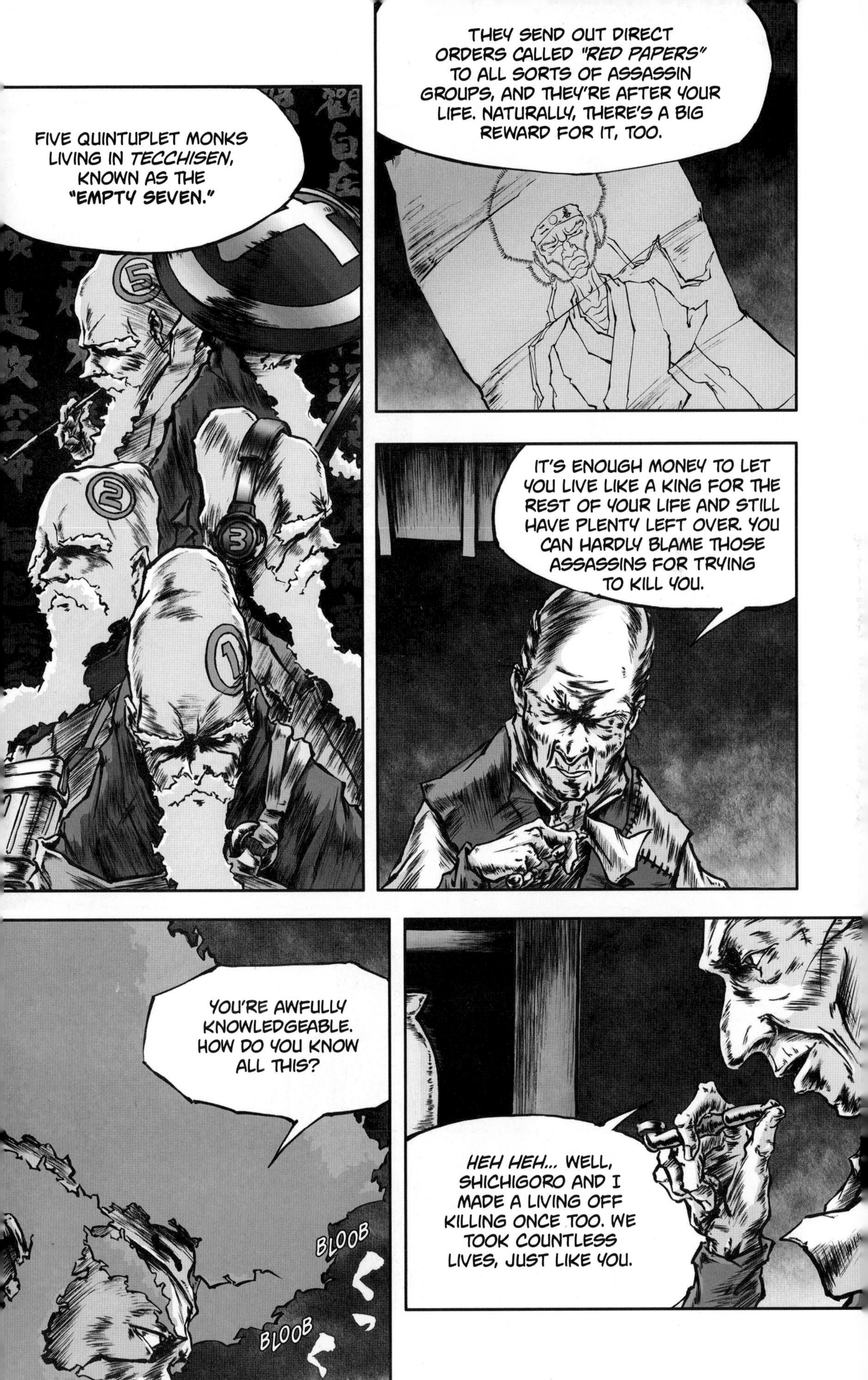
FIVE QUINTUPLET MONKS LIVING IN *TECCHISEN*, KNOWN AS THE "EMPTY SEVEN."
THEY SEND OUT DIRECT ORDERS CALLED *"RED PAPERS"* TO ALL SORTS OF ASSASSIN GROUPS, AND THEY'RE AFTER YOUR LIFE. NATURALLY, THERE'S A BIG REWARD FOR IT, TOO.
IT'S ENOUGH MONEY TO LET YOU LIVE LIKE A KING FOR THE REST OF YOUR LIFE AND STILL HAVE PLENTY LEFT OVER. YOU CAN HARDLY BLAME THOSE ASSASSINS FOR TRYING TO KILL YOU.
YOU'RE AWFULLY KNOWLEDGEABLE. HOW DO YOU KNOW ALL THIS?
BLOOB
BLOOB
HEH HEH... WELL, SHICHIGORO AND I MADE A LIVING OFF KILLING ONCE TOO. WE TOOK COUNTLESS LIVES, JUST LIKE YOU.

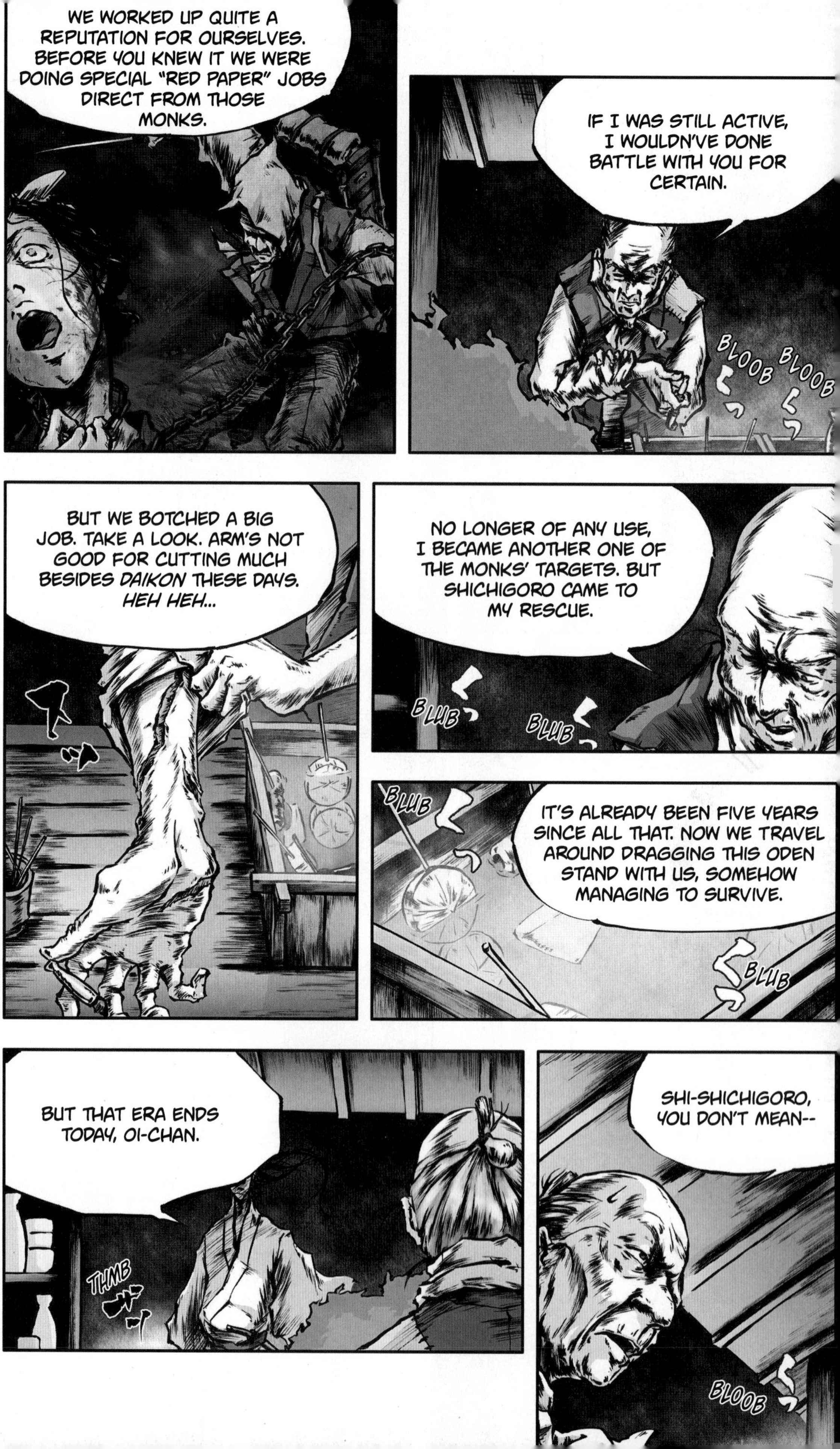
WE WORKED UP QUITE A REPUTATION FOR OURSELVES. BEFORE YOU KNEW IT WE WERE DOING SPECIAL "RED PAPER" JOBS DIRECT FROM THOSE MONKS.
IF I WAS STILL ACTIVE, I WOULDN'VE DONE BATTLE WITH YOU FOR CERTAIN.
BLOOB
BLOOB
BUT WE BOTCHED A BIG JOB. TAKE A LOOK. ARM'S NOT GOOD FOR CUTTING MUCH BESIDES DAIKON THESE DAYS. HEH HEH...
NO LONGER OF ANY USE, I BECAME ANOTHER ONE OF THE MONKS' TARGETS. BUT SHICHIGORO CAME TO MY RESCUE.
BLUB
BLUB
BLUB
IT'S ALREADY BEEN FIVE YEARS SINCE ALL THAT. NOW WE TRAVEL AROUND DRAGGING THIS ODEN STAND WITH US, SOMEHOW MANAGING TO SURVIVE.
BLUB
BUT THAT ERA ENDS TODAY, OI-CHAN.
THMB
SHI-SHICHIGORO, YOU DON'T MEAN--
BLOOB

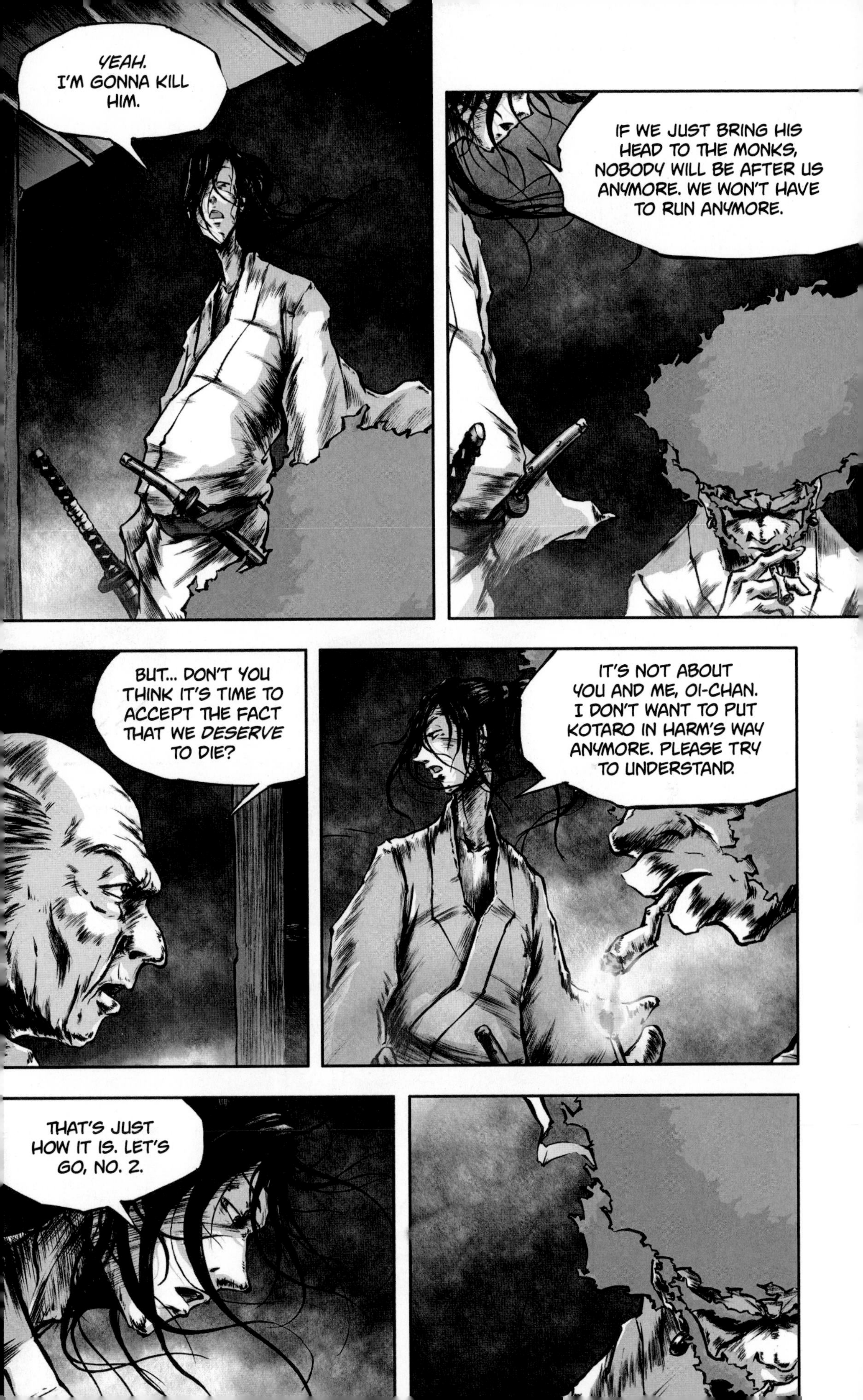
YEAH. I'M GONNA KILL HIM.
IF WE JUST BRING HIS HEAD TO THE MONKS, NOBODY WILL BE AFTER US ANYMORE. WE WON'T HAVE TO RUN ANYMORE.
BUT... DON'T YOU THINK IT'S TIME TO ACCEPT THE FACT THAT WE *DESERVE* TO DIE?
IT'S NOT ABOUT YOU AND ME, OI-CHAN. I DON'T WANT TO PUT KOTARO IN HARM'S WAY ANYMORE. PLEASE TRY TO UNDERSTAND.
THAT'S JUST HOW IT IS. LET'S GO, NO. 2.

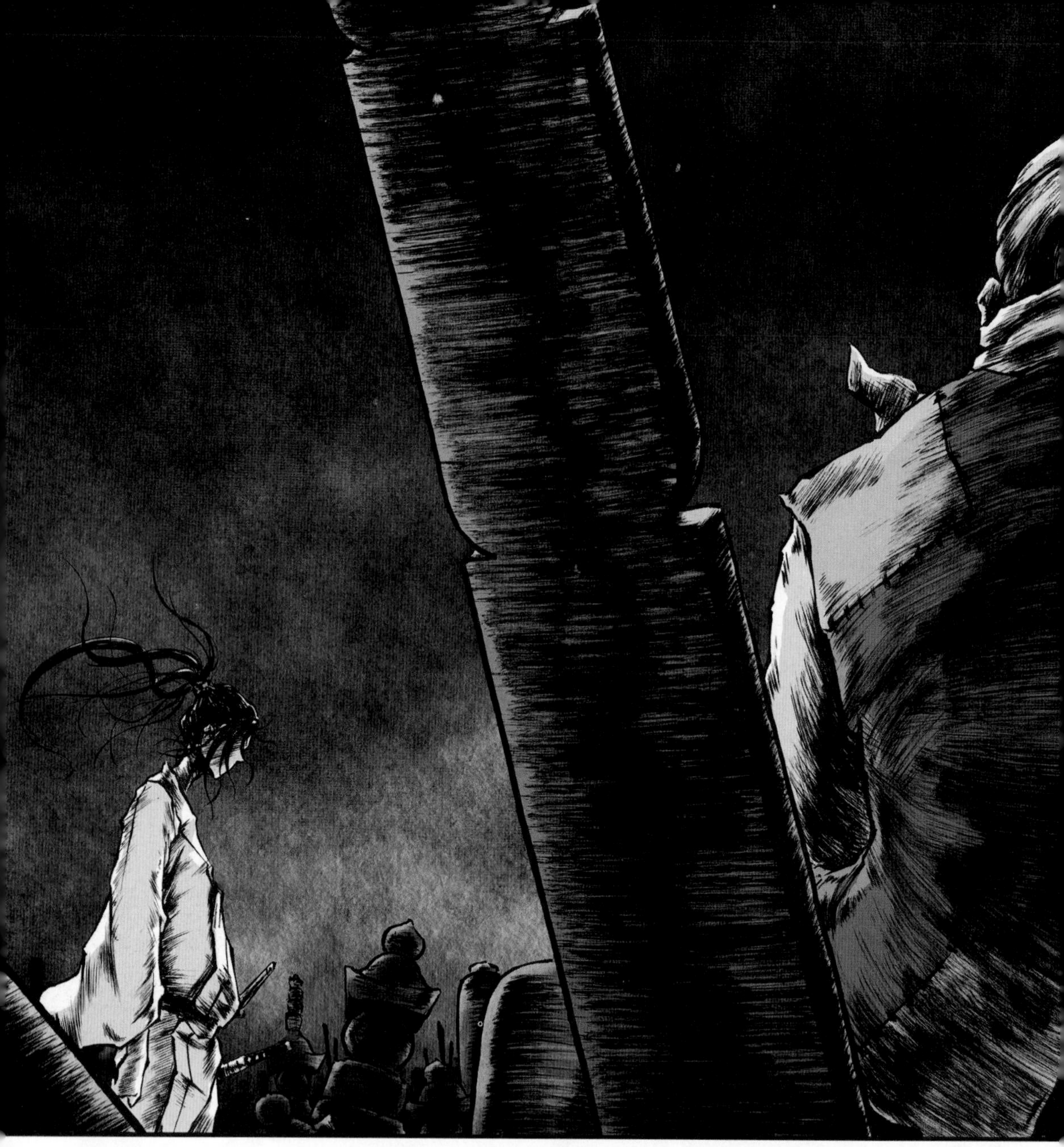
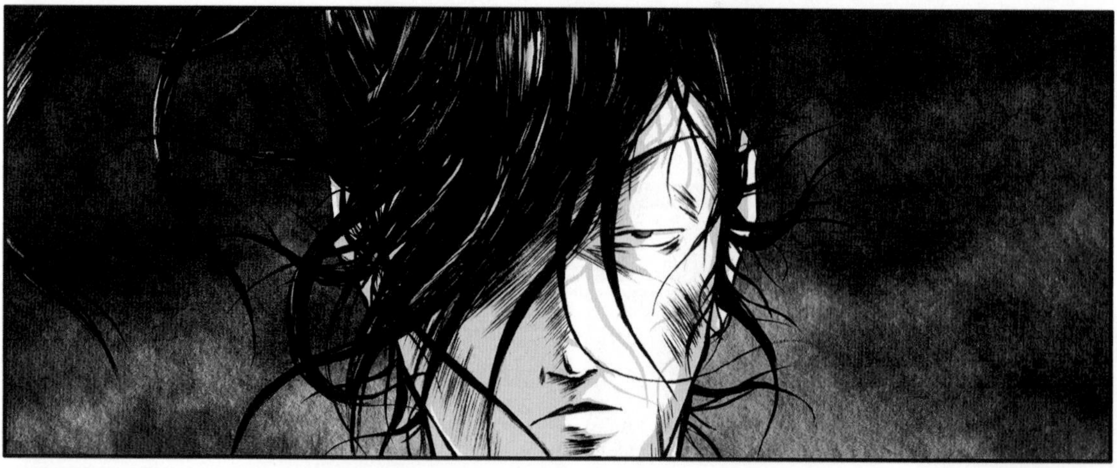

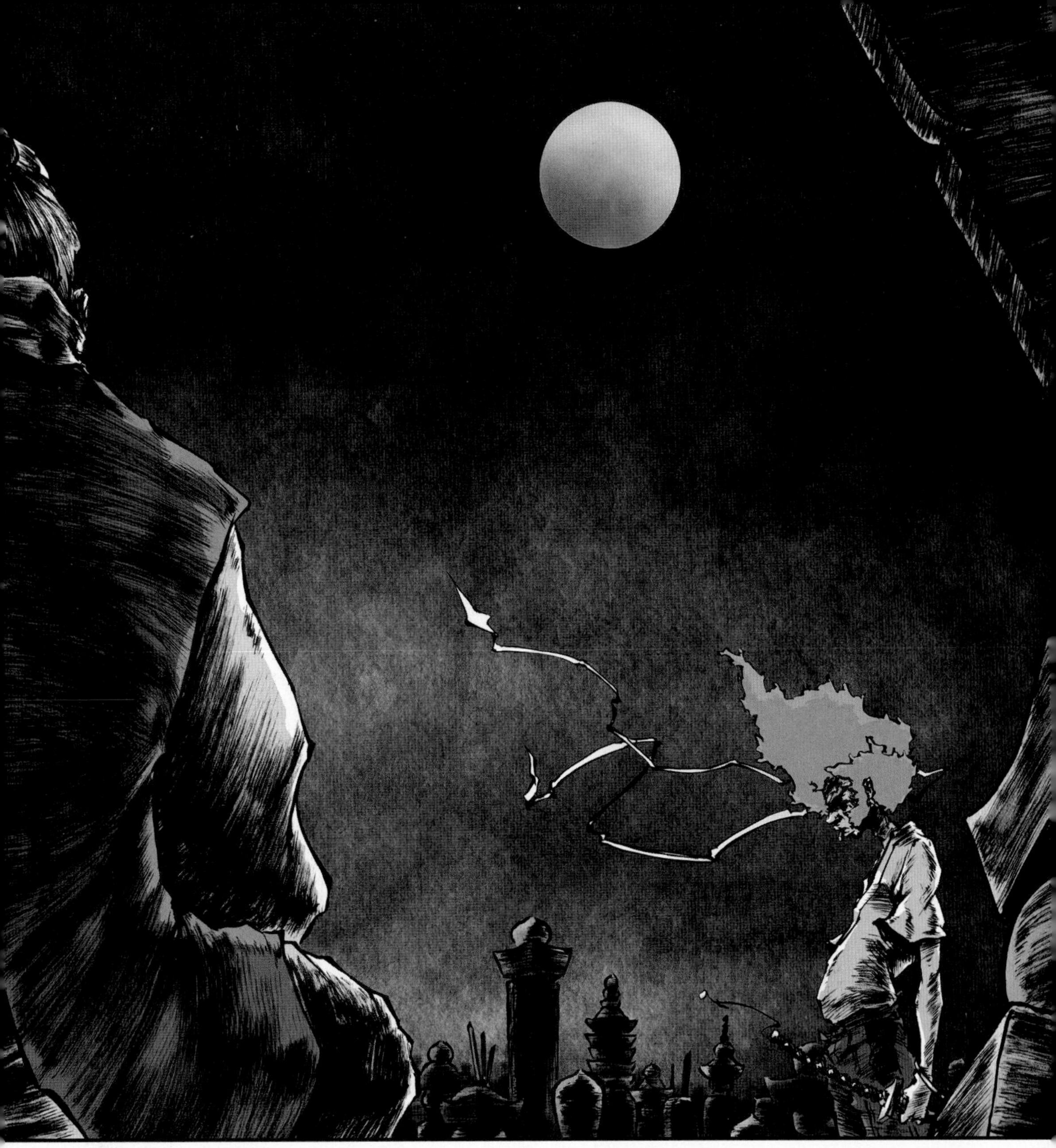
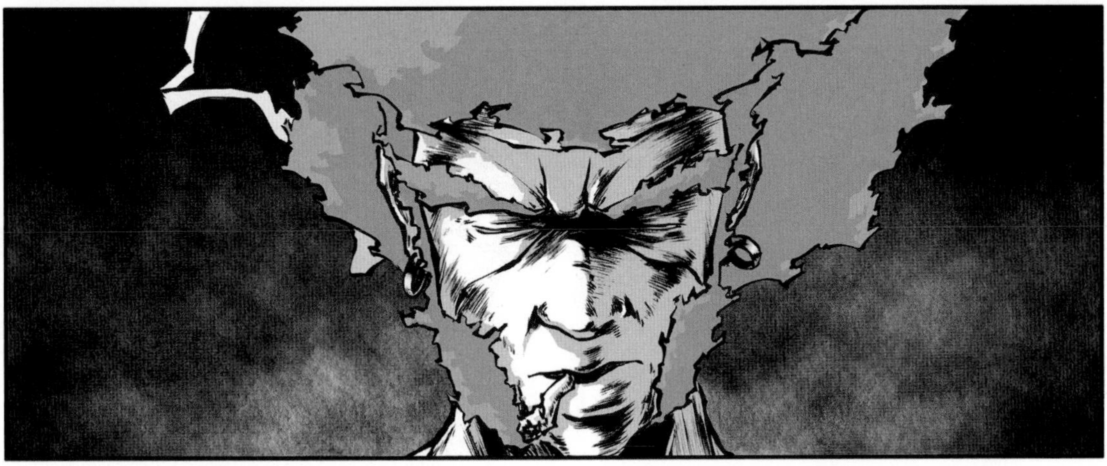

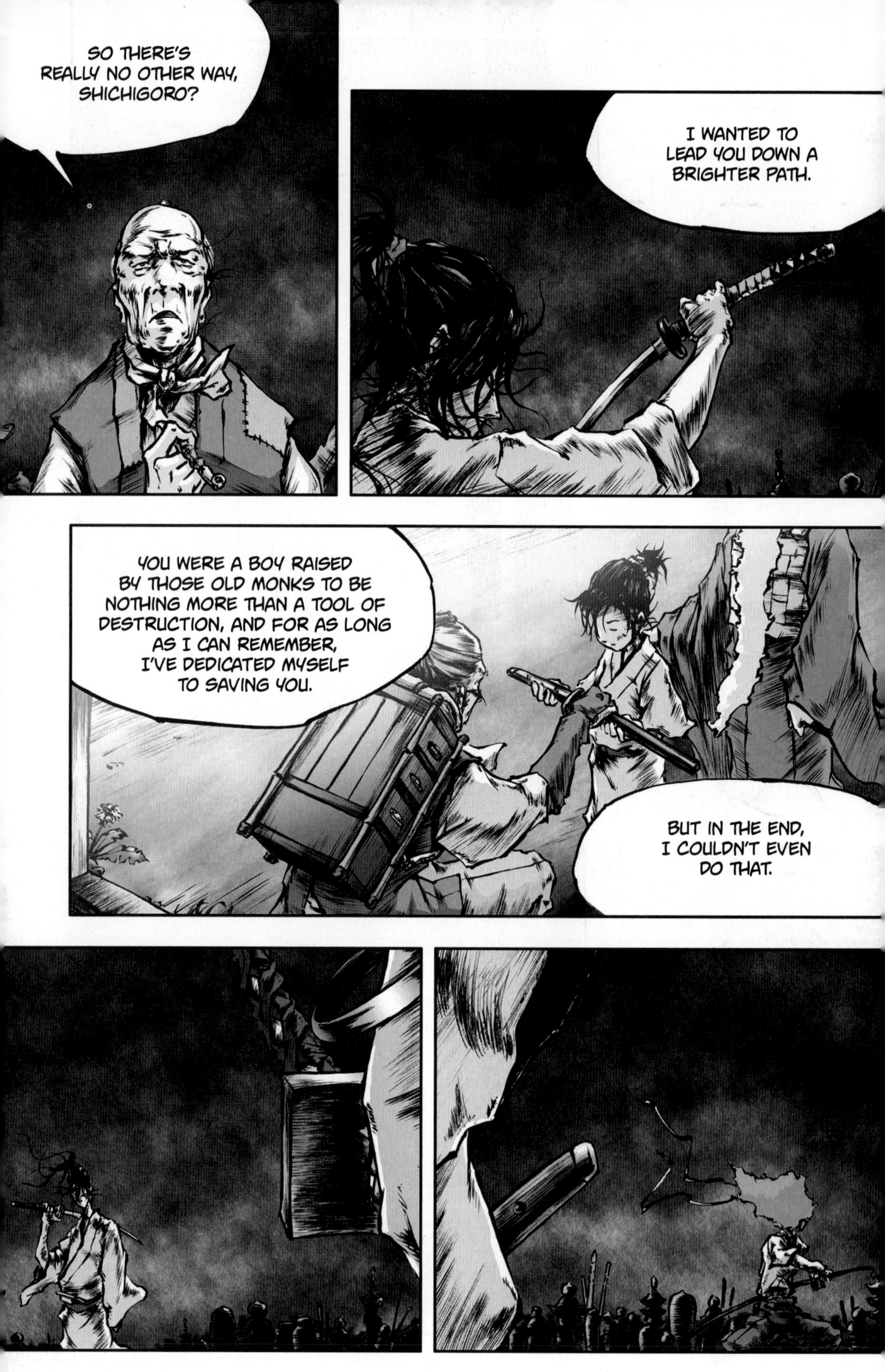
SO THERE'S REALLY NO OTHER WAY, SHICHIGORO?
I WANTED TO LEAD YOU DOWN A BRIGHTER PATH.
YOU WERE A BOY RAISED BY THOSE OLD MONKS TO BE NOTHING MORE THAN A TOOL OF DESTRUCTION, AND FOR AS LONG AS I CAN REMEMBER, I'VE DEDICATED MYSELF TO SAVING YOU.
BUT IN THE END, I COULDN'T EVEN DO THAT.

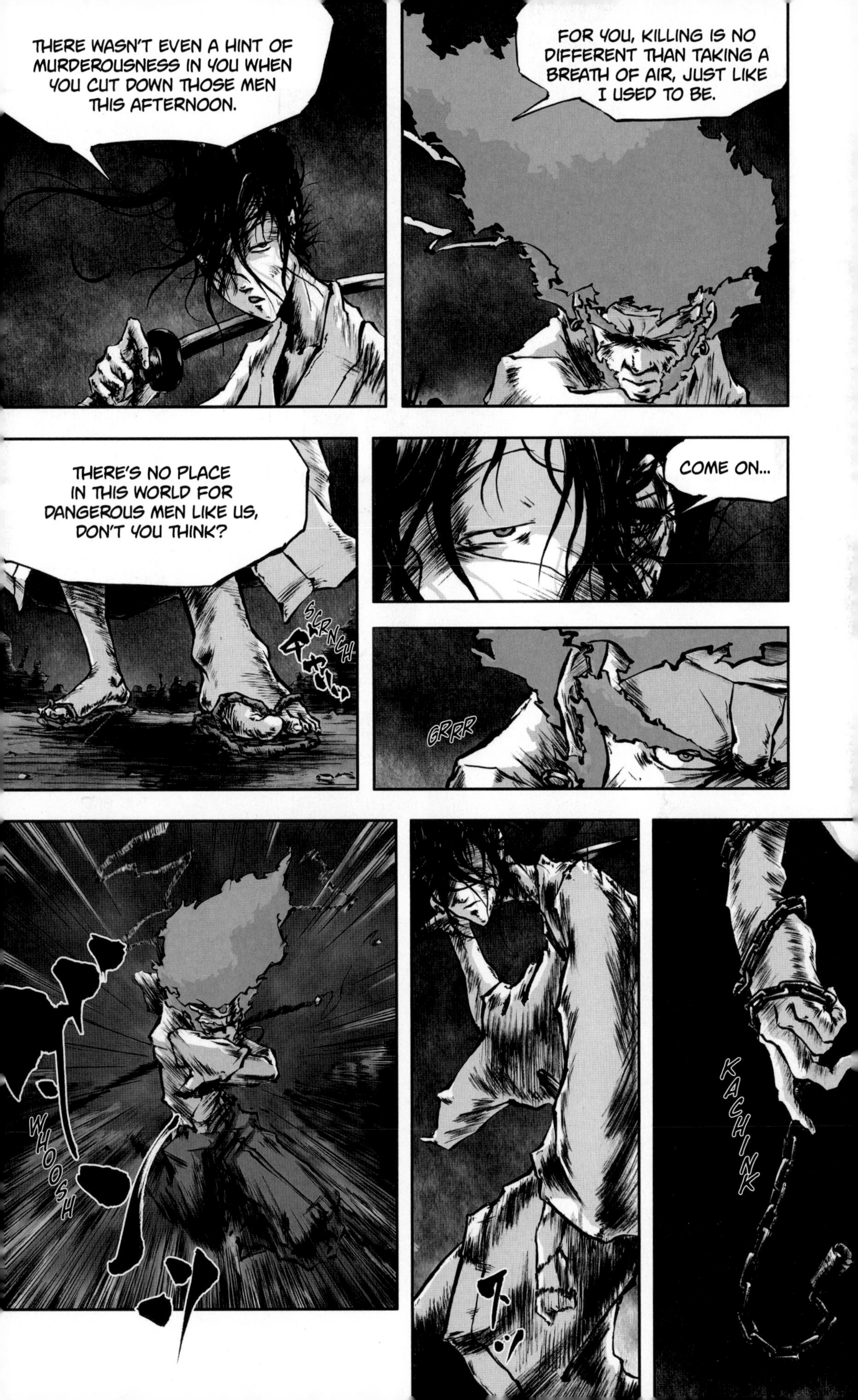
THERE WASN'T EVEN A HINT OF MURDEROUSNESS IN YOU WHEN YOU CUT DOWN THOSE MEN THIS AFTERNOON.
FOR YOU, KILLING IS NO DIFFERENT THAN TAKING A BREATH OF AIR, JUST LIKE I USED TO BE.
THERE'S NO PLACE IN THIS WORLD FOR DANGEROUS MEN LIKE US, DON'T YOU THINK?
SCRNCH
COME ON...
GRRR
WHOOSH
KACHINK

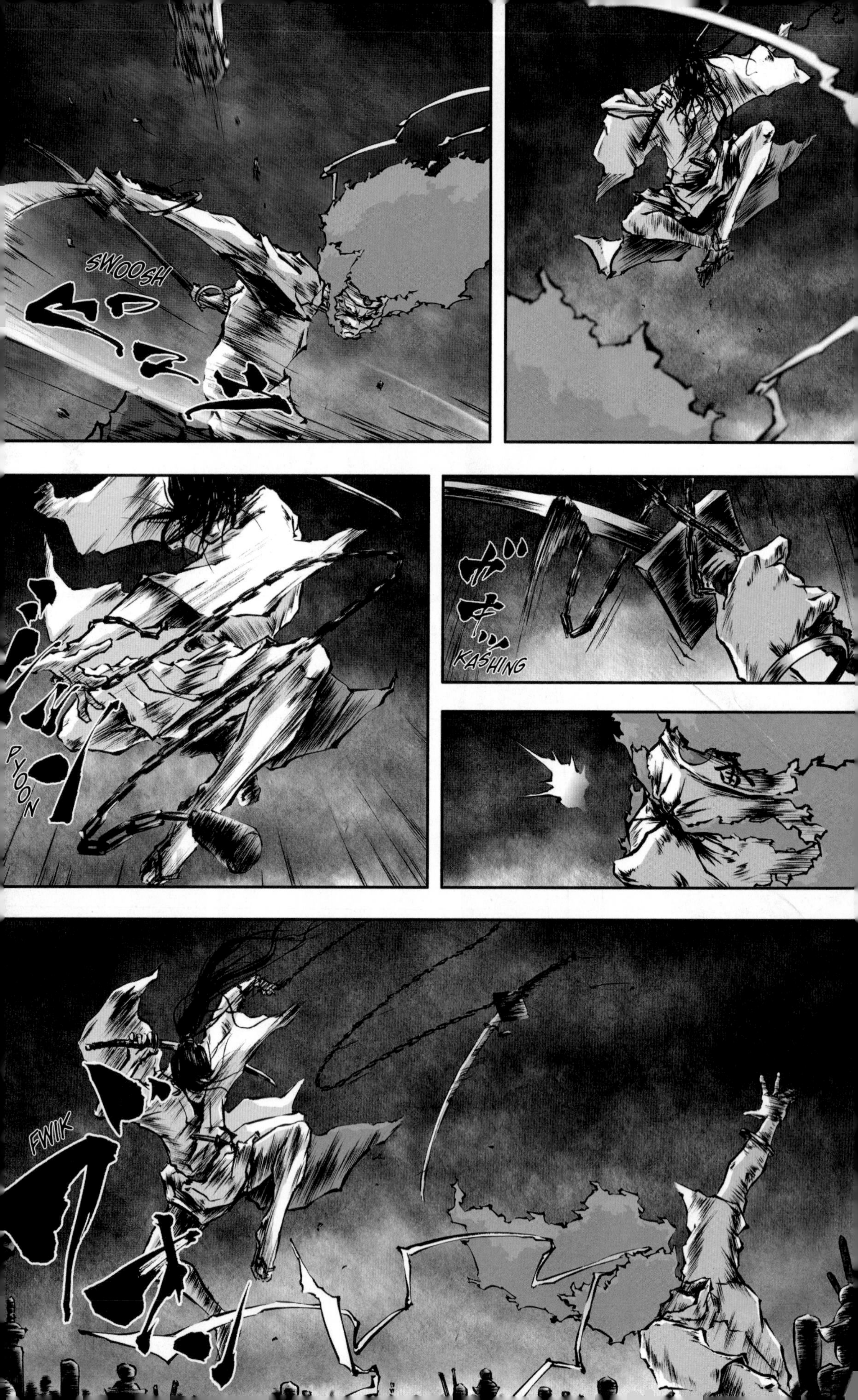
SWOOSH
PYOON
KASHING
FWIIK

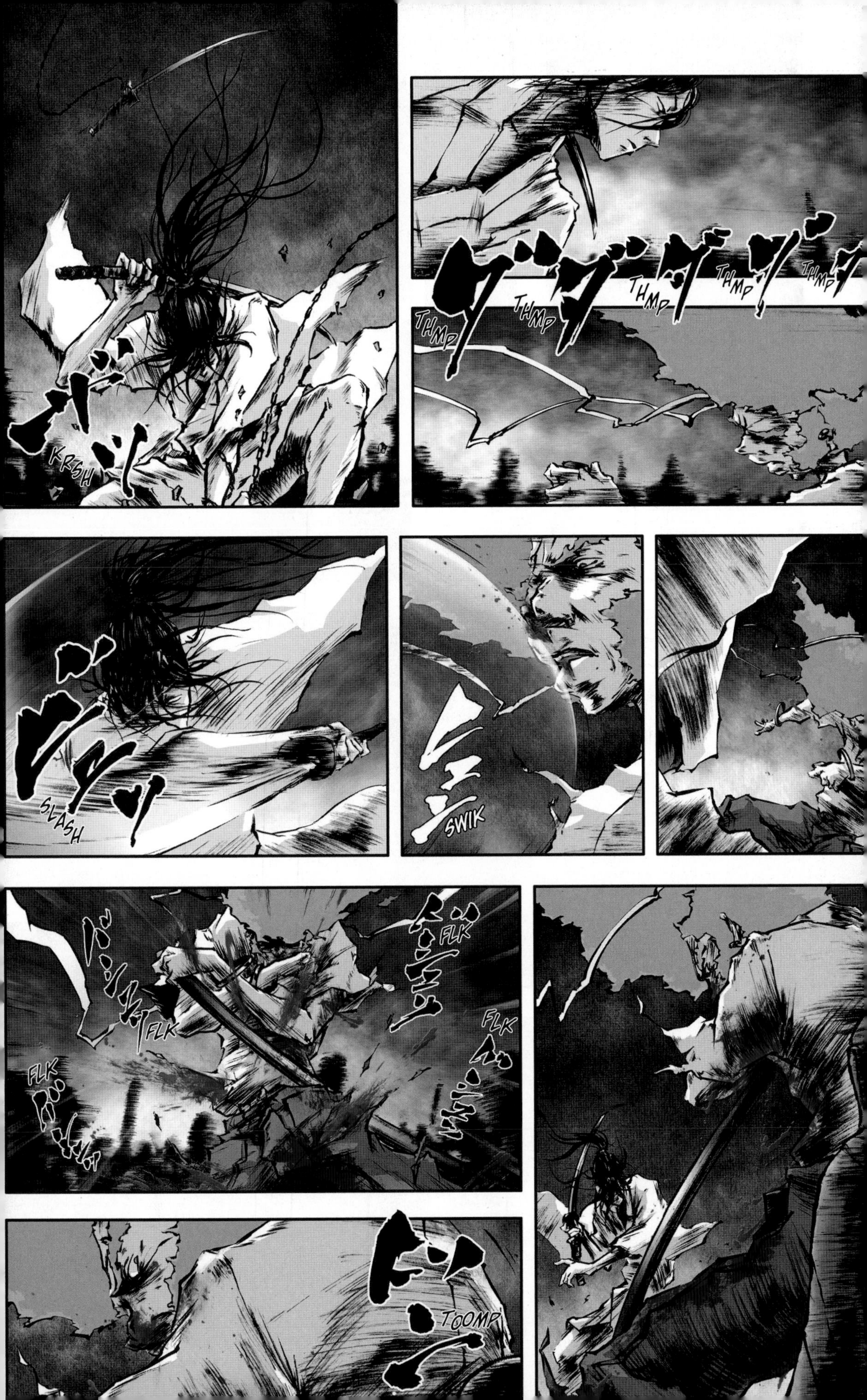
KRSH
THMP
THMP
THMP
THMP
THMP
SLASH
SWIK
FLK
FLK
FLK
FLK
TOOMP

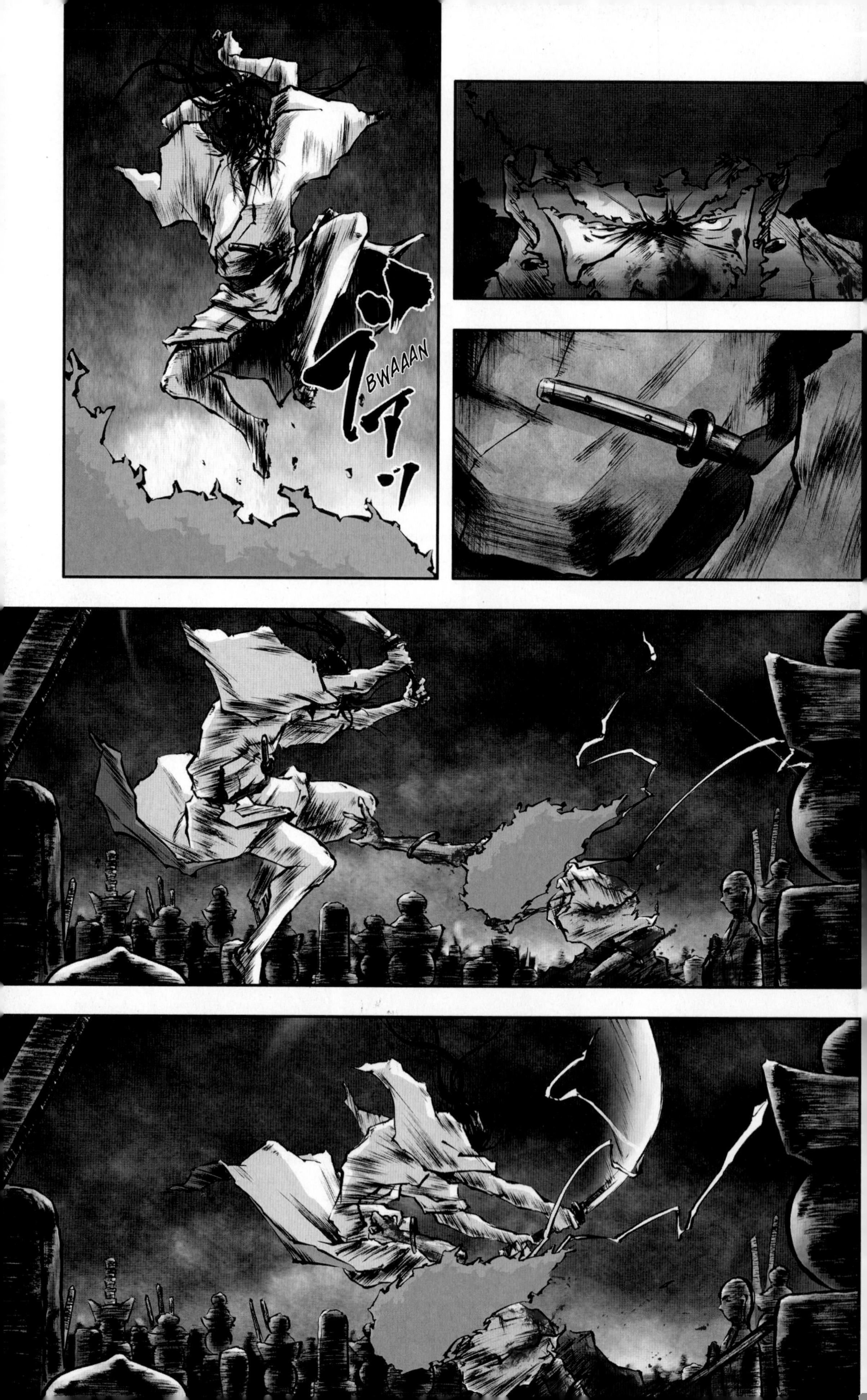
BWAAAN

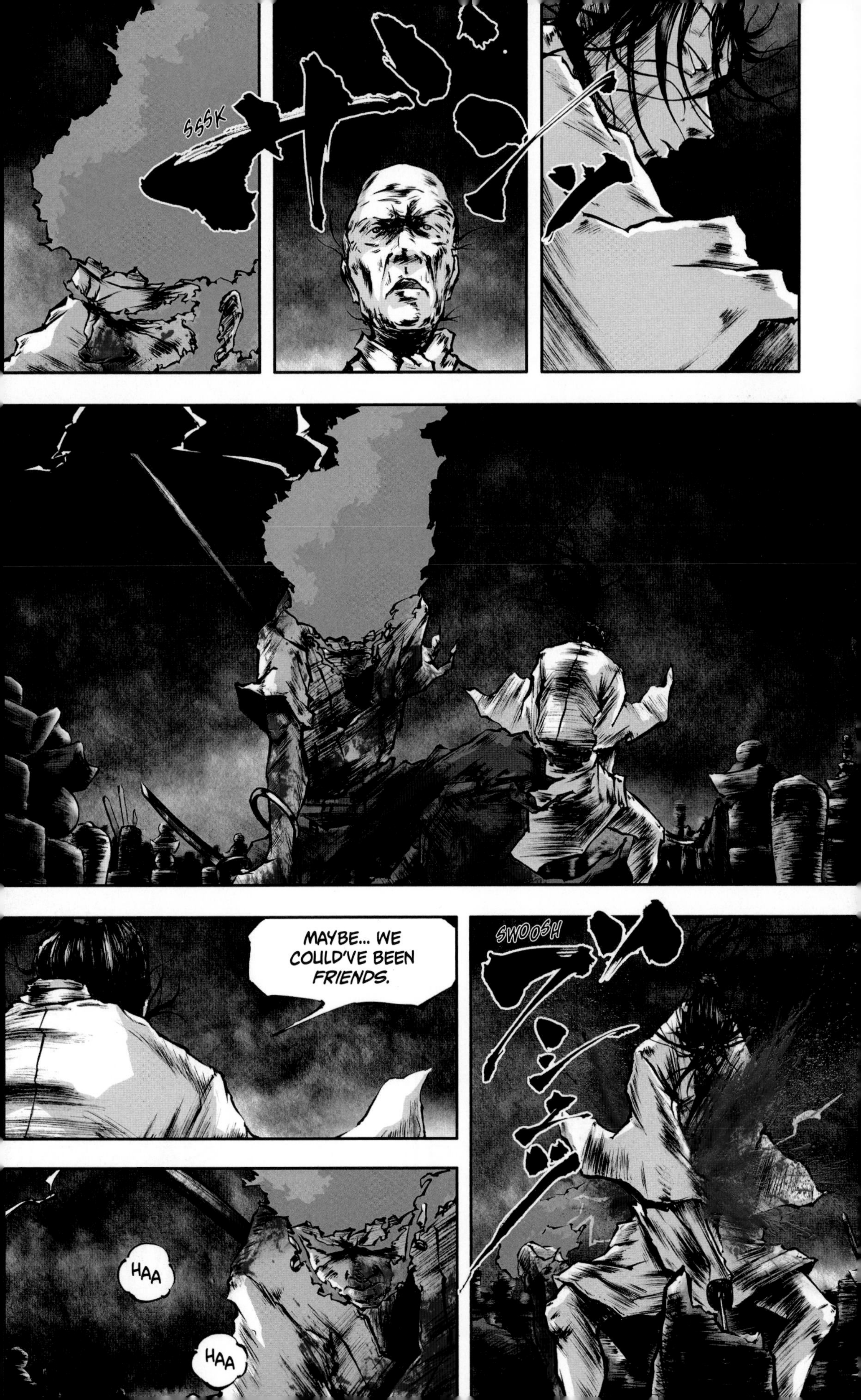
SSSK
MAYBE... WE COULD'VE BEEN FRIENDS.
HAA
HAA
SWOOSH

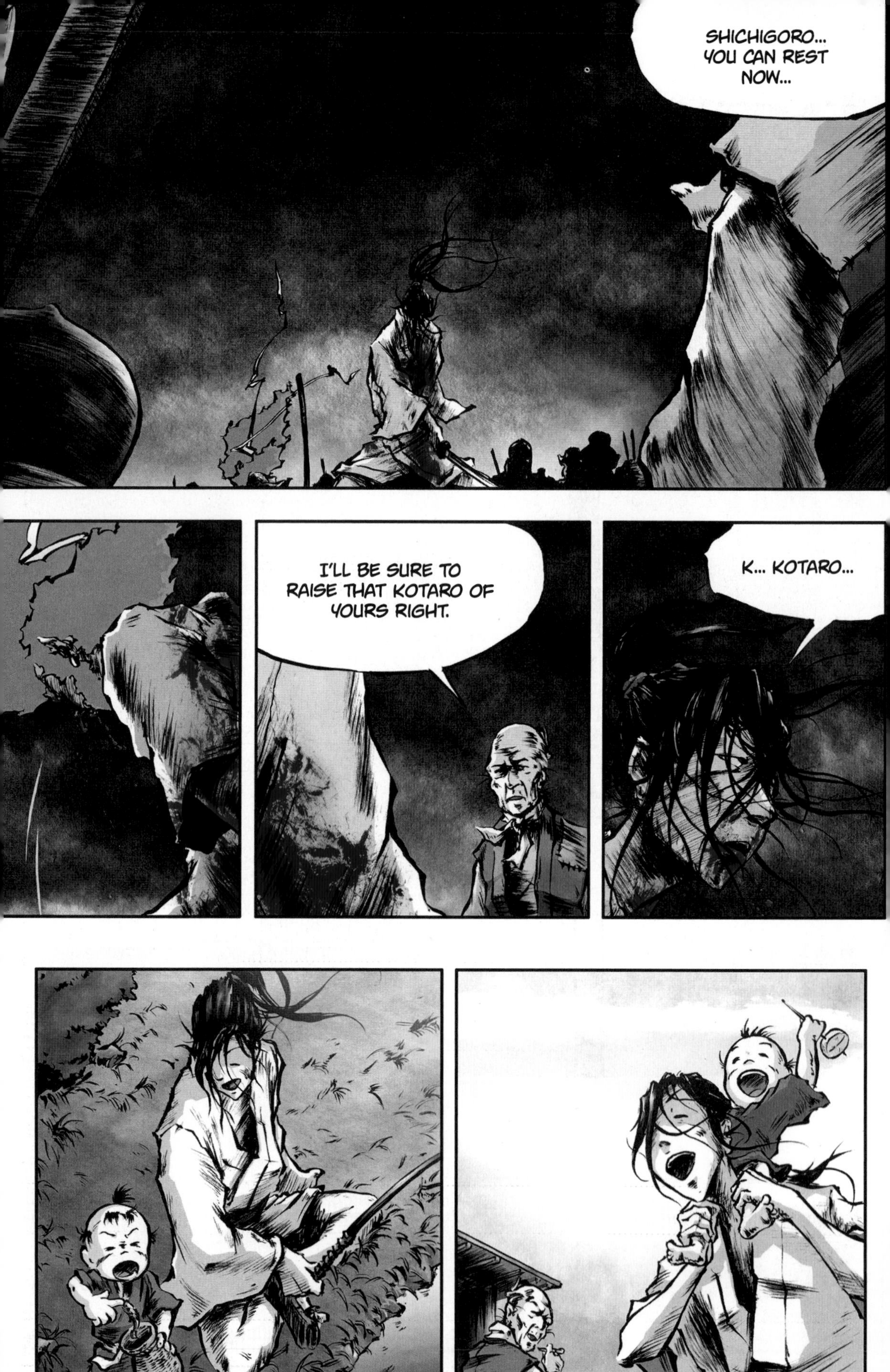
SHICHIGORO... YOU CAN REST NOW...
I'LL BE SURE TO RAISE THAT KOTARO OF YOURS RIGHT.
K... KOTARO...

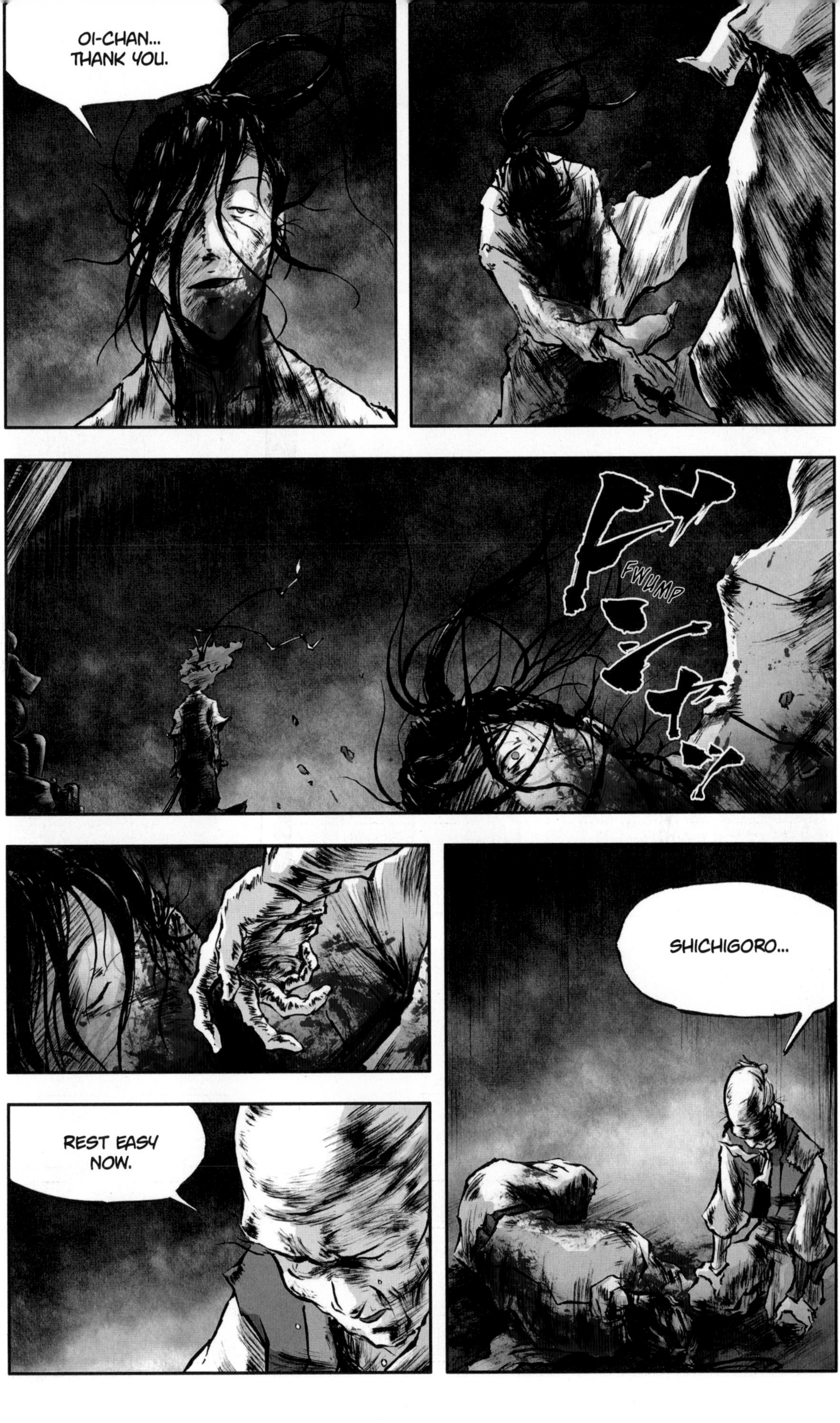
OI-CHAN... THANK YOU.
FWUMP
REST EASY NOW.
SHICHIGORO...

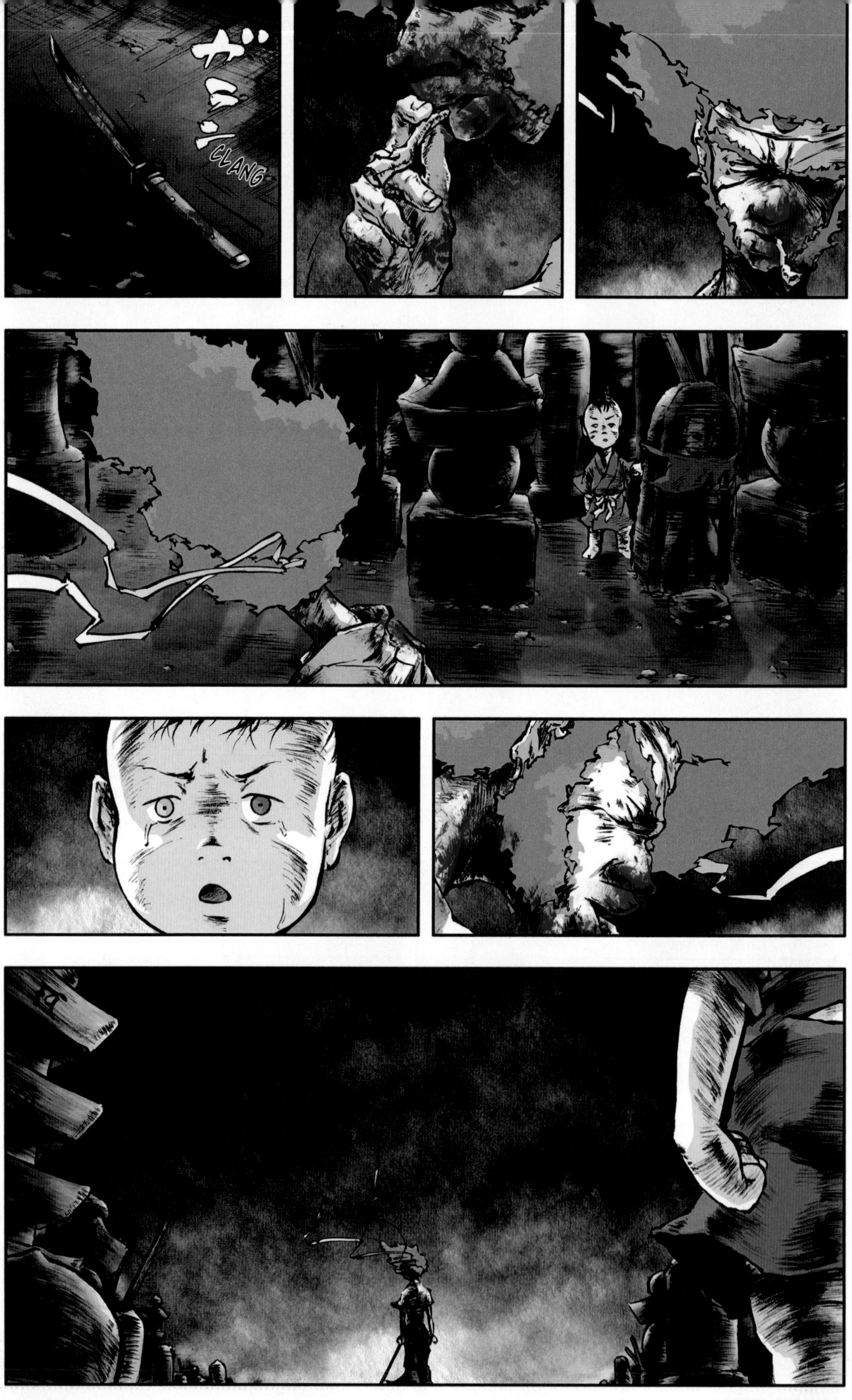
CLANG

END OF #02

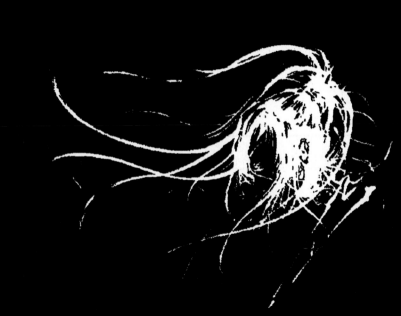

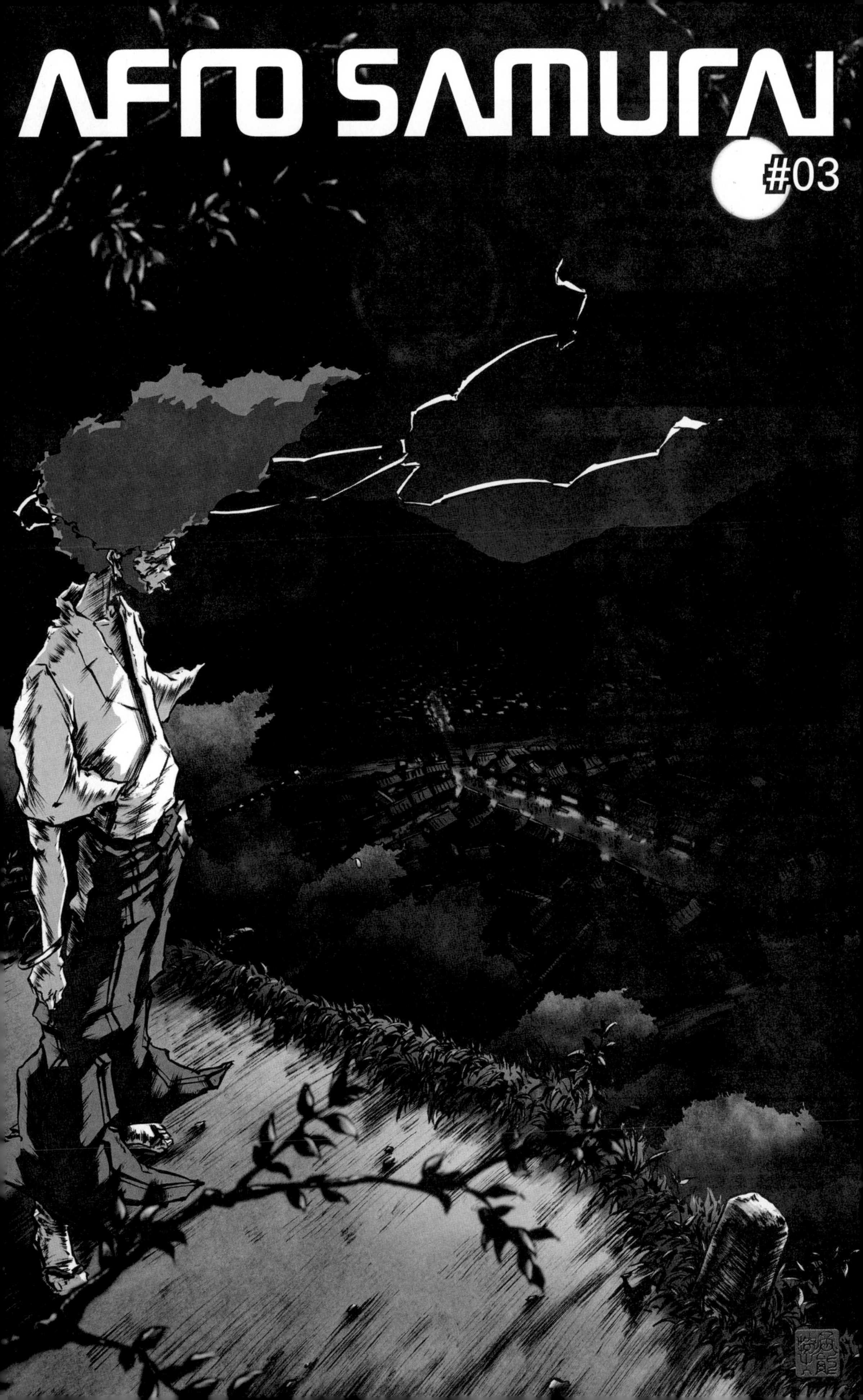
AFRO SAMURAI
#03

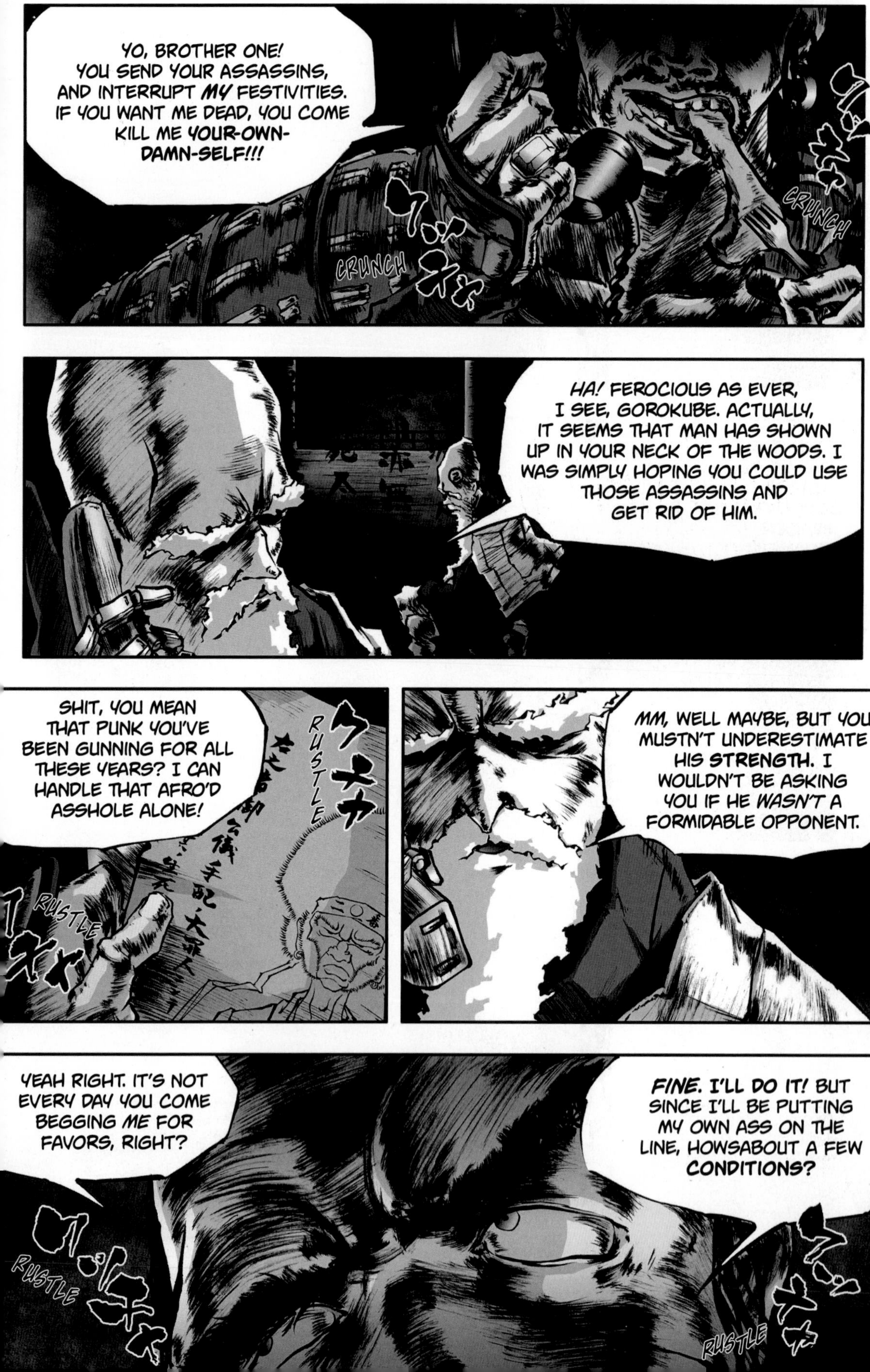
YO, BROTHER ONE! YOU SEND YOUR ASSASSINS, AND INTERRUPT *MY* FESTIVITIES. IF YOU WANT ME DEAD, YOU COME KILL ME YOUR-OWN-DAMN-SELF!!!
CRUNCH
CRUNCH
HA! FEROCIOUS AS EVER, I SEE, GOROKUBE. ACTUALLY, IT SEEMS THAT MAN HAS SHOWN UP IN YOUR NECK OF THE WOODS. I WAS SIMPLY HOPING YOU COULD USE THOSE ASSASSINS AND GET RID OF HIM.
SHIT, YOU MEAN THAT PUNK YOU'VE BEEN GUNNING FOR ALL THESE YEARS? I CAN HANDLE THAT AFRO'D ASSHOLE ALONE!
RUSTLE
RUSTLE
MM, WELL MAYBE, BUT YOU MUSTN'T UNDERESTIMATE HIS **STRENGTH**. I WOULDN'T BE ASKING YOU IF HE *WASN'T* A FORMIDABLE OPPONENT.
YEAH RIGHT. IT'S NOT EVERY DAY YOU COME BEGGING *ME* FOR FAVORS, RIGHT?
FINE. **I'LL DO IT!** BUT SINCE I'LL BE PUTTING MY OWN ASS ON THE LINE, HOWSABOUT A FEW **CONDITIONS?**
RUSTLE
RUSTLE

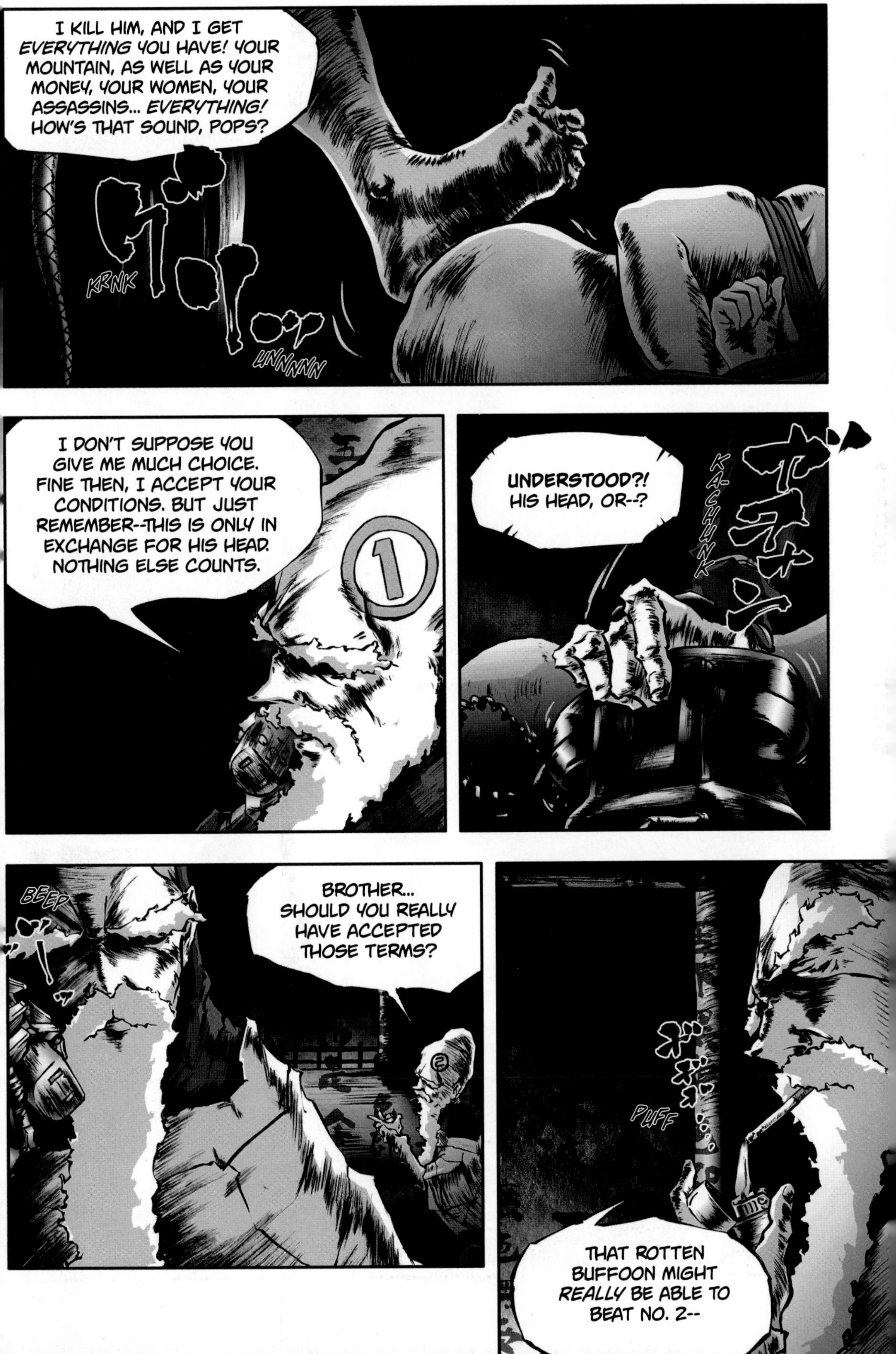
I KILL HIM, AND I GET EVERYTHING YOU HAVE! YOUR MOUNTAIN, AS WELL AS YOUR MONEY, YOUR WOMEN, YOUR ASSASSINS... EVERYTHING! HOW'S THAT SOUND, POPS?
KRNK
UNNNNN
I DON'T SUPPOSE YOU GIVE ME MUCH CHOICE. FINE THEN, I ACCEPT YOUR CONDITIONS. BUT JUST REMEMBER--THIS IS ONLY IN EXCHANGE FOR HIS HEAD. NOTHING ELSE COUNTS.
1
UNDERSTOOD?! HIS HEAD, OR--?
KA-CHUNK
BEEP
BROTHER... SHOULD YOU REALLY HAVE ACCEPTED THOSE TERMS?
PUFF
THAT ROTTEN BUFFOON MIGHT REALLY BE ABLE TO BEAT NO. 2--

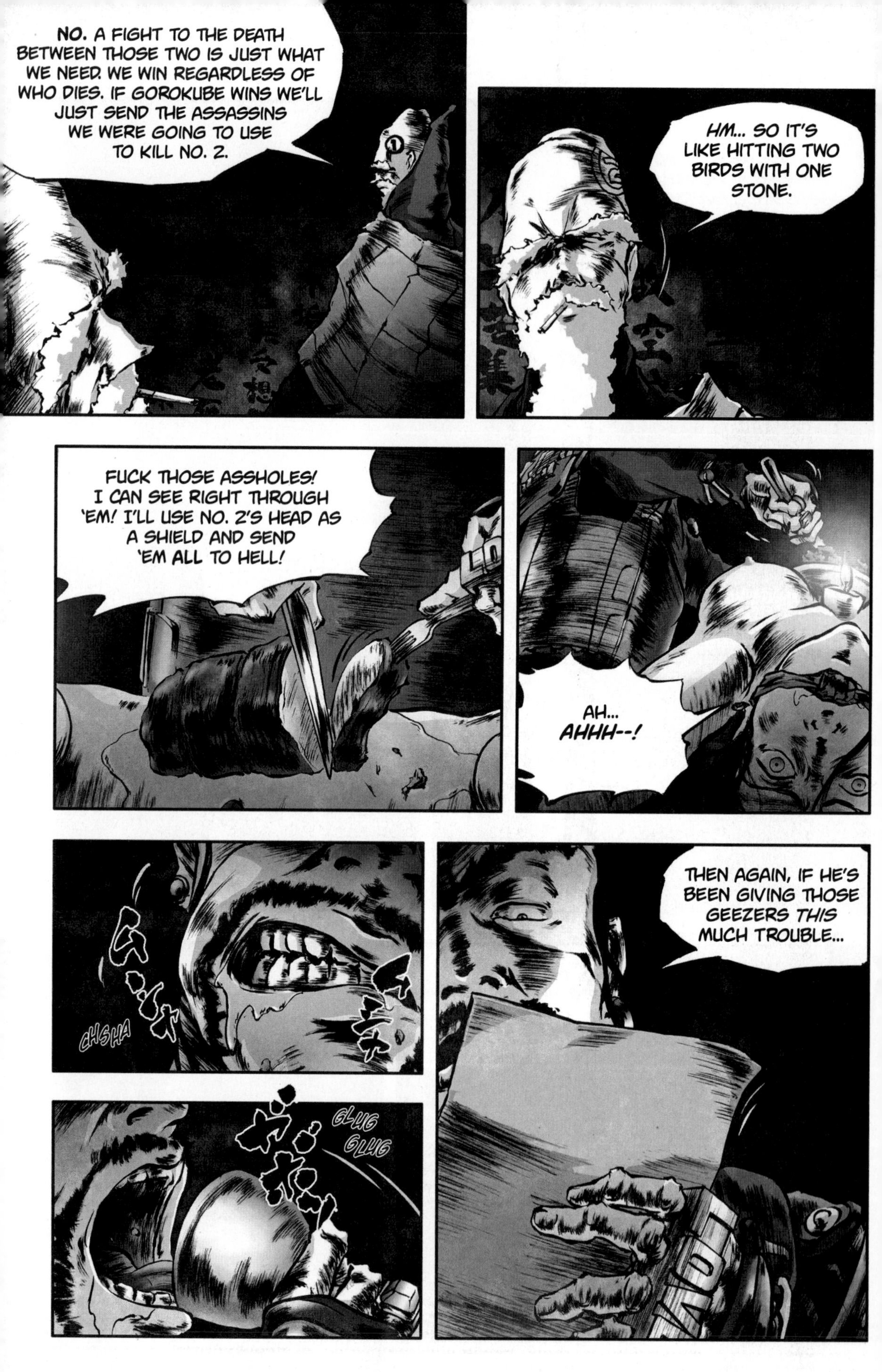
NO. A FIGHT TO THE DEATH BETWEEN THOSE TWO IS JUST WHAT WE NEED. WE WIN REGARDLESS OF WHO DIES. IF GOROKUBE WINS WE'LL JUST SEND THE ASSASSINS WE WERE GOING TO USE TO KILL NO. 2.
HM... SO IT'S LIKE HITTING TWO BIRDS WITH ONE STONE.
FUCK THOSE ASSHOLES! I CAN SEE RIGHT THROUGH 'EM! I'LL USE NO. 2'S HEAD AS A SHIELD AND SEND 'EM ALL TO HELL!
AH... AHHH--!
CHSHA
GLUG GLUG
THEN AGAIN, IF HE'S BEEN GIVING THOSE GEEZERS THIS MUCH TROUBLE...

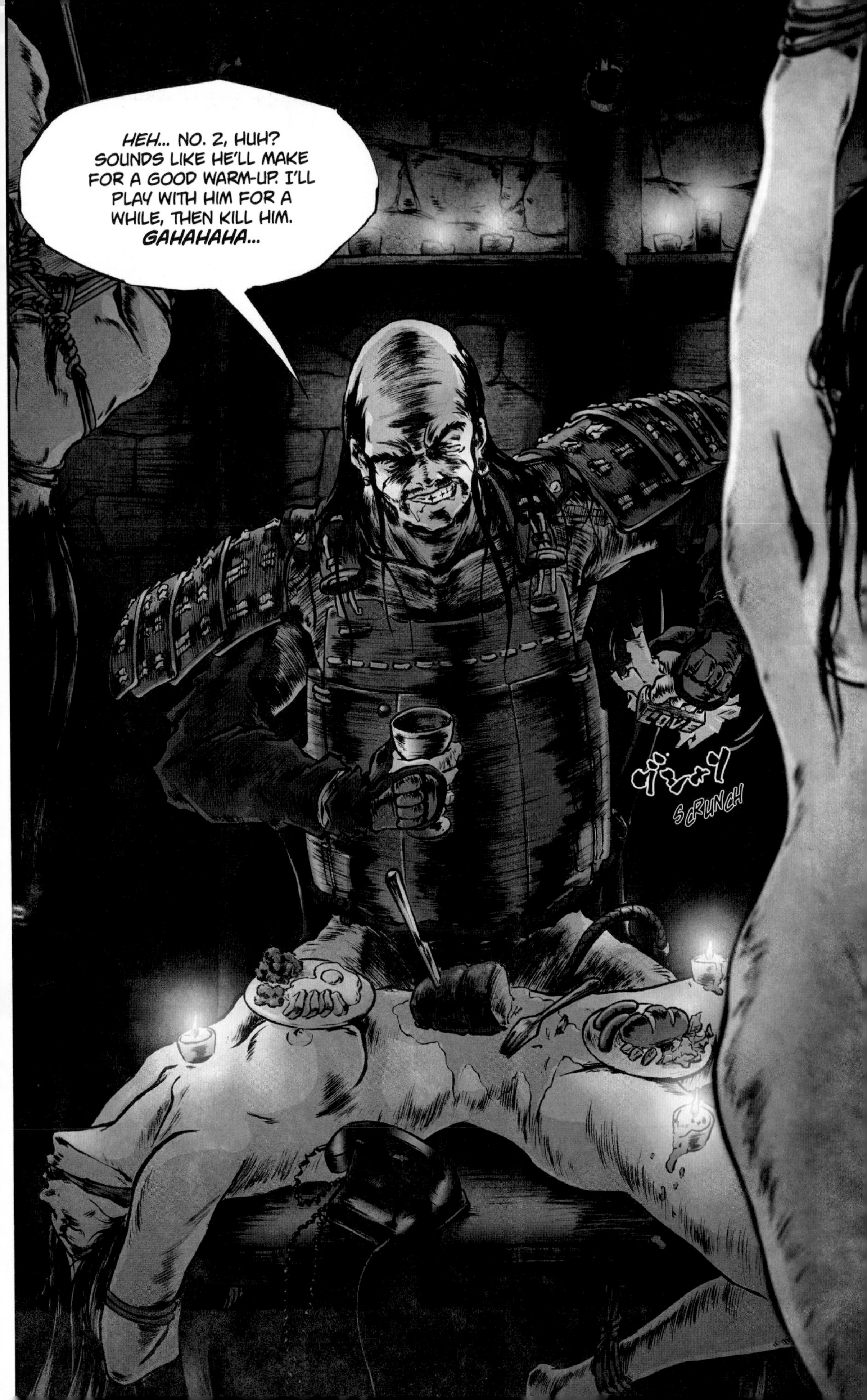
HEH... NO. 2, HUH? SOUNDS LIKE HE'LL MAKE FOR A GOOD WARM-UP. I'LL PLAY WITH HIM FOR A WHILE, THEN KILL HIM. GAHAHAHA...
LOVE
ぐしゃり
SCRUNCH

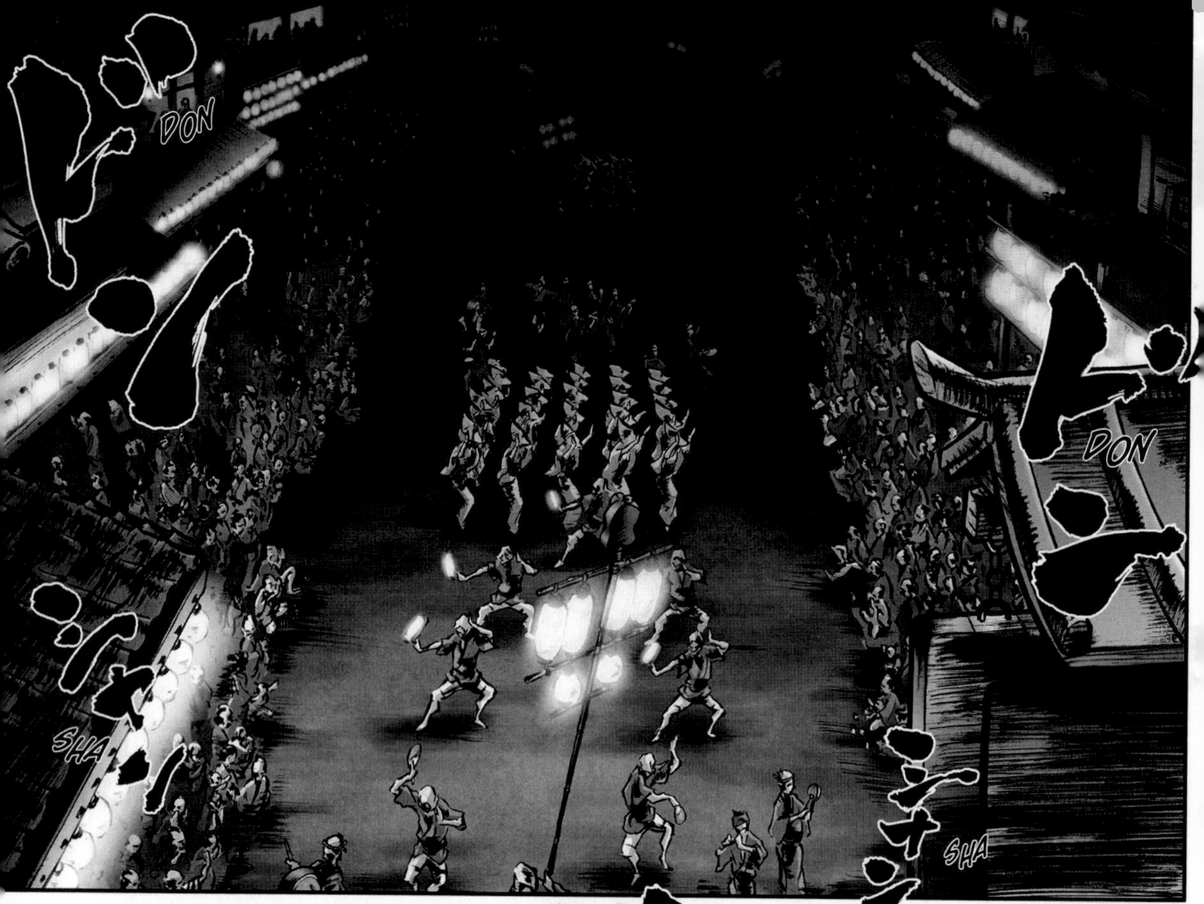
DON
SHA
DON
SHA

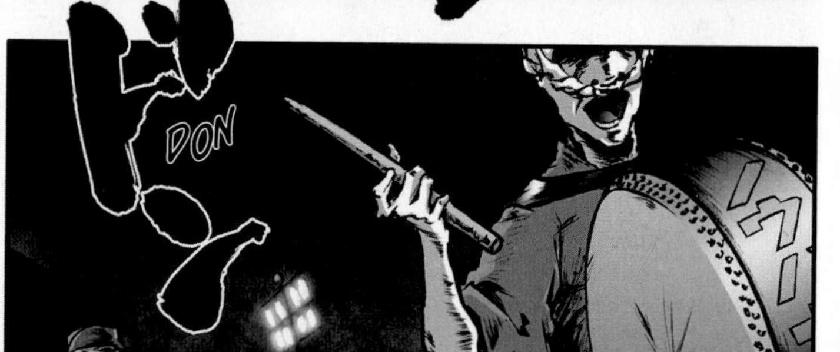
DON

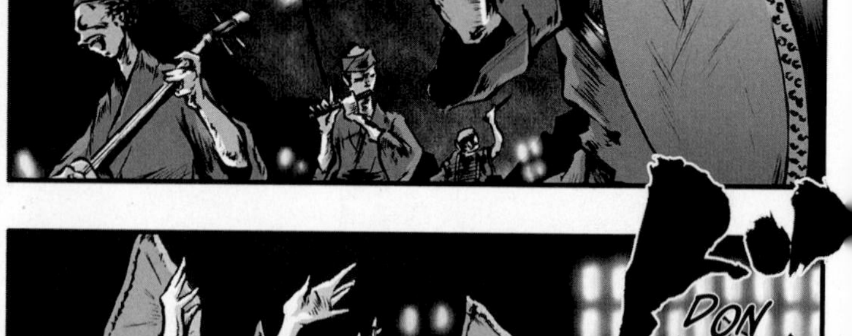
DON

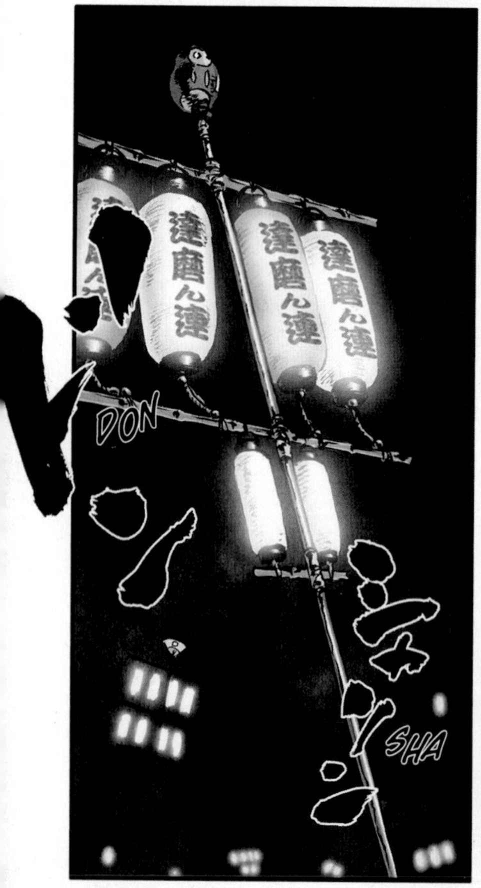
達磨ん連
達磨ん連
達磨ん連
DON
SHA

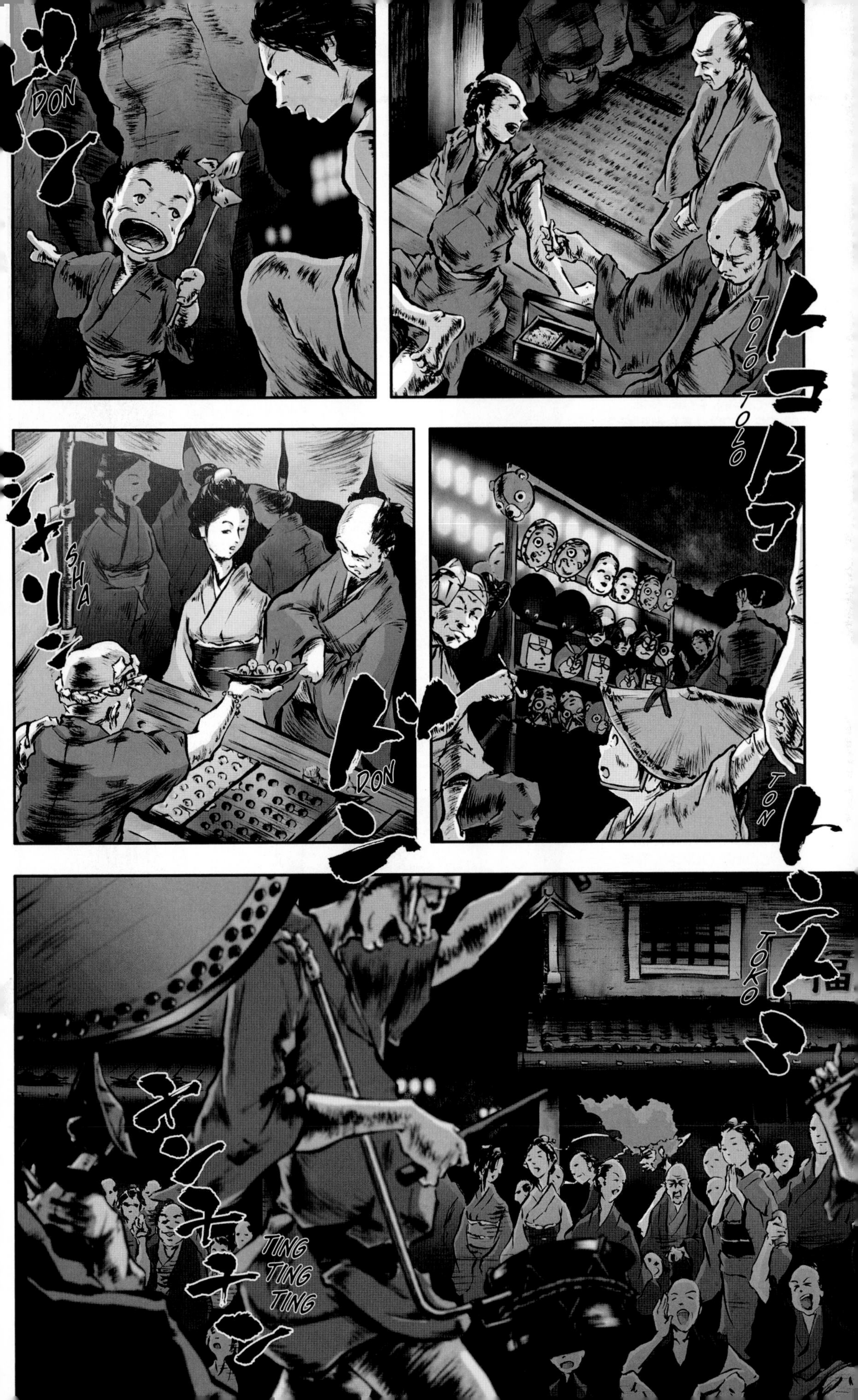
DON
TOLO TOLO
SHA
DON
TON
TOKO
TING TING TING

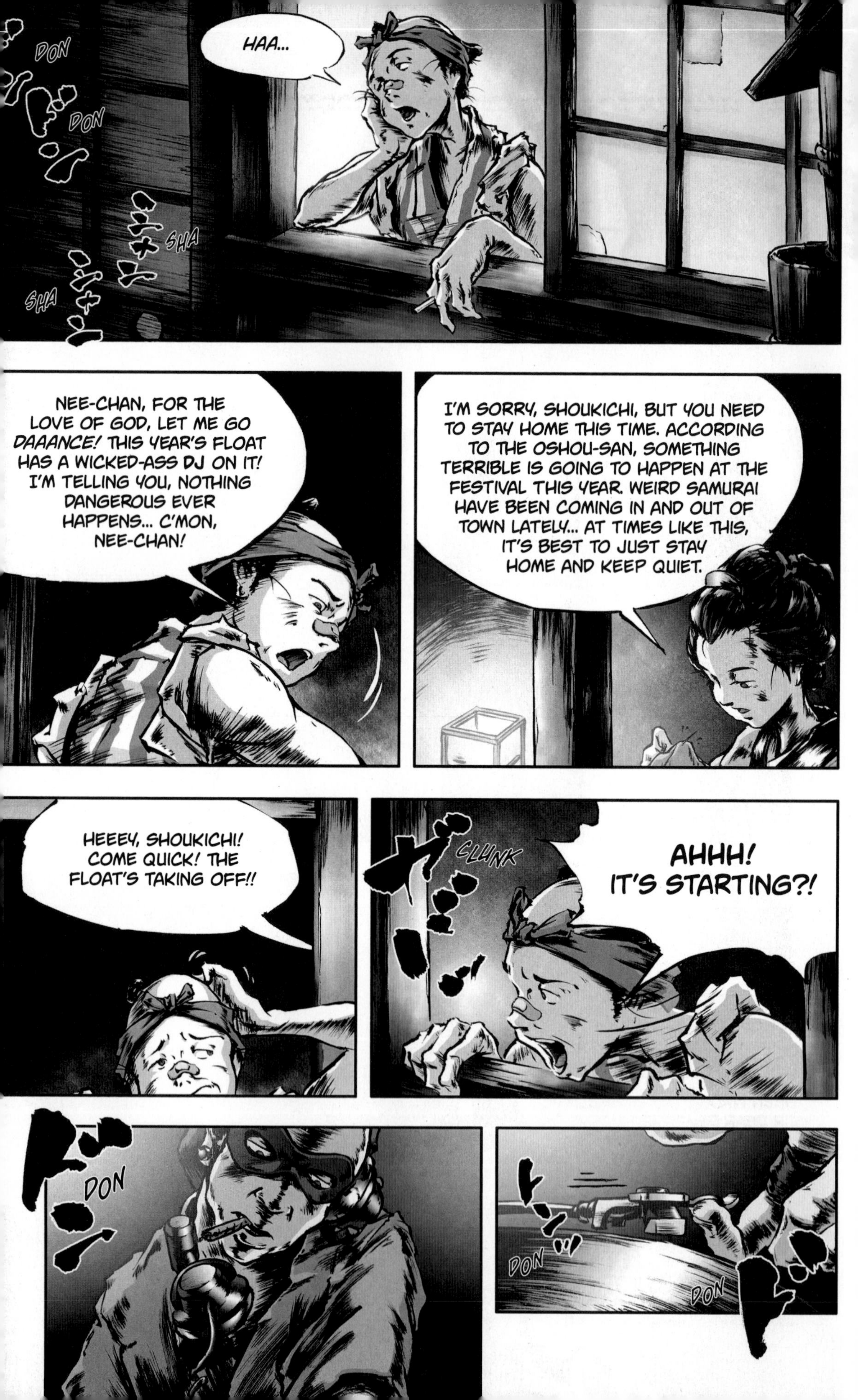
DON
DON
SHA
SHA
HAA...
NEE-CHAN, FOR THE LOVE OF GOD, LET ME GO DAAANCE! THIS YEAR'S FLOAT HAS A WICKED-ASS DJ ON IT! I'M TELLING YOU, NOTHING DANGEROUS EVER HAPPENS... C'MON, NEE-CHAN!
I'M SORRY, SHOUKICHI, BUT YOU NEED TO STAY HOME THIS TIME. ACCORDING TO THE OSHOU-SAN, SOMETHING TERRIBLE IS GOING TO HAPPEN AT THE FESTIVAL THIS YEAR. WEIRD SAMURAI HAVE BEEN COMING IN AND OUT OF TOWN LATELY... AT TIMES LIKE THIS, IT'S BEST TO JUST STAY HOME AND KEEP QUIET.
HEEEY, SHOUKICHI! COME QUICK! THE FLOAT'S TAKING OFF!!
CLUNK
AHHH! IT'S STARTING?!
DON
DON
DON

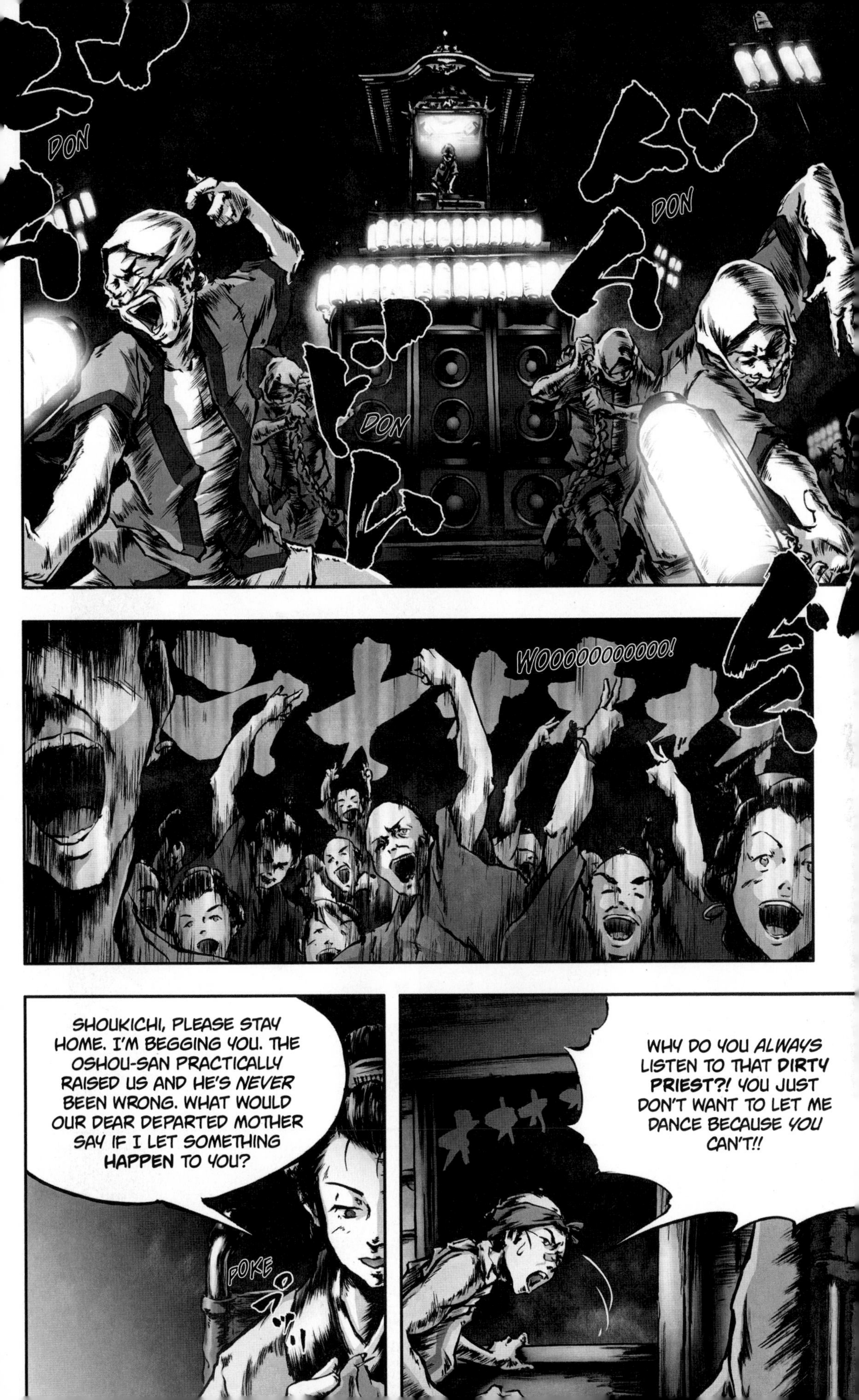
DON
DON
DON
WOOOOOOOOOOO!
SHOUKICHI, PLEASE STAY HOME. I'M BEGGING YOU. THE OSHOU-SAN PRACTICALLY RAISED US AND HE'S *NEVER* BEEN WRONG. WHAT WOULD OUR DEAR DEPARTED MOTHER SAY IF I LET SOMETHING HAPPEN TO YOU?
POKE
WHY DO YOU *ALWAYS* LISTEN TO THAT **DIRTY PRIEST?!** YOU JUST DON'T WANT TO LET ME DANCE BECAUSE *YOU* CAN'T!!

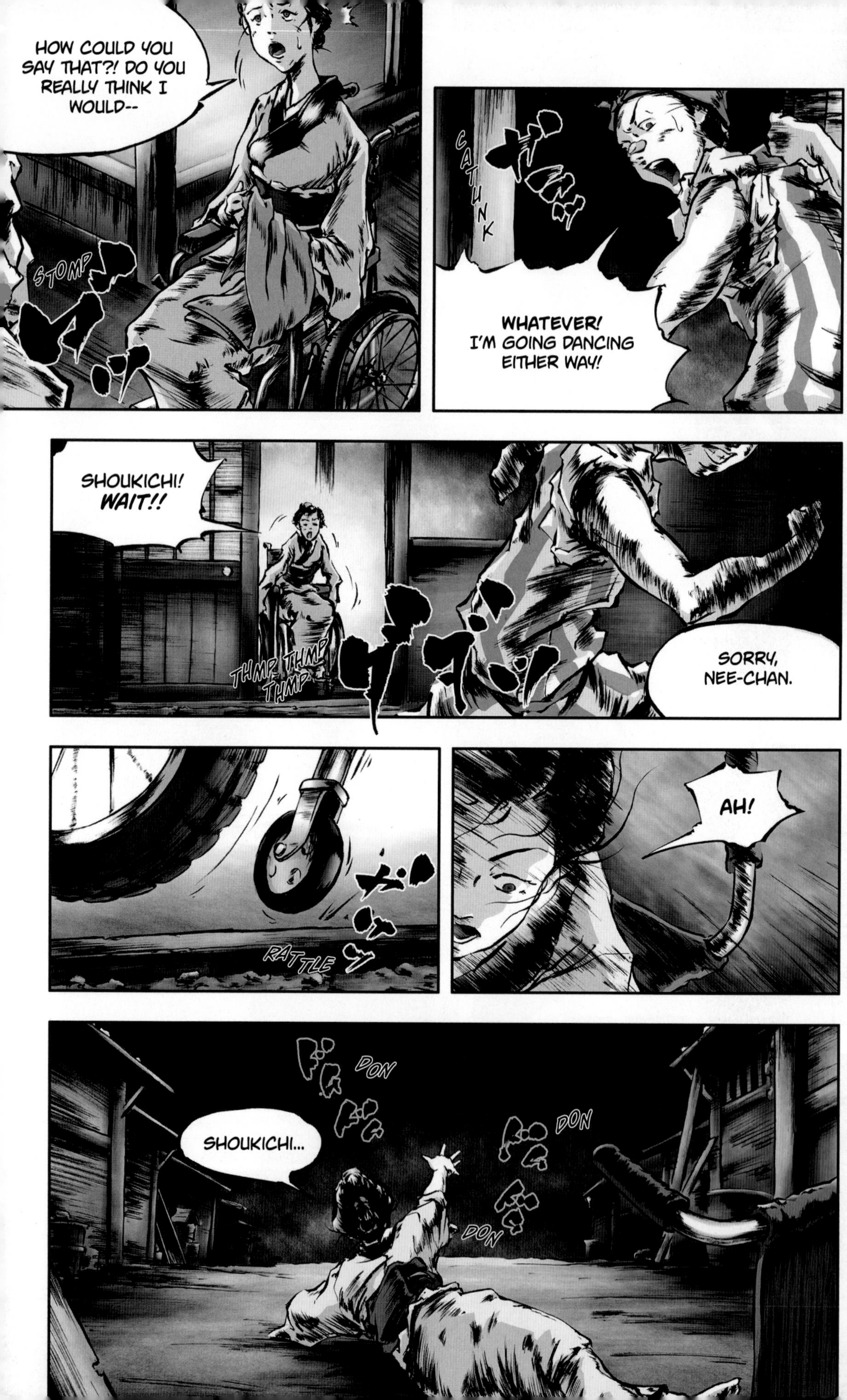
HOW COULD YOU SAY THAT?! DO YOU REALLY THINK I WOULD--
STOMP
CATUNK
WHATEVER! I'M GOING DANCING EITHER WAY!
SHOUKICHI! WAIT!!
THMP THMP THMP
SORRY, NEE-CHAN.
RATTLE
AH!
DON
SHOUKICHI...
DON
DON

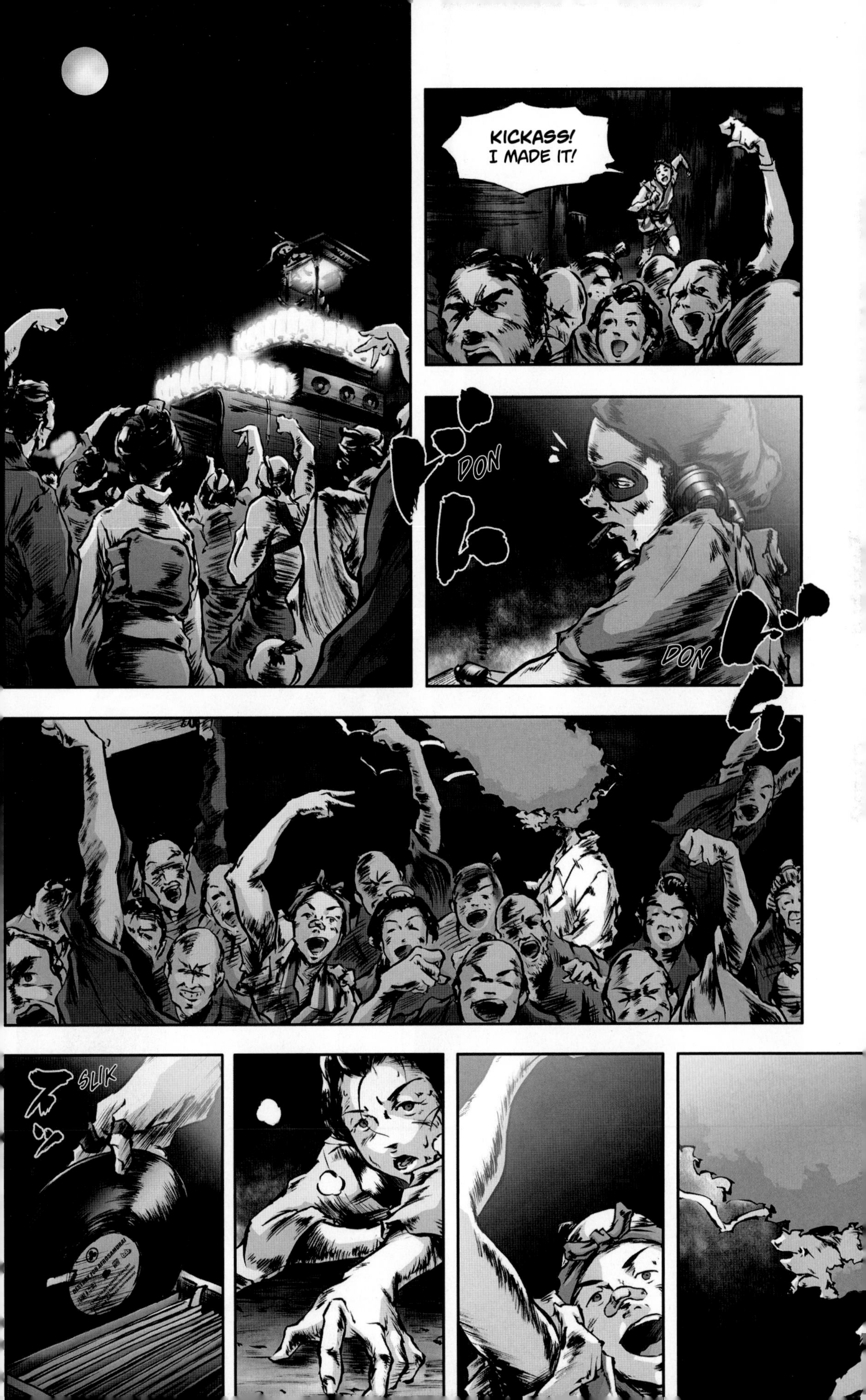
KICKASS! I MADE IT!
DON
DON
SLIK

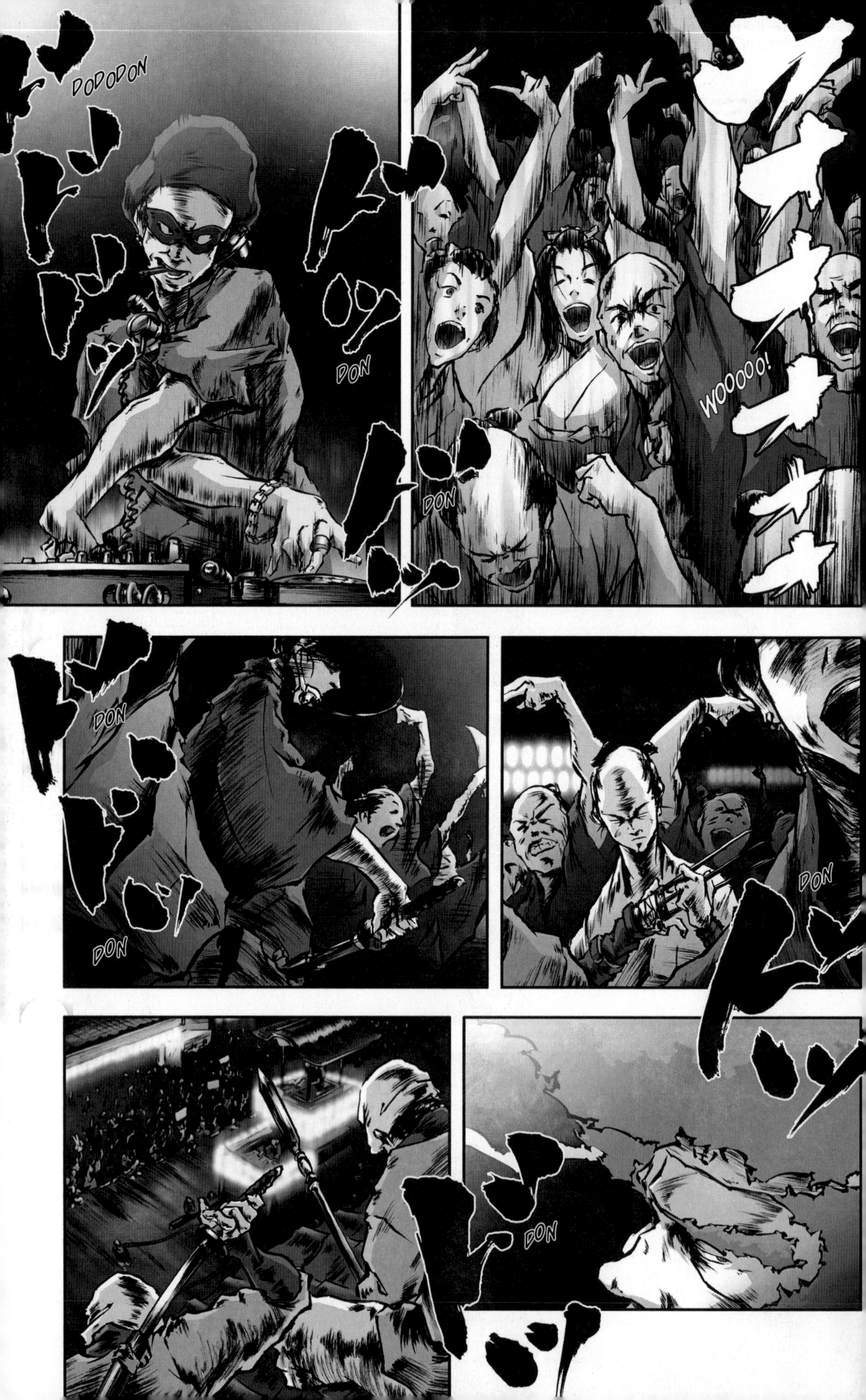

DODODON
DON
DON
WOOOOO!
DON
DON
DON
DON

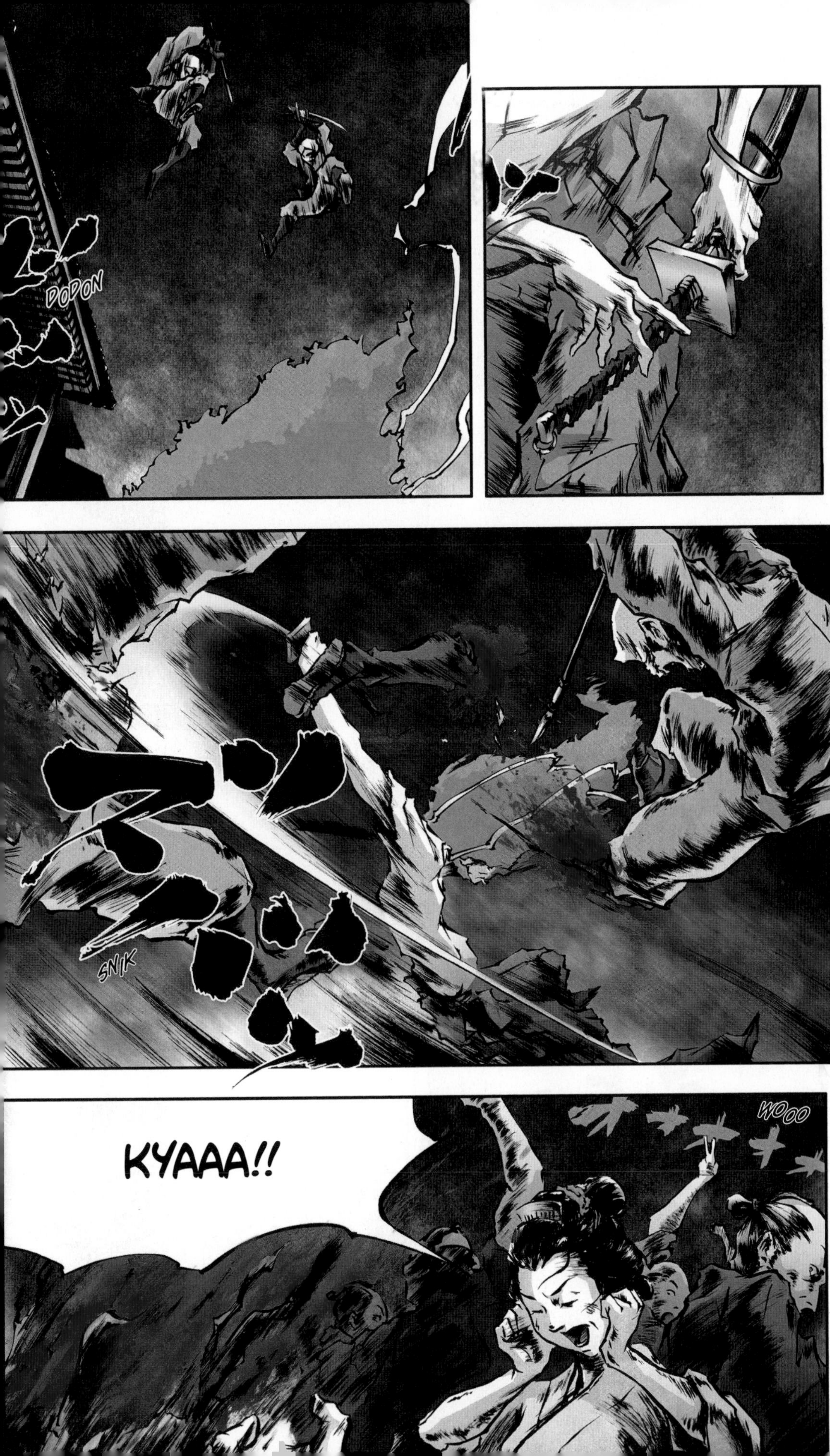
DODON
SNIK
KYAAA!!
WOOO

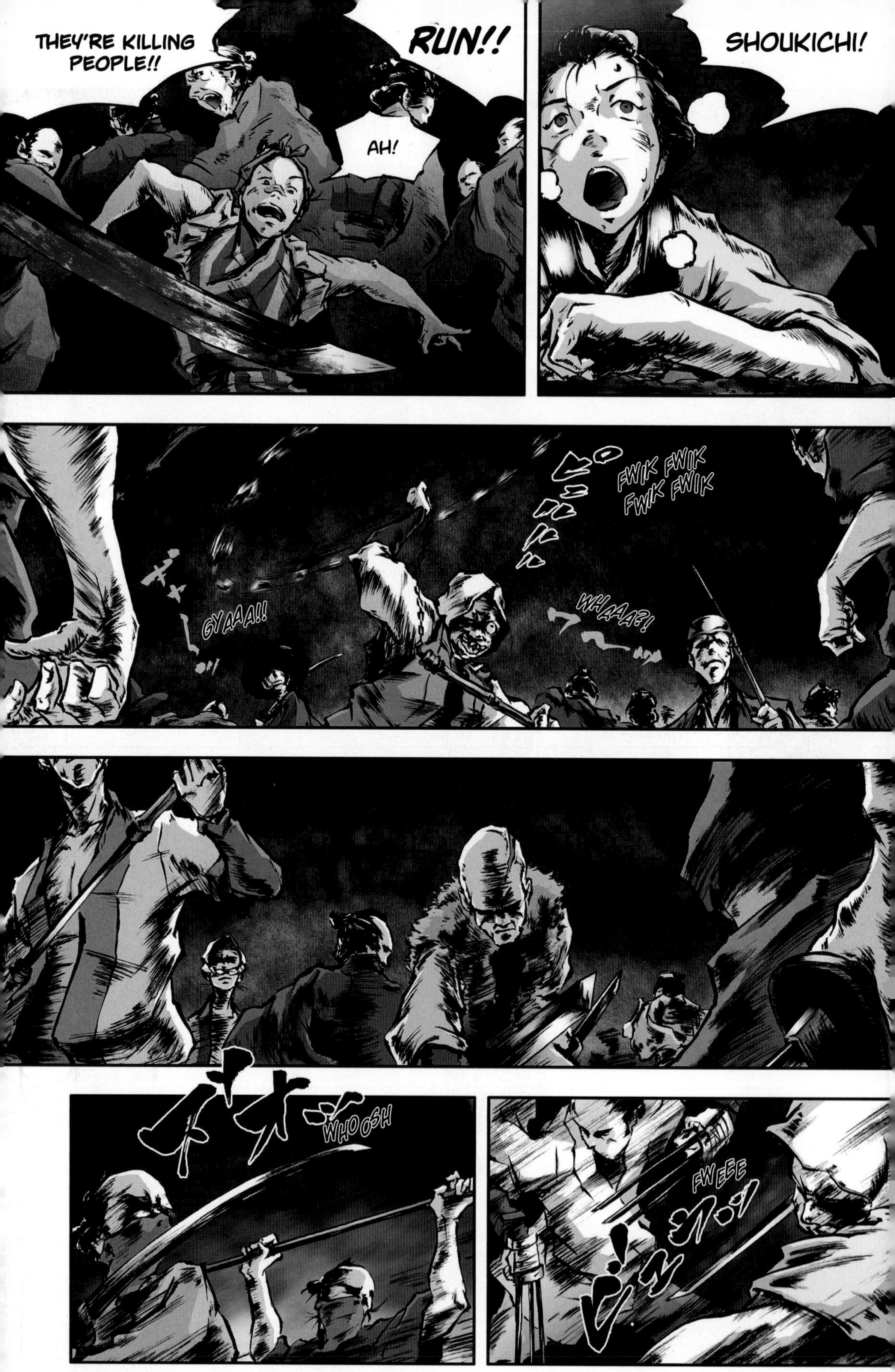
THEY'RE KILLING PEOPLE!!
RUN!!
AH!
SHOUKICHI!
FWIK FWIK
FWIK FWIK
GYAAA!!
WHAAA?!
WHOOSH
FWEEE

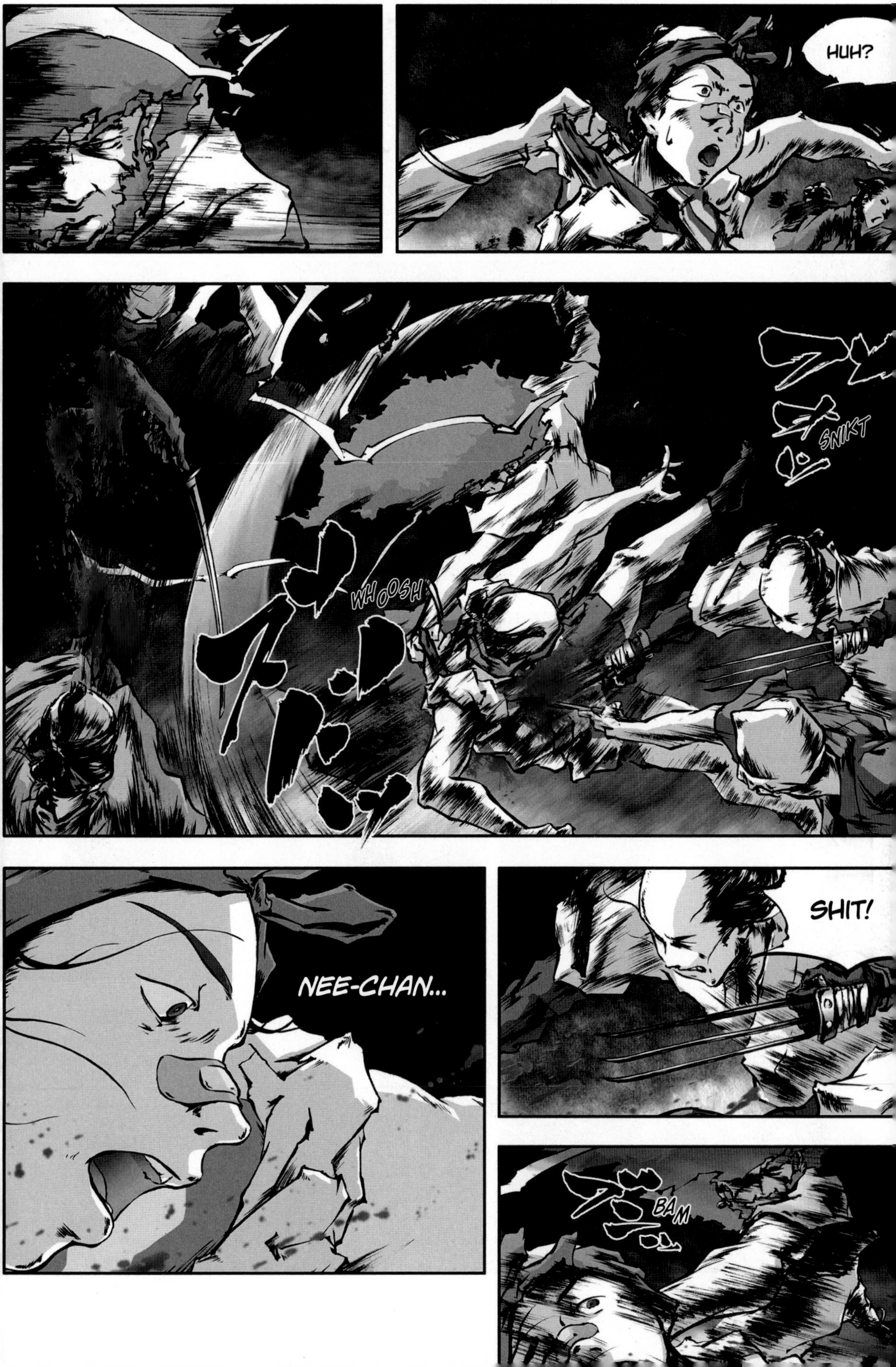
HUH?
SNIKT
WHOOSH
NEE-CHAN...
SHIT!
BAM

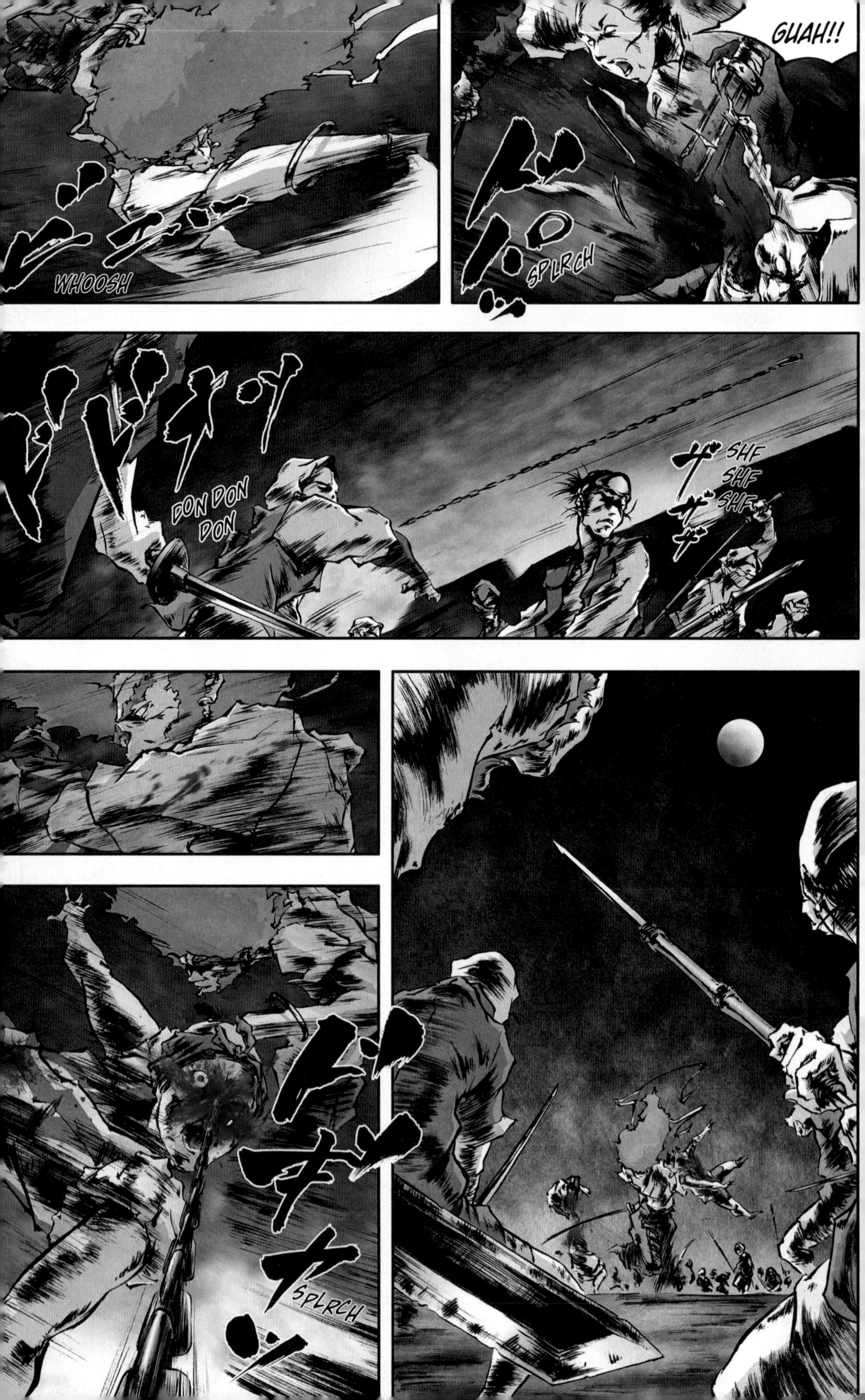
WHOOSH
GUAH!!
SPLRCH
DON DON DON
SHF SHF SHF
SPLRCH

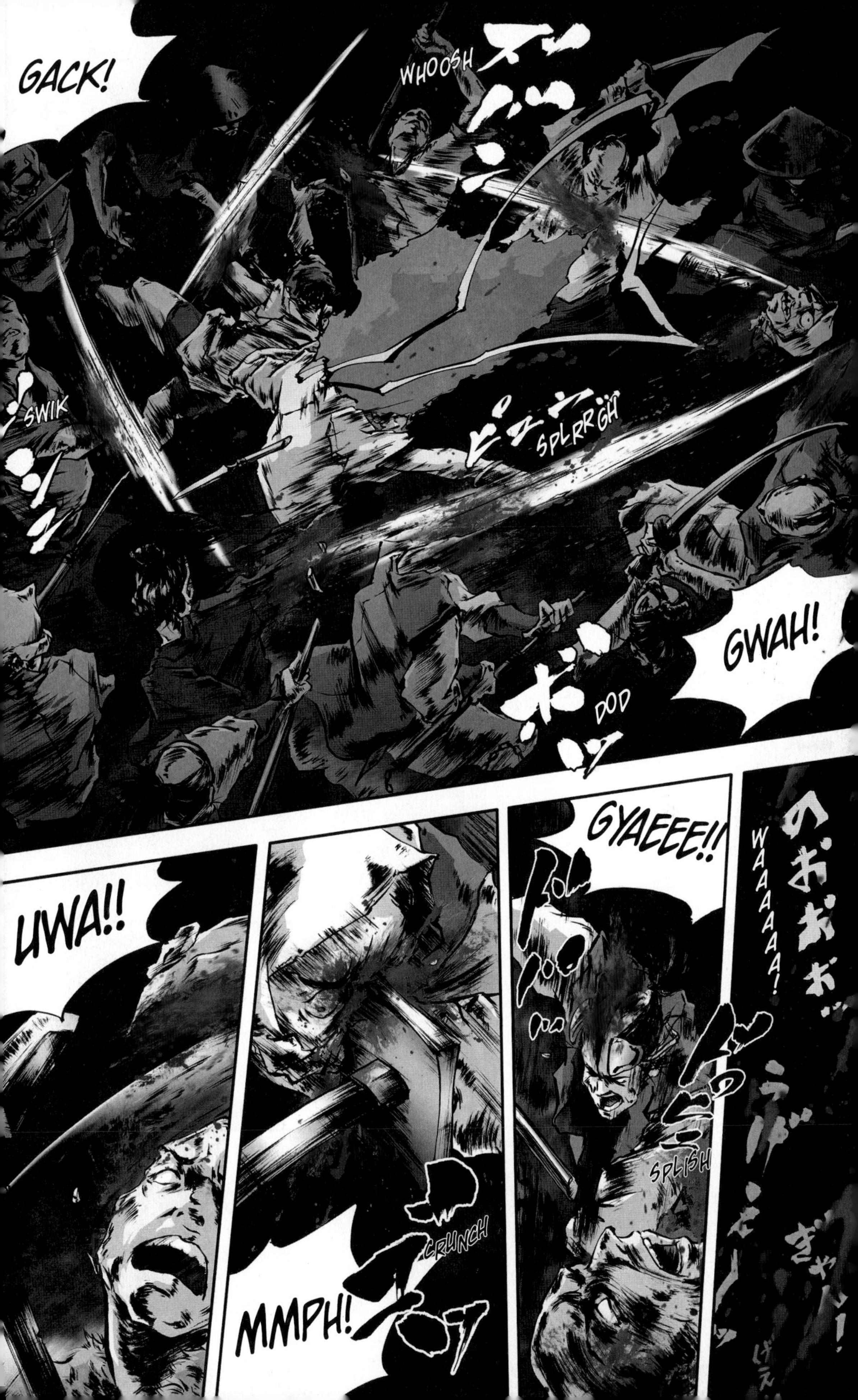
GACK!
WHOOSH
SWIK
SPLRRGH
GWAH!
DOD
UWA!!
MMPH!
CRUNCH
GYAEEE!!
SPLISH
WAAAAAA!

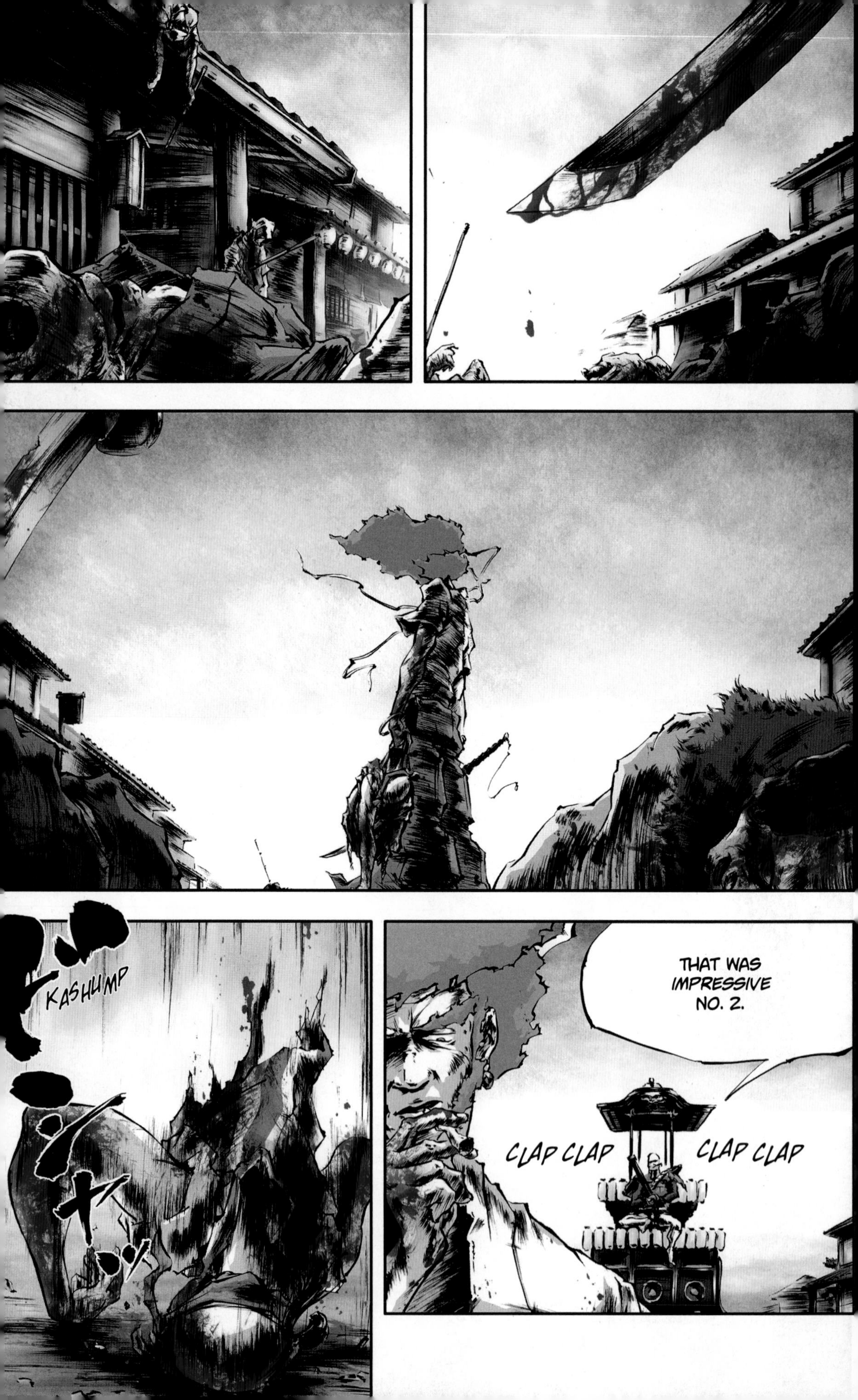
KASHUMP
THAT WAS IMPRESSIVE NO. 2.
CLAP CLAP
CLAP CLAP

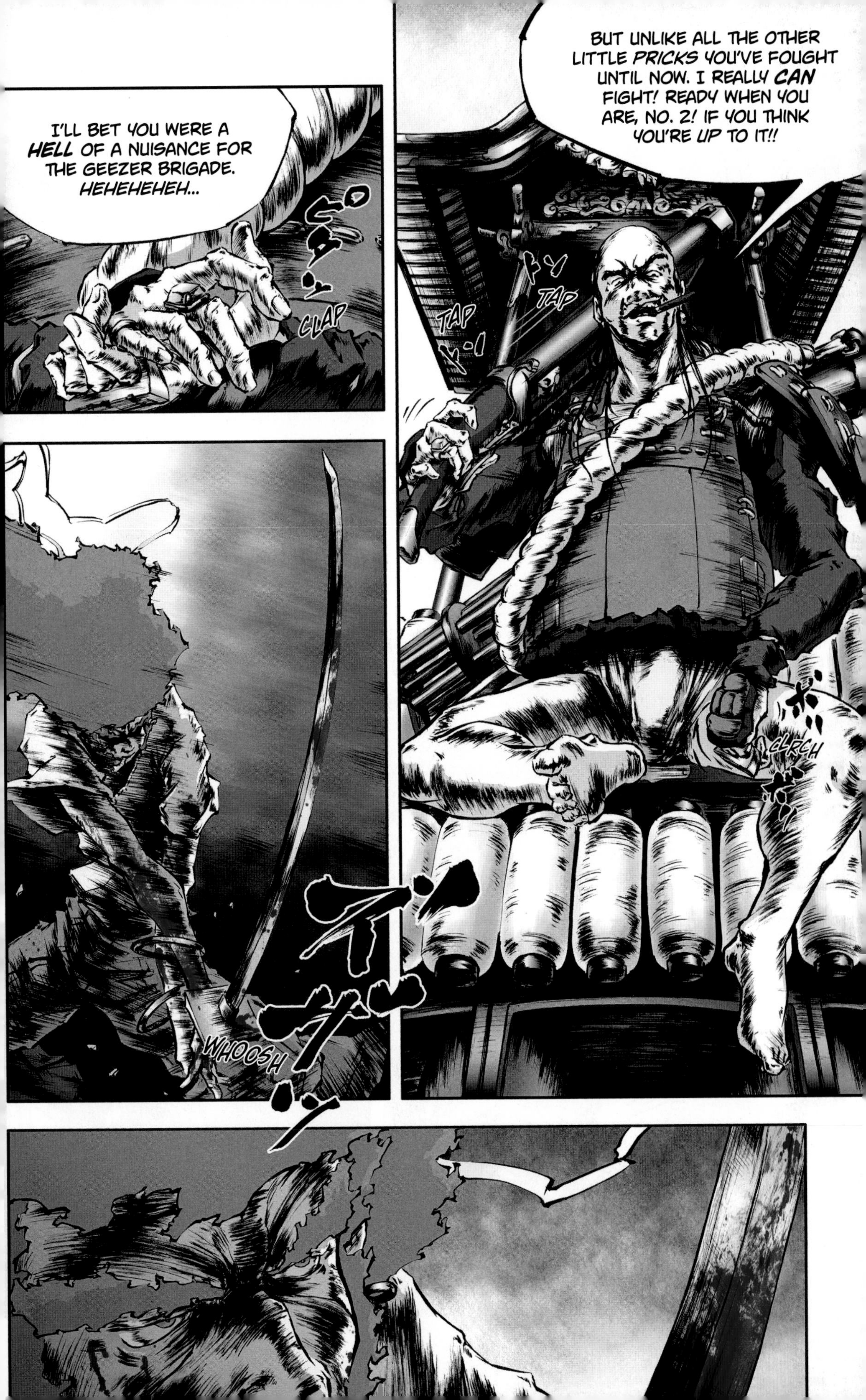
I'LL BET YOU WERE A HELL OF A NUISANCE FOR THE GEEZER BRIGADE. HEHEHEHEH...
CLAP
WHOOSH
BUT UNLIKE ALL THE OTHER LITTLE PRICKS YOU'VE FOUGHT UNTIL NOW. I REALLY CAN FIGHT! READY WHEN YOU ARE, NO. 2! IF YOU THINK YOU'RE UP TO IT!!
TAP
TAP
CLRCH

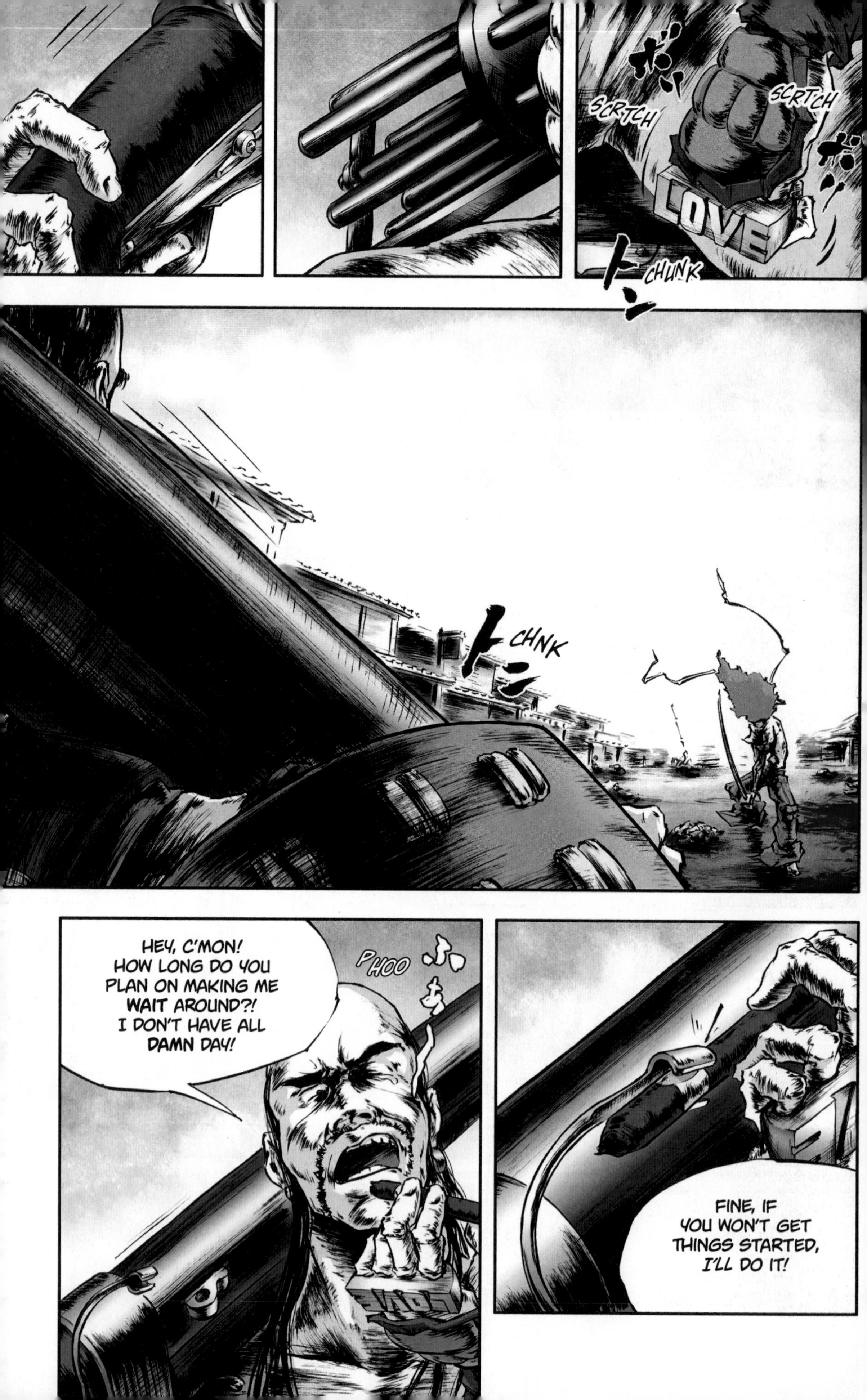
SCRTCH
SCRTCH
LOVE
CHUNK
CHNK
HEY, C'MON! HOW LONG DO YOU PLAN ON MAKING ME WAIT AROUND?! I DON'T HAVE ALL DAMN DAY!
PHOO
FINE, IF YOU WON'T GET THINGS STARTED, I'LL DO IT!

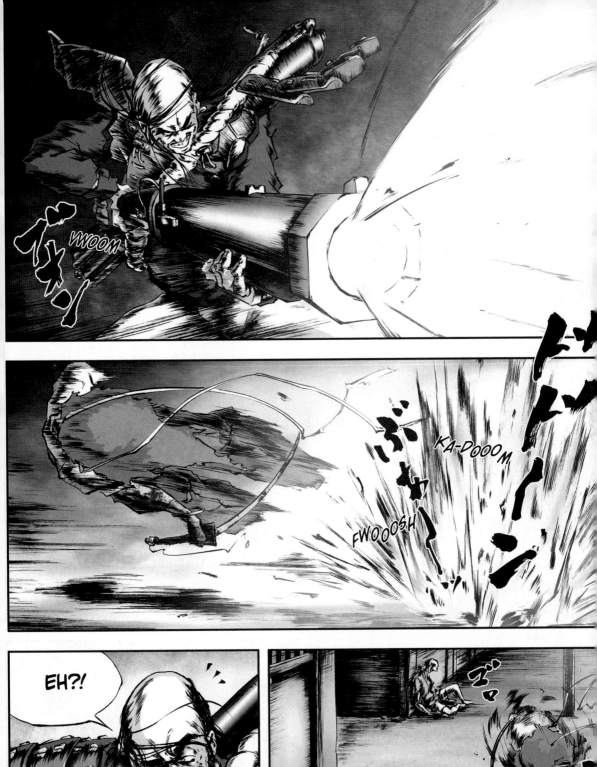

VWOOM

KA-DOOOM

FWOOOSH

EH?!

ROLL

GAAAHAHAHA! EVEN THE GREAT NO. 2 CAN'T DO NOTHIN' BESIDES RUN OFF AND *HIDE* AT THE SIGHT OF MY GREAT BIG CANNON!

BUT HIDING WON'T DO YA ANY GOOD!

WE'VE JUST GOTTEN STARTED. DON'T GO DYING ON ME JUST YET...

SSSSSZZZZZ

LET ME HAVE A TINY BIT MORE FUN FIRST... HEHEH...

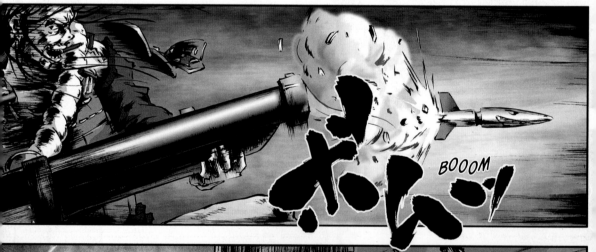

BOOOM

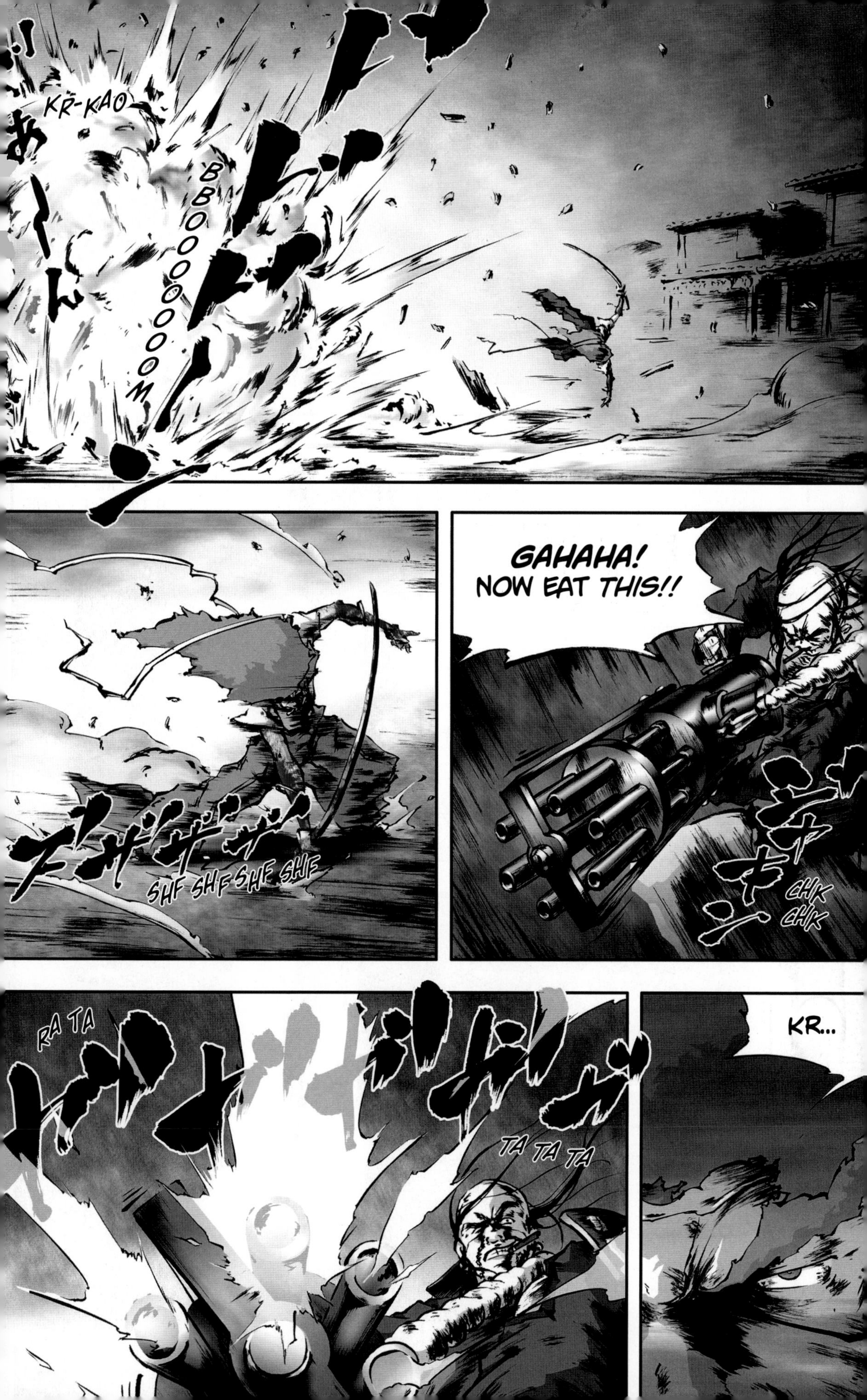
KR-KAO
あ〜ん
BBOOOOOOOOM
SHF SHF SHF SHF
GAHAHA!
NOW EAT THIS!!
CHK
CHK
RA TA
TA TA TA
KR...

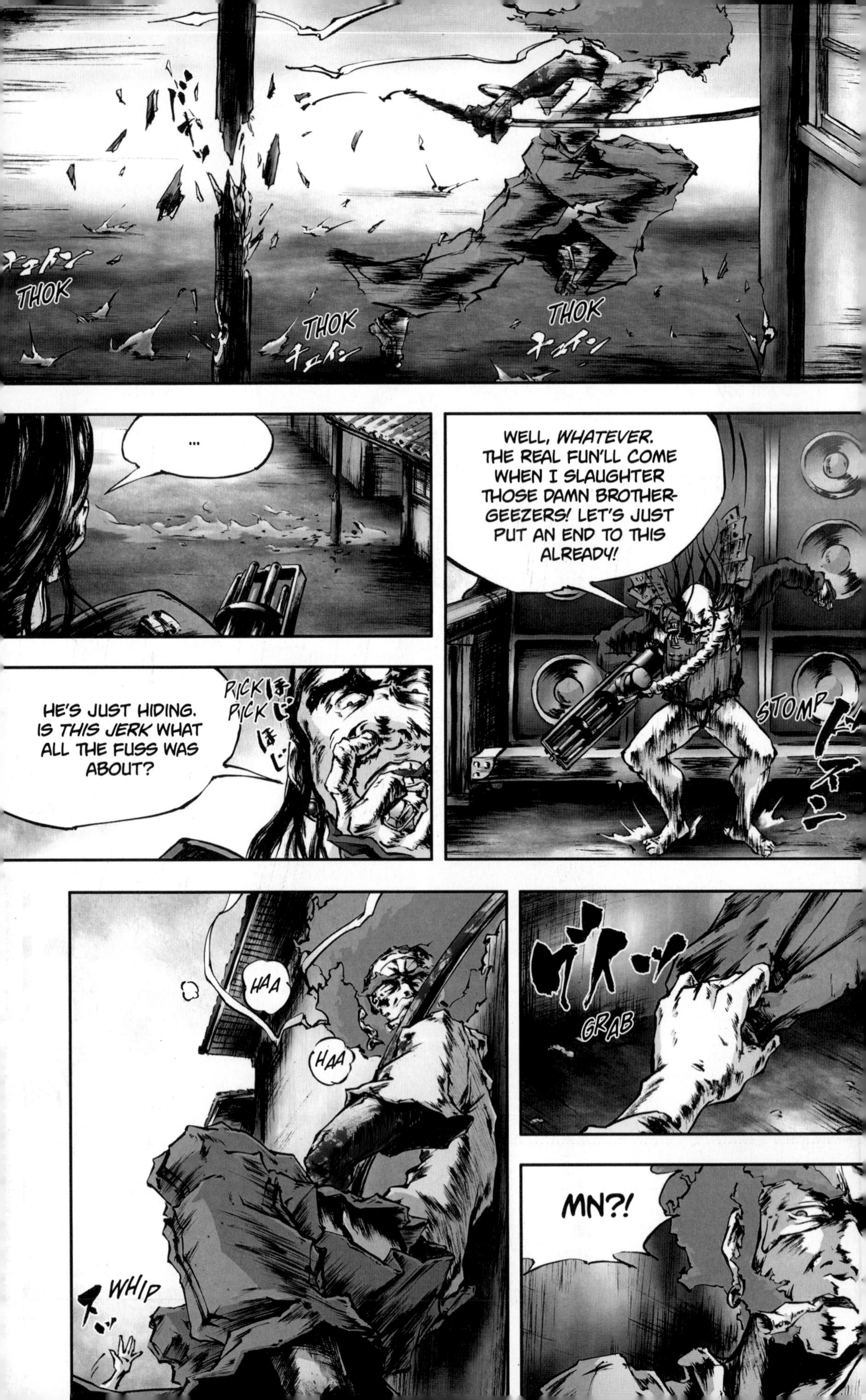
THOK
THOK
THOK
...
HE'S JUST HIDING. IS *THIS JERK* WHAT ALL THE FUSS WAS ABOUT?
PICK PICK
WELL, *WHATEVER.* THE REAL FUN'LL COME WHEN I SLAUGHTER THOSE DAMN BROTHER-GEEZERS! LET'S JUST PUT AN END TO THIS ALREADY!
STOMP
HAA
HAA
WHIP
GRAB
MN?!

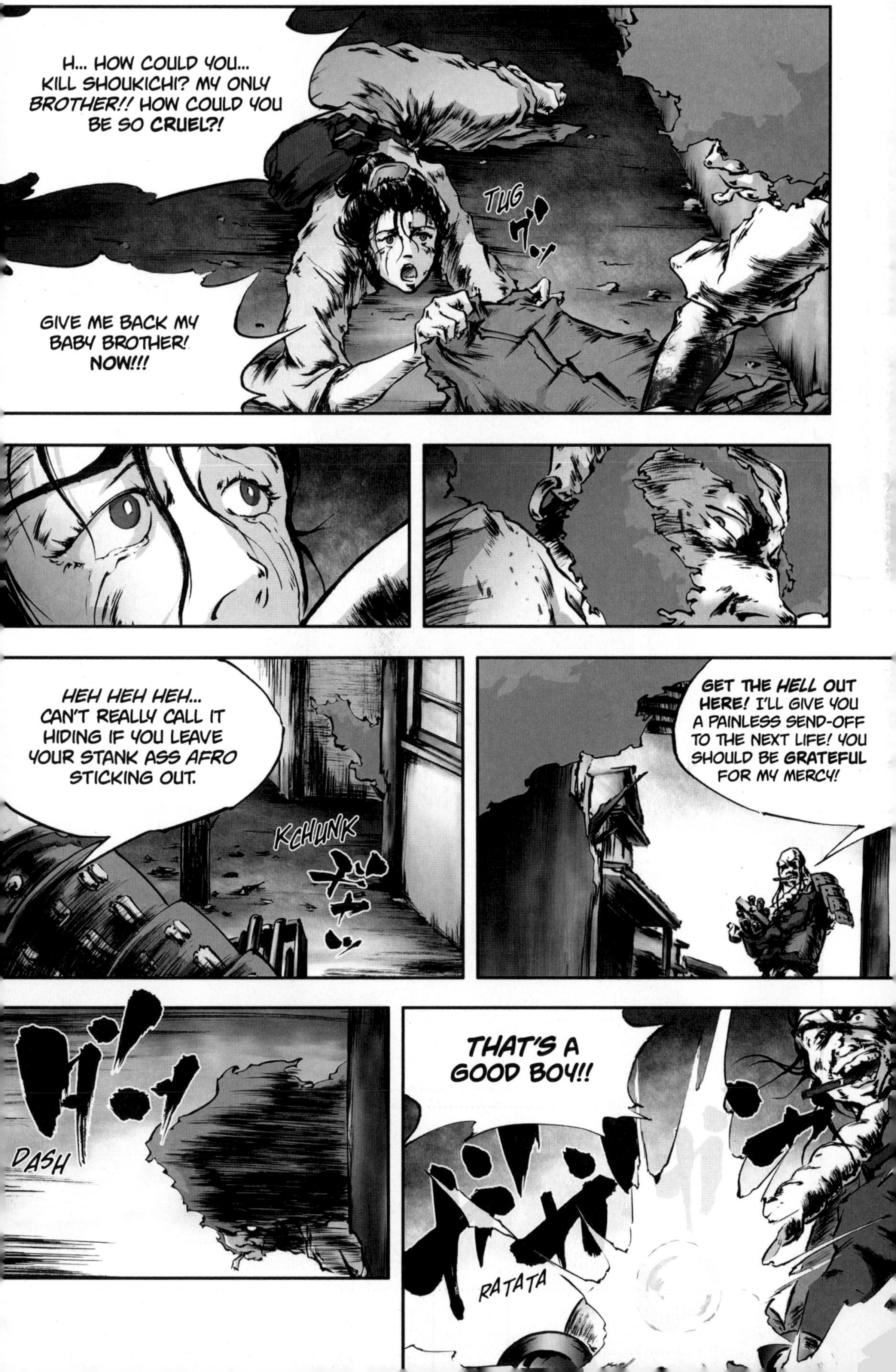
H... HOW COULD YOU... KILL SHOUKICHI? MY ONLY BROTHER!! HOW COULD YOU BE SO CRUEL?!
TUG
GIVE ME BACK MY BABY BROTHER! NOW!!!
HEH HEH HEH... CAN'T REALLY CALL IT HIDING IF YOU LEAVE YOUR STANK ASS AFRO STICKING OUT.
KCHUNK
GET THE HELL OUT HERE! I'LL GIVE YOU A PAINLESS SEND-OFF TO THE NEXT LIFE! YOU SHOULD BE GRATEFUL FOR MY MERCY!
DASH
THAT'S A GOOD BOY!!
RATATA

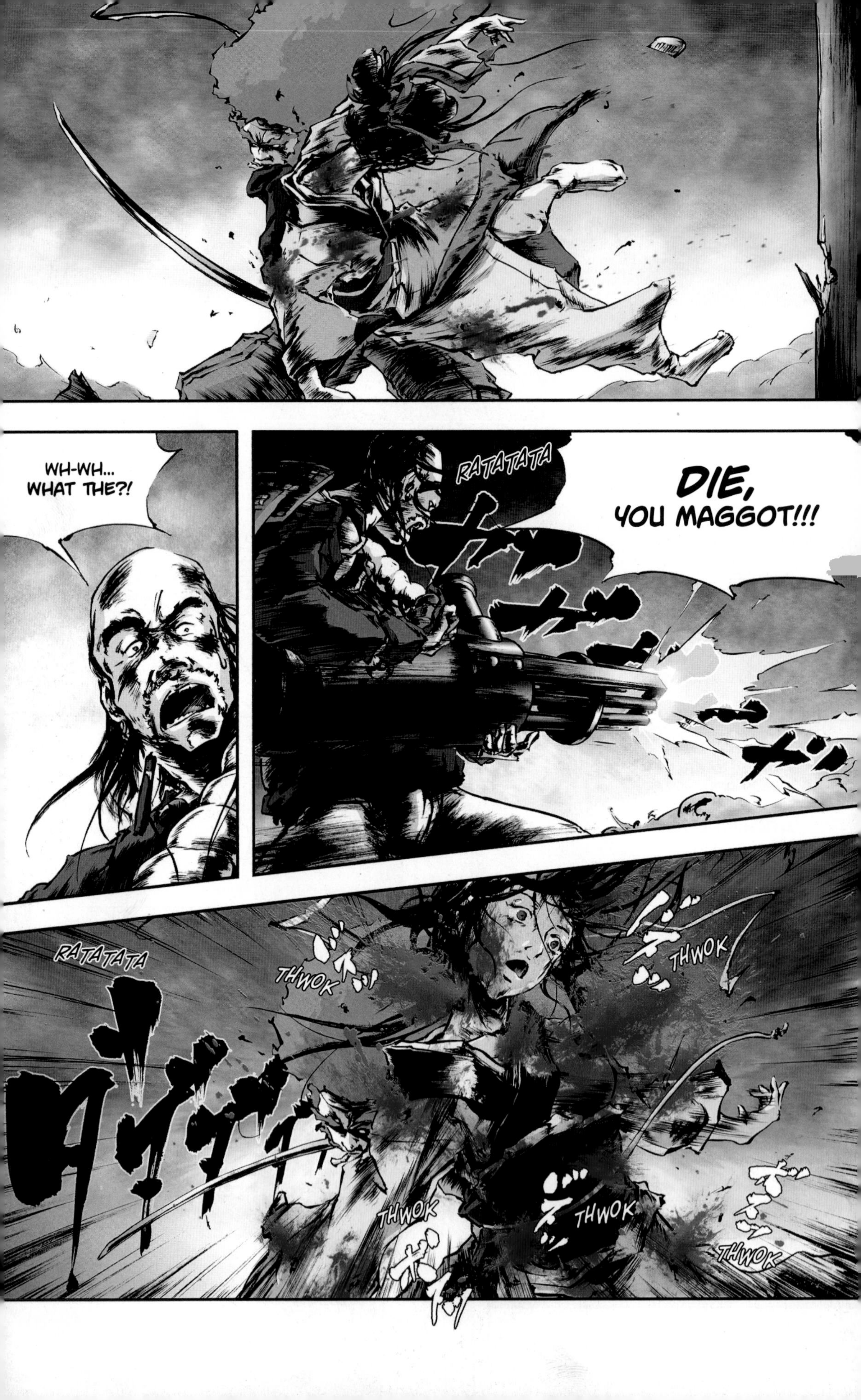
WH-WH... WHAT THE?!
RATATATA
DIE, YOU MAGGOT!!!
RATATATA
THWOK
THWOK
THWOK
THWOK
THWOK

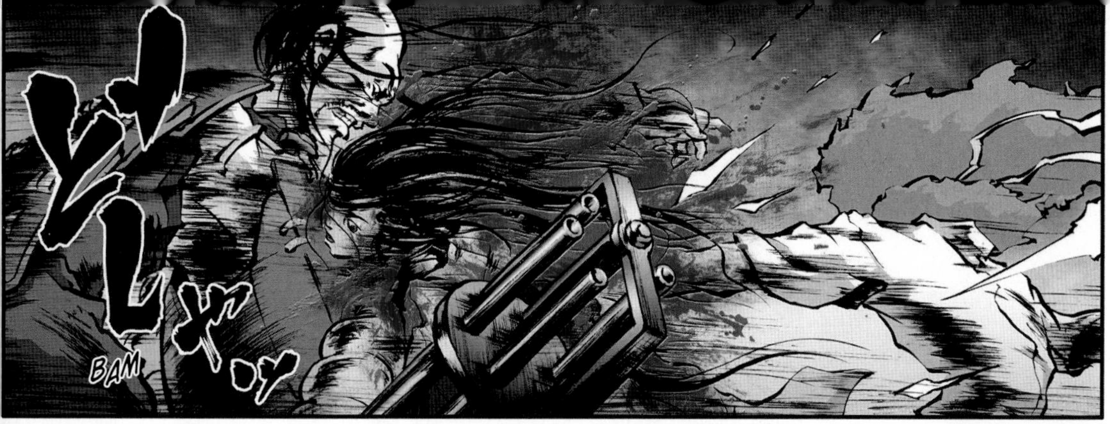
BAM

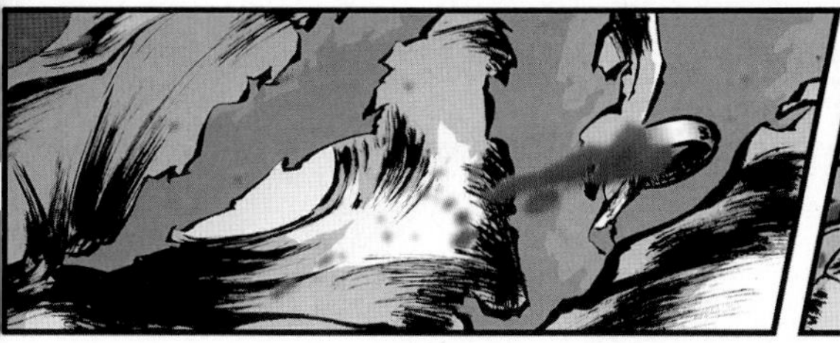

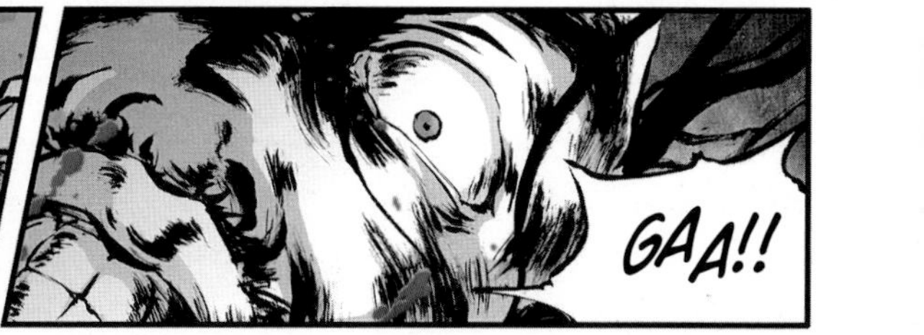
GAA!!

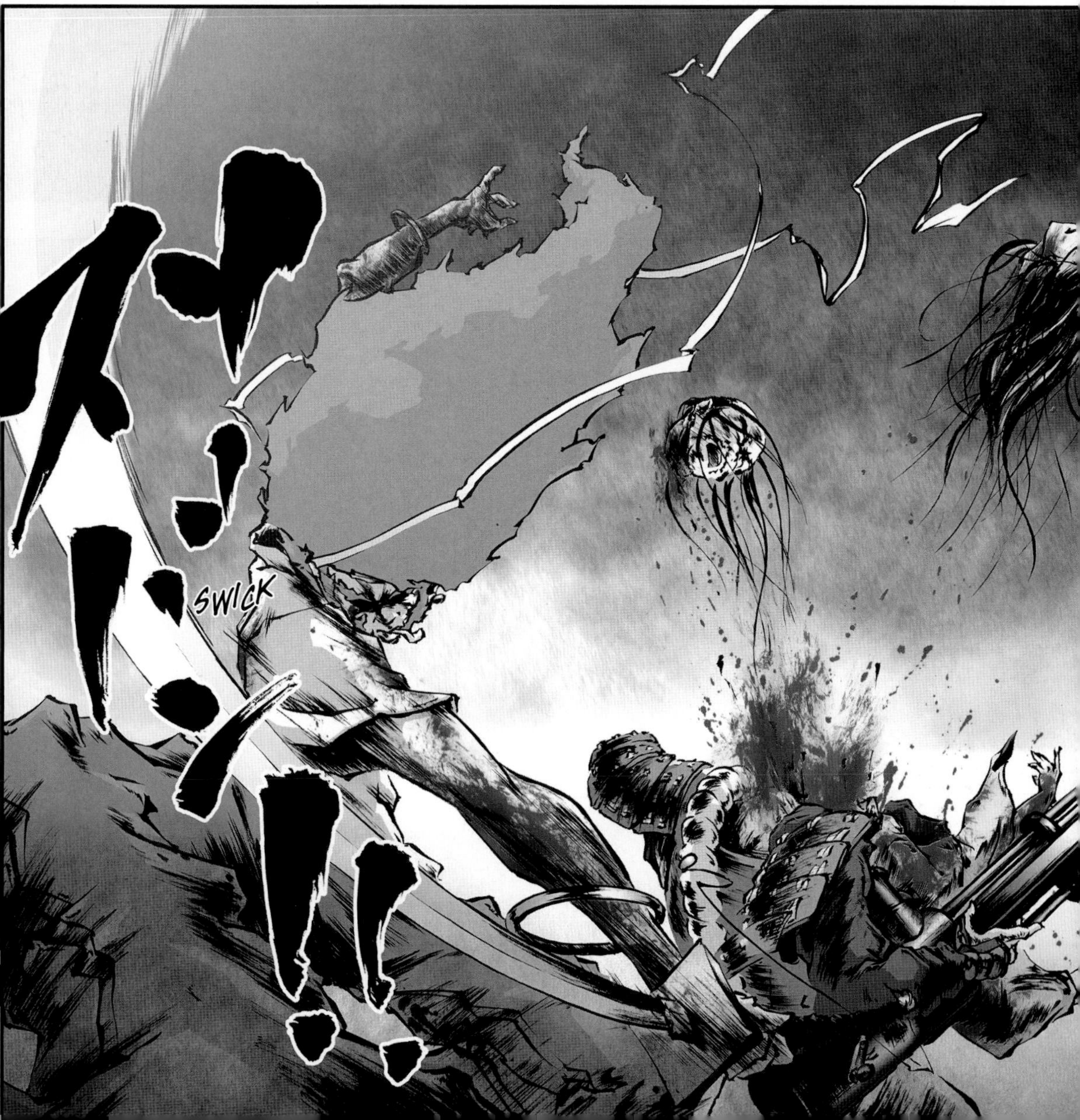
SWICK

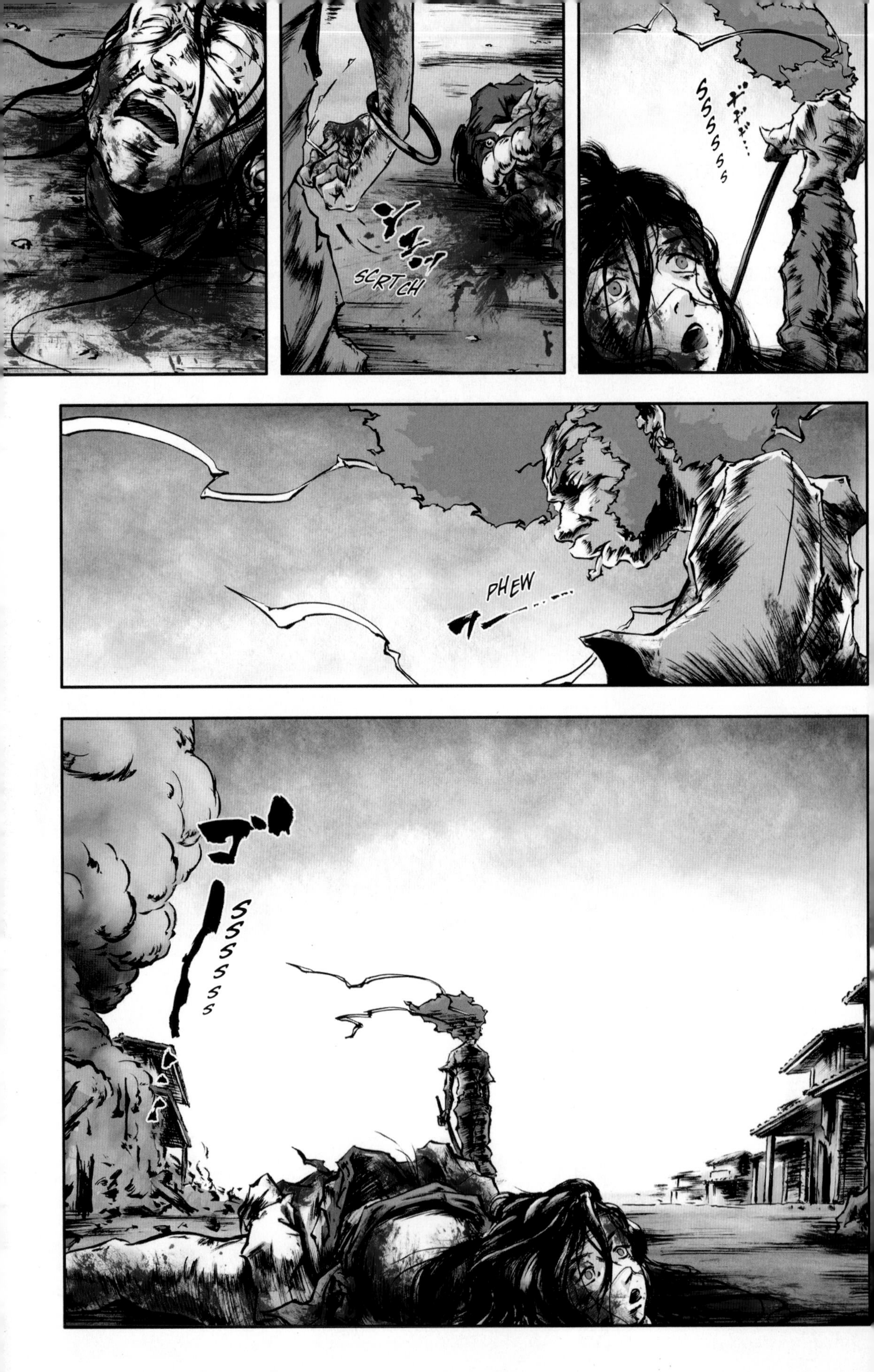

SCRTCH
SSSSSSS
PHEW
SSSSSSS

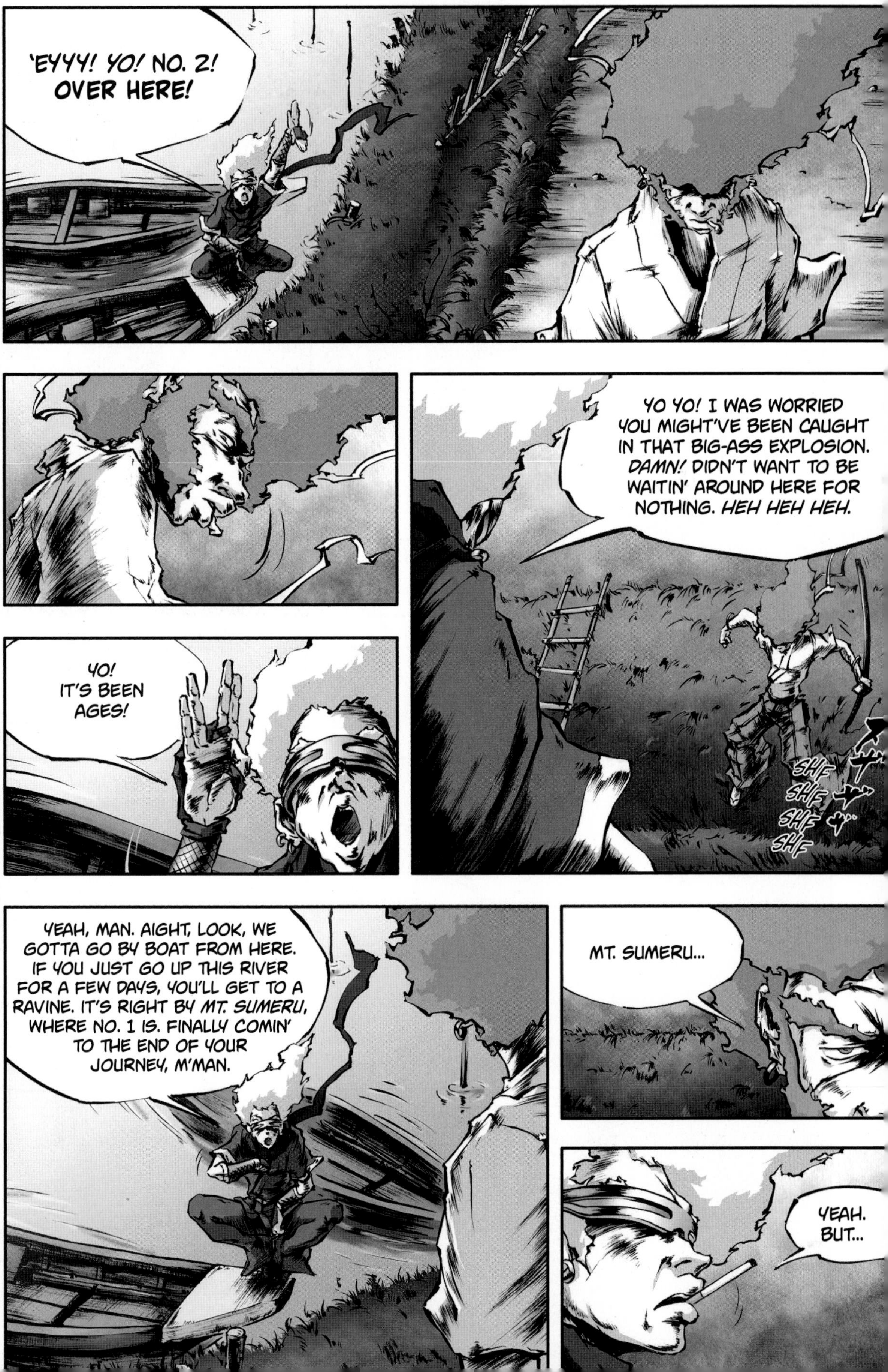
'EYYY! YO! NO. 2! OVER HERE!
YO! IT'S BEEN AGES!
YO YO! I WAS WORRIED YOU MIGHT'VE BEEN CAUGHT IN THAT BIG-ASS EXPLOSION. DAMN! DIDN'T WANT TO BE WAITIN' AROUND HERE FOR NOTHING. HEH HEH HEH.
SHF SHF SHF SHF
YEAH, MAN. AIGHT, LOOK, WE GOTTA GO BY BOAT FROM HERE. IF YOU JUST GO UP THIS RIVER FOR A FEW DAYS, YOU'LL GET TO A RAVINE. IT'S RIGHT BY MT. SUMERU, WHERE NO. 1 IS. FINALLY COMIN' TO THE END OF YOUR JOURNEY, M'MAN.
MT. SUMERU...
YEAH. BUT...

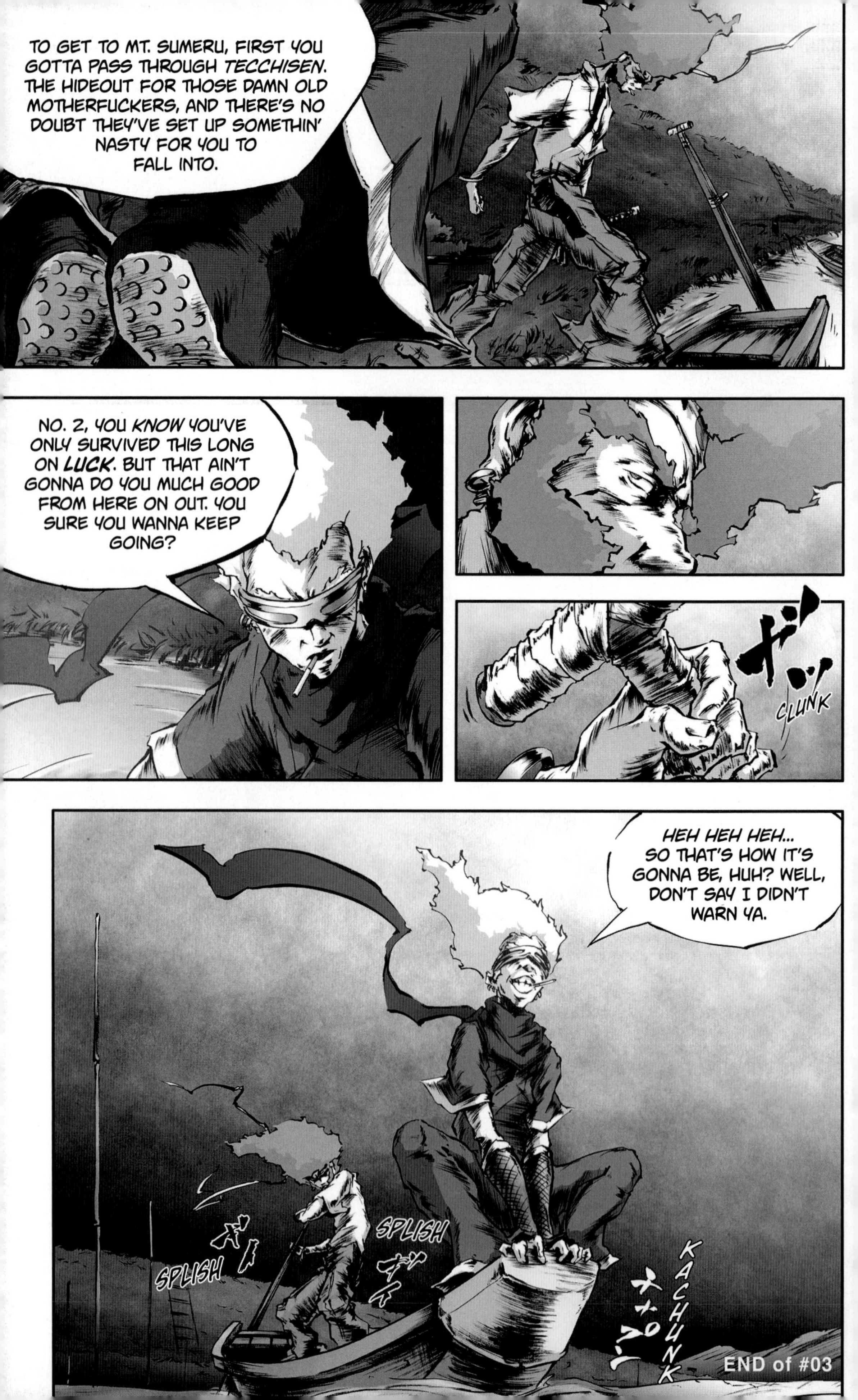
TO GET TO MT. SUMERU, FIRST YOU GOTTA PASS THROUGH *TECCHISEN*. THE HIDEOUT FOR THOSE DAMN OLD MOTHERFUCKERS, AND THERE'S NO DOUBT THEY'VE SET UP SOMETHIN' NASTY FOR YOU TO FALL INTO.
NO. 2, YOU *KNOW* YOU'VE ONLY SURVIVED THIS LONG ON ***LUCK***. BUT THAT AIN'T GONNA DO YOU MUCH GOOD FROM HERE ON OUT. YOU SURE YOU WANNA KEEP GOING?
CLUNK
HEH HEH HEH... SO THAT'S HOW IT'S GONNA BE, HUH? WELL, DON'T SAY I DIDN'T WARN YA.
SPLISH
SPLISH
KACHUNK
END of #03

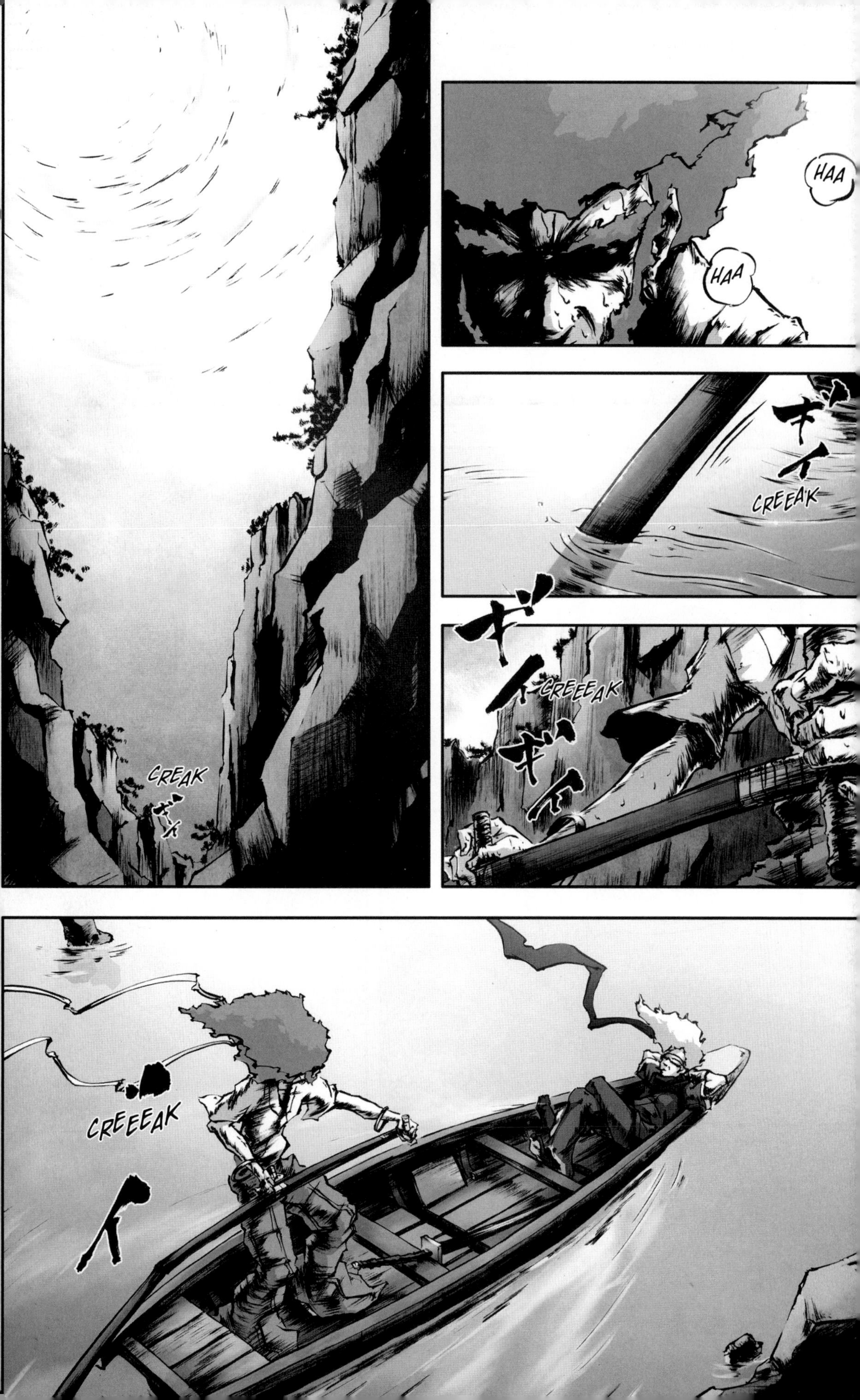
CREAK
ギィ
HAA
HAA
ギィ
CREEAK
ギィ
CREEEAK
ギィ
CREEEAK
ギィ

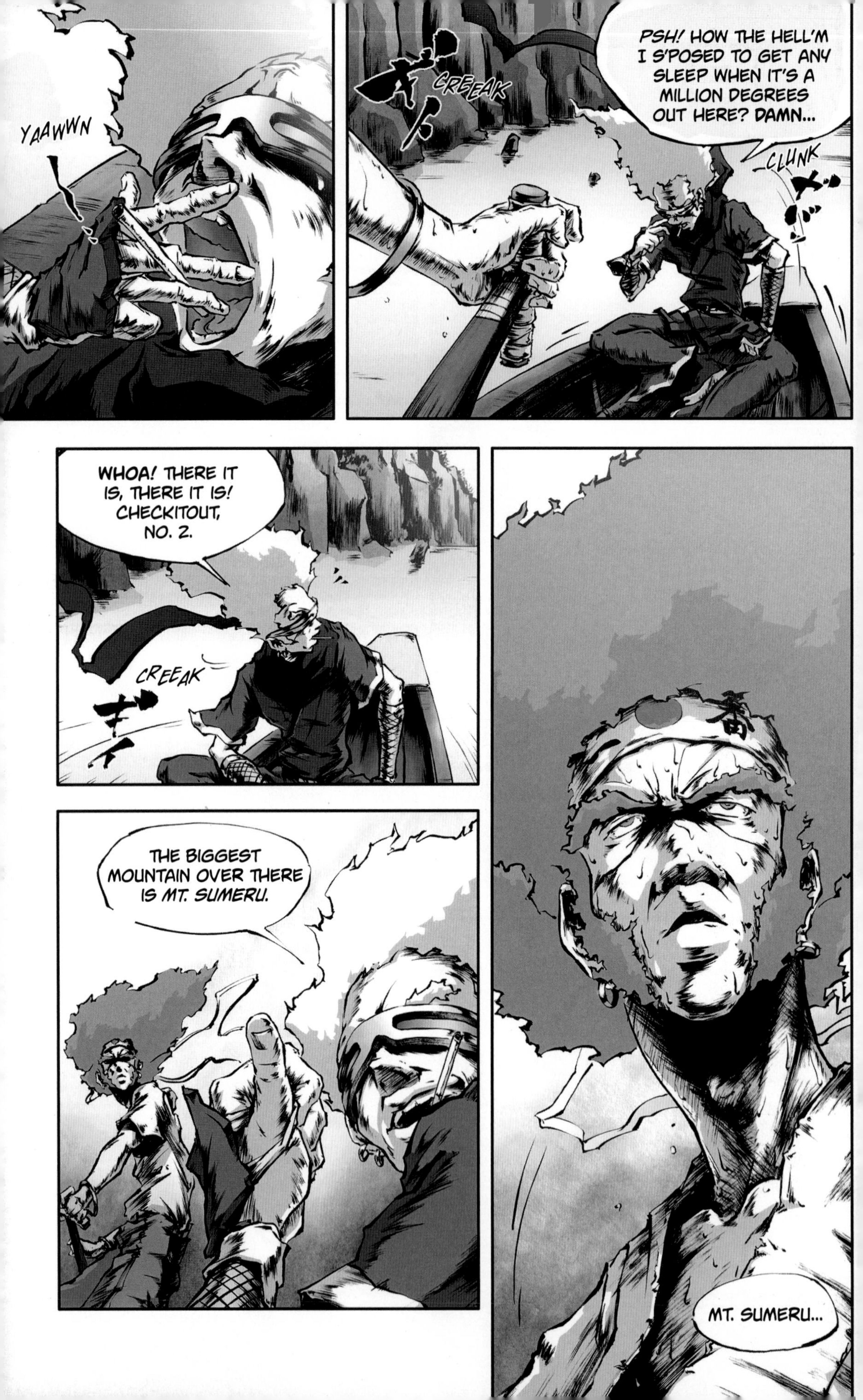
YAAWWN
CREEAK
PSH! HOW THE HELL'M I S'POSED TO GET ANY SLEEP WHEN IT'S A MILLION DEGREES OUT HERE? DAMN...
CLUNK
WHOA! THERE IT IS, THERE IT IS! CHECKITOUT, NO. 2.
CREEAK
THE BIGGEST MOUNTAIN OVER THERE IS MT. SUMERU.
MT. SUMERU...

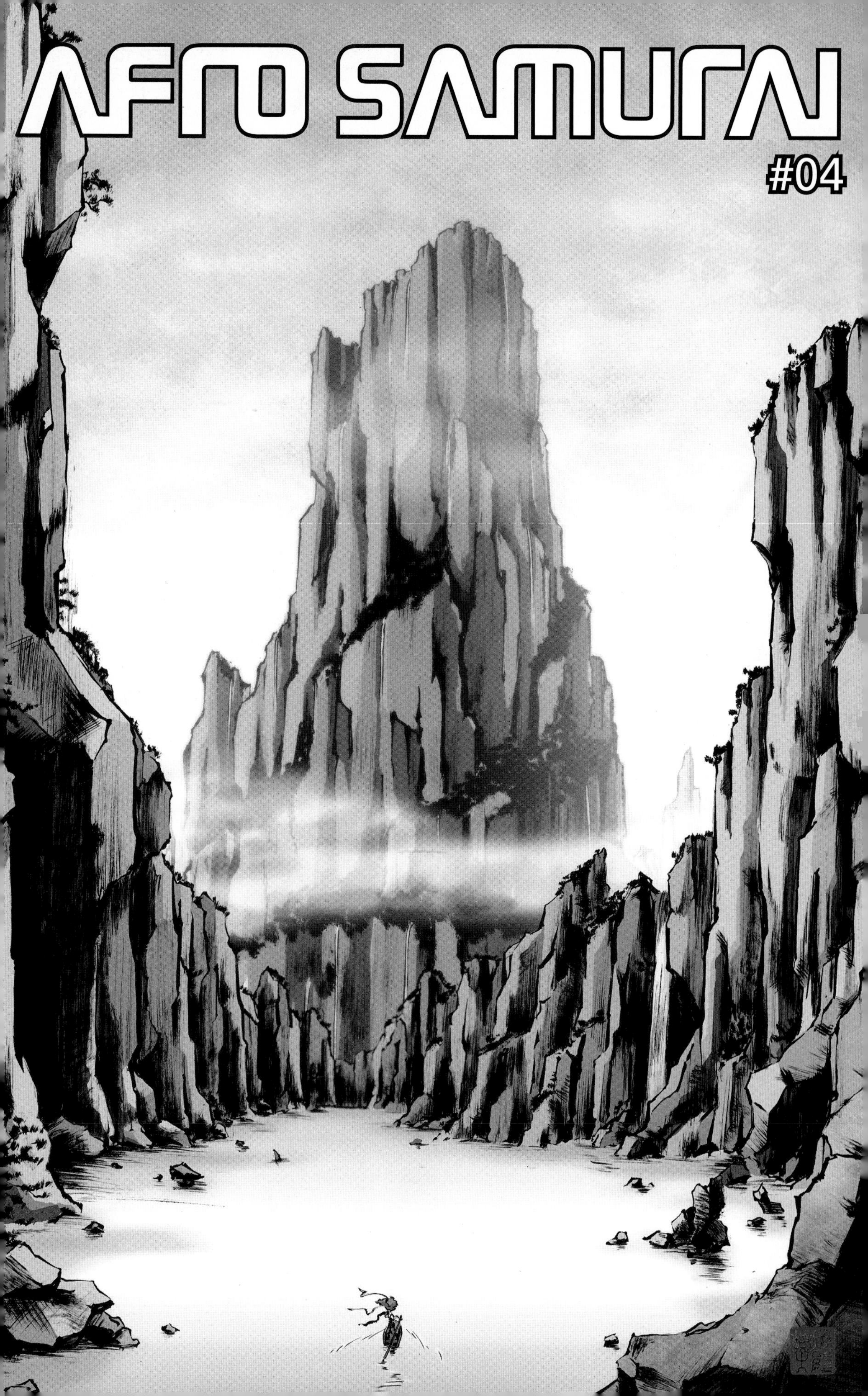
AFRO SAMURAI
#04

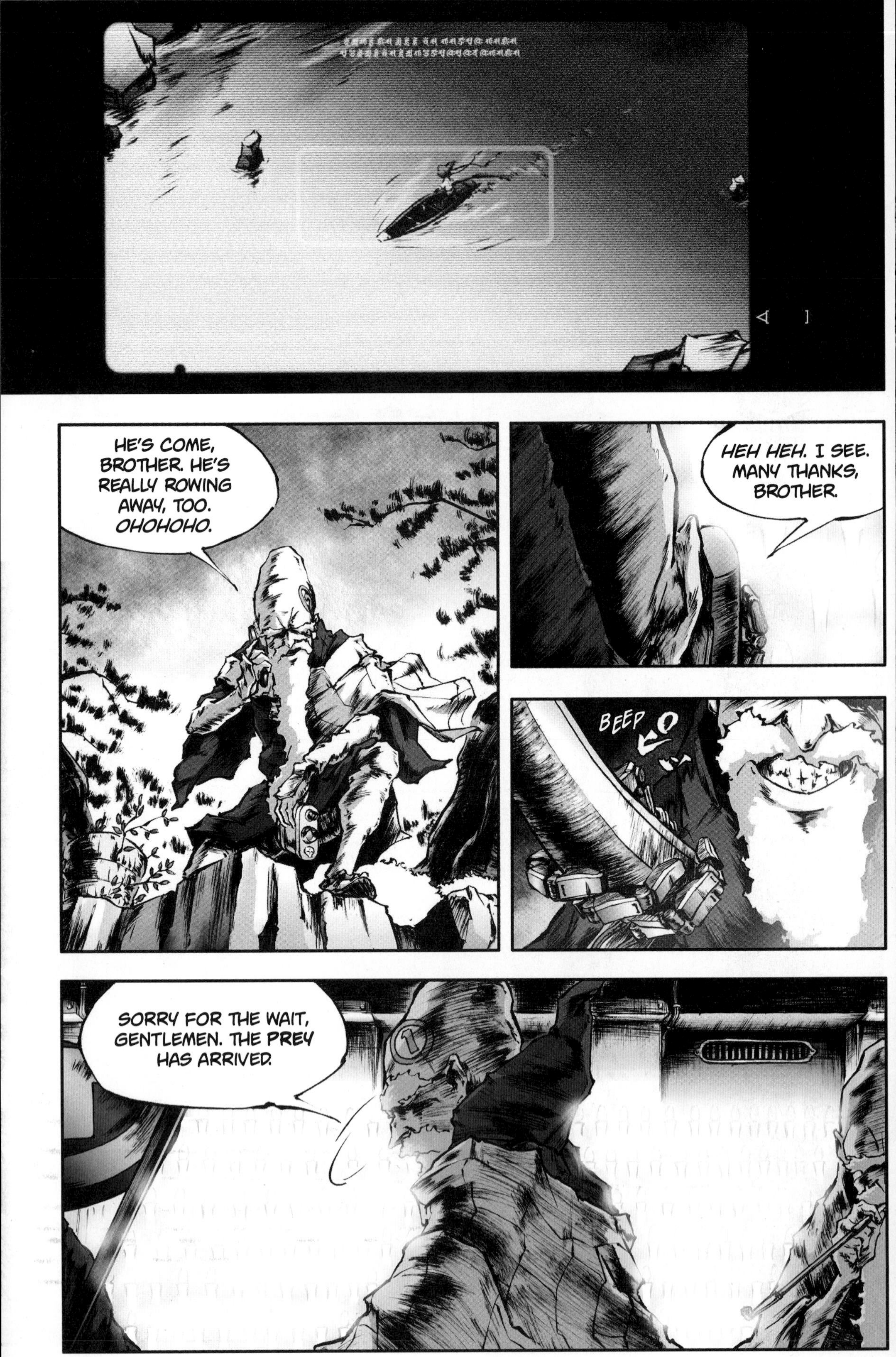
HE'S COME, BROTHER. HE'S REALLY ROWING AWAY, TOO. OHOHOHO.
HEH HEH. I SEE. MANY THANKS, BROTHER.
BEEP
SORRY FOR THE WAIT, GENTLEMEN. THE PREY HAS ARRIVED.

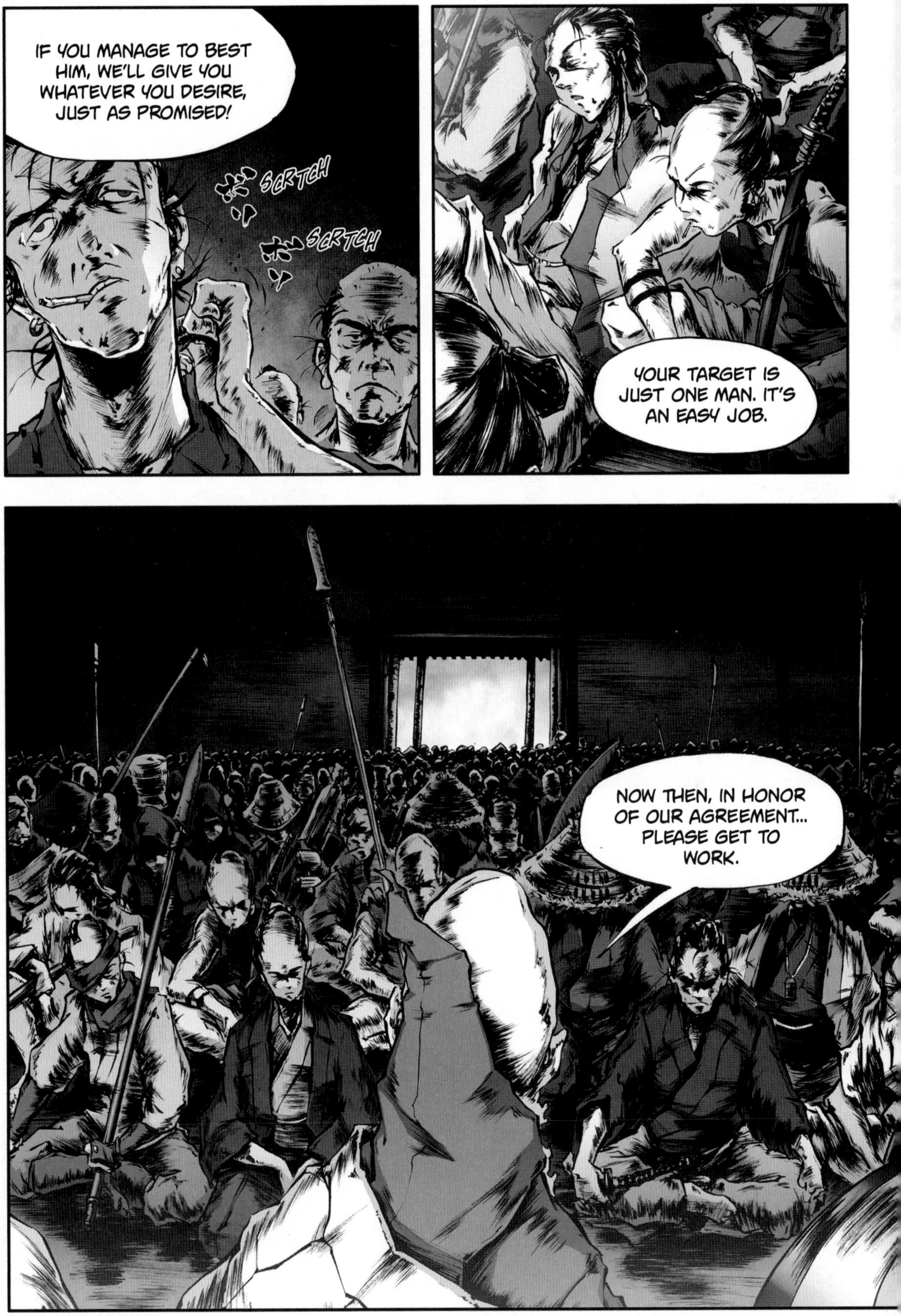
IF YOU MANAGE TO BEST HIM, WE'LL GIVE YOU WHATEVER YOU DESIRE, JUST AS PROMISED!
SCRTCH
SCRTCH
YOUR TARGET IS JUST ONE MAN. IT'S AN EASY JOB.
NOW THEN, IN HONOR OF OUR AGREEMENT... PLEASE GET TO WORK.

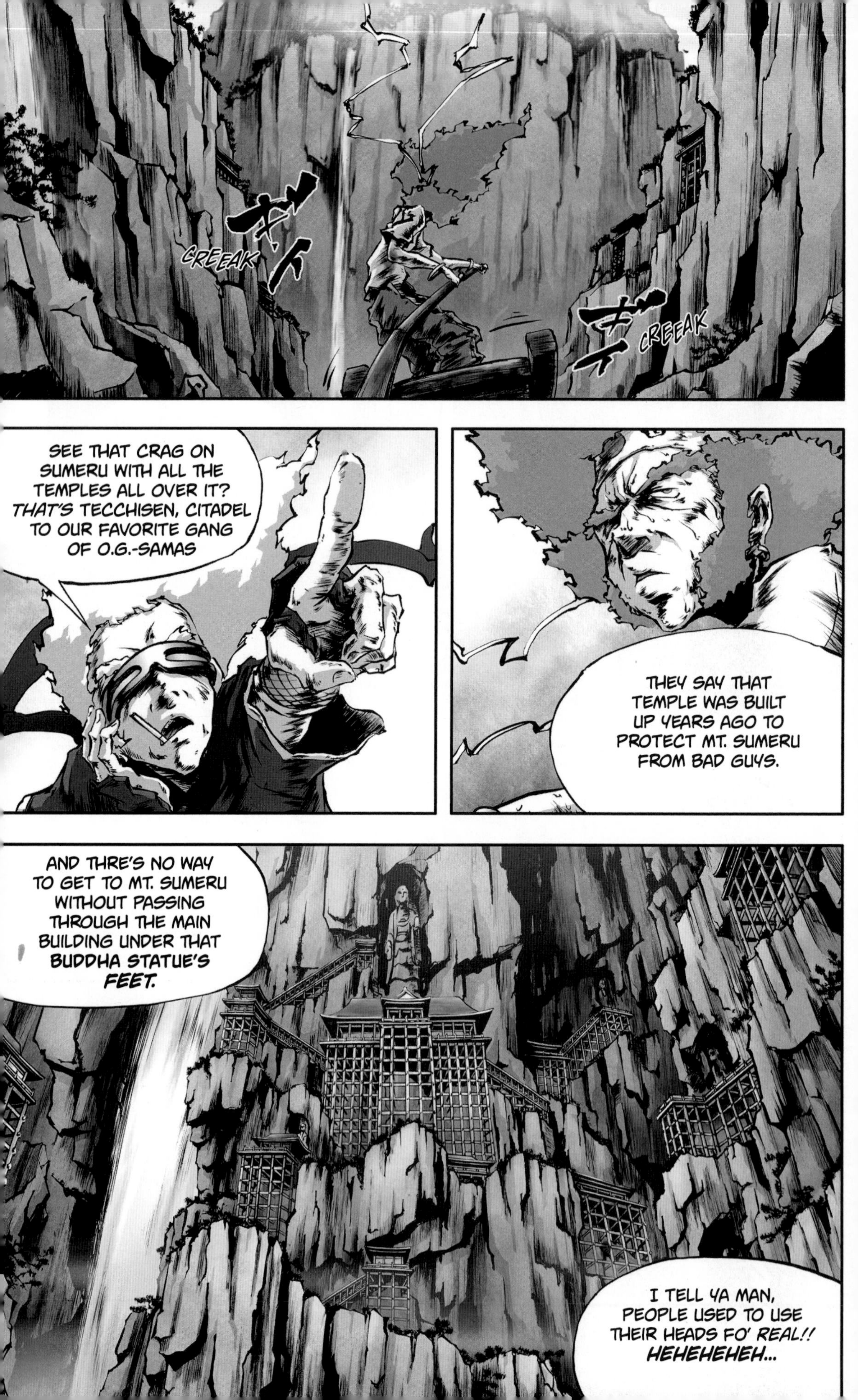
CREEAK
CREEAK
SEE THAT CRAG ON SUMERU WITH ALL THE TEMPLES ALL OVER IT? *THAT'S* TECCHISEN, CITADEL TO OUR FAVORITE GANG OF O.G.-SAMAS
THEY SAY THAT TEMPLE WAS BUILT UP YEARS AGO TO PROTECT MT. SUMERU FROM BAD GUYS.
AND THRE'S NO WAY TO GET TO MT. SUMERU WITHOUT PASSING THROUGH THE MAIN BUILDING UNDER THAT BUDDHA STATUE'S *FEET.*
I TELL YA MAN, PEOPLE USED TO USE THEIR HEADS FO' *REAL!!* ***HEHEHEHEH...***

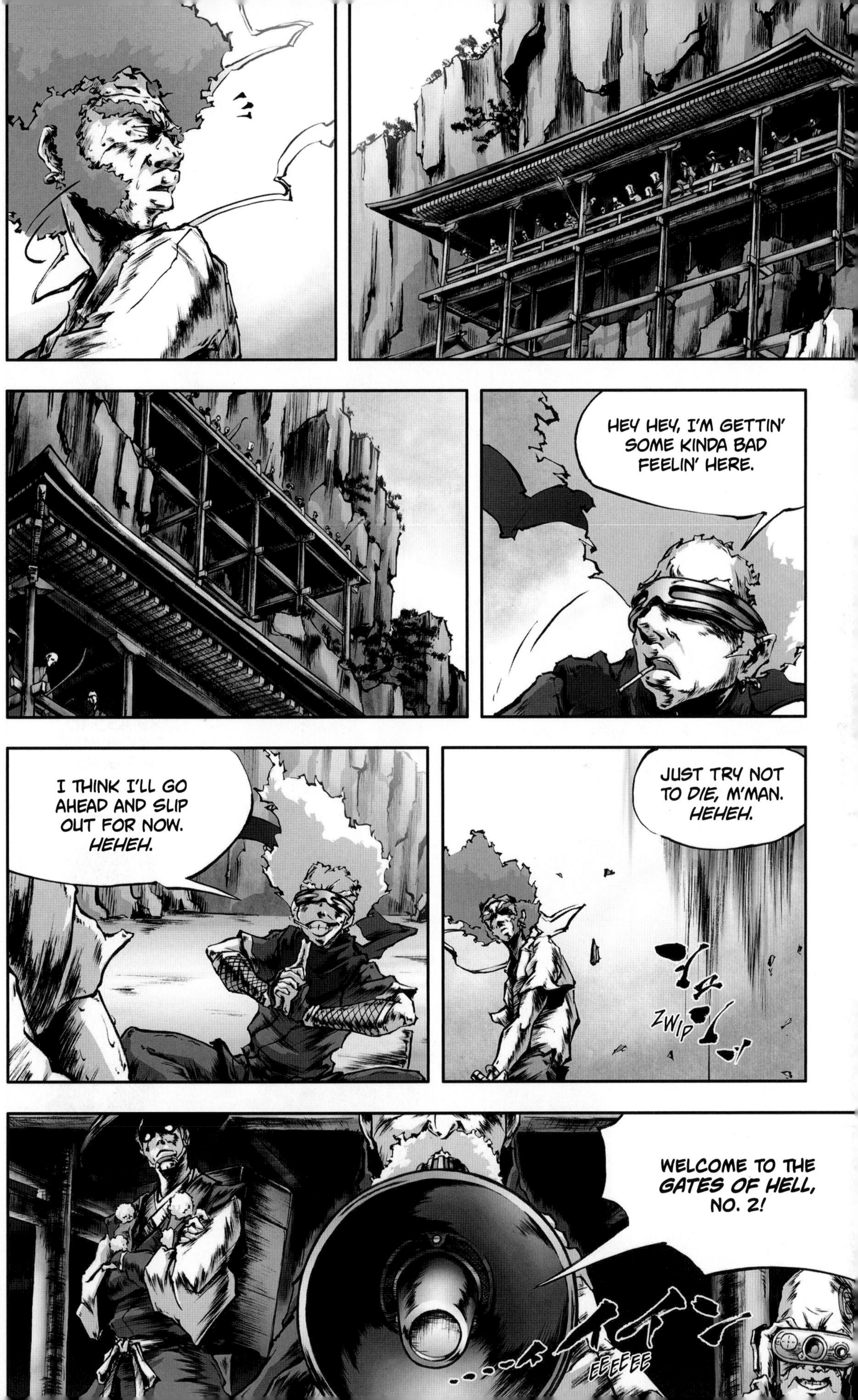
HEY HEY, I'M GETTIN' SOME KINDA BAD FEELIN' HERE.
I THINK I'LL GO AHEAD AND SLIP OUT FOR NOW. *HEHEH.*
JUST TRY NOT TO *DIE*, M'MAN. *HEHEH.*
ZWIP
WELCOME TO THE *GATES OF HELL*, NO. 2!
EEEEEE

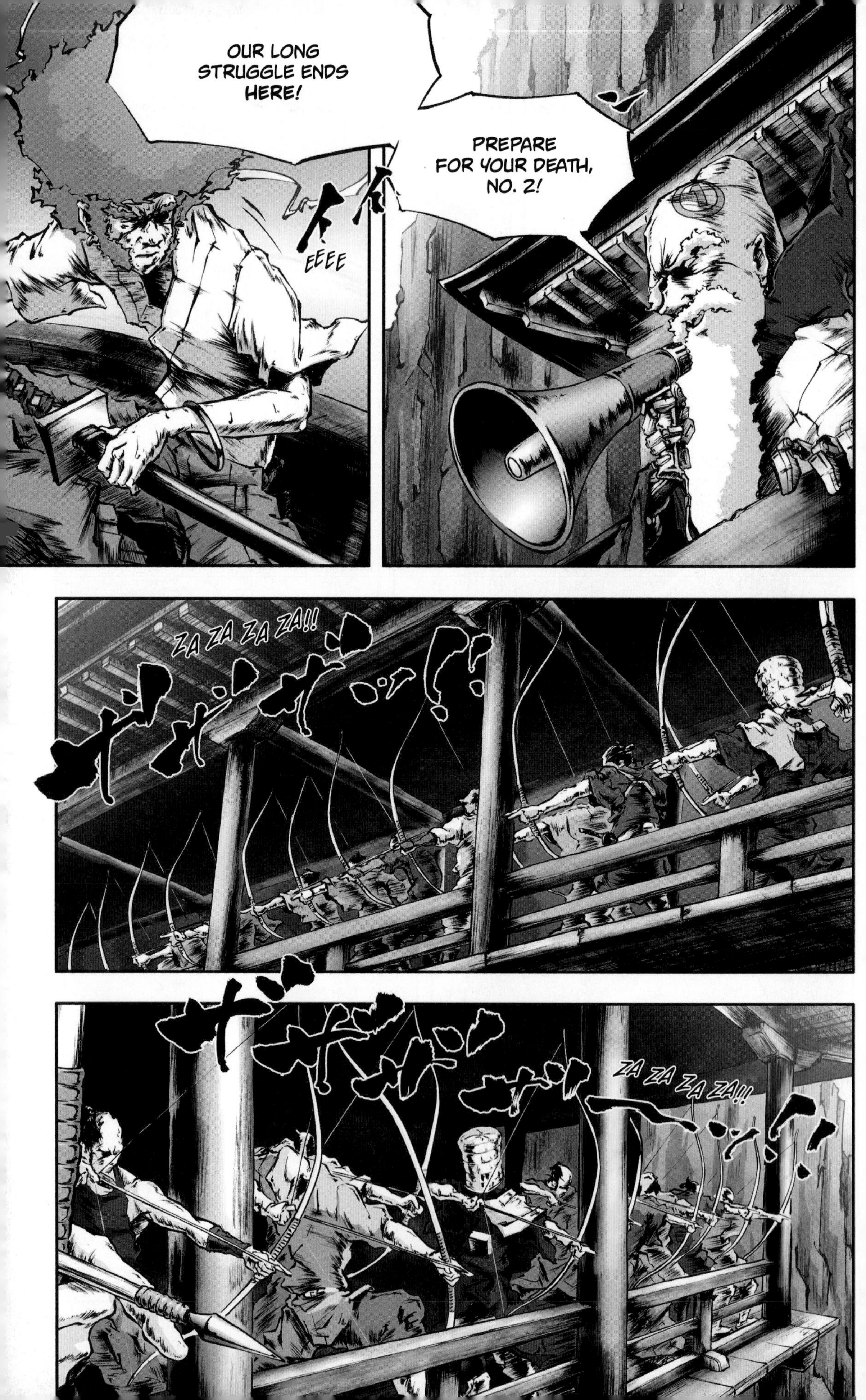
OUR LONG STRUGGLE ENDS HERE!
EEEE
PREPARE FOR YOUR DEATH, NO. 2!
ZA ZA ZA ZA!!
ZA ZA ZA ZA!!

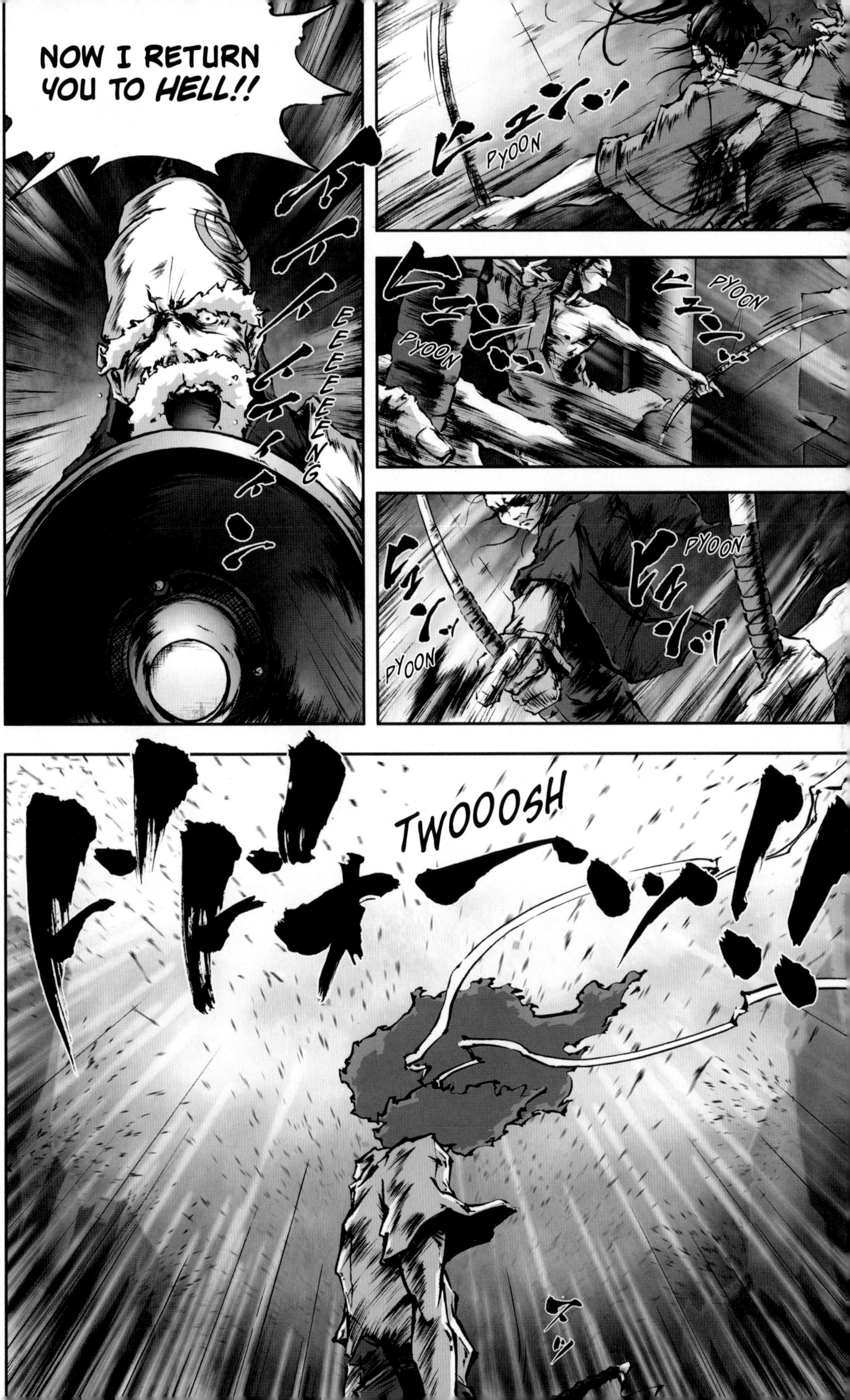
NOW I RETURN YOU TO HELL!!
EEEEEEEENG
PYOON
PYOON
PYOON
PYOON
PYOON
TWOOOSH

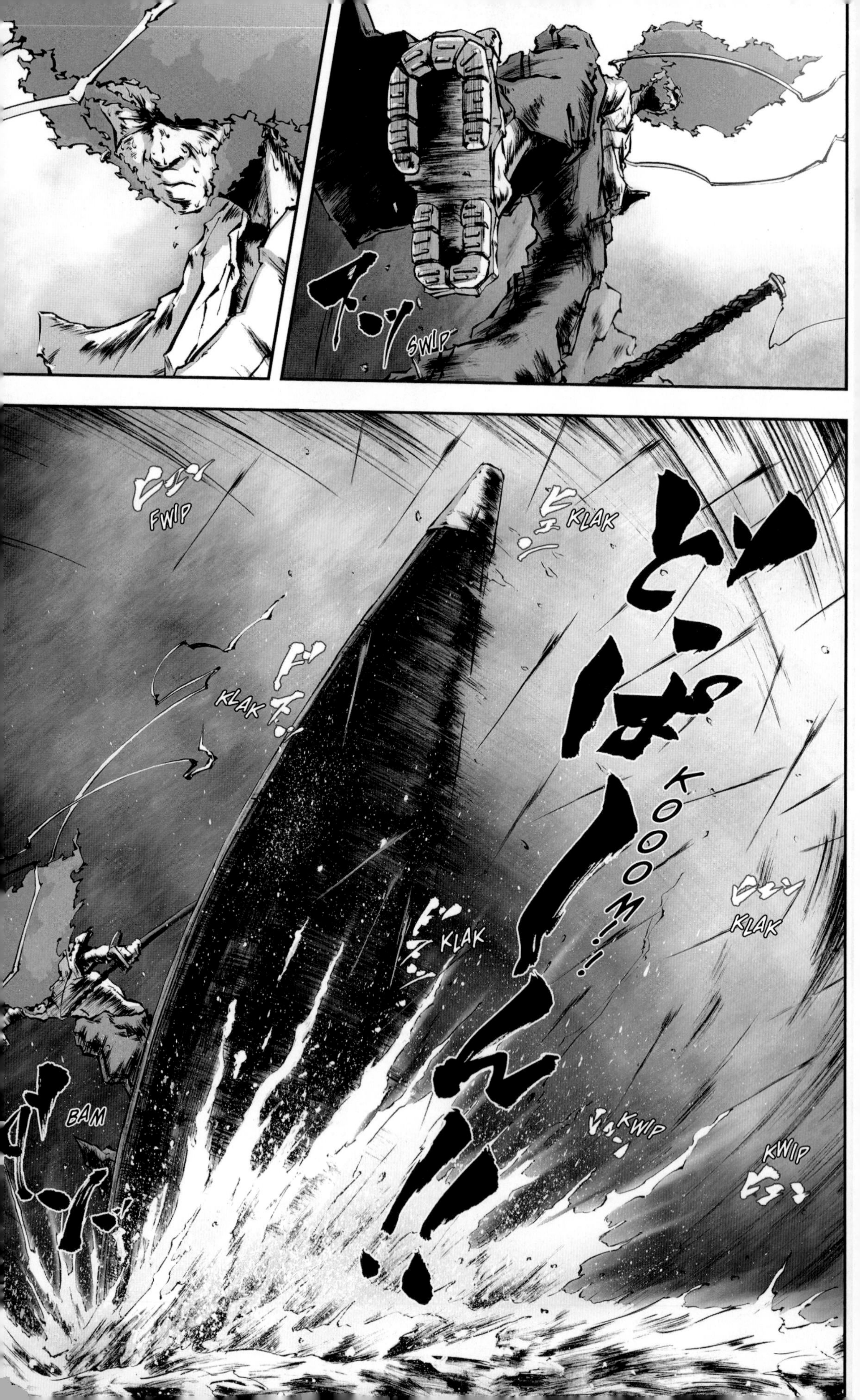
SWIP
FWIP
KLAK
KLAK
どぱーん!!
KOOOOM!!!
KLAK
KLAK
BAM
KWIP
KWIP

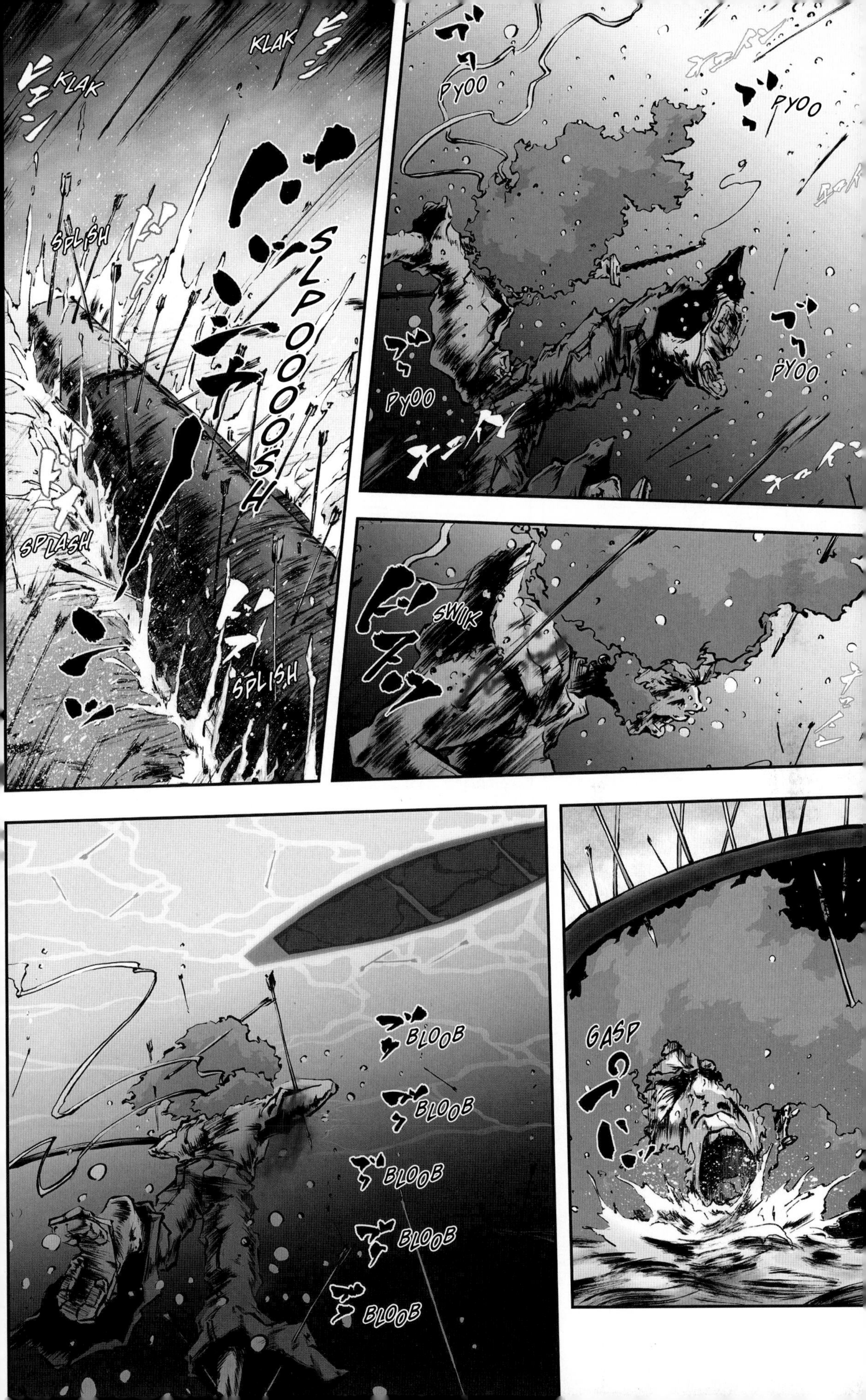
KLAK
KLAK
SPLISH
SLPOOOOOOSH
SPLASH
SPLISH
PYOO
PYOO
PYOO
PYOO
SWIK
BLOOB
BLOOB
BLOOB
BLOOB
BLOOB
GASP

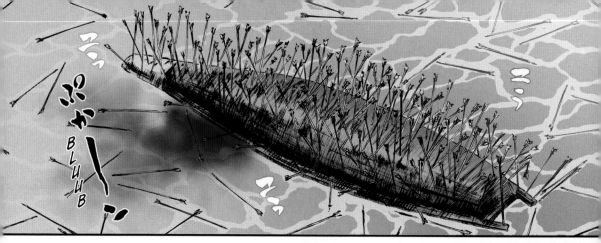

BLUUB

HMPH... PATHETIC. I GUESS NO. 2 WAS HUMAN AFTER ALL.

ROKUTA. WHEN THE BOAT REACHES LAND, GO OUT THERE AND RETRIEVE THE HEADBAND. ONCE YOU'VE DONE THAT, GET STARTED ON EXTERMINATING THOSE ASSASSINS.

AS YOU WISH.

HMMM... IT'S HARD TO BELIEVE NO. 2 WOULD GO DOWN SO EASY.

CREEEAK

ROKUTA. DO NOT LET YOUR GUARD DOWN UNTIL YOU'VE REMOVED HIS HEAD! I'M STILL NOT CONVINCED...

HEH... THERE'S NO NEED TO WORRY, BROTHER TWO. HE'S ALREADY DEAD.

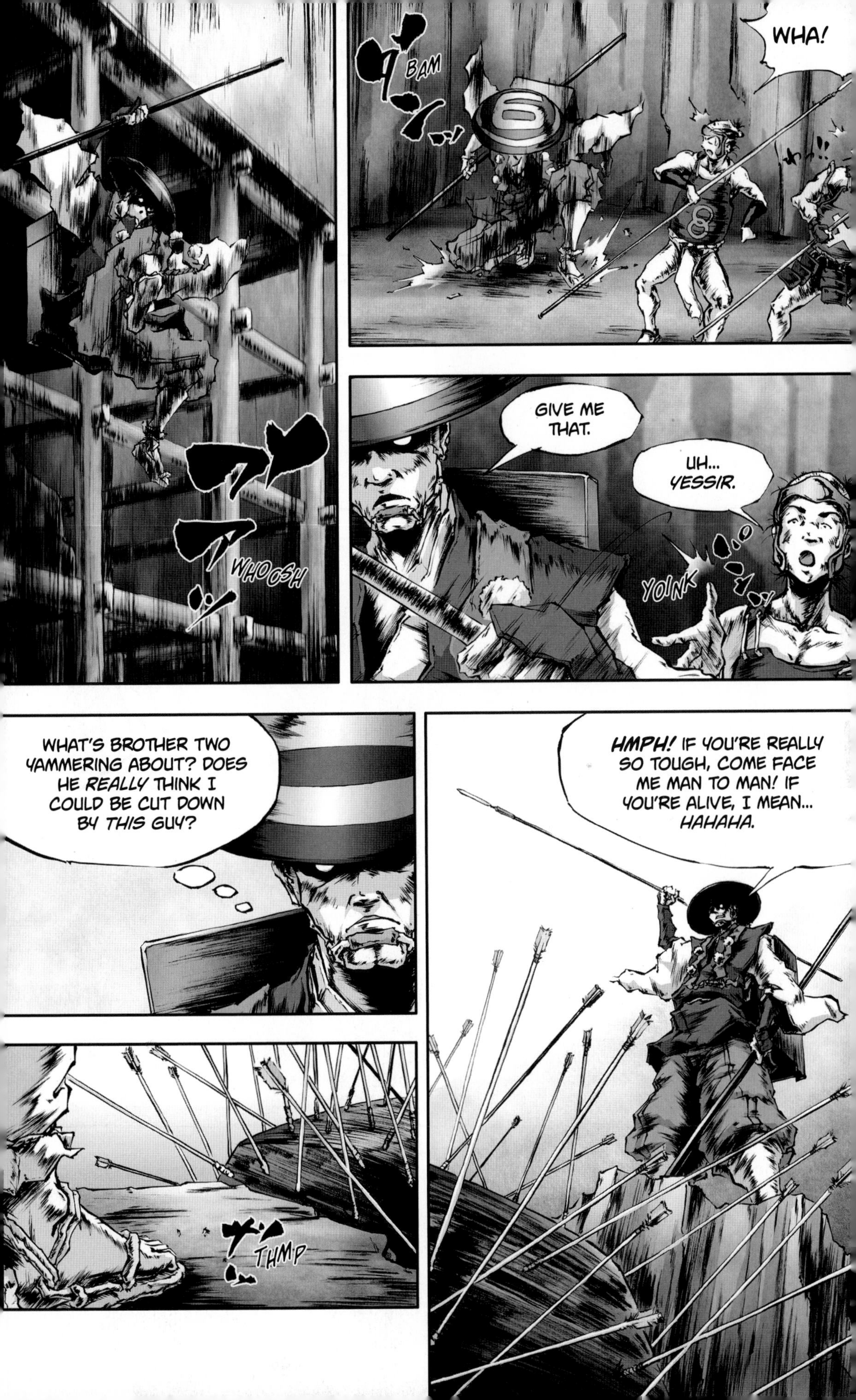
WHOOSH
BAM
WHA!
GIVE ME THAT.
UH... YESSIR.
YOINK
WHAT'S BROTHER TWO YAMMERING ABOUT? DOES HE *REALLY* THINK I COULD BE CUT DOWN BY *THIS GUY*?
THMP
HMPH! IF YOU'RE REALLY SO TOUGH, COME FACE ME MAN TO MAN! IF YOU'RE ALIVE, I MEAN... *HAHAHA.*

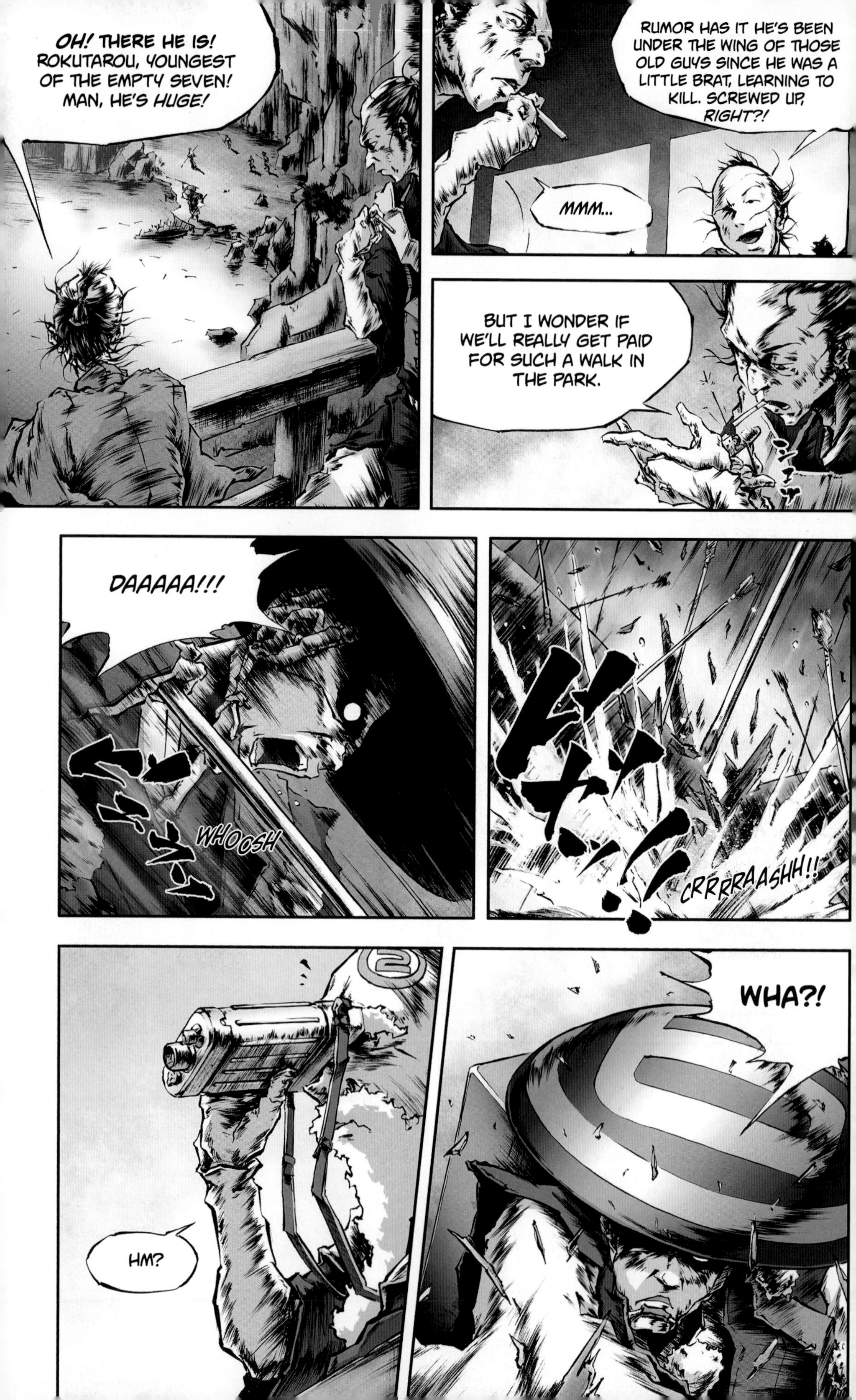
OH! THERE HE IS! ROKUTAROU, YOUNGEST OF THE EMPTY SEVEN! MAN, HE'S HUGE!
RUMOR HAS IT HE'S BEEN UNDER THE WING OF THOSE OLD GUYS SINCE HE WAS A LITTLE BRAT, LEARNING TO KILL. SCREWED UP, RIGHT?!
MMM...
BUT I WONDER IF WE'LL REALLY GET PAID FOR SUCH A WALK IN THE PARK.
DAAAAA!!!
WHOOSH
CRRRRAASHH!!
HM?
WHA?!

OH, COME ON, WE DID OUR JOBS, DIDN'T WE? *HAHAHA!*

SNAP

SCRITCH

SCRITCH

HAHAHA. YEAH RIGHT.

Y'KNOW, I'M THINKING OF GOING STRAIGHT AFTER THIS JOB.

IT SEEMS KIND OF DUMB TO BE MAKING A LIVING PUTTING YOUR ASS ON THE LINE.

SO WHAT ARE YOU GOING TO ASK FOR? WE CAN ASK FOR AS MUCH AS WE WANT FROM THE BROTHERS, RIGHT?

EHH, ENOUGH TO FOOL AROUND THE REST OF MY LIFE, I GUESS. THREE THOUSAND RYOU, MAYBE?

KA-TUNK

K-SPLAT

WHAT, *SERIOUSLY?* WOW, THEN I GUESS I'LL ASK FOR THE SA...?!

?

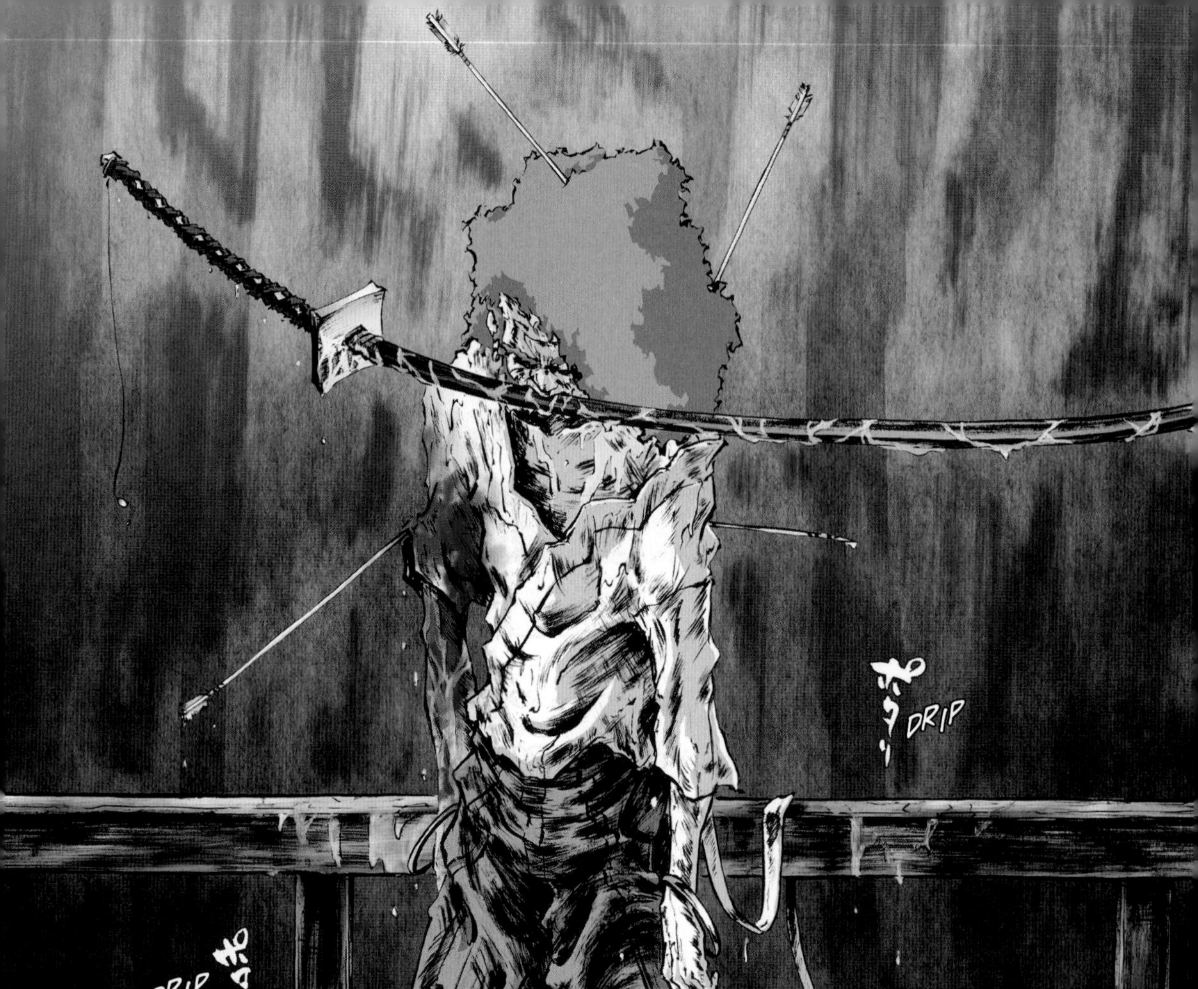
DRIP
DRIP
KSPLRCH
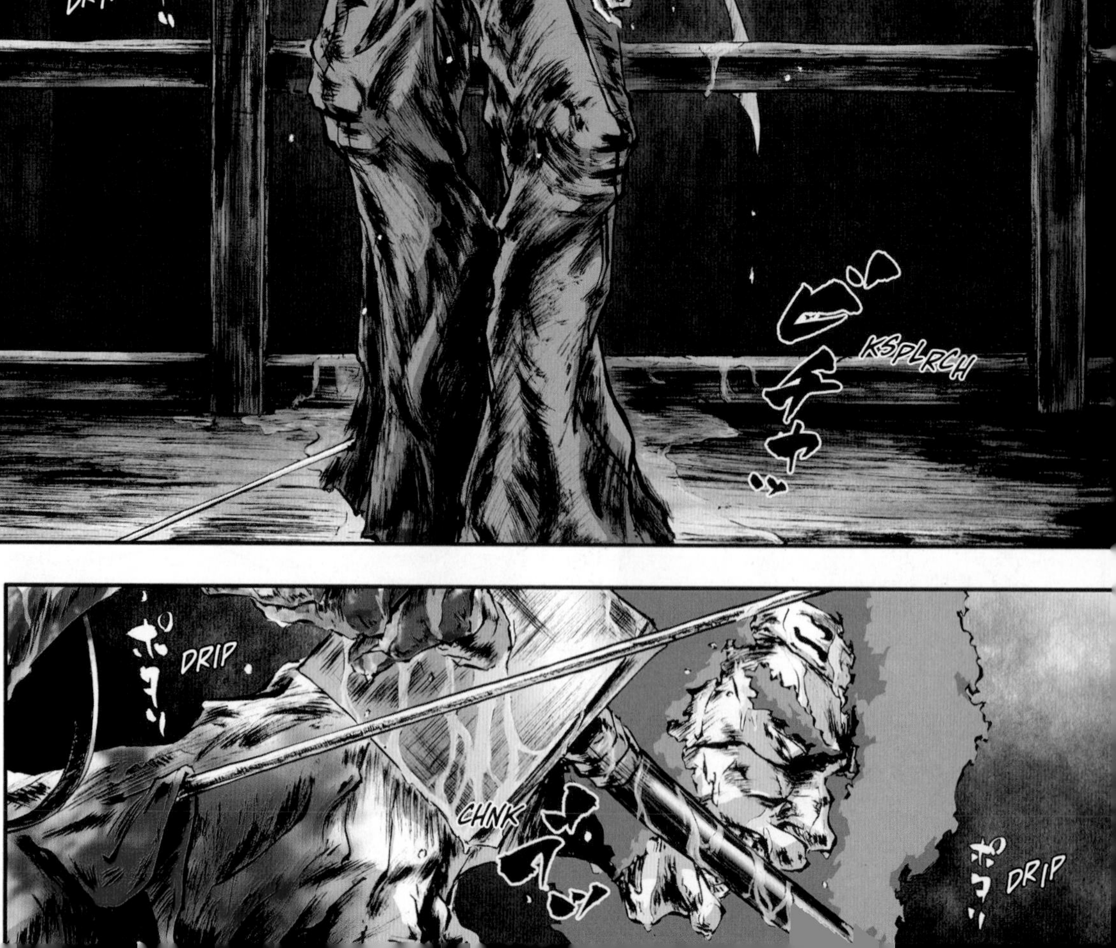
DRIP
CHNK
DRIP

HM?!

GYAAA!

UMA!

HYAA!

BROTHER! COME LOOK! HE ISN'T DEAD YET!

WHAT?!

WHAT THE *HELL* ARE ROKUTA AND THE ASSASSINS DOING?!

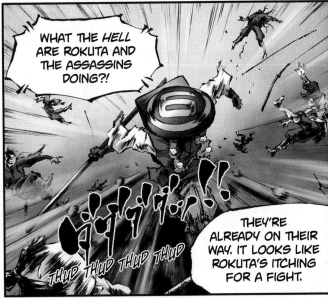

THUD THUD THUD THUD

THEY'RE ALREADY ON THEIR WAY. IT LOOKS LIKE ROKUTA'S ITCHING FOR A FIGHT.

SO... AFRO SURVIVED OUR ATTACK... WHAT'S HIS *CONDITION*?!

?

CLUNK

HE'S SLICING THROUGH OUR ASSASSINS, BUT HE'S *WOUNDED* HIS DOMINANT ARM.

HE MIGHT GET PAST THOSE BOTTOM-FEEDERS, BUT HE'LL *NEVER* LAST IN A FIGHT WITH ROKUTA. *HEHEHEH!*

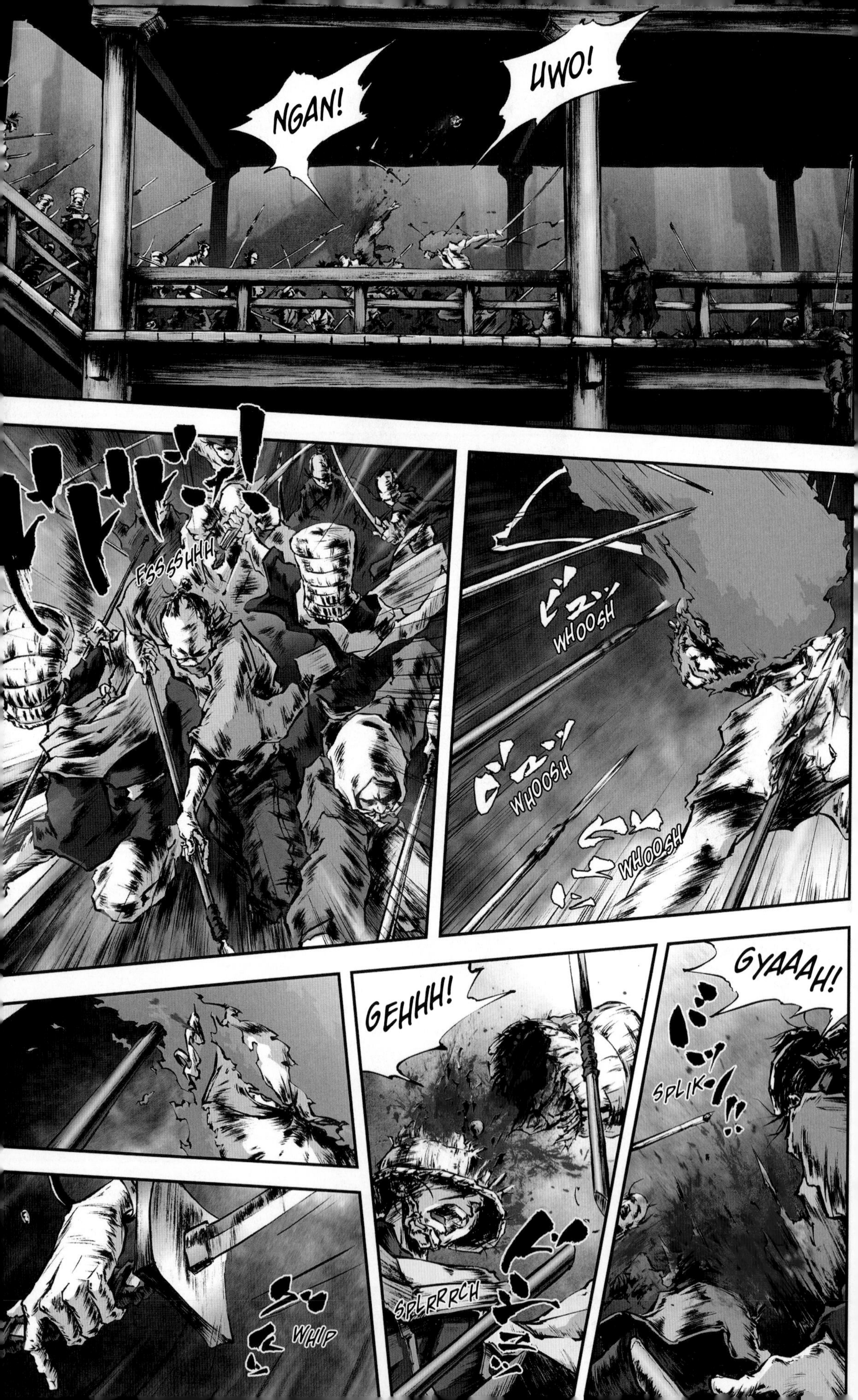
NGAN!
UWO!
FSSSSHHH
ビュッ
WHOOSH
ビュッ
WHOOSH
WHOOSH
WHIP
GEHHH!
SPLRRRCH
GYAAAH!
SPLIK
!!

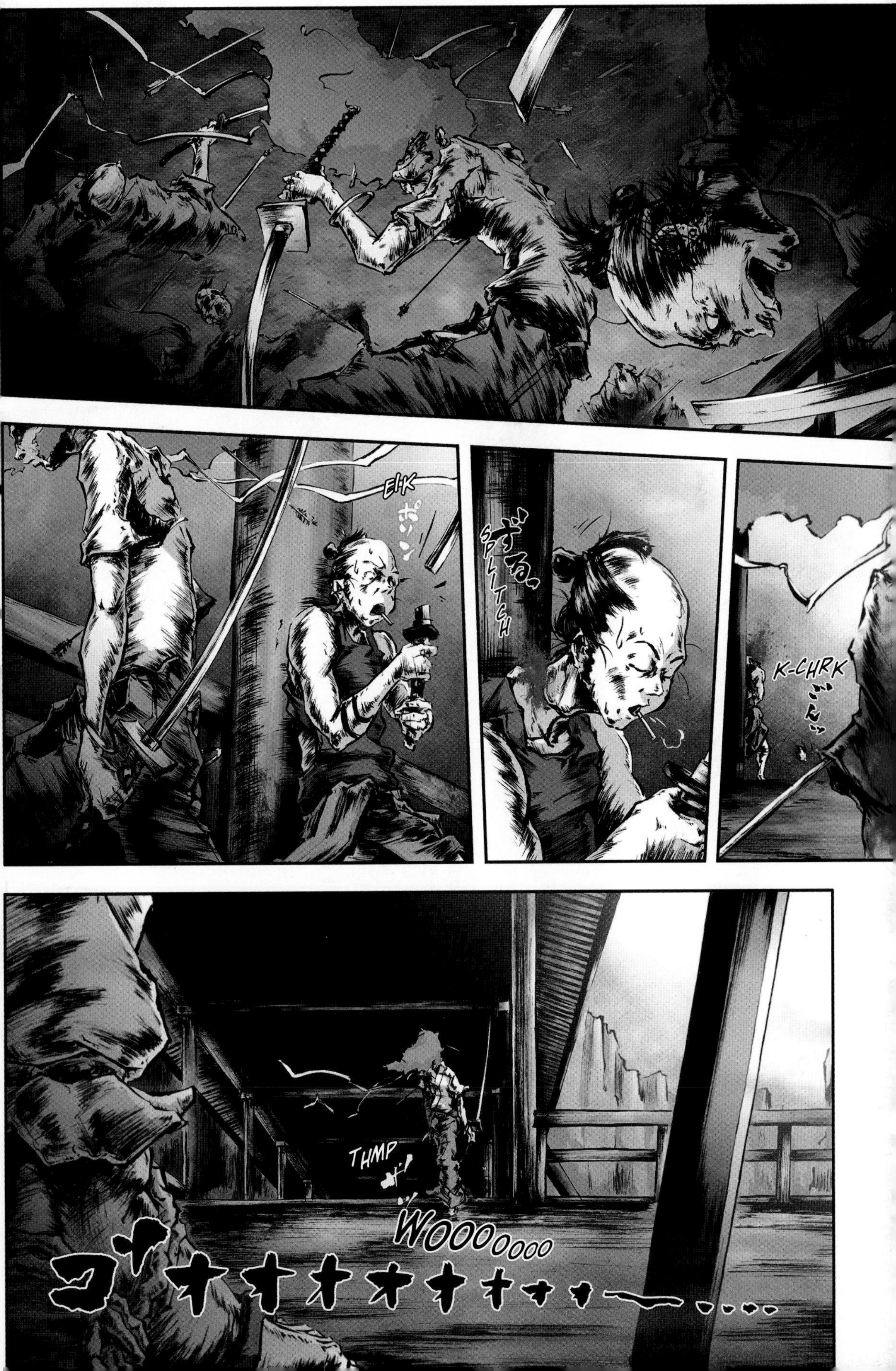
EEK
ポソン
ずるっ
SPLITCH
K-CHRK
ごんッ
THMP
ドッ
WOOOoooo
ゴオオオオオオォォ〜……

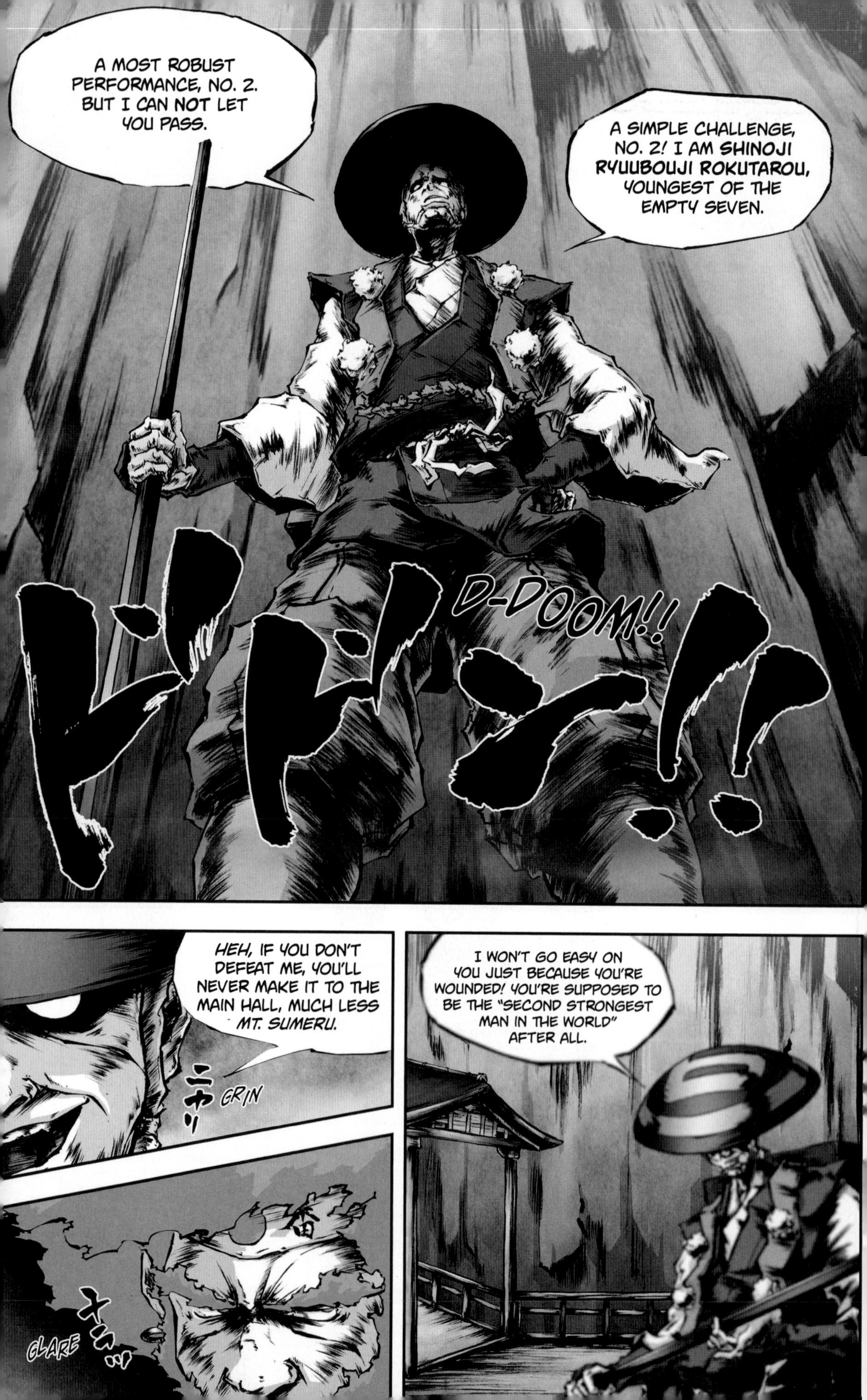
A MOST ROBUST PERFORMANCE, NO. 2. BUT I CAN NOT LET YOU PASS.
A SIMPLE CHALLENGE, NO. 2! I AM SHINOJI RYUUBOUJI ROKUTAROU, YOUNGEST OF THE EMPTY SEVEN.
ドドン!!
D-DOOM!!
HEH, IF YOU DON'T DEFEAT ME, YOU'LL NEVER MAKE IT TO THE MAIN HALL, MUCH LESS MT. SUMERU.
ニヤリ
GRIN
ギロッ
GLARE
I WON'T GO EASY ON YOU JUST BECAUSE YOU'RE WOUNDED! YOU'RE SUPPOSED TO BE THE "SECOND STRONGEST MAN IN THE WORLD" AFTER ALL.

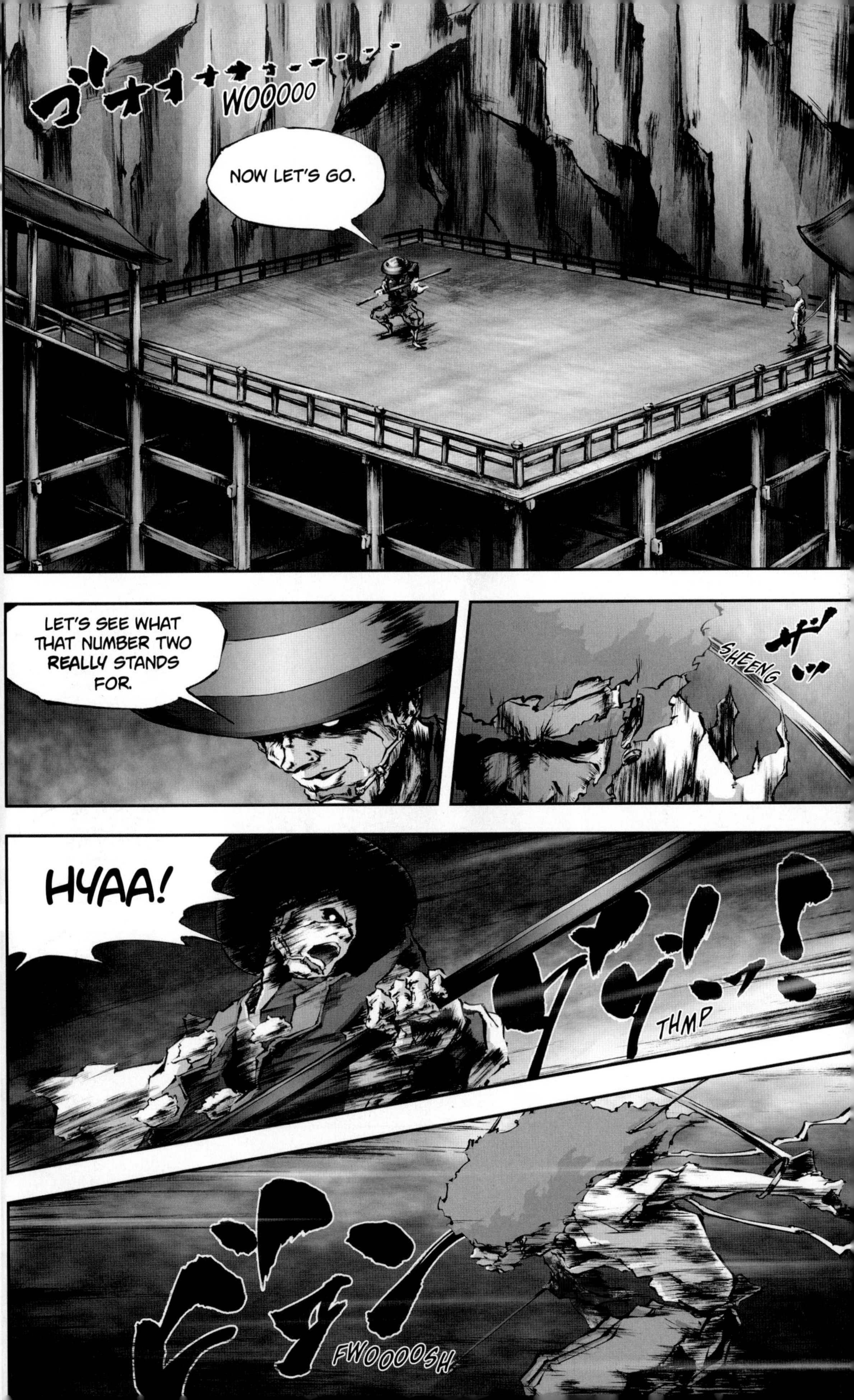
ゴオオオオォォォ…
WOOOOO
NOW LET'S GO.
LET'S SEE WHAT THAT NUMBER TWO REALLY STANDS FOR.
ザッ
SHEENG
HYAA!
ダッ!
THMP
FWOOOOSH

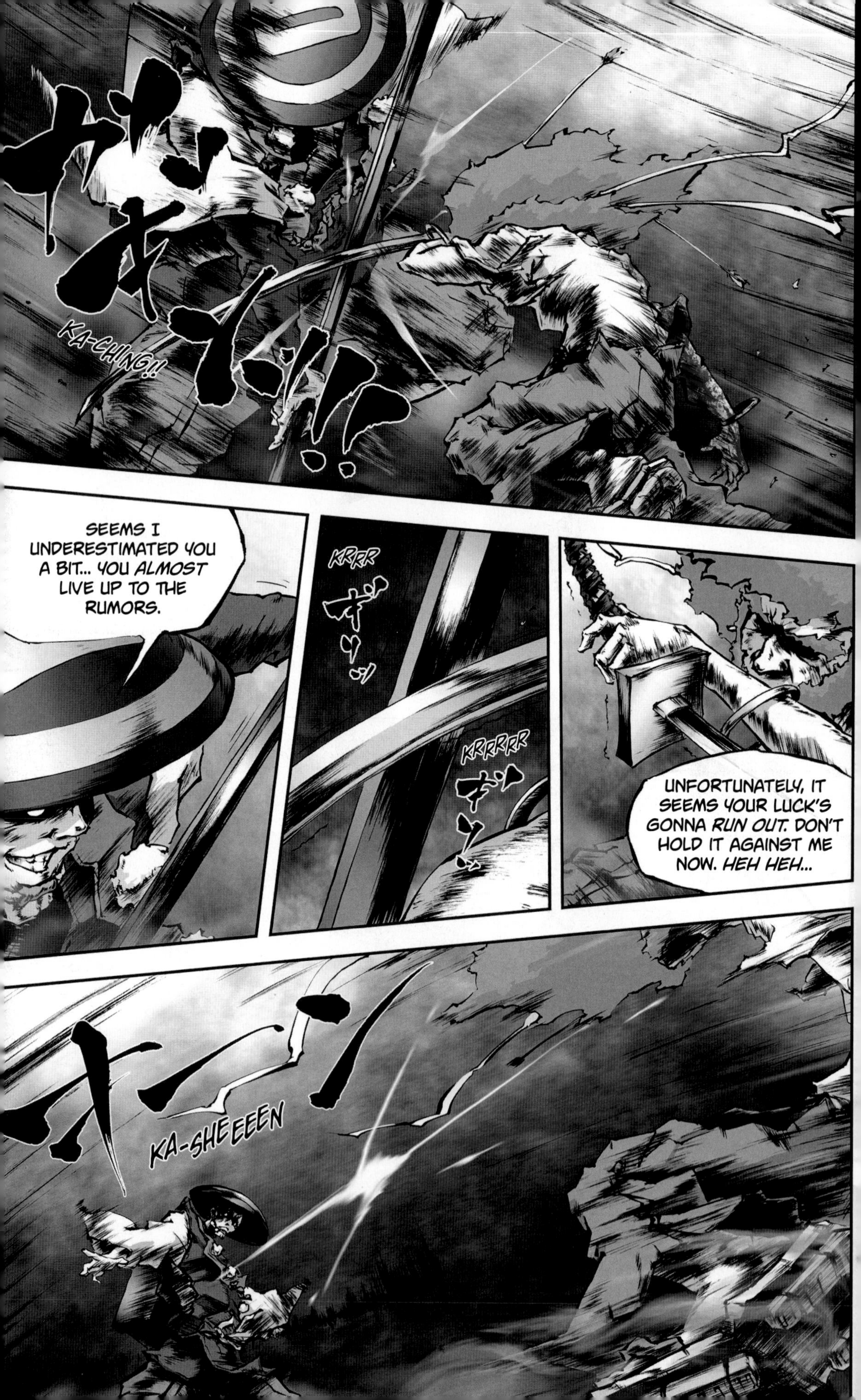
KA-CHING!!
SEEMS I UNDERESTIMATED YOU A BIT... YOU *ALMOST* LIVE UP TO THE RUMORS.
KRRR
KRRRRR
UNFORTUNATELY, IT SEEMS YOUR LUCK'S GONNA *RUN OUT.* DON'T HOLD IT AGAINST ME NOW. *HEH HEH...*
KA-SHEEEEN

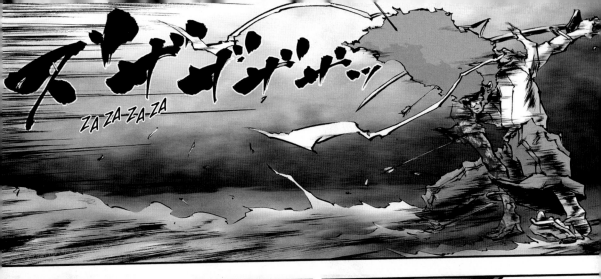

ZA ZA-ZA-ZA

K-CHNK

CHNK

HEHEH, YOU'RE WASTING TIME, NO. 2!

FWOOOSH

WHOOOSH

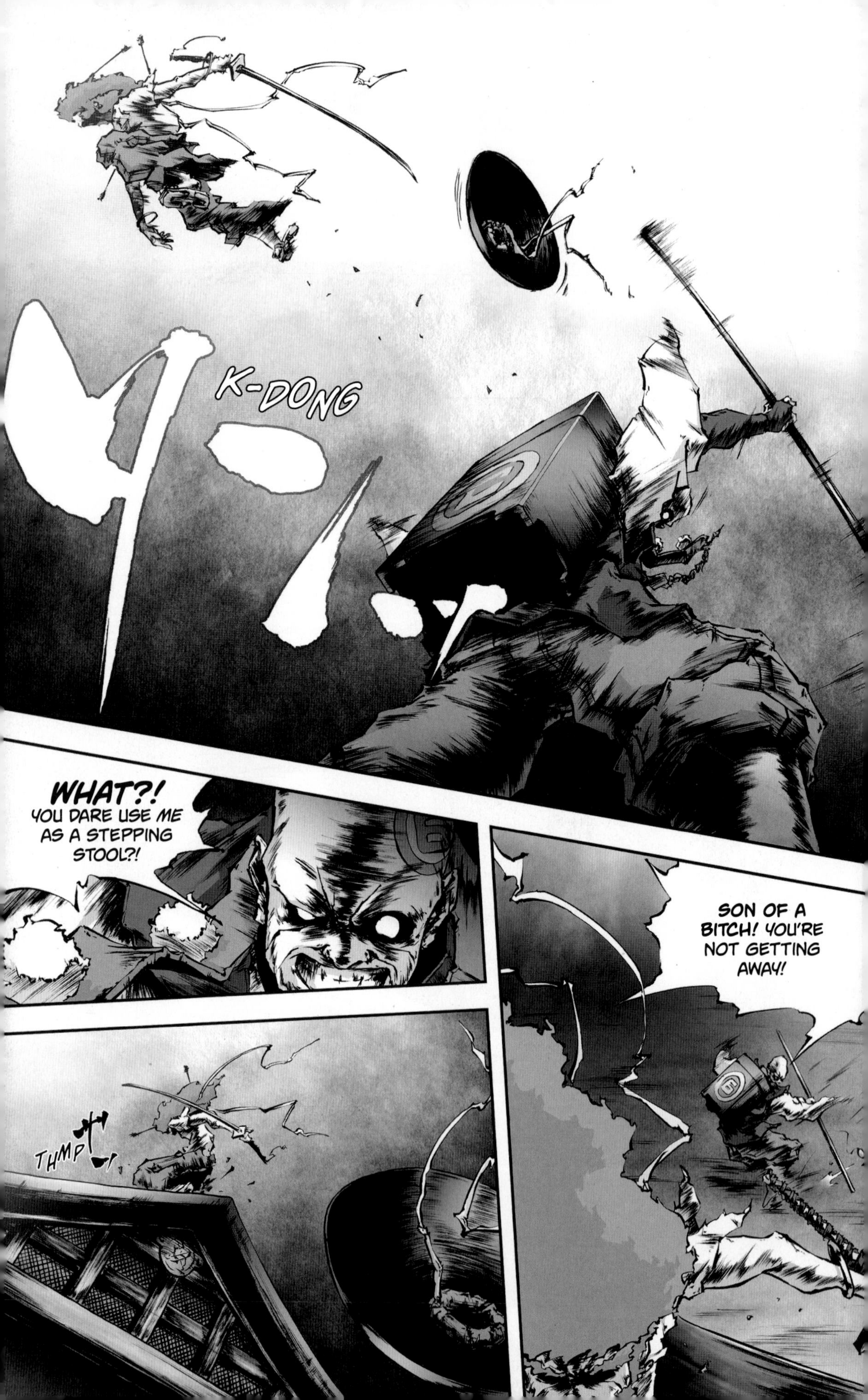
K-DONG
WHAT?! YOU DARE USE ME AS A STEPPING STOOL?!
THMP
SON OF A BITCH! YOU'RE NOT GETTING AWAY!

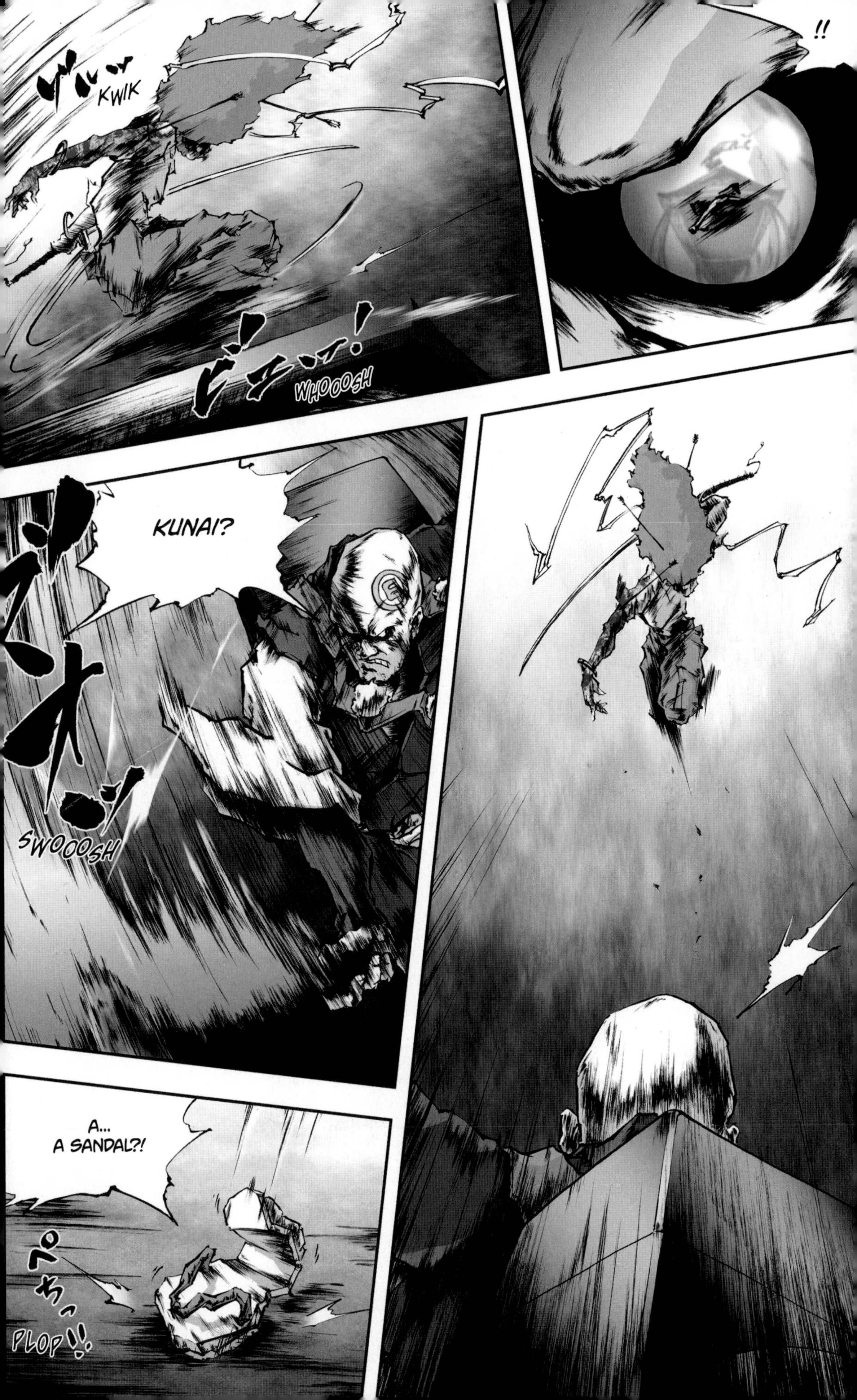
KWIK
WHOOOSH
!!
KUNAI?
SWOOOSH
A...
A SANDAL?!
PLOP!!

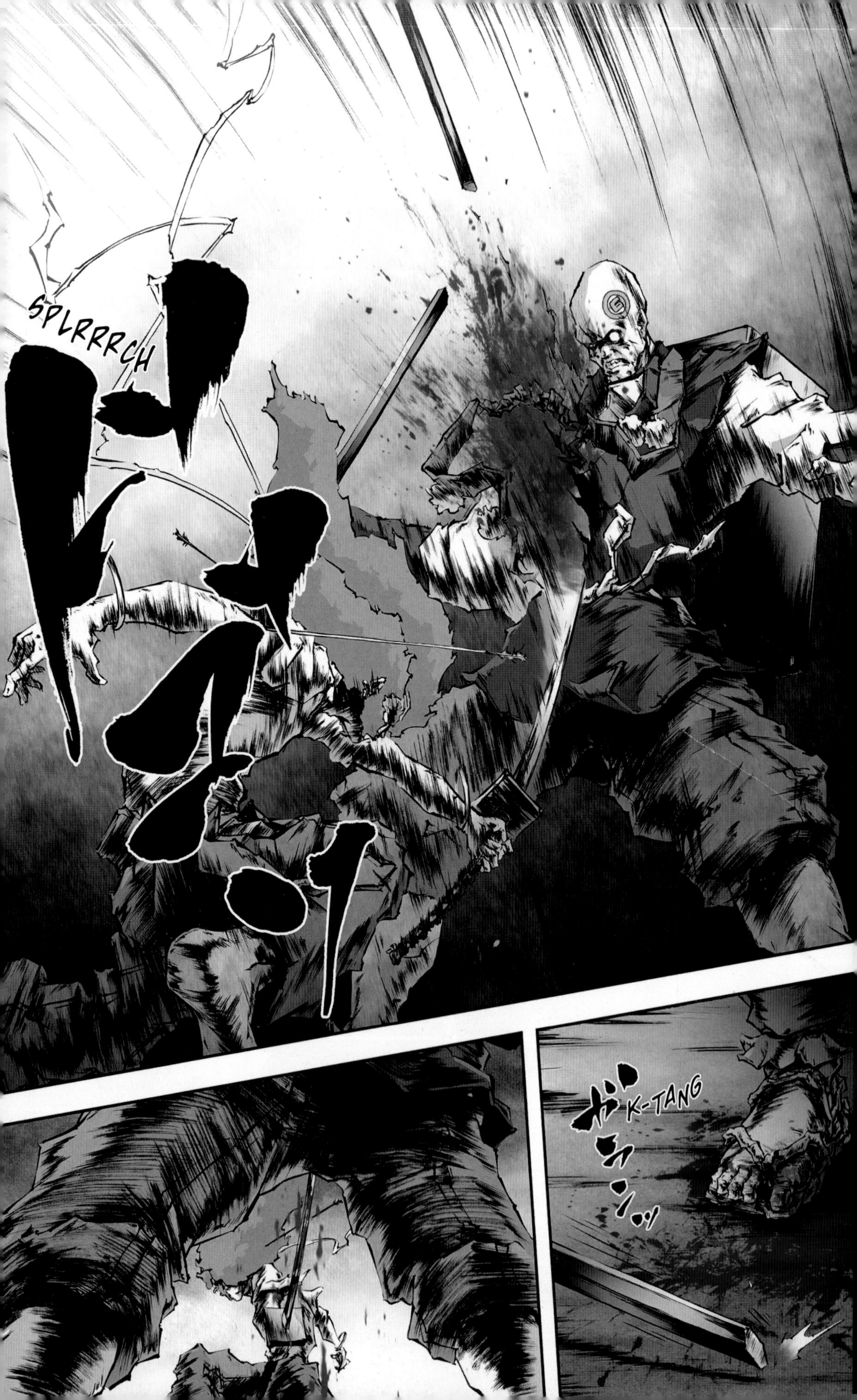
SPLRRRCH
K-TANG

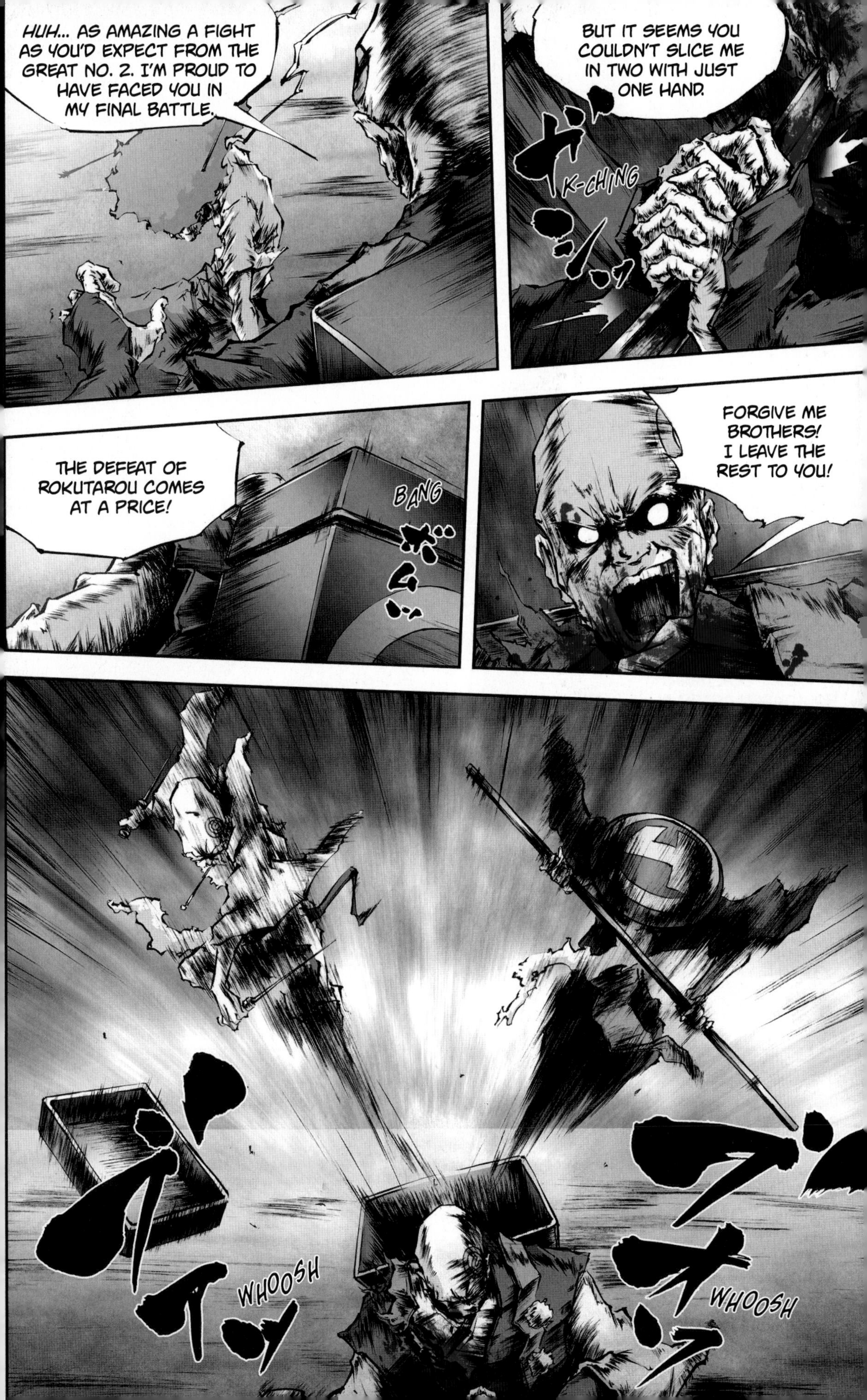
HUH... AS AMAZING A FIGHT AS YOU'D EXPECT FROM THE GREAT NO. 2. I'M PROUD TO HAVE FACED YOU IN MY FINAL BATTLE.
BUT IT SEEMS YOU COULDN'T SLICE ME IN TWO WITH JUST ONE HAND.
K-CHING
THE DEFEAT OF ROKUTAROU COMES AT A PRICE!
BANG
FORGIVE ME BROTHERS! I LEAVE THE REST TO YOU!
WHOOSH
WHOOSH

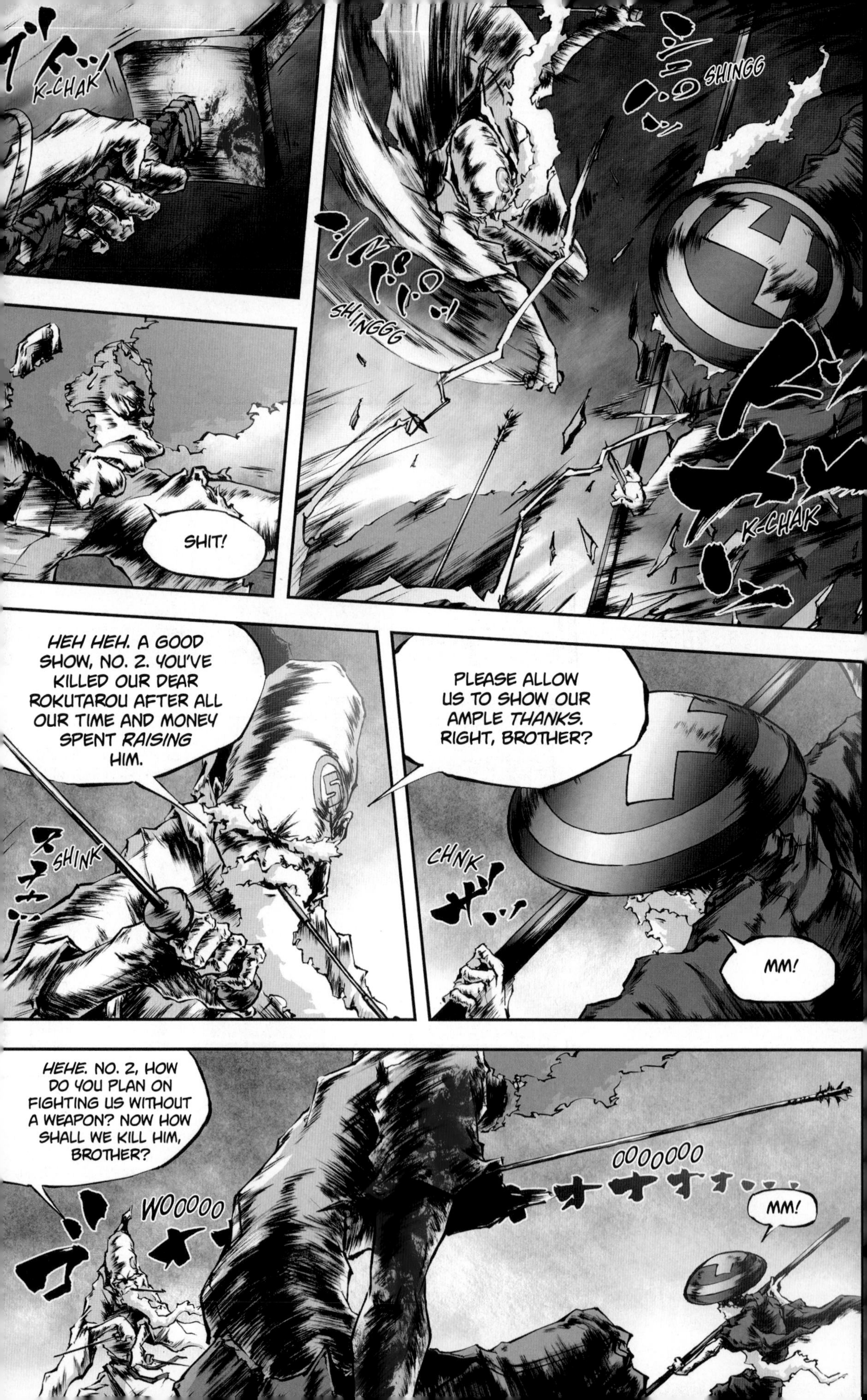
K-CHAK!
SHIT!
SHINGG
SHINGGG
K-CHAK
HEH HEH. A GOOD SHOW, NO. 2. YOU'VE KILLED OUR DEAR ROKUTAROU AFTER ALL OUR TIME AND MONEY SPENT *RAISING* HIM.
SHINK
PLEASE ALLOW US TO SHOW OUR AMPLE *THANKS.* RIGHT, BROTHER?
CHNK
MM!
HEHE. NO. 2, HOW DO YOU PLAN ON FIGHTING US WITHOUT A WEAPON? NOW HOW SHALL WE KILL HIM, BROTHER?
WOOOOO
OOOOOOO
MM!

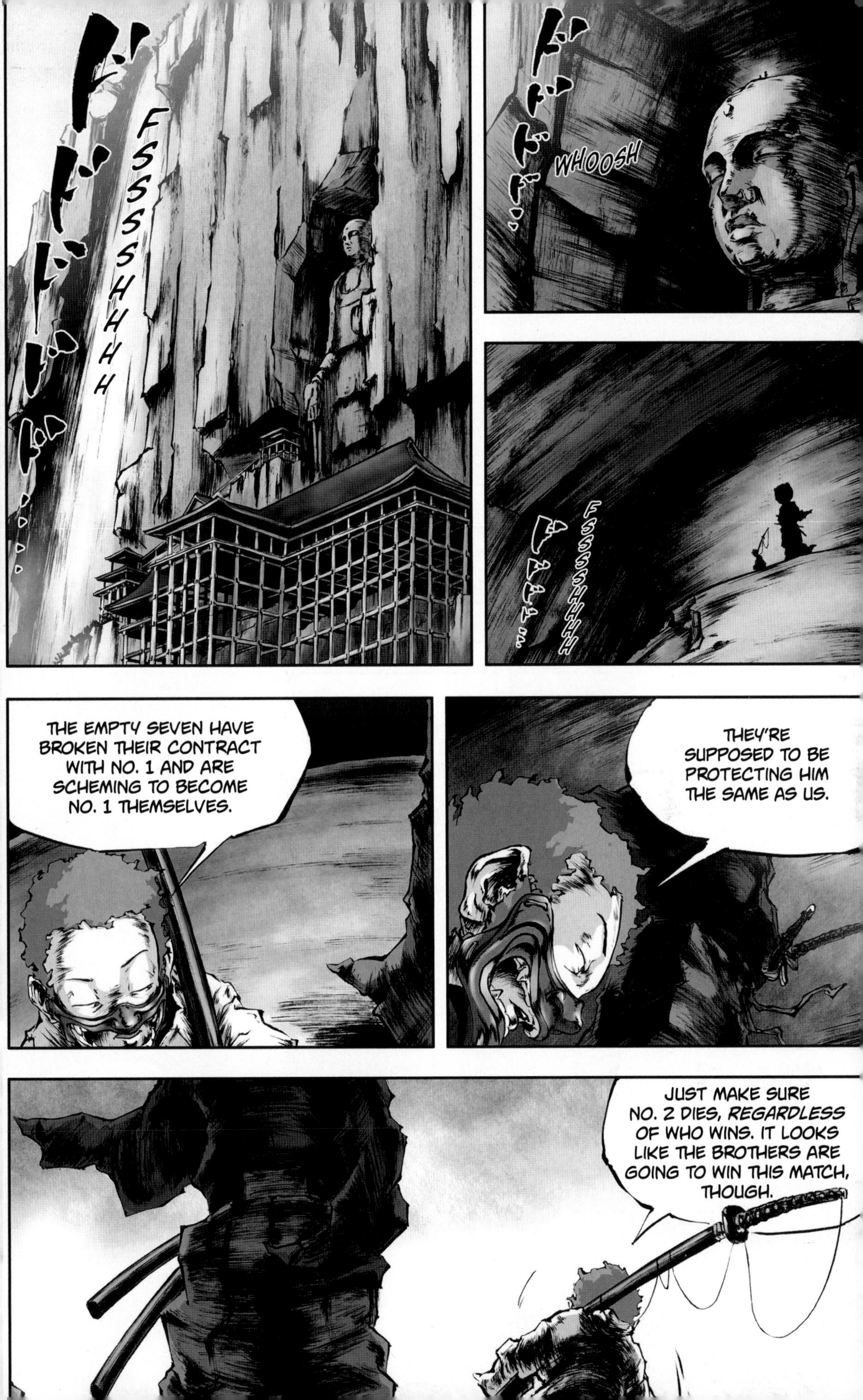
ドドドドド…
FSSSSHHHH
ドドドド…
WHOOSH
FSSSSHHHH
ドドド…
THE EMPTY SEVEN HAVE BROKEN THEIR CONTRACT WITH NO. 1 AND ARE SCHEMING TO BECOME NO. 1 THEMSELVES.
THEY'RE SUPPOSED TO BE PROTECTING HIM THE SAME AS US.
JUST MAKE SURE NO. 2 DIES, *REGARDLESS* OF WHO WINS. IT LOOKS LIKE THE BROTHERS ARE GOING TO WIN THIS MATCH, THOUGH.

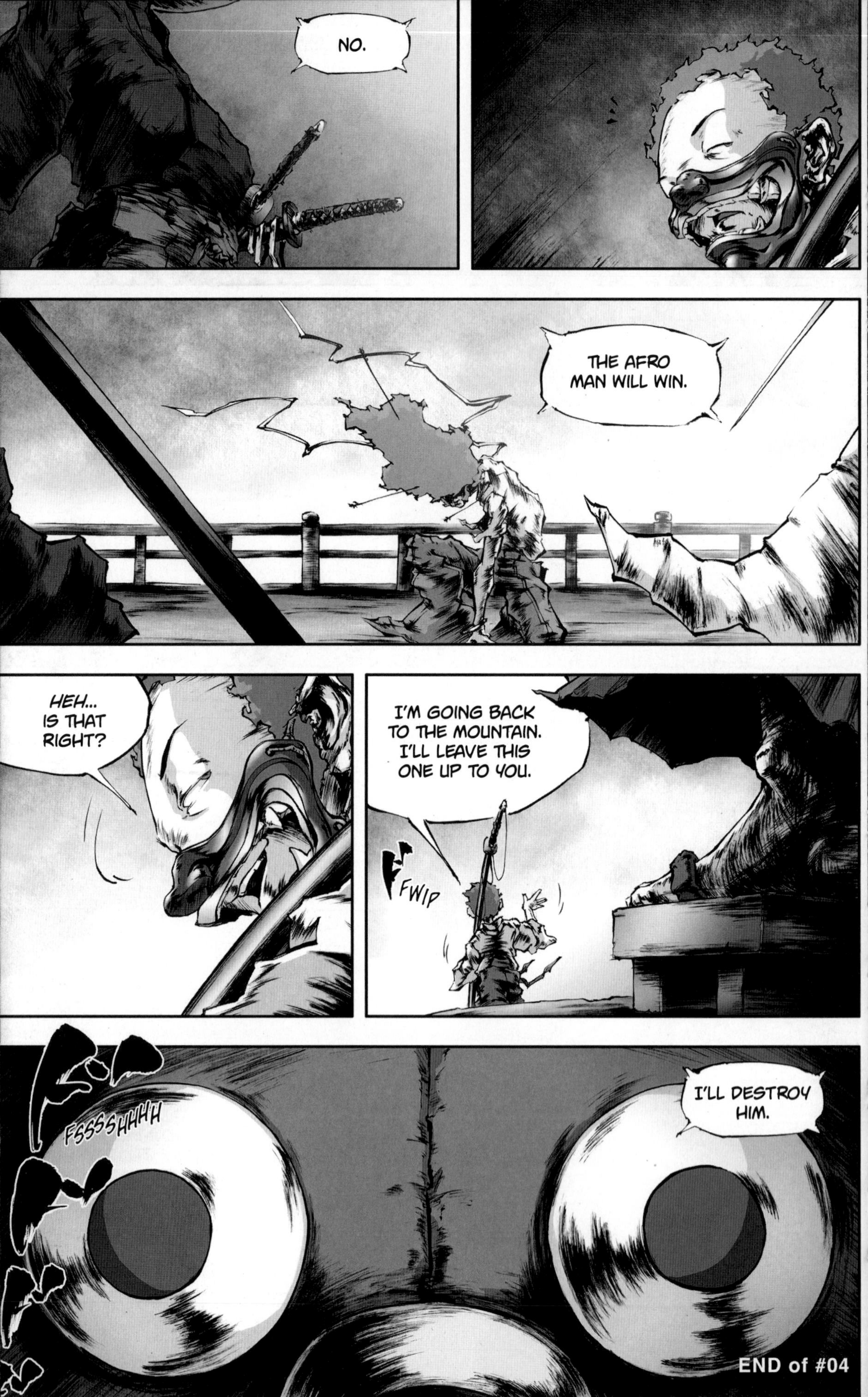
NO.
THE AFRO MAN WILL WIN.
HEH... IS THAT RIGHT?
I'M GOING BACK TO THE MOUNTAIN. I'LL LEAVE THIS ONE UP TO YOU.
FWIP
FSSSSHHHH
I'LL DESTROY HIM.
END of #04

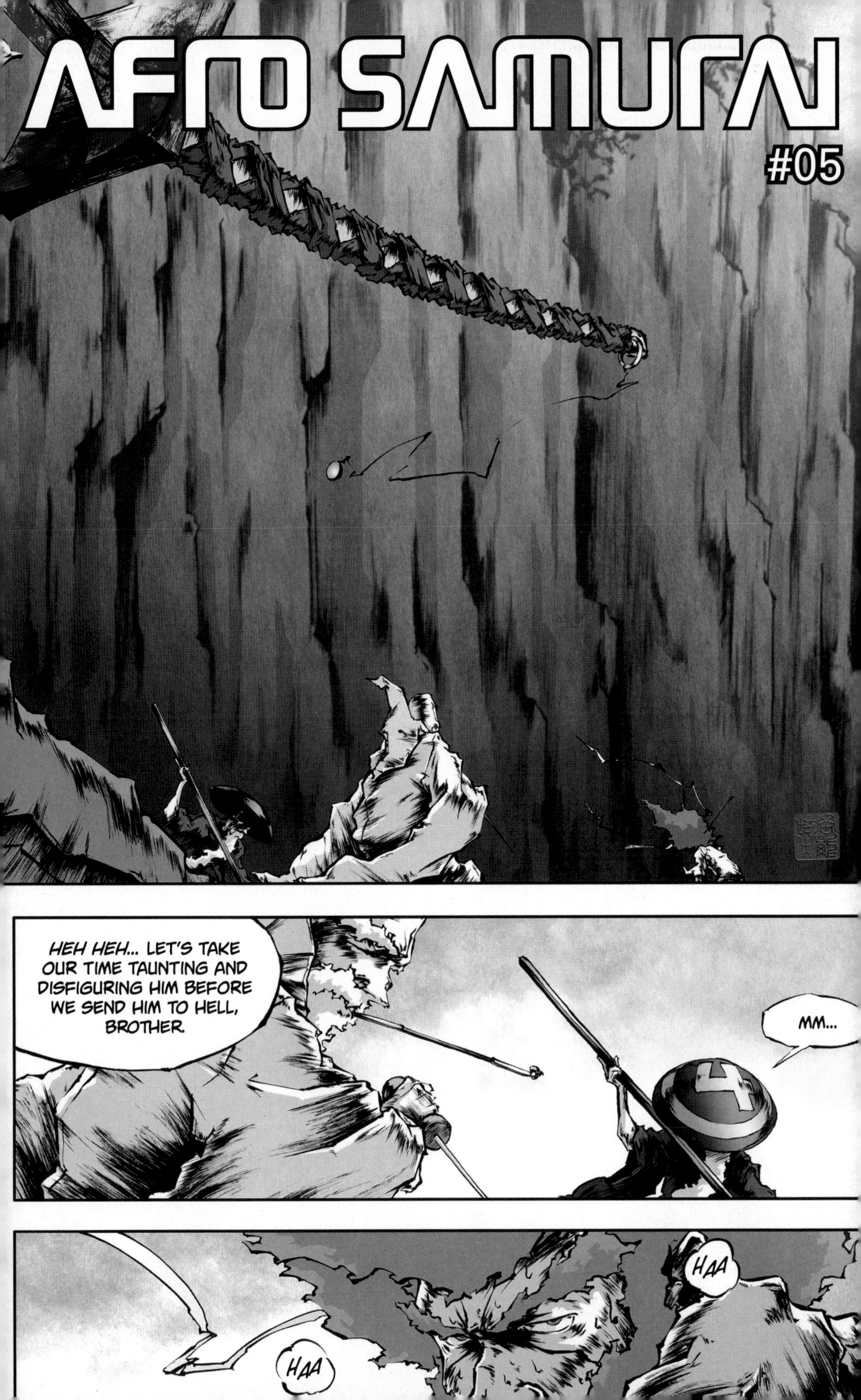
AFRO SAMURAI
#05
HEH HEH... LET'S TAKE OUR TIME TAUNTING AND DISFIGURING HIM BEFORE WE SEND HIM TO HELL, BROTHER.
MM...
HAA
HAA

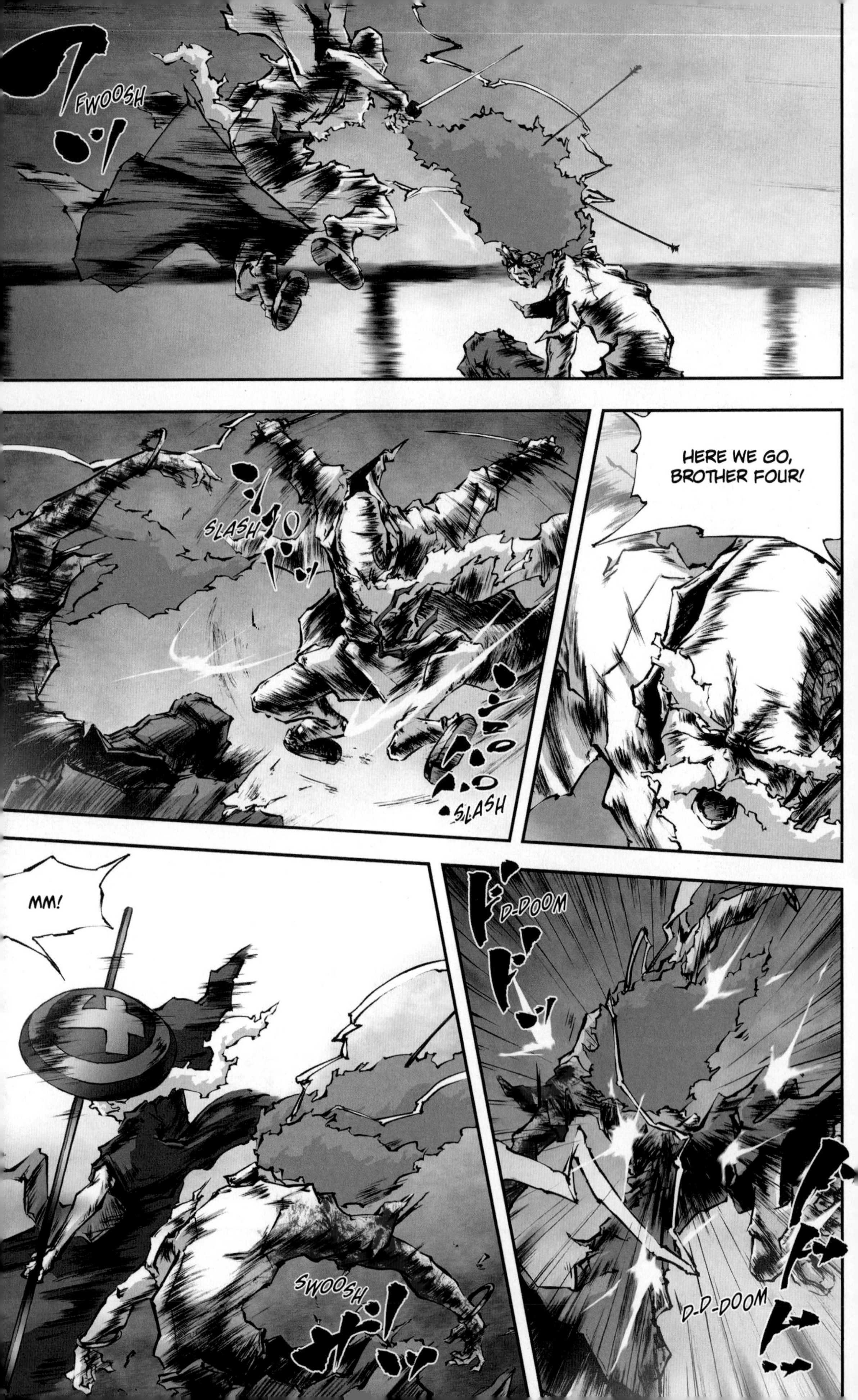
FWOOSH
SLASH
SLASH
HERE WE GO, BROTHER FOUR!
MM!
SWOOSH
D-DOOM
D-D-DOOM

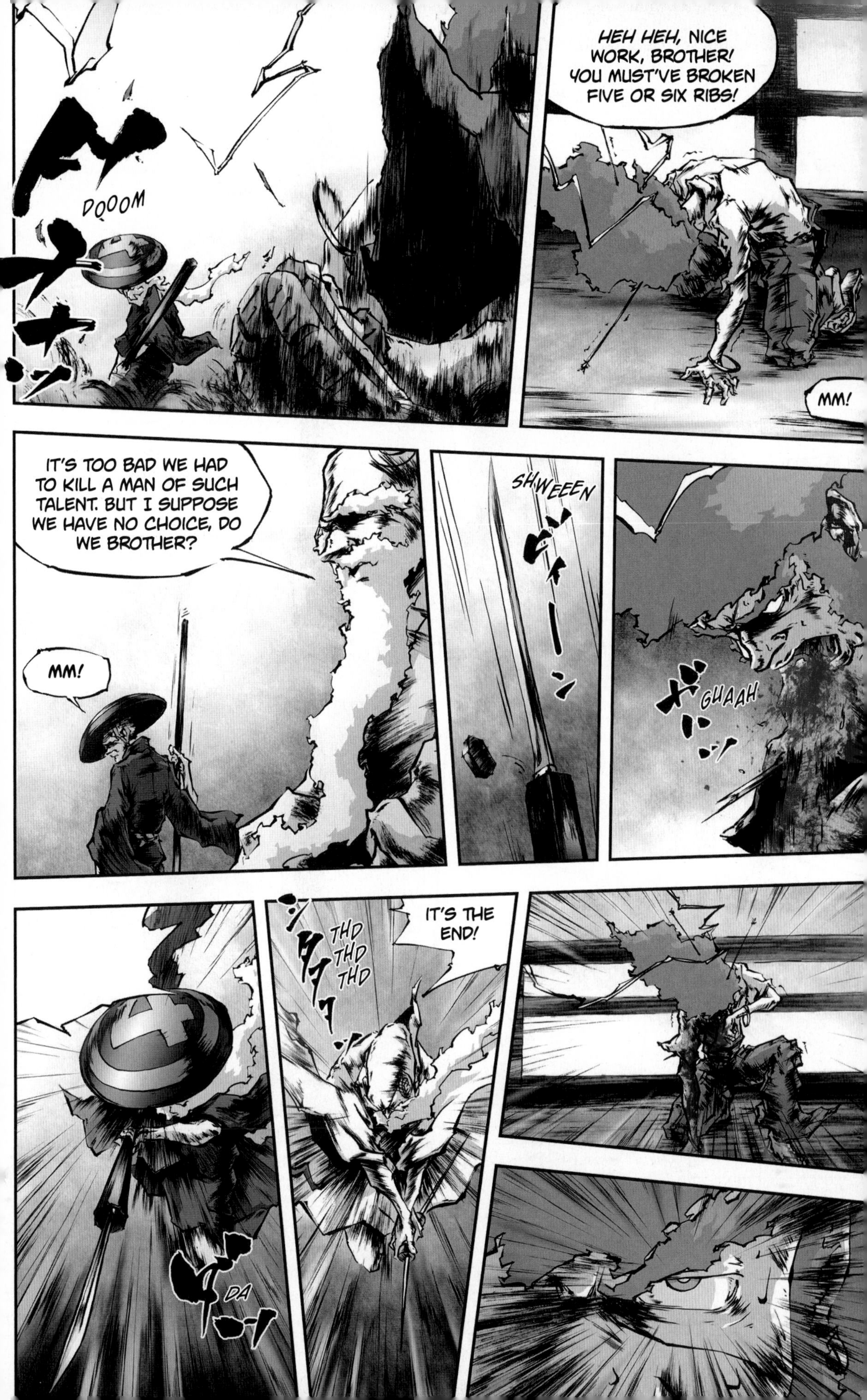
DOOOM
HEH HEH, NICE WORK, BROTHER! YOU MUST'VE BROKEN FIVE OR SIX RIBS!
MM!
IT'S TOO BAD WE HAD TO KILL A MAN OF SUCH TALENT. BUT I SUPPOSE WE HAVE NO CHOICE, DO WE BROTHER?
MM!
SHWEEEN
GUAAH
DA
THD THD THD
IT'S THE END!

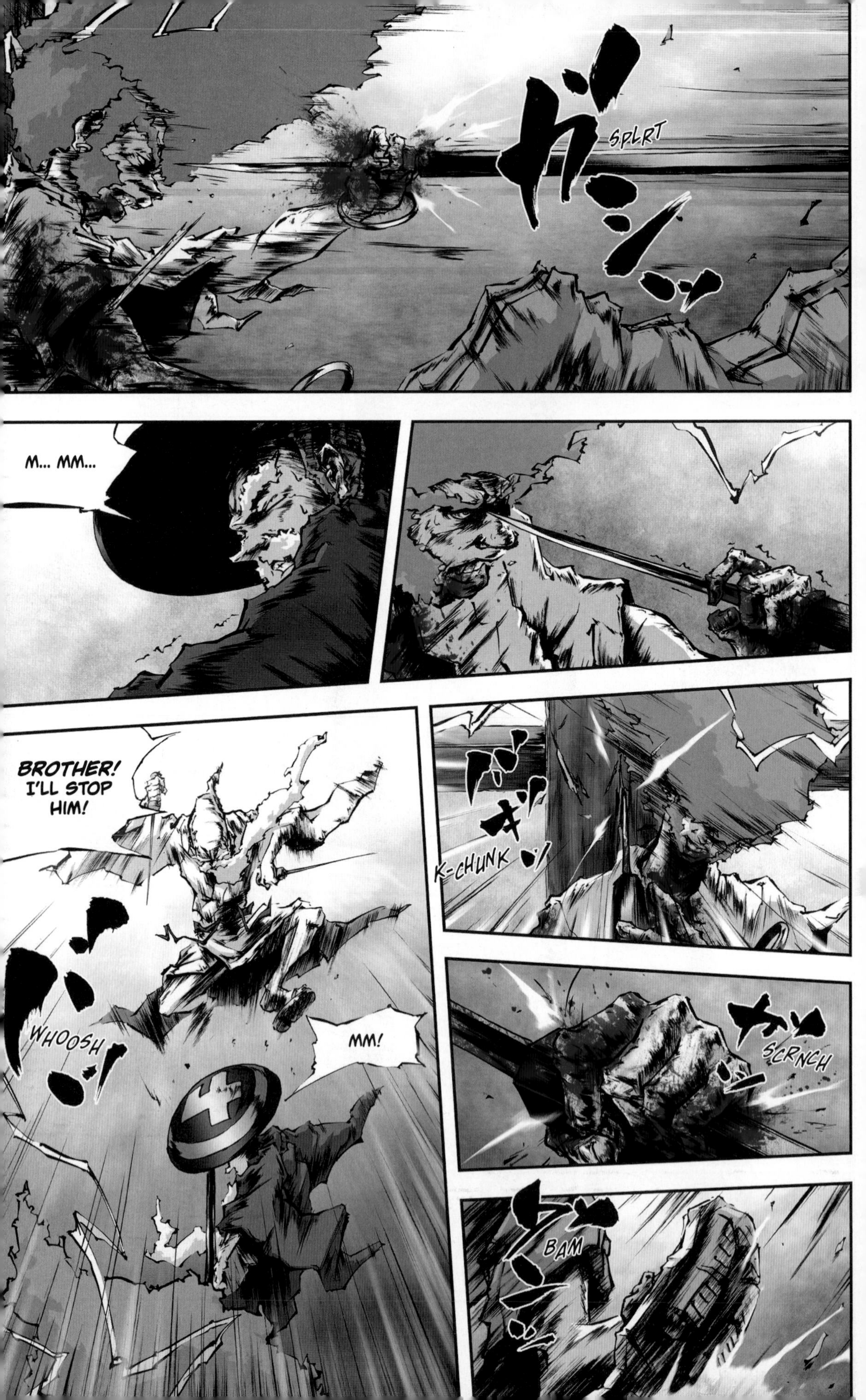
SPLRT
M... MM...
BROTHER! I'LL STOP HIM!
WHOOSH
MM!
K-CHUNK
SCRNCH
BAM

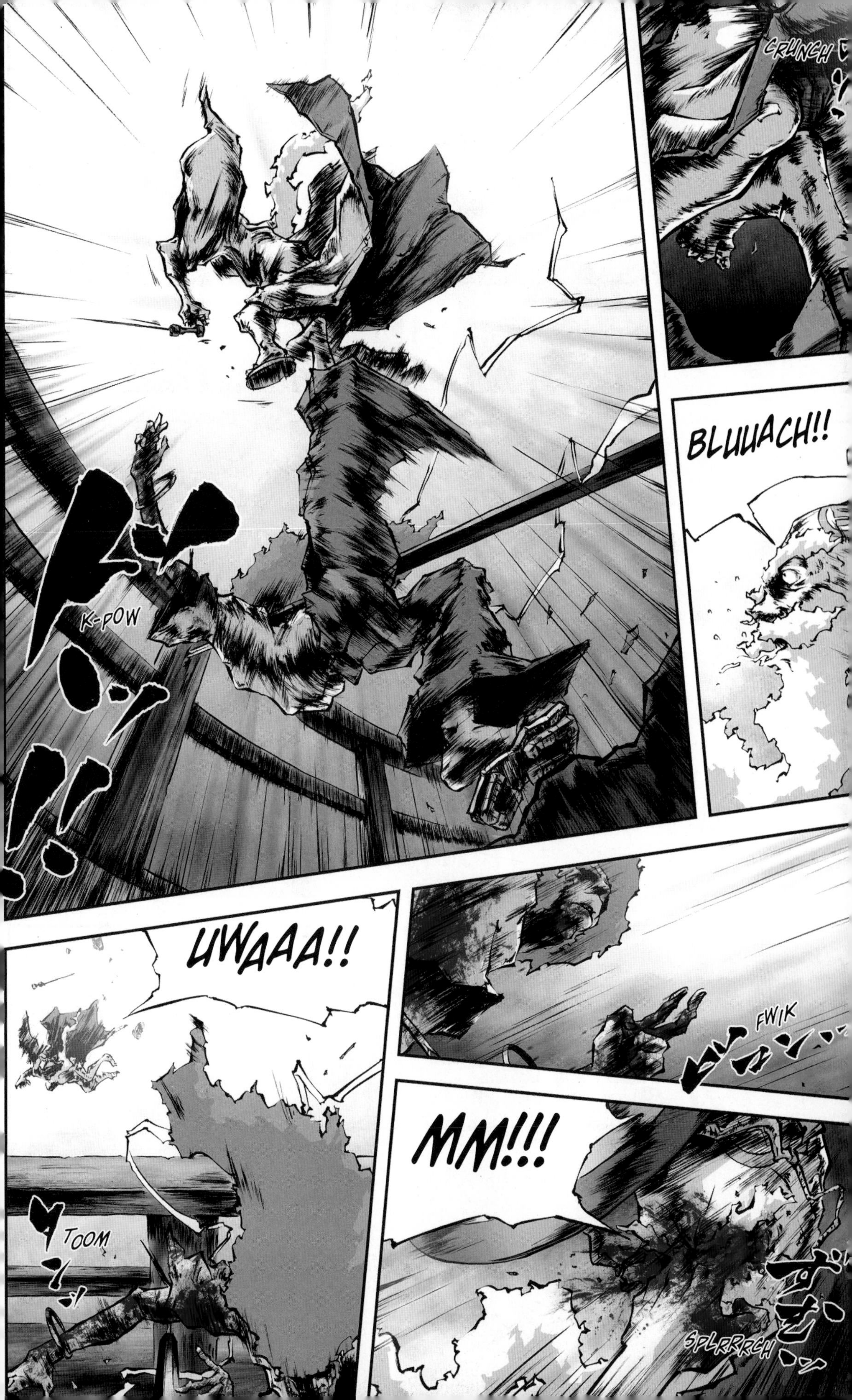
K-POW
CRUNCH
BLUUACH!!
UWAAA!!
TOOM
FWIK
MM!!!
SPLRRRCH

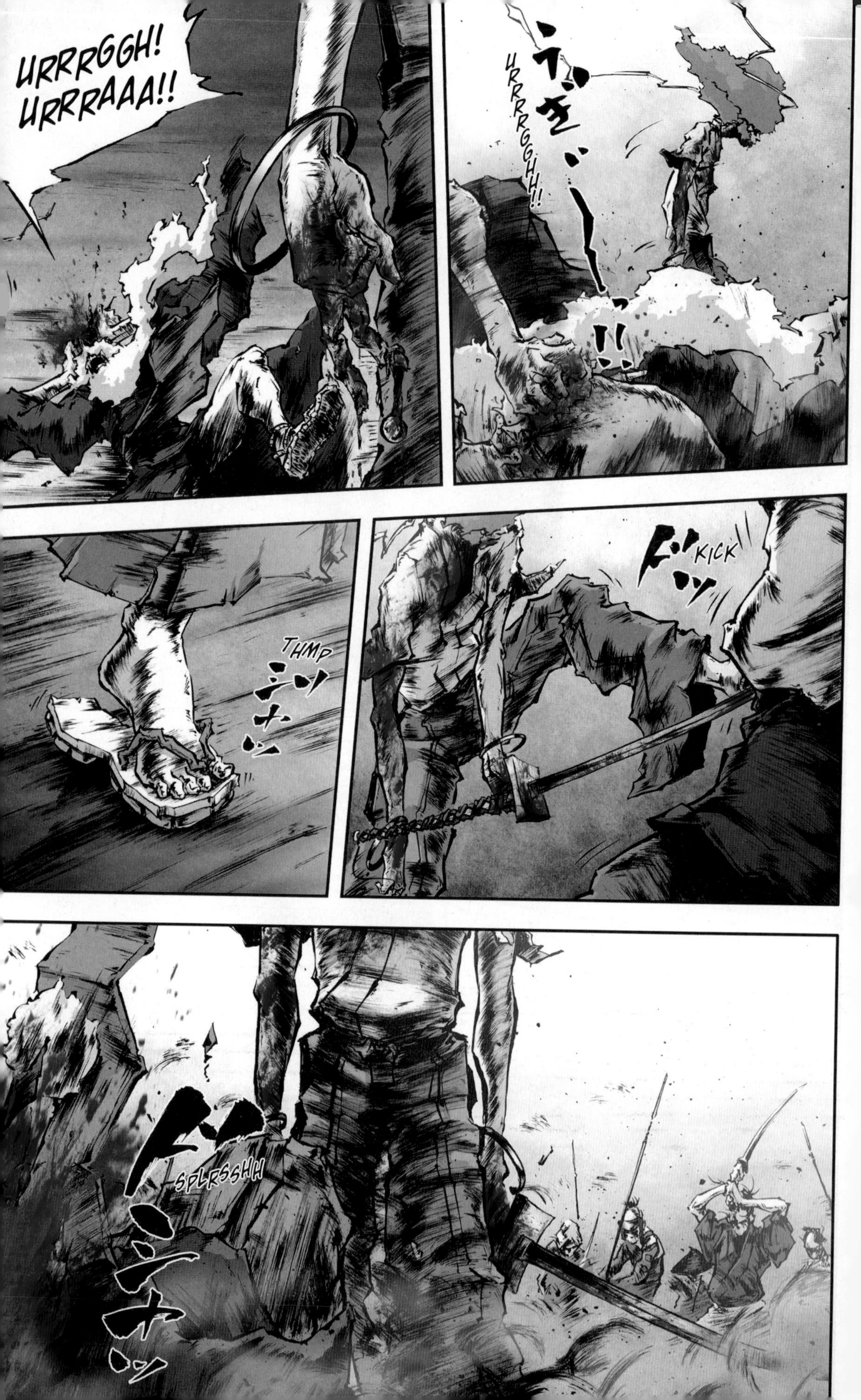
URRRGGH!
URRRAAA!!
URRRRGGHH!!
THMP
KICK
SPLRSSHH

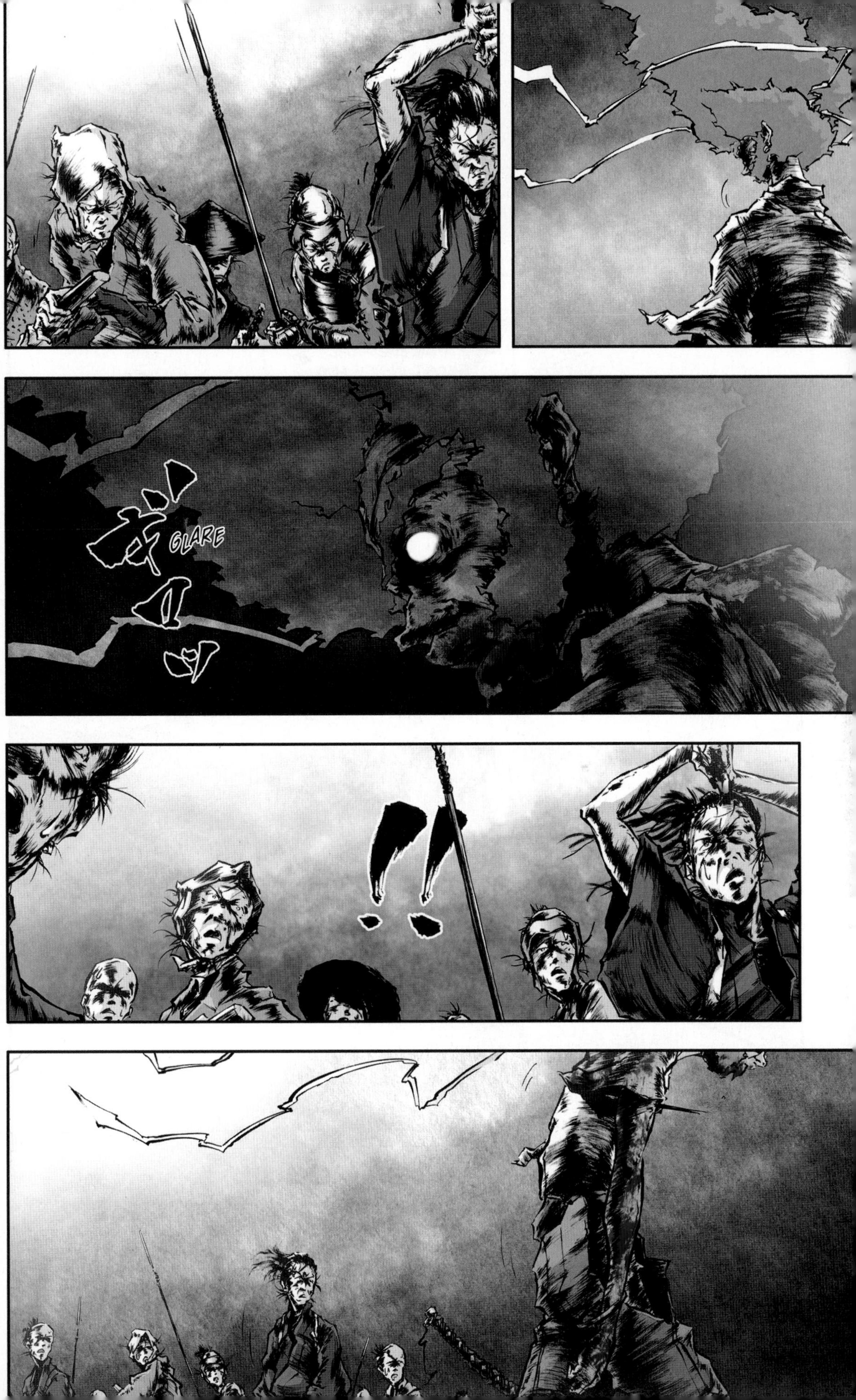
ギロッ
GLARE
!!

BROTHER FOUR, BROTHER FIVE, ROKUTAROU... REST IN PEACE. *NAMANDABU NAMANDABU...*

FSSSSHHHH

BROTHER, IT SEEMS OUR COAXING HAS AWAKENED THE BEAST INSIDE HIM.

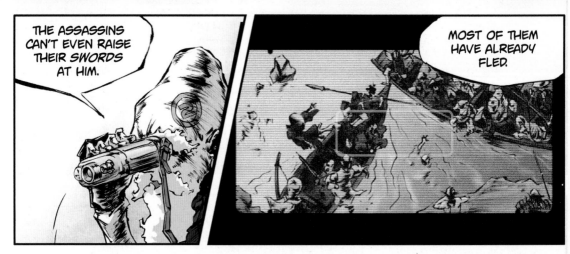

THE ASSASSINS CAN'T EVEN RAISE THEIR *SWORDS* AT HIM.

MOST OF THEM HAVE ALREADY FLED.

THIS HAS BECOME A MEANINGLESS ENDEAVOR. LET US *FLEE* AS WELL. WE DON'T HAVE MANY YEARS LEFT AHEAD OF US ANYWAY. IT WOULDN'T BE SO BAD TO LIVE OUT OUR REMAINING TIME PEACEFULLY IN SOME VILLAGE.

I'VE LIVED LONG ENOUGH...

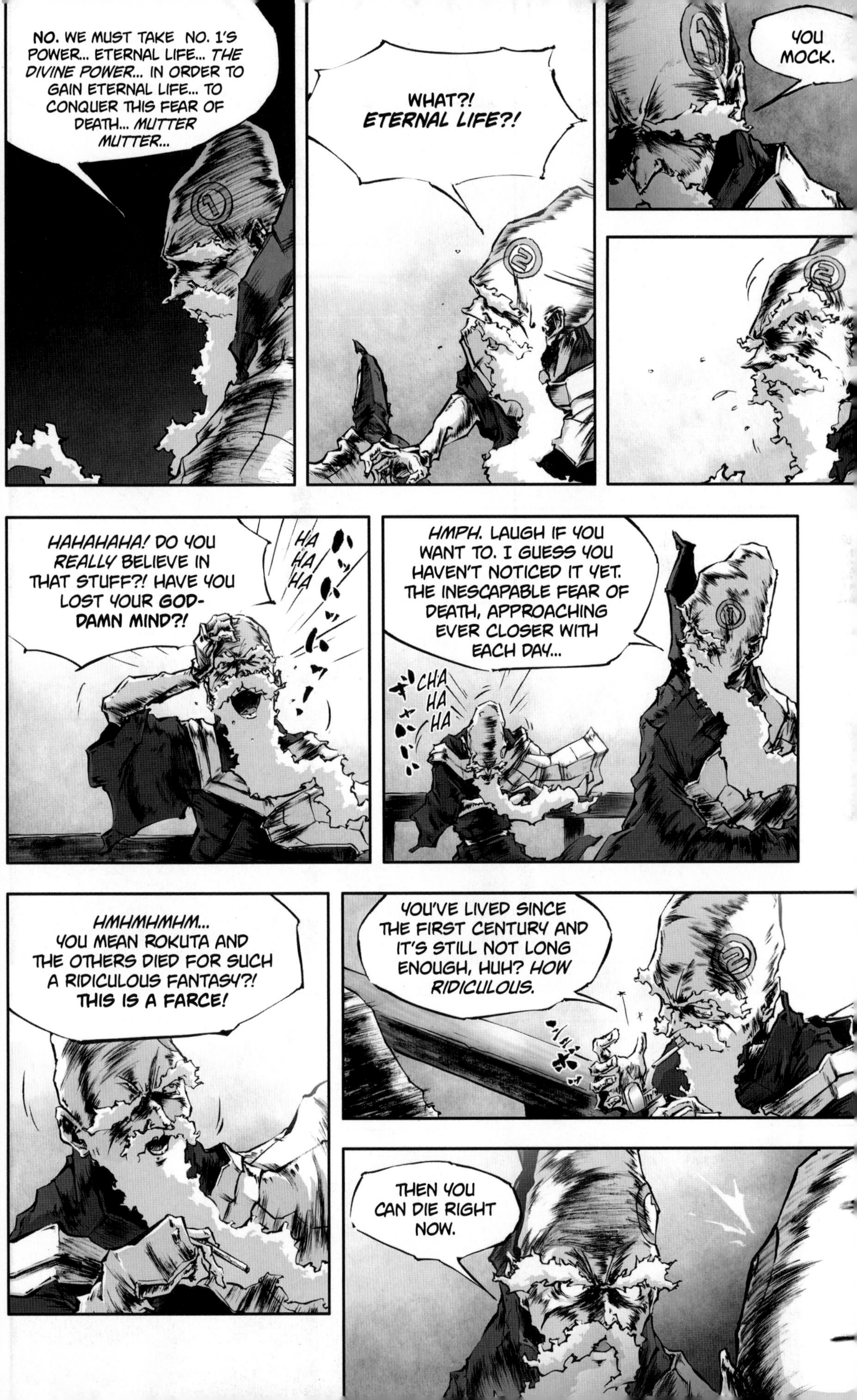
NO. WE MUST TAKE NO. 1'S POWER... ETERNAL LIFE... *THE DIVINE POWER*... IN ORDER TO GAIN ETERNAL LIFE... TO CONQUER THIS FEAR OF DEATH... *MUTTER MUTTER*...
WHAT?! *ETERNAL LIFE?!*
YOU MOCK.
HAHAHAHA! DO YOU *REALLY* BELIEVE IN THAT STUFF?! HAVE YOU LOST YOUR GOD-DAMN MIND?!
HA HA HA
HMPH. LAUGH IF YOU WANT TO. I GUESS YOU HAVEN'T NOTICED IT YET. THE INESCAPABLE FEAR OF DEATH, APPROACHING EVER CLOSER WITH EACH DAY...
CHA HA HA
HMHMHMHM... YOU MEAN ROKUTA AND THE OTHERS DIED FOR SUCH A RIDICULOUS FANTASY?! THIS IS A FARCE!
YOU'VE LIVED SINCE THE FIRST CENTURY AND IT'S STILL NOT LONG ENOUGH, HUH? *HOW RIDICULOUS.*
THEN YOU CAN DIE RIGHT NOW.

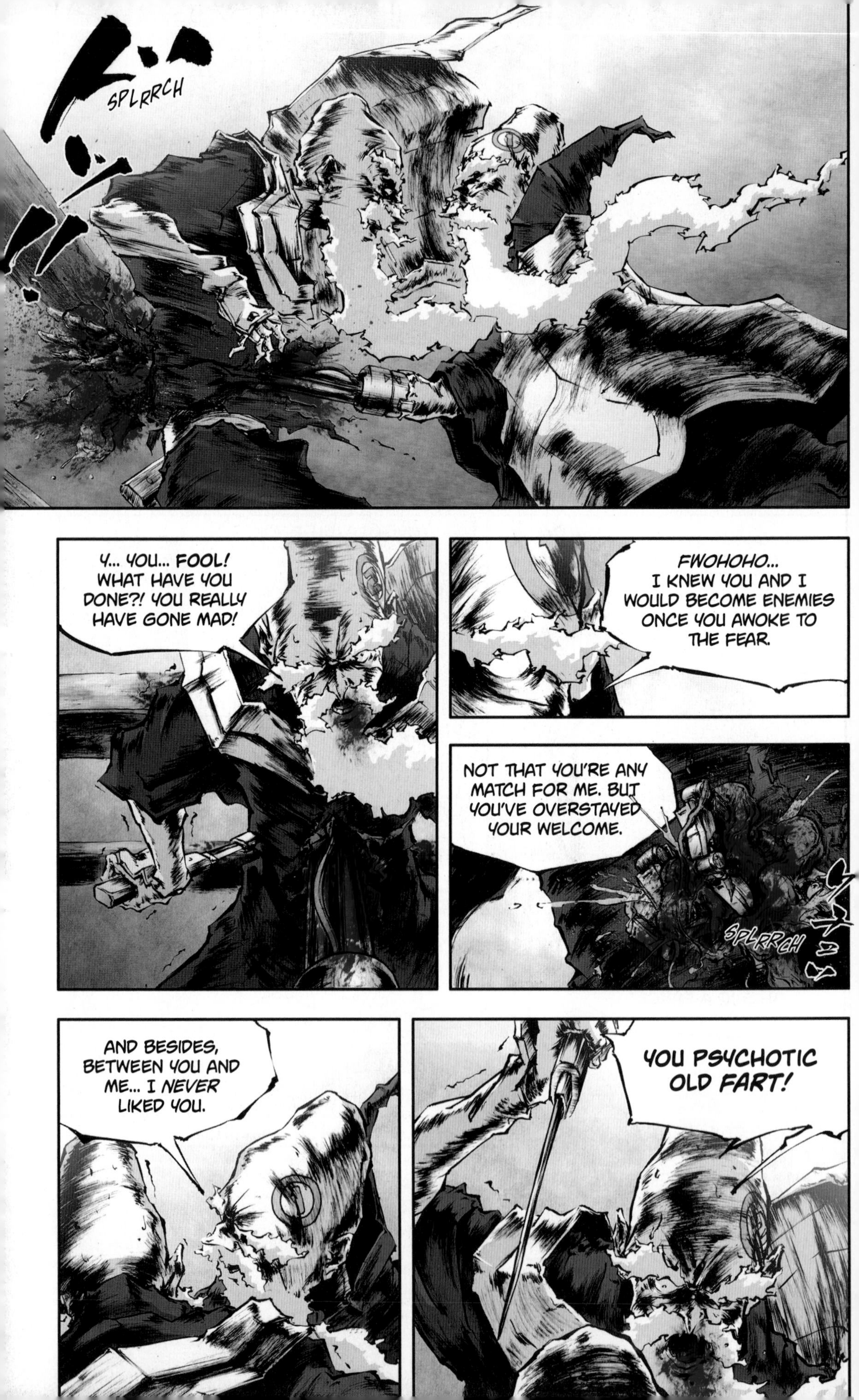
SPLRRCH
Y... YOU... FOOL! WHAT HAVE YOU DONE?! YOU REALLY HAVE GONE MAD!
FWOHOHO... I KNEW YOU AND I WOULD BECOME ENEMIES ONCE YOU AWOKE TO THE FEAR.
NOT THAT YOU'RE ANY MATCH FOR ME. BUT YOU'VE OVERSTAYED YOUR WELCOME.
SPLRRCH
AND BESIDES, BETWEEN YOU AND ME... I NEVER LIKED YOU.
YOU PSYCHOTIC OLD FART!

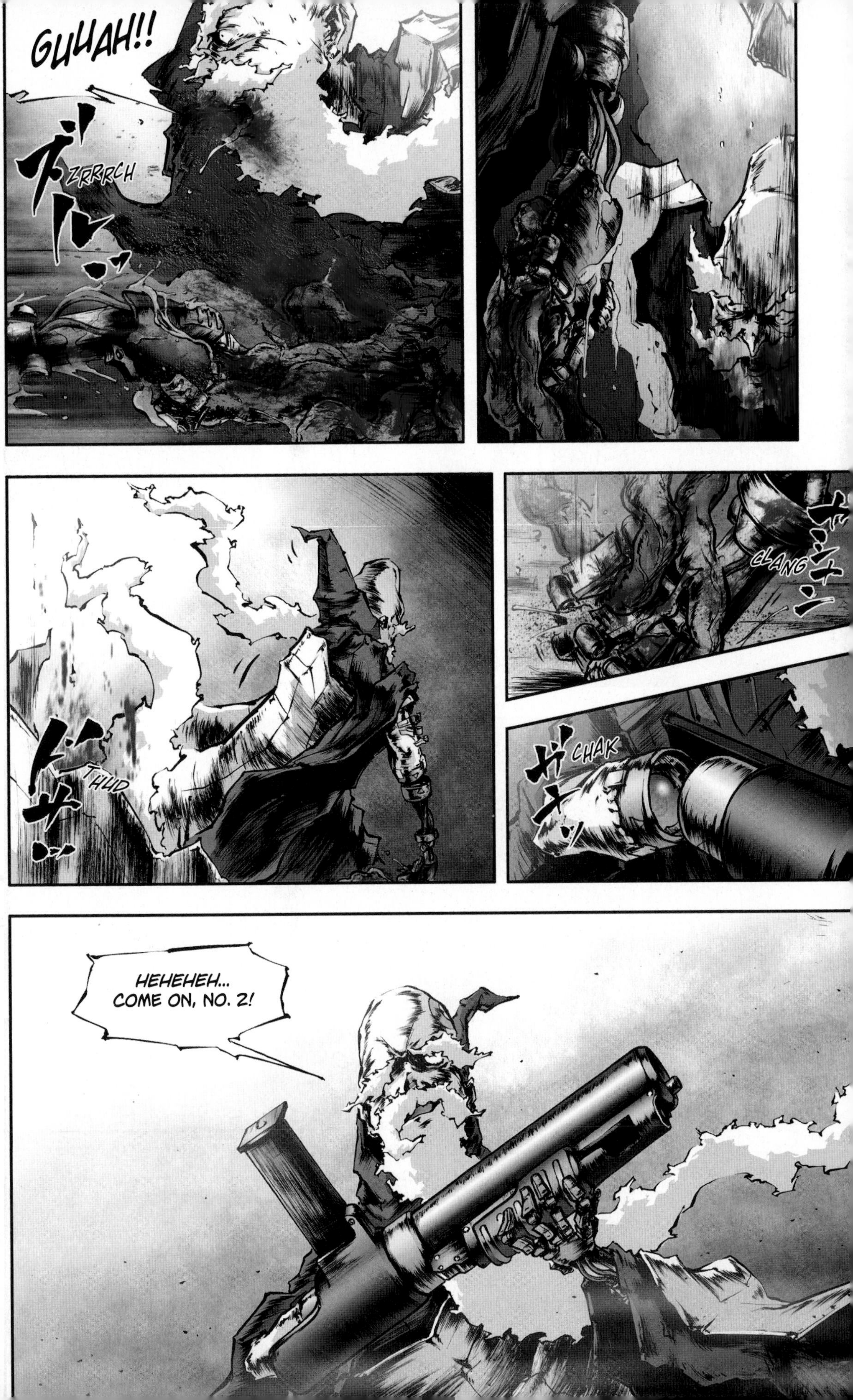
GUUAH!!
ZRRRCH
THUD
CLANG
CHAK
HEHEHEH... COME ON, NO. 2!

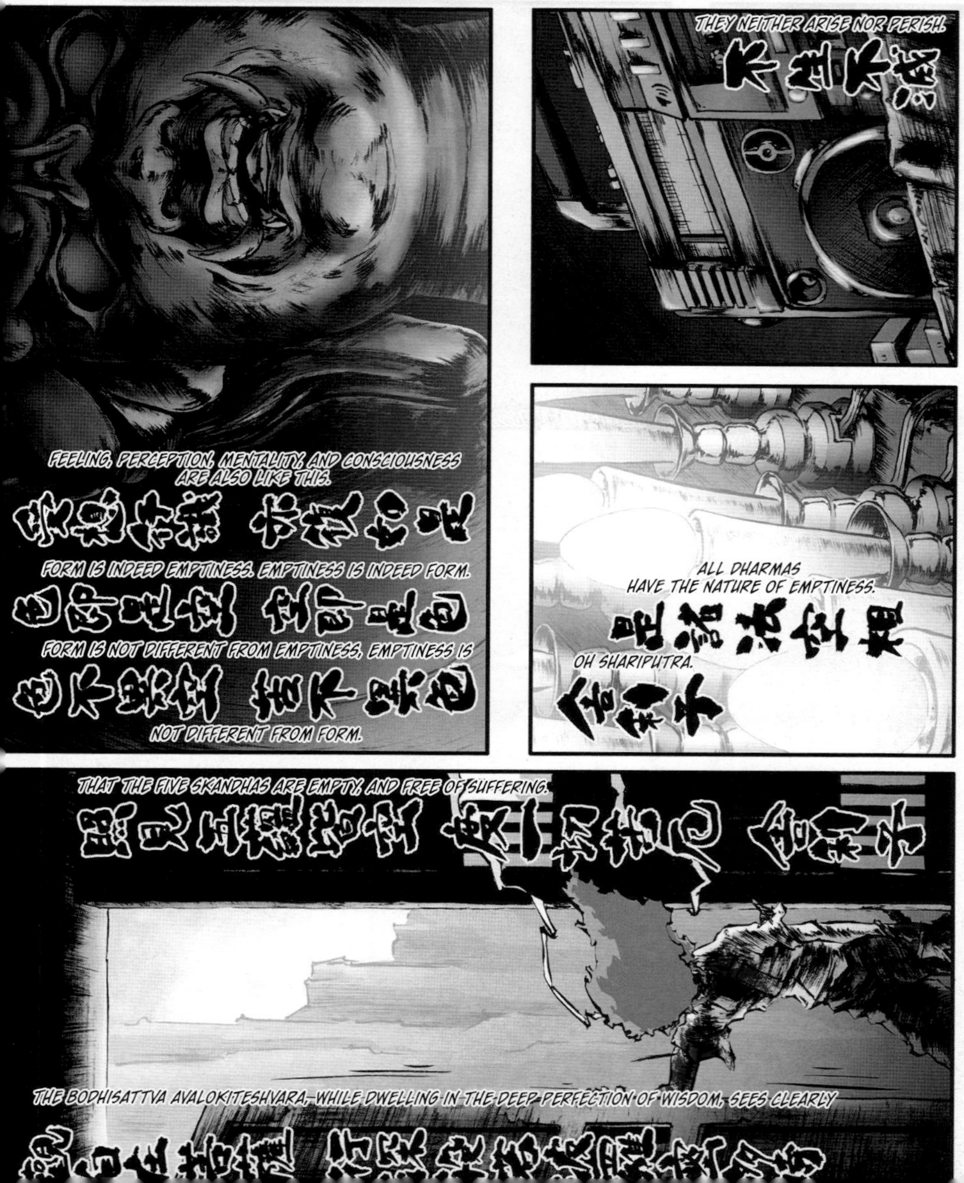
FEELING, PERCEPTION, MENTALITY, AND CONSCIOUSNESS ARE ALSO LIKE THIS.
受想行識 亦復如是
FORM IS INDEED EMPTINESS. EMPTINESS IS INDEED FORM.
色即是空 空即是色
FORM IS NOT DIFFERENT FROM EMPTINESS, EMPTINESS IS NOT DIFFERENT FROM FORM.
色不異空 空不異色
THEY NEITHER ARISE NOR PERISH.
不生不滅
ALL DHARMAS HAVE THE NATURE OF EMPTINESS.
是諸法空相
OH SHARIPUTRA.
舍利子
THAT THE FIVE SKANDHAS ARE EMPTY, AND FREE OF SUFFERING.
照見五蘊皆空 度一切苦厄 舍利子
THE BODHISATTVA AVALOKITESHVARA, WHILE DWELLING IN THE DEEP PERFECTION OF WISDOM, SEES CLEARLY
觀自在菩薩 行深般若波羅蜜多時
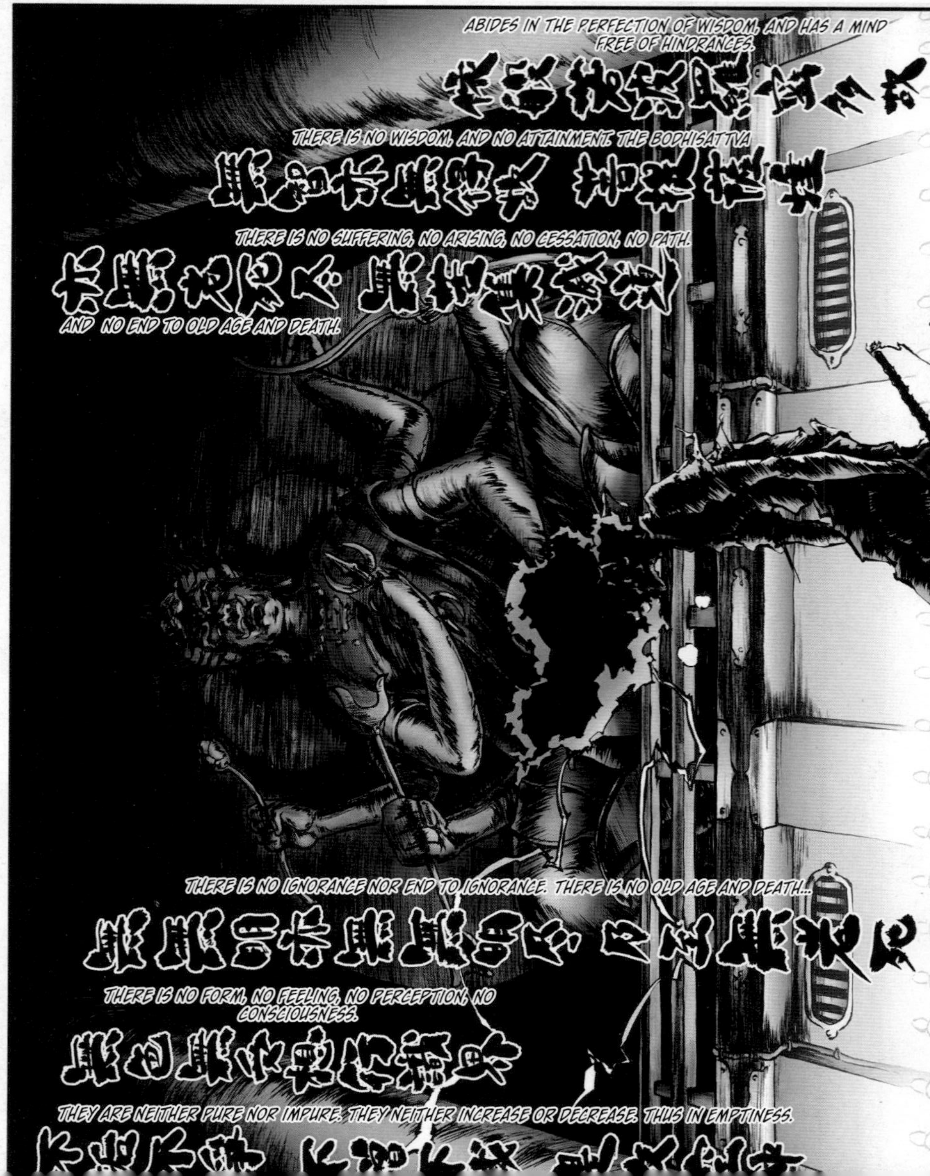
ABIDES IN THE PERFECTION OF WISDOM, AND HAS A MIND FREE OF HINDRANCES.
依般若波羅蜜多故
THERE IS NO WISDOM, AND NO ATTAINMENT. THE BODHISATTVA
無智亦無得以 菩提薩埵
THERE IS NO SUFFERING, NO ARISING, NO CESSATION, NO PATH.
亦無老死尽 無苦集滅道
AND NO END TO OLD AGE AND DEATH.
THERE IS NO IGNORANCE NOR END TO IGNORANCE. THERE IS NO OLD AGE AND DEATH...
無無明亦無無明尽 乃至無老死
THERE IS NO FORM, NO FEELING, NO PERCEPTION, NO CONSCIOUSNESS.
無色無受想行識界
THEY ARE NEITHER PURE NOR IMPURE. THEY NEITHER INCREASE OR DECREASE. THUS IN EMPTINESS.
不垢不浄 不増不減 是故空中

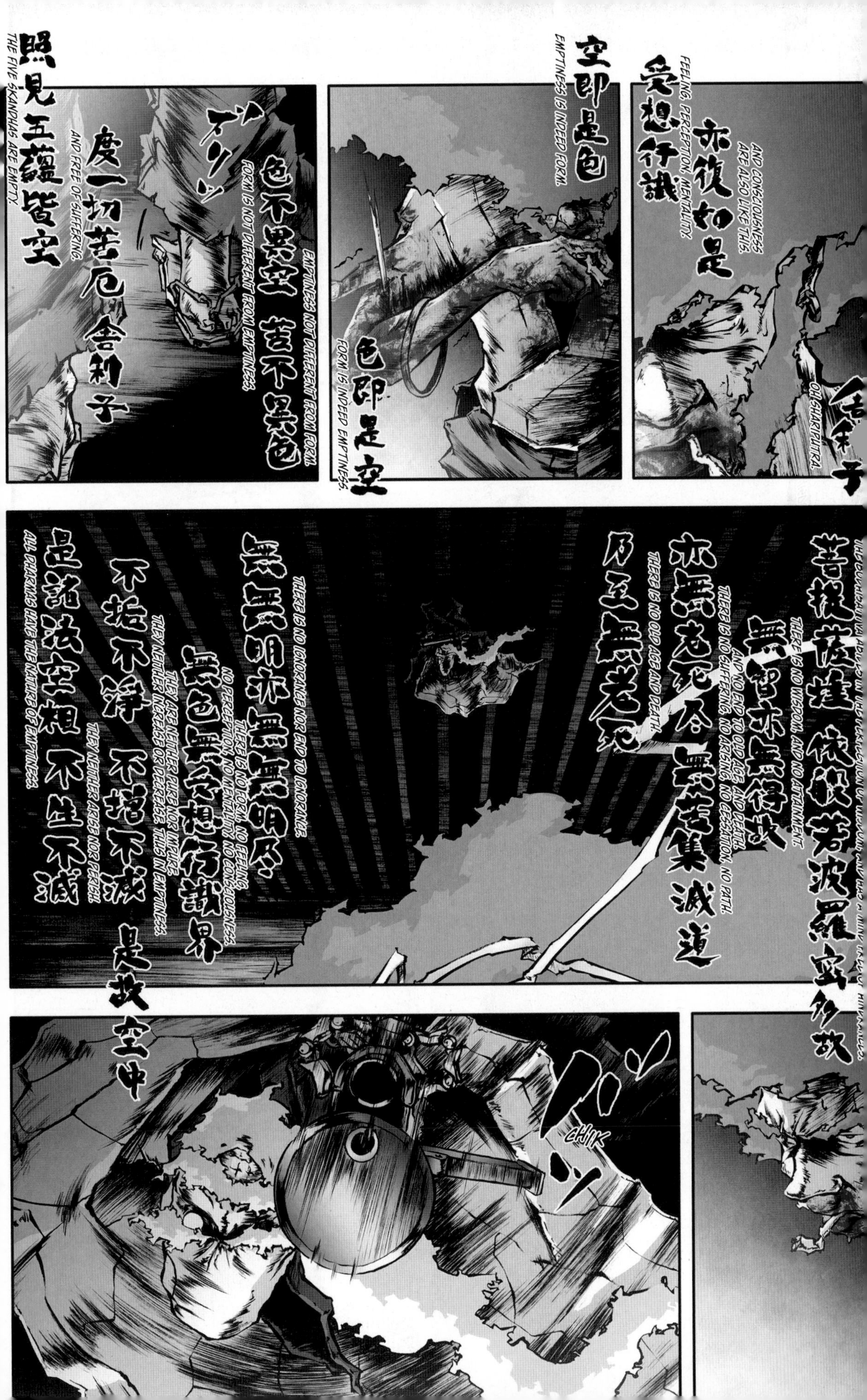
照見五蘊皆空
THE FIVE SKANDHAS ARE EMPTY.
度一切苦厄 舍利子
AND FREE OF SUFFERING.
ズリッ
色不異空 空不異色
EMPTINESS NOT DIFFERENT FROM FORM.
FORM IS NOT DIFFERENT FROM EMPTINESS.
色即是空
FORM IS INDEED EMPTINESS.
空即是色
EMPTINESS IS INDEED FORM.
受想行識
FEELING, PERCEPTION, MENTALITY.
亦復如是
AND CONSCIOUSNESS ARE ALSO LIKE THIS.
舍利子
OH SHARIPUTRA.
是諸法空相 不生不滅
ALL DHARMAS HAVE THE NATURE OF EMPTINESS.
THEY NEITHER ARISE NOR PERISH.
不垢不浄 不増不減 是故空中
THEY NEITHER PURE NOR IMPURE.
THEY ARE NEITHER INCREASE OR DECREASE. THUS IN EMPTINESS.
無色無受想行識界
NO PERCEPTION, NO MENTALITY, NO CONSCIOUSNESS.
THERE IS NOT FORM, NO FEELING.
無無明亦無無明尽
THERE IS NO IGNORANCE NOR END TO IGNORANCE.
乃至無老死
THERE IS NO OLD AGE AND DEATH.
亦無老死尽 無苦集滅道
AND NO END TO OLD AGE AND DEATH.
THERE IS NO SUFFERING, NO ARISING, NO CESSATION, NO PATH.
無智亦無得以無所得故
THERE IS NO WISDOM, AND NO ATTAINMENT.
菩提薩埵 依般若波羅蜜多故
CHIK

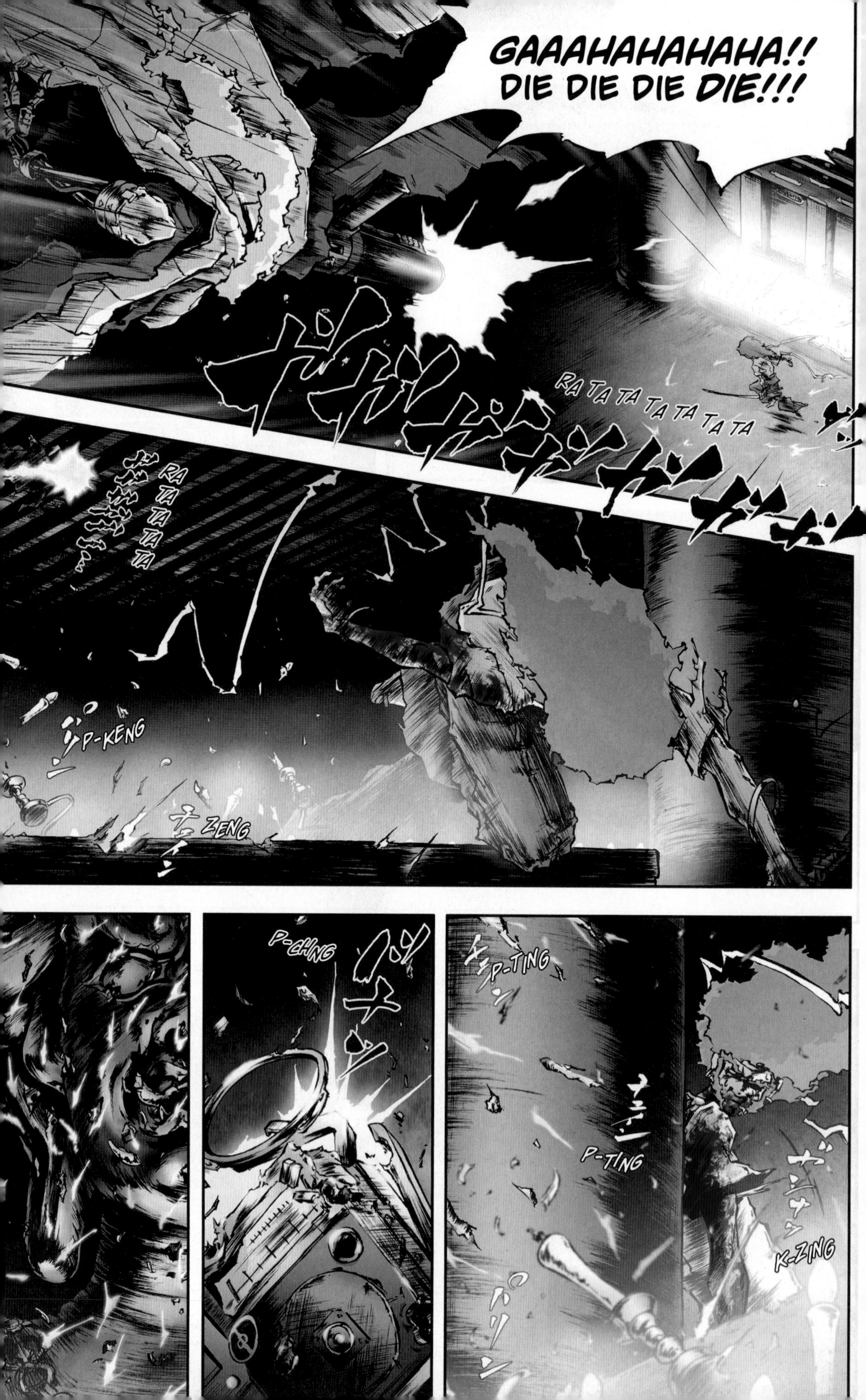
GAAAHAHAHAHA!!
DIE DIE DIE DIE!!!
RA TA TA TA TA TA TA TA
RA TA TA TA TA
P-KENG
ZENG
P-CHNG
P-TING
P-TING
K-ZING

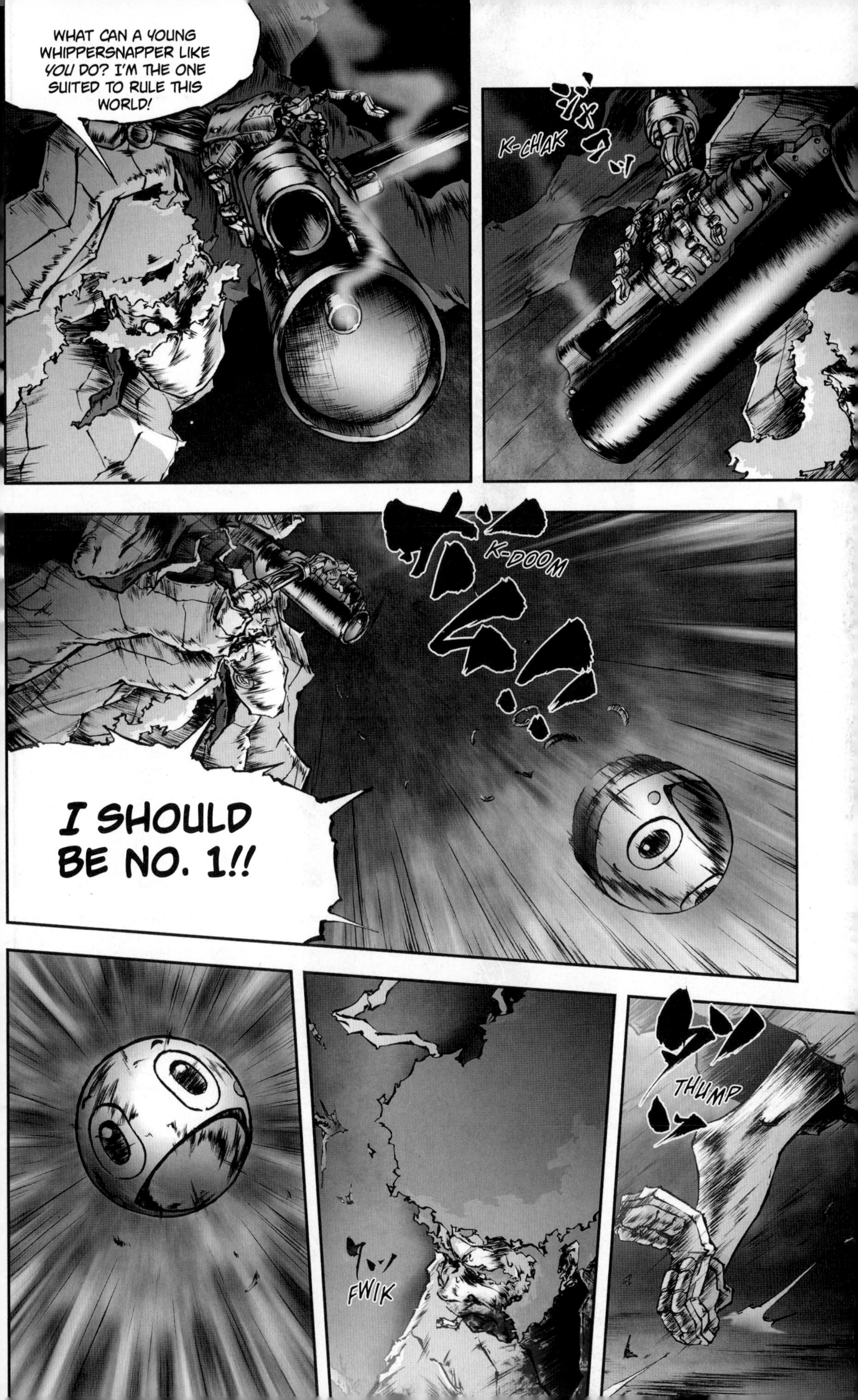
WHAT CAN A YOUNG WHIPPERSNAPPER LIKE *YOU* DO? I'M THE ONE SUITED TO RULE THIS WORLD!
K-CHAK
K-DOOM
I SHOULD BE NO. 1!!
FWIK
THUMP

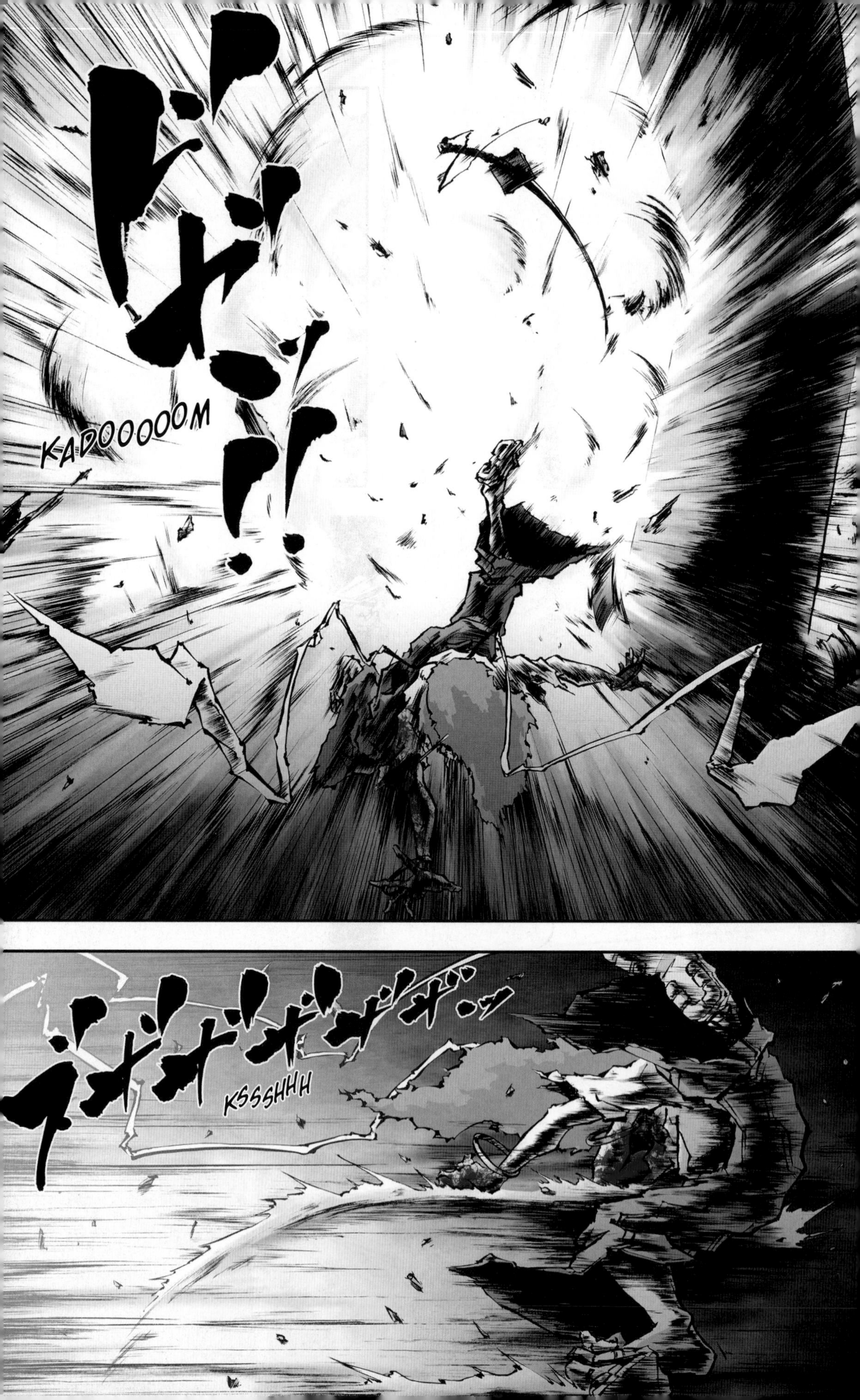
KADOOOOOM
KSSSHHH

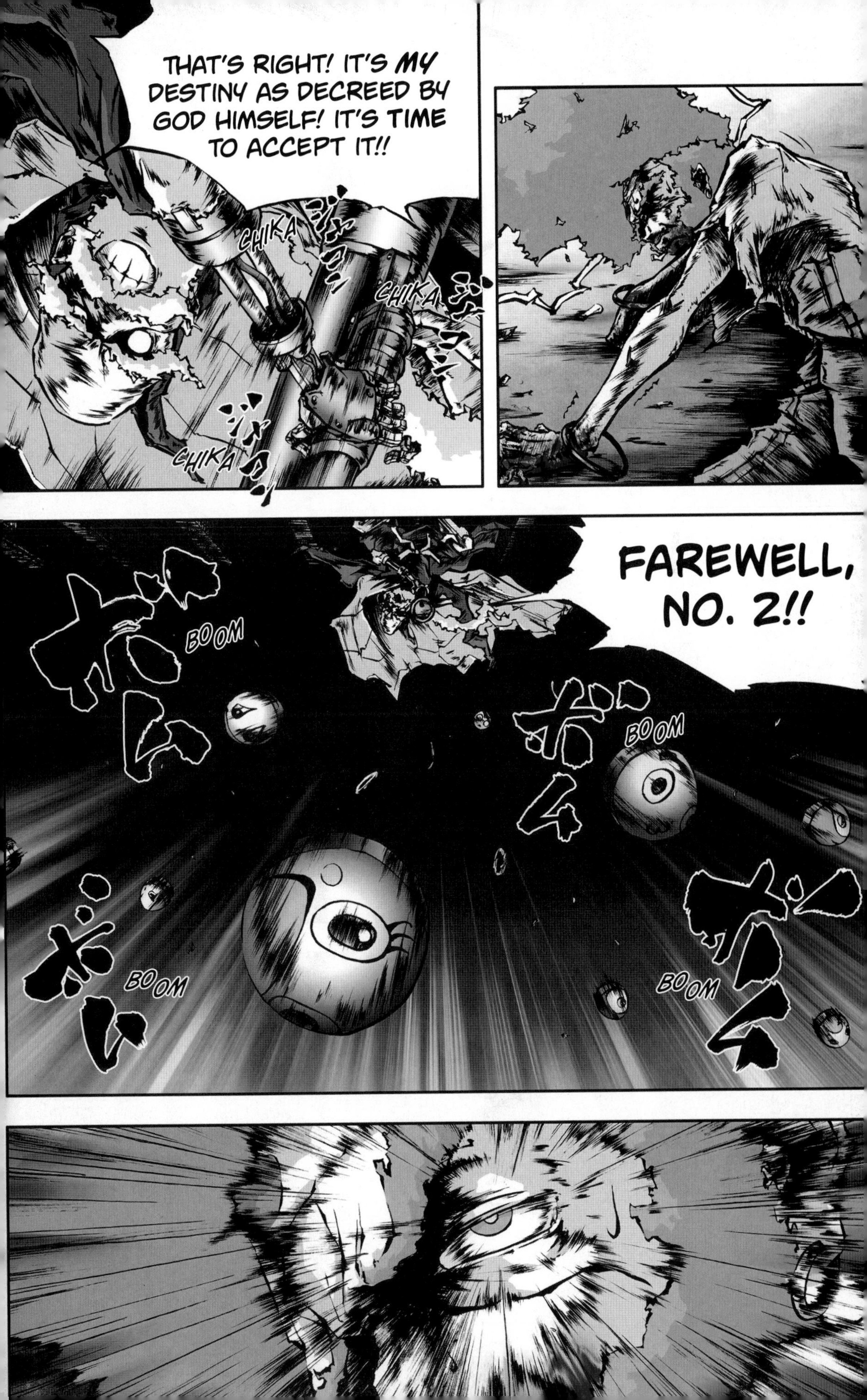
THAT'S RIGHT! IT'S MY DESTINY AS DECREED BY GOD HIMSELF! IT'S TIME TO ACCEPT IT!!
CHIKA
CHIKA
CHIKA
FAREWELL, NO. 2!!
BOOM
BOOM
BOOM
BOOM

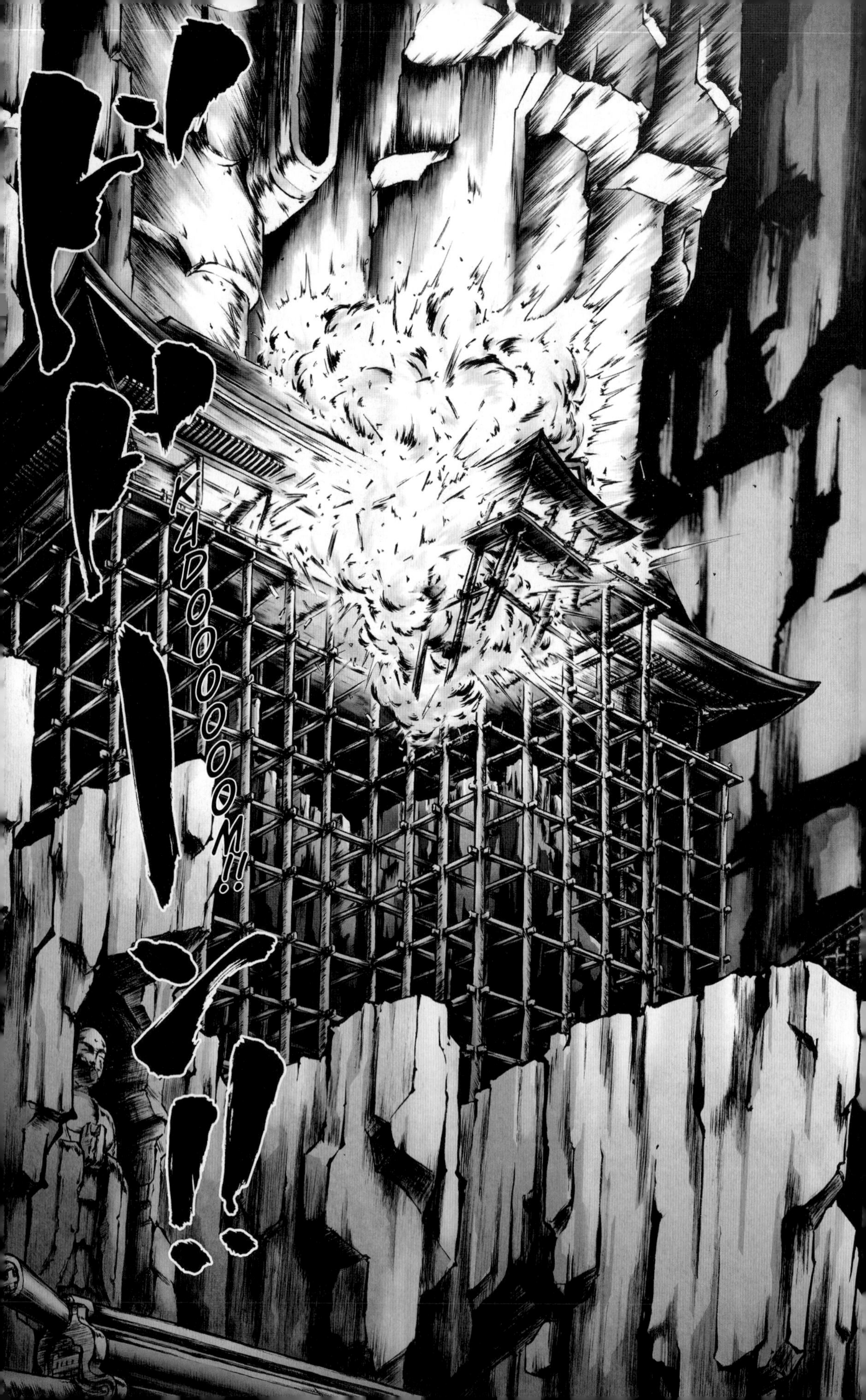
KADOOOOOOM!!

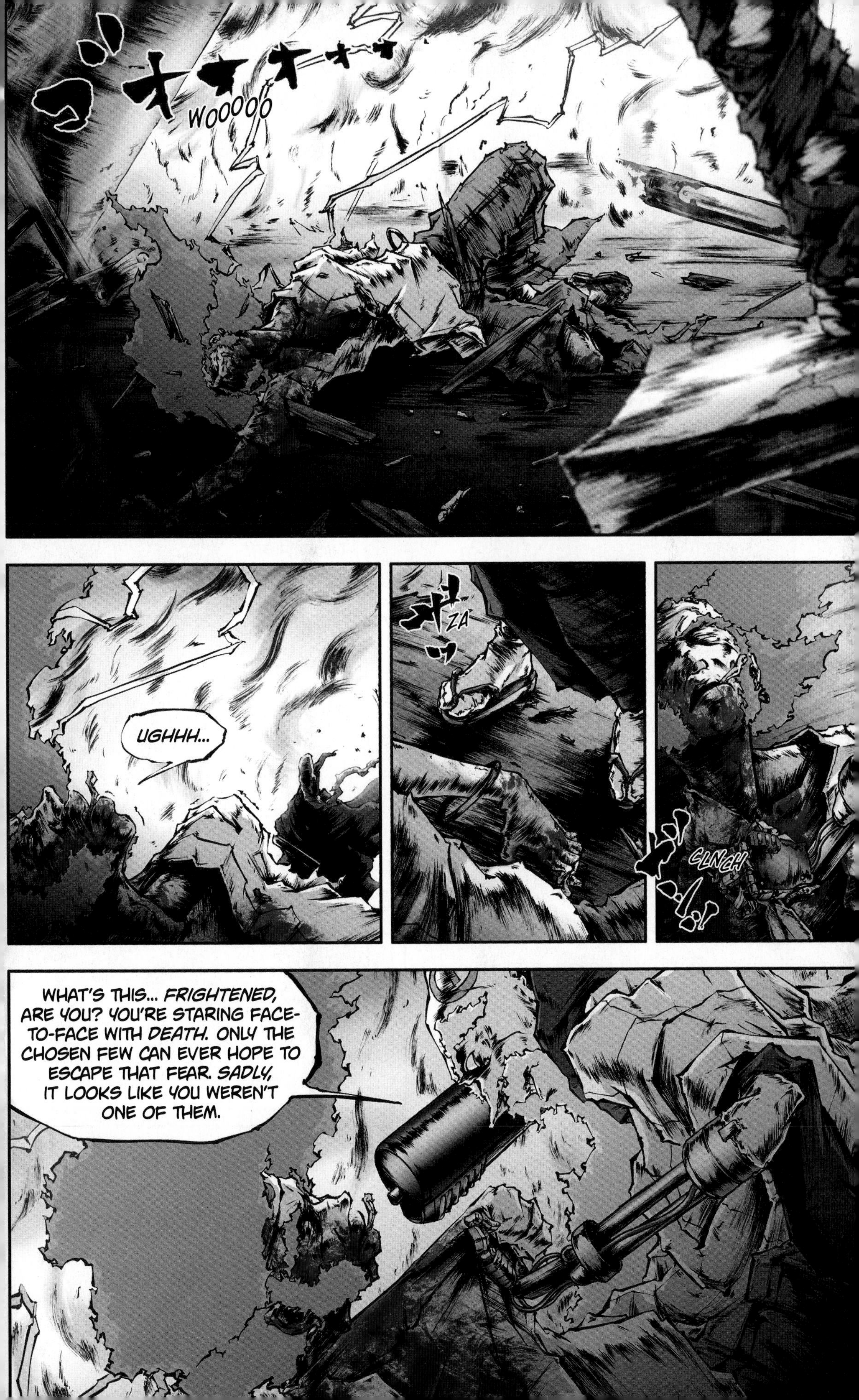
WOOOOO
UGHHH...
ZA
CLNCH
WHAT'S THIS... *FRIGHTENED*, ARE YOU? YOU'RE STARING FACE-TO-FACE WITH *DEATH*. ONLY THE CHOSEN FEW CAN EVER HOPE TO ESCAPE THAT FEAR. *SADLY*, IT LOOKS LIKE YOU WEREN'T ONE OF THEM.

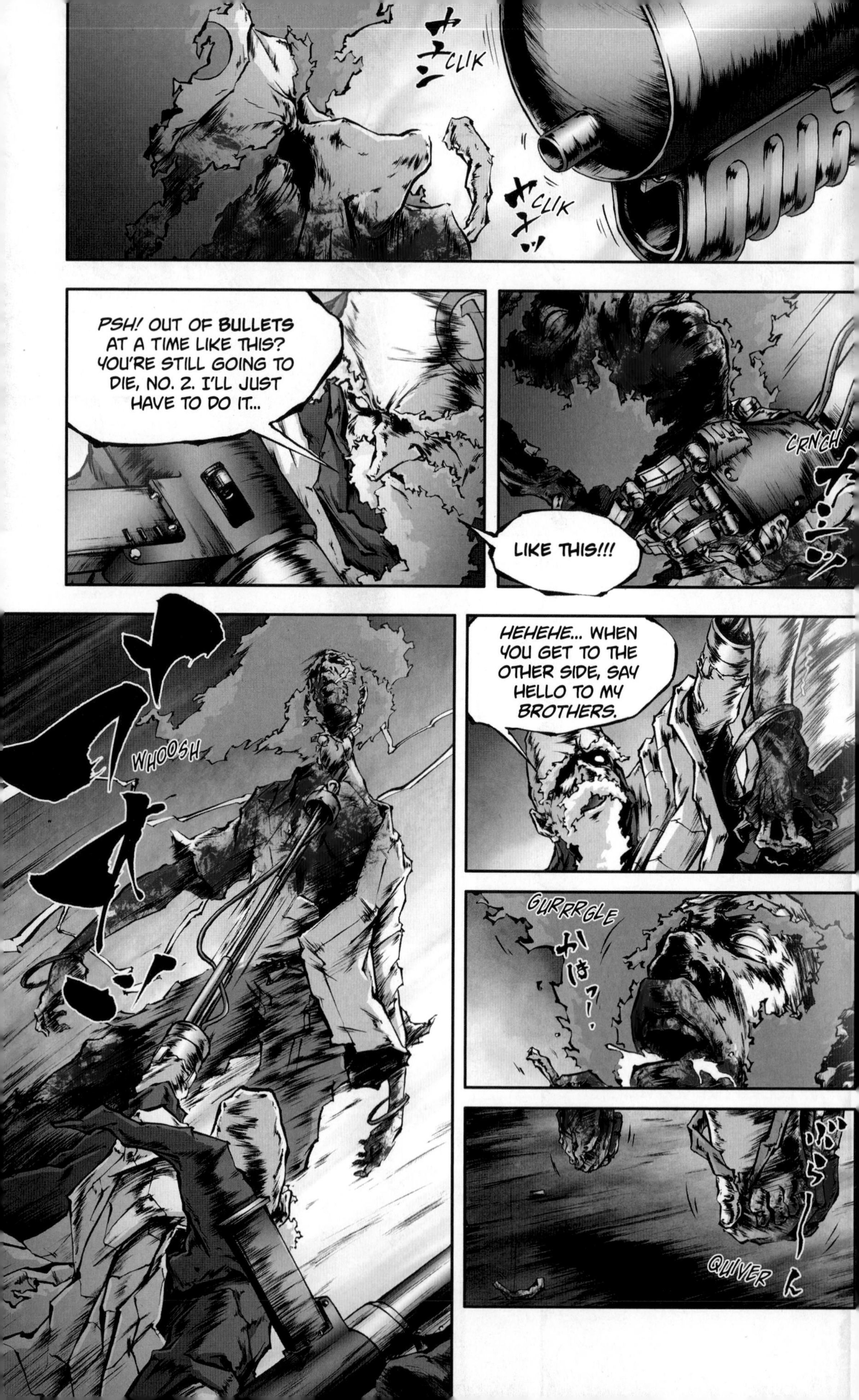
CLIK
CLIK
PSH! OUT OF BULLETS AT A TIME LIKE THIS? YOU'RE STILL GOING TO DIE, NO. 2. I'LL JUST HAVE TO DO IT...
LIKE THIS!!!
CRNCH
WHOOSH
HEHEHE... WHEN YOU GET TO THE OTHER SIDE, SAY HELLO TO MY BROTHERS.
GURRRGLE
QUIVER

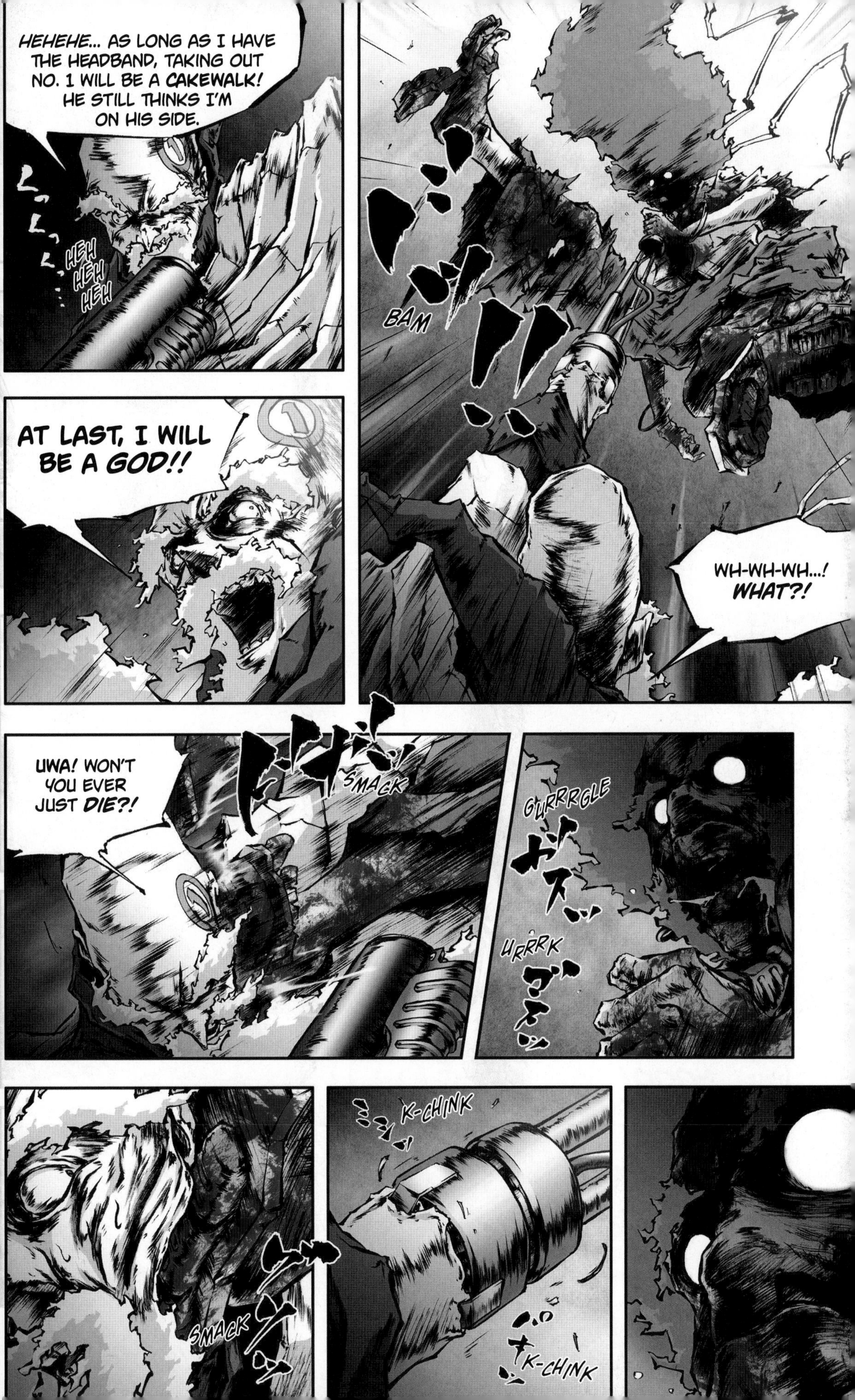
HEHEHE... AS LONG AS I HAVE THE HEADBAND, TAKING OUT NO. 1 WILL BE A CAKEWALK! HE STILL THINKS I'M ON HIS SIDE.
HEH HEH HEH
AT LAST, I WILL BE A GOD!!
BAM
WH-WH-WH...! WHAT?!
UWA! WON'T YOU EVER JUST DIE?!
SMACK
GURRRGLE
URRRK
SMACK
K-CHINK
K-CHINK

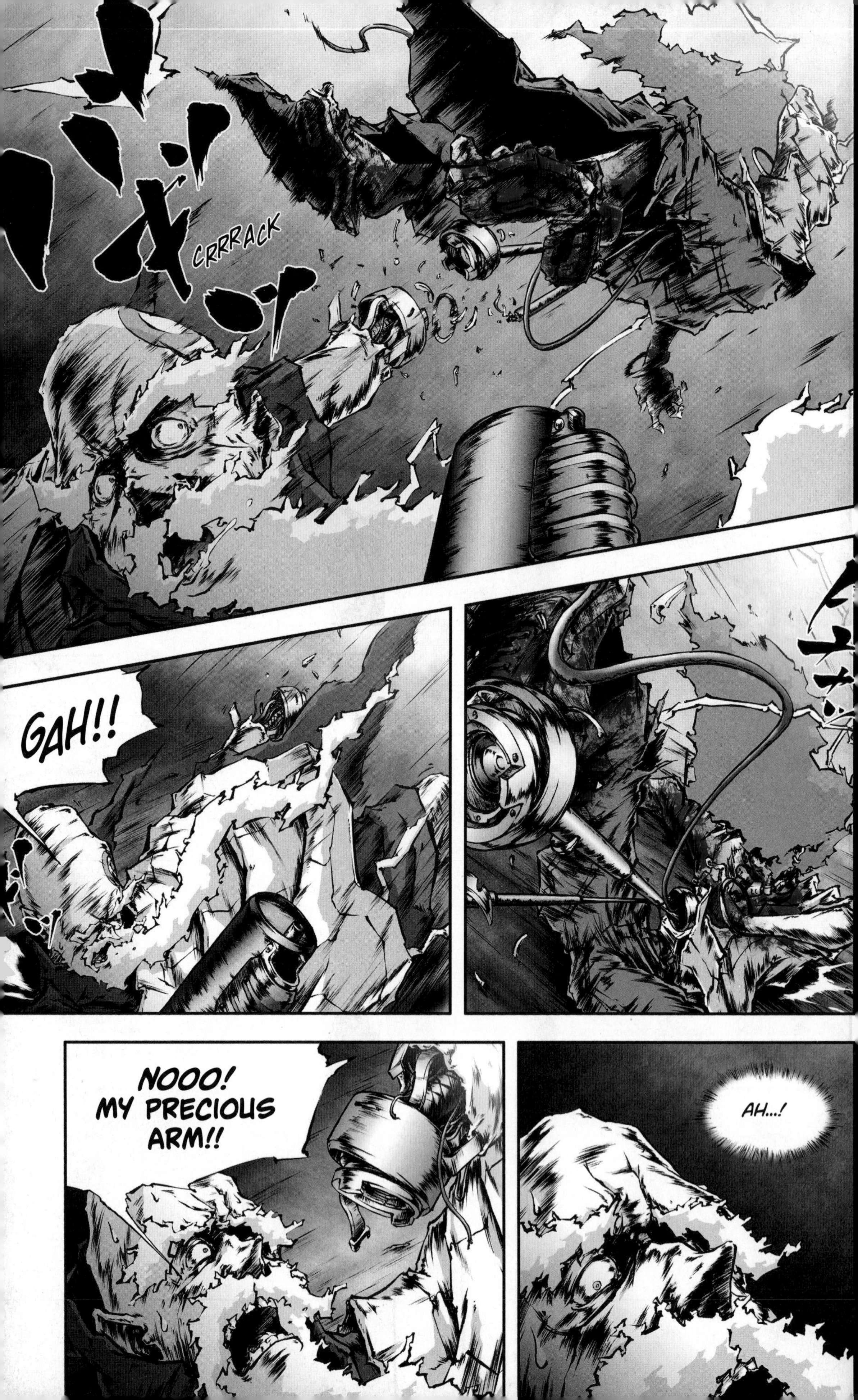
CRRRACK
GAH!!
NOOO! MY PRECIOUS ARM!!
AH...!

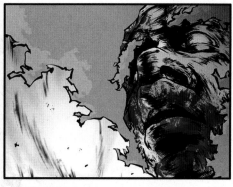

ゴォ★★★★★★
WOOOOO

NO... I...

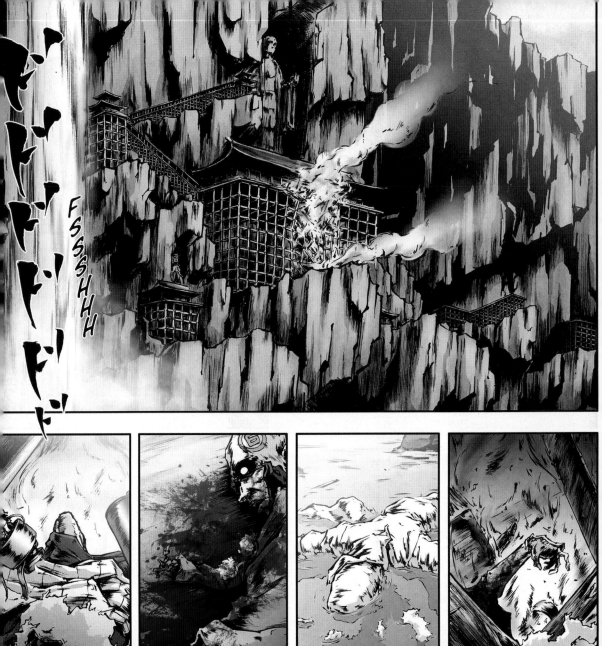

FSSSHHH

FSSSHHH

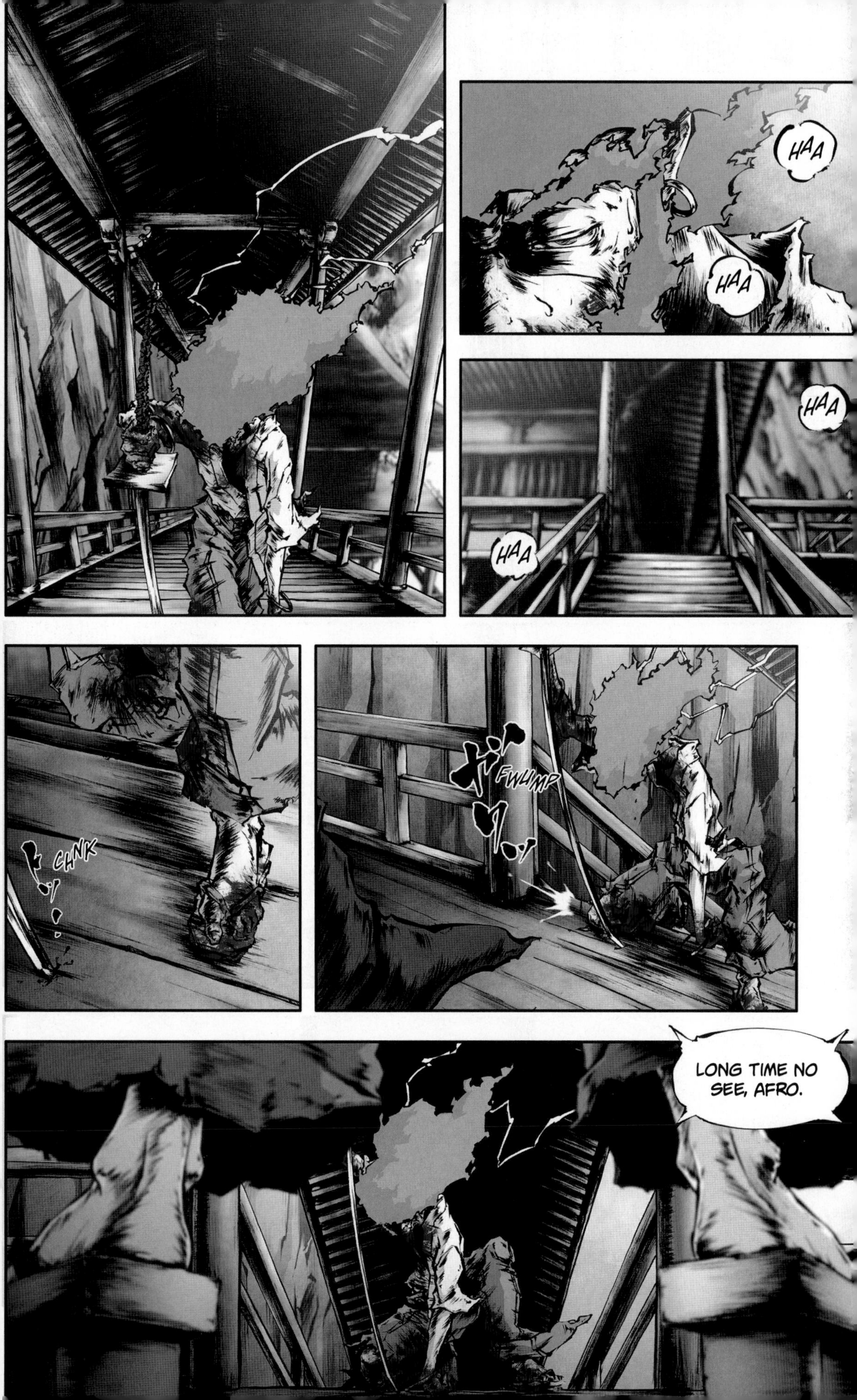
HAA
HAA
HAA
HAA
CHNK
FWUMP
LONG TIME NO SEE, AFRO.

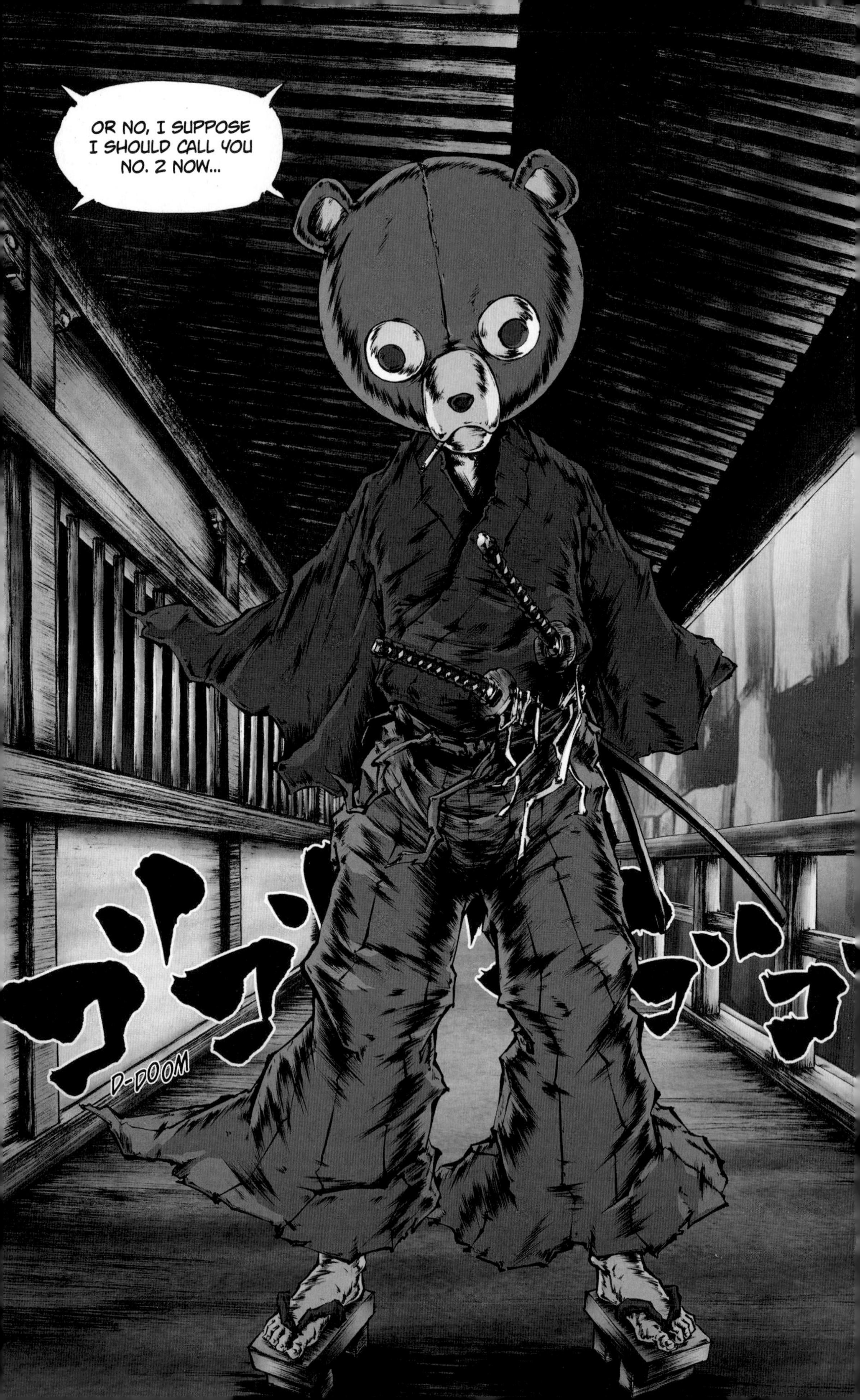
OR NO, I SUPPOSE I SHOULD CALL YOU NO. 2 NOW...
D-DOOM

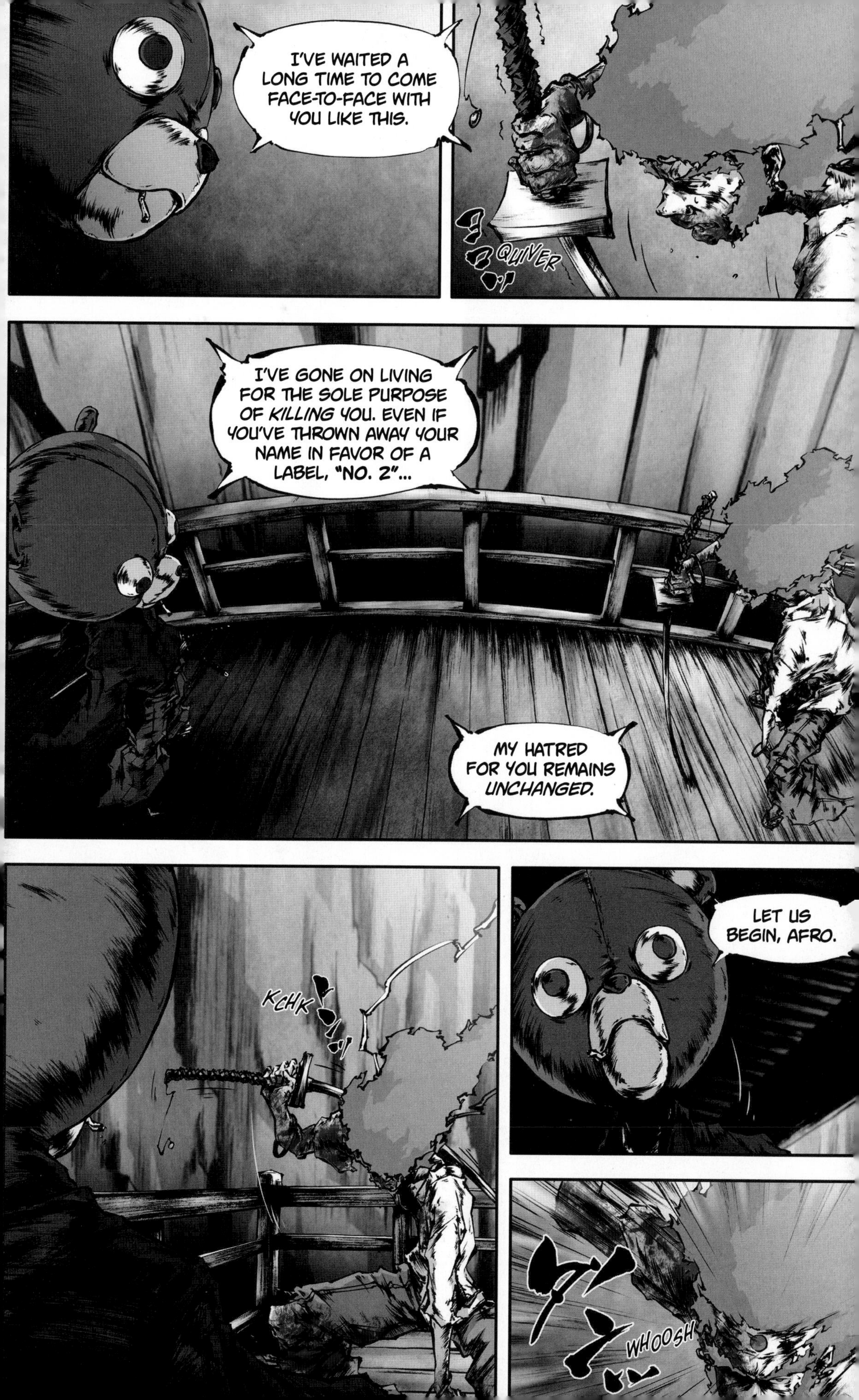
I'VE WAITED A LONG TIME TO COME FACE-TO-FACE WITH YOU LIKE THIS.
QUIVER
I'VE GONE ON LIVING FOR THE SOLE PURPOSE OF *KILLING* YOU. EVEN IF YOU'VE THROWN AWAY YOUR NAME IN FAVOR OF A LABEL, "NO. 2"...
MY HATRED FOR YOU REMAINS *UNCHANGED.*
KCHK
LET US BEGIN, AFRO.
WHOOSH

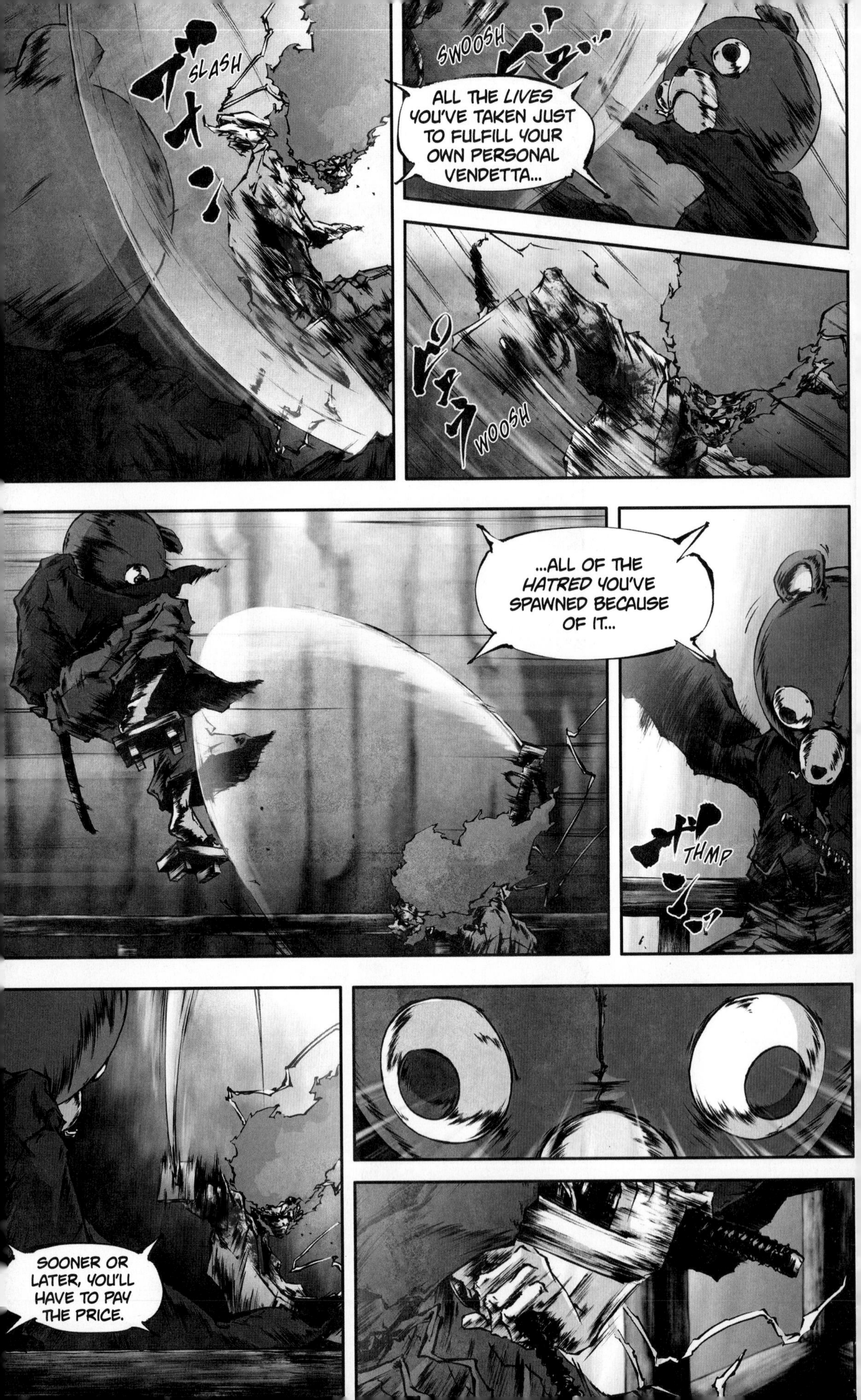
SLASH
SWOOSH
ALL THE *LIVES* YOU'VE TAKEN JUST TO FULFILL YOUR OWN PERSONAL VENDETTA...
WOOSH
...ALL OF THE *HATRED* YOU'VE SPAWNED BECAUSE OF IT...
THMP
SOONER OR LATER, YOU'LL HAVE TO PAY THE PRICE.

KASHWEEEN!!

CLURCH

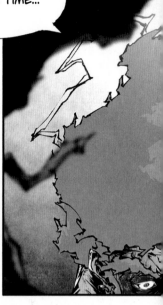

BUT NOW IS NOT THE TIME...

YOUR DEATH IS FATED TO BE FAR MORE AGONIZING, ROASTING ON FLAMES OF HATRED.

KSH

DON'T THINK YOU'LL BE PUT DOWN EASY, AFRO, THE NEXT TIME WE MEET...

THAT WILL BE THE TIME.

WOOSH

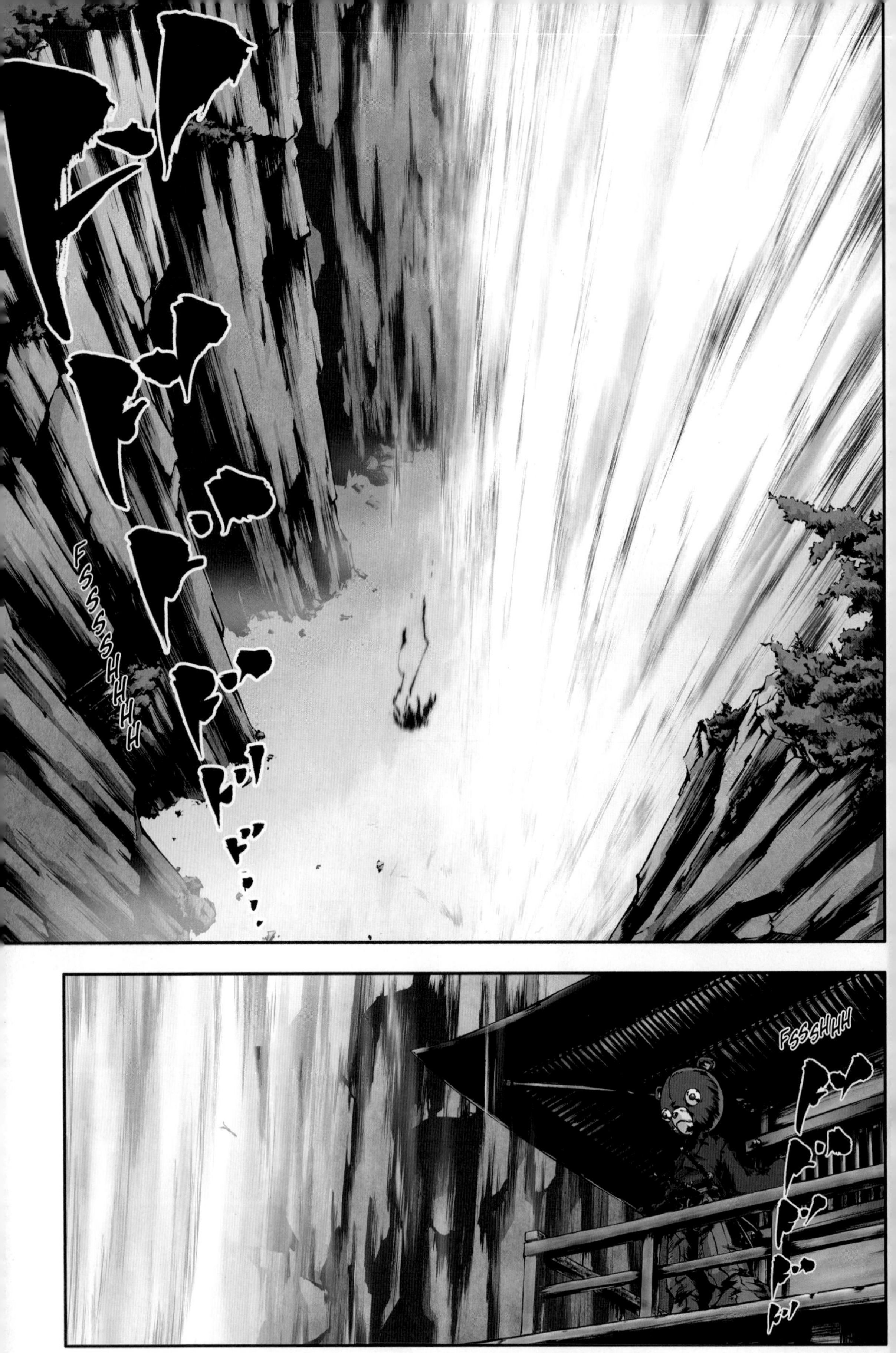
FSSSSHHHH
FSSSHHH

END OF #05

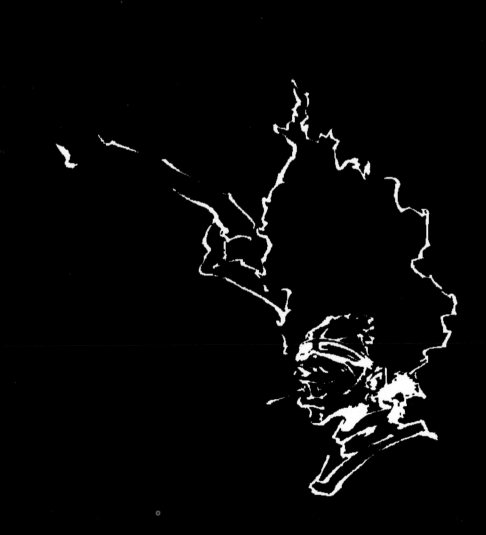

TRANSLATION NOTES

CHAPTER 1

Page 22
In the Japanese, the bandit leader scoffs at Afro for attempting an *"iai"* with such a long sword. Iai is a technique in which the samurai unsheathes his sword and slices his opponent all in one swift, fluid motion, not unlike a western quick-draw. *Iaido* is a martial art still practised today.

Page 27
"Brother" is derived from the Japanese *"ani-ja."*

Page 31
"Jii-sama" or *"grandfather."*

Page 33
The name *"Brother One"* is derived from the Japanese *"Ichi-no-ji,"* meaning *"the digit 1."*

Page 35
Mt. Sumeru - A legendary mountain said to tower over the center of the Earth and serves as a meeting place for the gods. Also known as *Shumisen.*

CHAPTER 2

Page 45
Tecchisen - A legendary mountain from the Buddhist world map. While Sumeru was found in the center of the Earth, Tecchisen lay on the very edge of it. Also known as *Cakravada Mountain.*

Page 49
Oden - A type of hotpot stew popular during the cold months.

Page 51
Occhan - A colloquial term of endearment for an elderly person, like "pops."

Page 56
Daikon - A large Japanese radish used in *oden.*

CHAPTER 3

Page 78
"Wicked" from the word *"sugee,"* a modern colloquialism meaning "amazing" or "cool" (from *"sugoi"*).

Oshou-san - A Buddhist priest of high rank.

Page 79
"Mother" - from *"kaa-san."*

Page 89
"Geezer brigade" taken from *"jijii-doo."*

CHAPTER 4

Page 108
"O.G.-samas" from *"jii-sama-tachi."*

Page 114
Rokuta is also known as "Brother Six" in the anime version of *Afro Samurai.* The Kanji for "Rokuta" are in fact the kanji for "six" (*"roku"*) and *"ta,"* a kanji common in male names.

Page 117
Ryou is an old type of Japanese coin. Evidently it was worth a lot more than the modern yen.

Page 127
Kunai - Throwing knives.

Page 130
Brother four's name in Japanese is *"Shi no Ji"* following the pattern for all the monk brothers' names, with *"shi"* meaning "four" and *"no ji"* meaning "the digit" or "the letter." The only difference is that in Brother Four's case, the *"shi"* is written with the kanji for "death", also pronounced "shi." So it looks like 死の字 instead of 四の字. The pun is lost in English, although an alternative translation could be "Brother Shi," which a fraction of readers would likely understand, since the four/death connection is one of the more well-spread factoids of Japanese cultural minutiae.

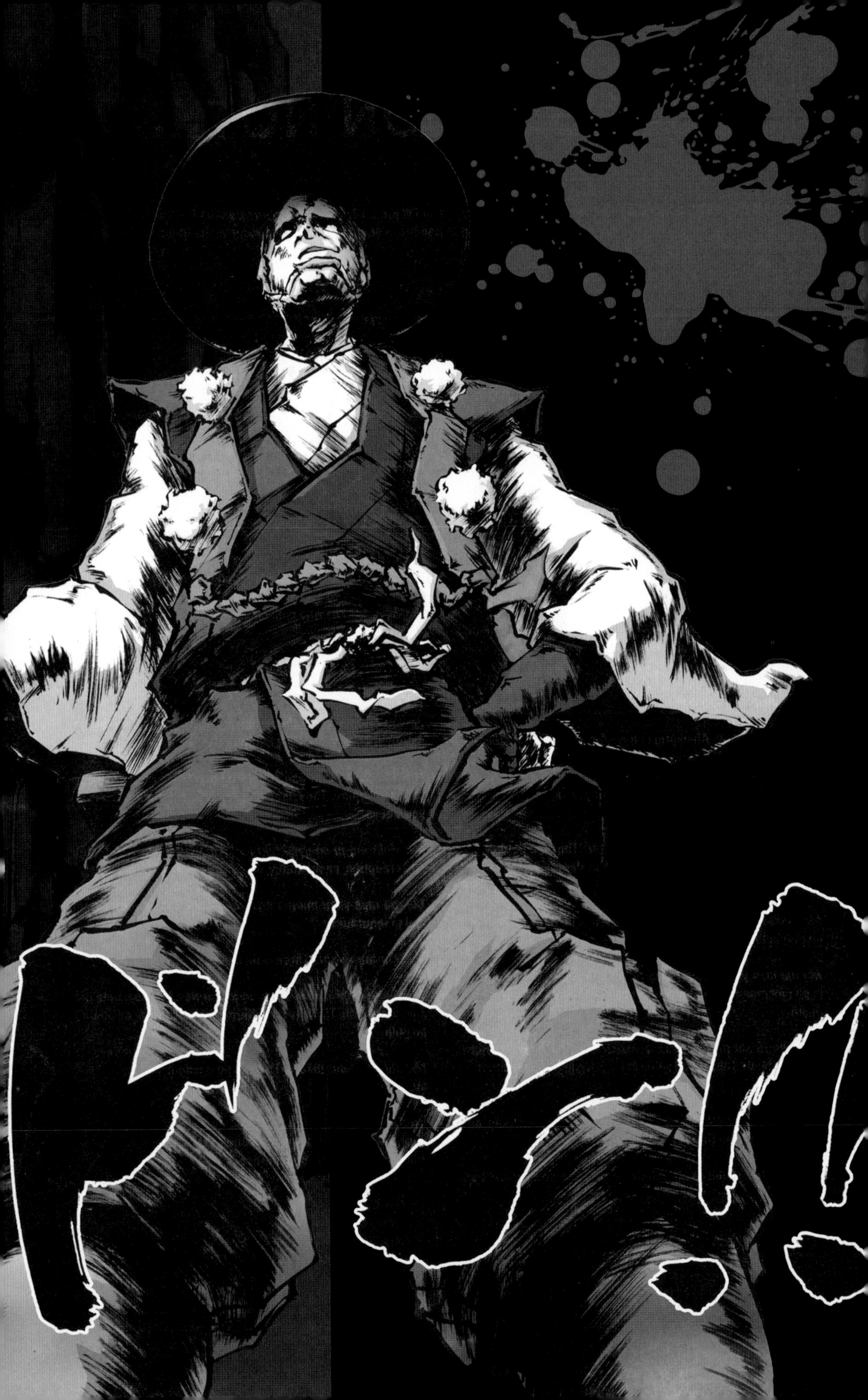
ドン!!

TRANSLATION NOTES

HEART SUTRA

The Heart Sutra is one of the most well-known sutras in Buddhism and is primarily chanted by Zen sects in East Asian Buddhism. As the shortest sutra, it is said to perfectly express the wisdom of Buddha in condensed form, focusing on the Buddhist doctrines of emptiness and non-attachment.

CHAPTER 5

Page 146

146.1
Kan-ji-zai-bo-satsu Gyô-jin-han-nya-ha-ra-mit-ta-ji **- The Bodhisattva Avalokiteshvara, while dwelling in the deep perfection of wisdom, sees clearly.**

Shô-ken-go-un-kai-kuu Do-is-sai-ku-yaku Sha-ri-shi **- That the five skandhas are empty, and free of suffering.**

146.2
Shiki-fu-j-kuu Ku-i-shiki **- Form is not different from emptiness, emptiness is not different from form.**

Shiki-fsoku-ze-kuu ku-soku-ze-shiki **- Form is indeed emptiness. Emptiness is indeed form.**

Ju-sô-gyô-shiki Yaku-bu-nyo-ze **- Feeling, perception, mentality, and consciousness are also like this.**

146.3
Sha-ri-shi **- Oh Shariputra.**

Ze-sho-hô-kuu-sô **- All dharmas have the nature of emptiness.**

146.4
Fu-shô-fu-metsu **- They neither arise nor perish.**

146..5
Fu-ku-fu-jô Fu-zô-fu-gen Ze-ko-kuu-chuu **- They are neither pure nor impure. They neither increase or decrease. Thus in emptiness.**

Mu-shiki-mu-ju-sô-gyô-shiki-kai **- There is no form, no feeling, no perception, no consciousness.**

Mu-mu-myô-yaku-mu-mu-myô-jin Nai-shi-mu-rô-shi **- There is no ignorance nor end to ignorance. There is no old age and death…**

Yaku-mu-rô-shi-jin Mu-ku-shuu-metsu-dô **- And no end to old age and death. There is no suffering, no arising, no cessation, no path.**

Mu-chi-yaku-mu-toku-i Bo-dai-sat-ta **- There is no wisdom, and no attainment. The Bodhisattva.**

E-han-nya-ha-ra-mit-ta-ko **- Abides in the perfection of wisdom, and has a mind free of hindrances.**

Page 147

147.1
Shô-ken-go-un-kai-kuu **- The five skandhas are empty.**

Do-is-ken-ku-yaku Sha-ri-shi **- And free of suffering.**

Shiki-fu-i-kuu Ku-fu-i-shiki **- Form is not different from emptiness, emptiness not different from form.**

147.2
Shiki-soku-ze-shiki **- Emptiness is indeed form.**

147.3
Ju-sô-gyô-shiki **- Feeling, perception, mentality.**

Yaku-bu-nyo-ze **- And consciousness are also like this.**

Sha-ri-shi **- Oh Shariputra.**

147.4
Ze-sho-hô-kuu-sô Fu-shô-fu-metsu **- All dharmas have the nature of emptiness. They neither arise nor perish.**

Fu-ku-fu-jô Fu-zô-fu-gen Ze-ko-kuu-chuu **- They are neither pure nor impure. They neither increase nor decrease. Thus in emptiness.**

Mu-shiki-mu-ju-sô-gyô-shiki-kai **- There is no form, no feeling, no perception, no mentality, no consciousness.**

Mu-mu-myô-yaku-mu-mu-myô-jin **- There is no ignorance nor end to ignorance.**

Mai-shi-mu-rô-shi **- There is no old age and death.**

Yaku-mu-rô-shi-jin Mu-ku-shuu-metsu-dô **- And no end to old age, and death. There is no suffering, no arising, no cessation, no path.**

Mu-chi-yaku-mu-toku-i **- There is no wisdom, and no attainment.**

Bo-dai-sat-ta E-han-nya-ha-ra-mit-ta-ko **- The Bodhisattva abides in the perfection of wisdom, and has a mind free of hindrances.**

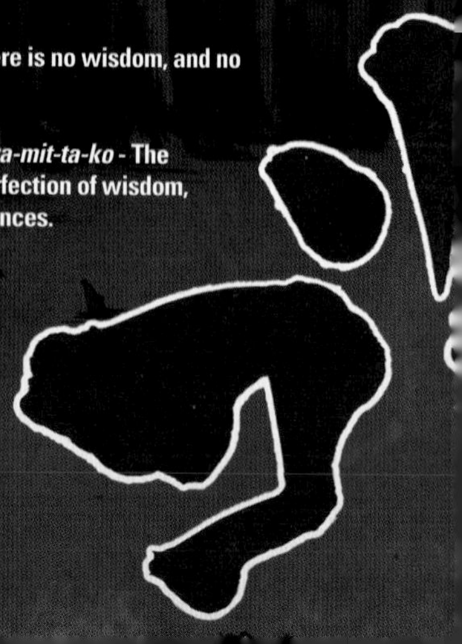

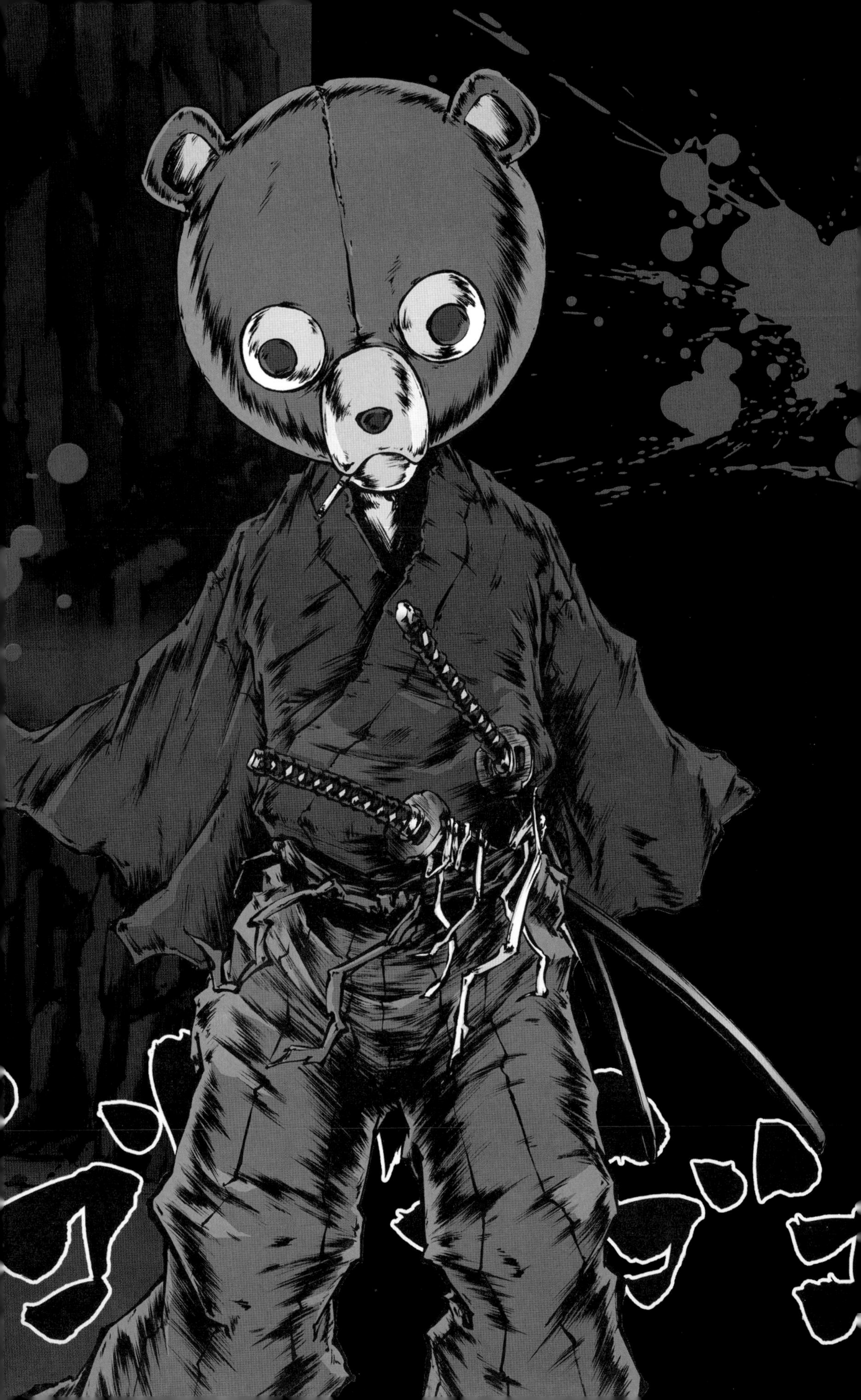

SUPPLEMENT MATERIAL

ORIGINAL DOUJINSHI PAGES

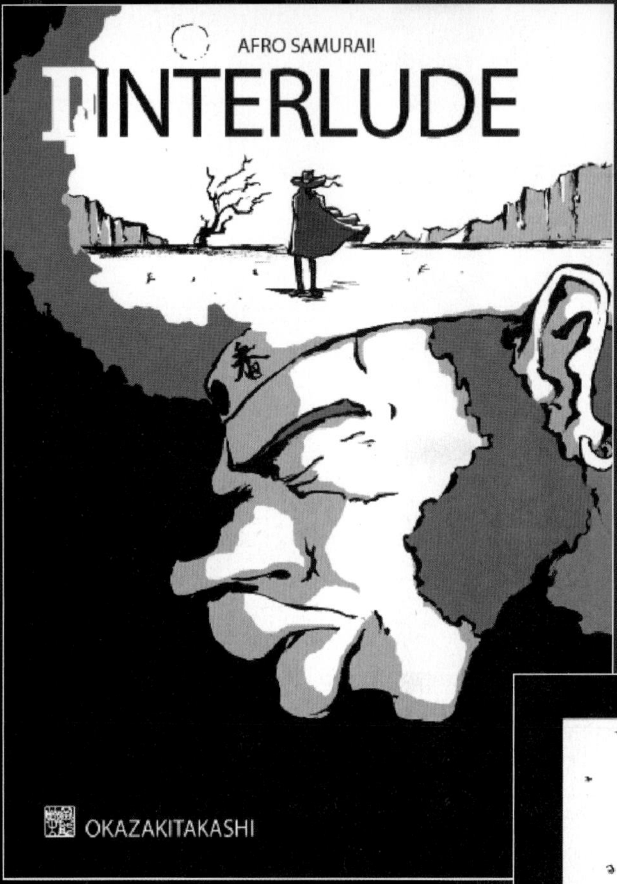
AFRO SAMURAI!
INTERLUDE
OKAZAKITAKASHI

Afro Samurai first began life as a *doujinshi* series in Japan before making the leap to animation and then back to manga. Presented here are eight of Okazaki-sensei's original Afro Samurai *doujinshi* pages featuring the iconic sequence that made Afro the bad-ass mutha he is today.

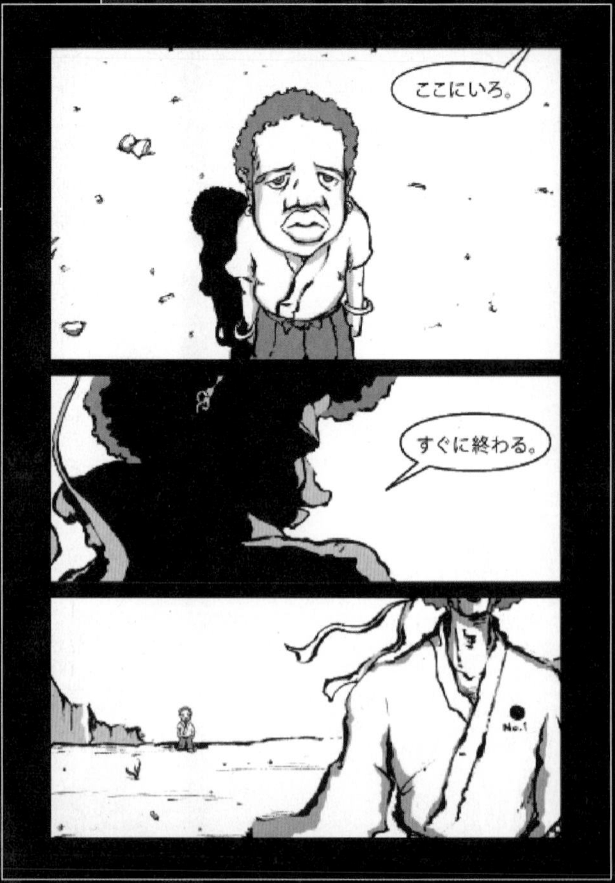
ここにいろ。
すぐに終わる。

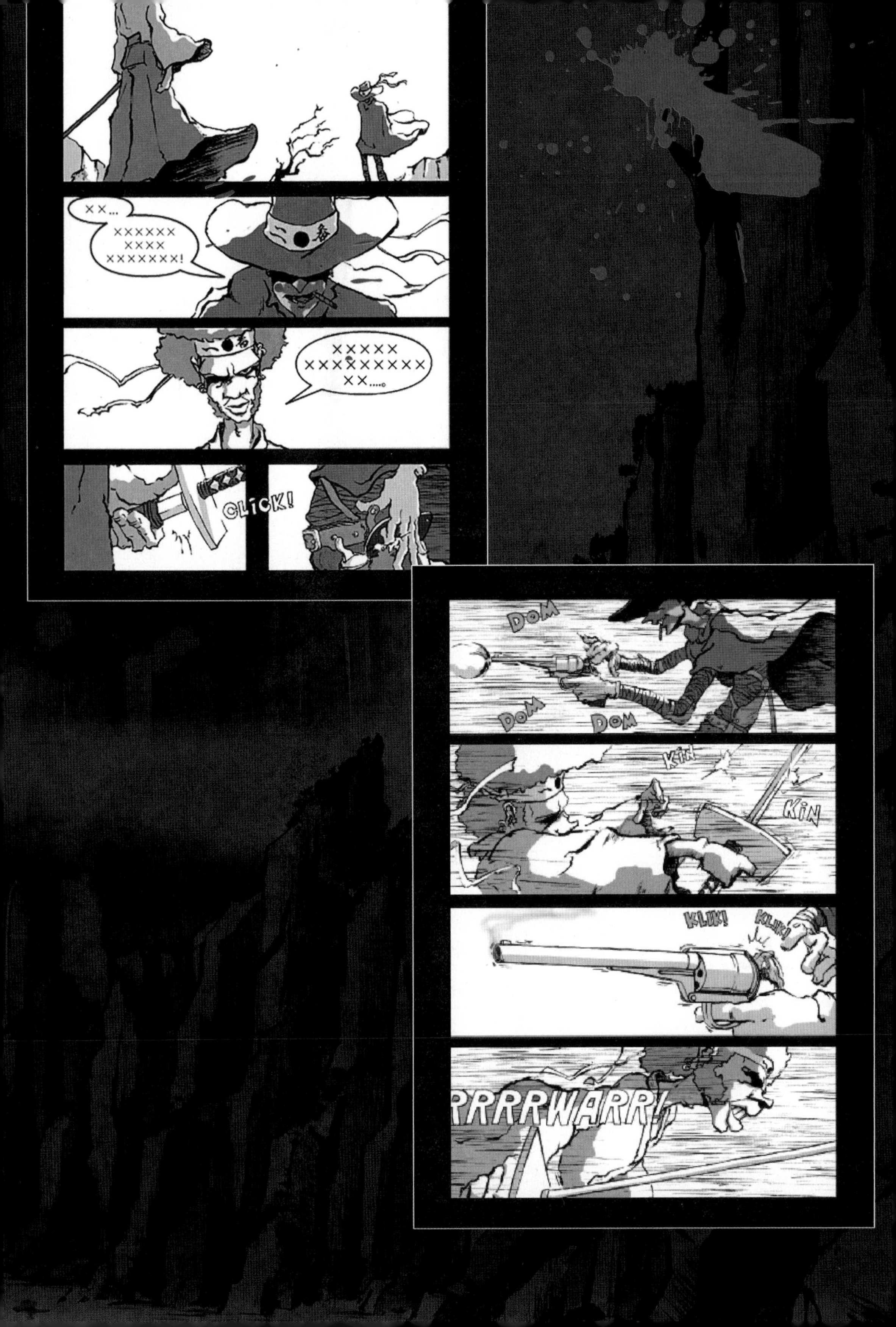

××...
×××××× ×××× ×××××××!
××××× ×××××××××× ××....
CLICK!
DOM
DOM
DOM
KIN
KIN
KLIK!
KLIK!
RRRRWARR!

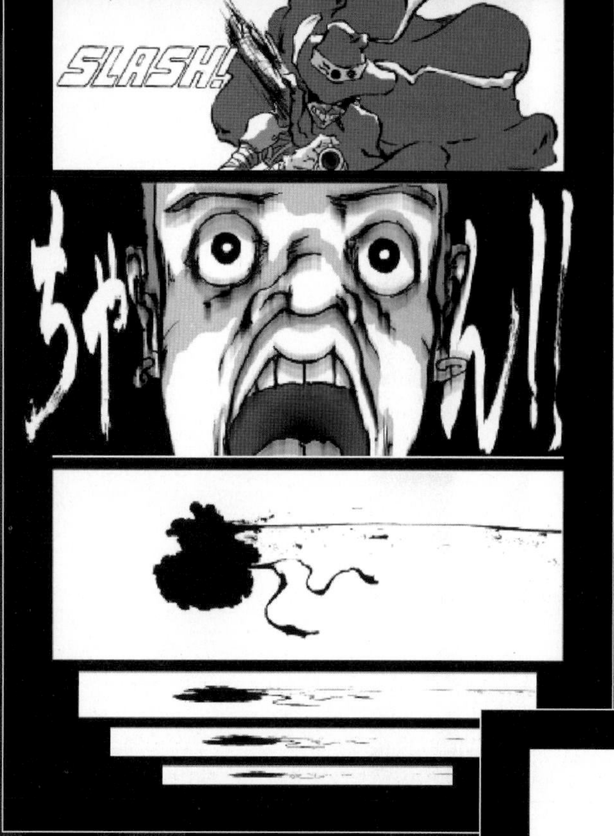
SLASH!
ちゃん!!

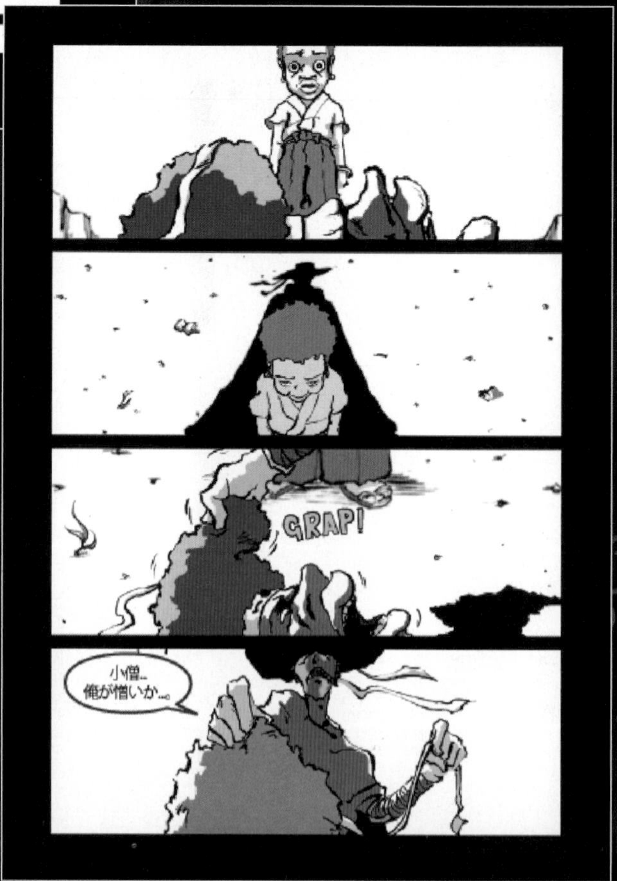
GRAP!
小僧…
俺が憎いか…。

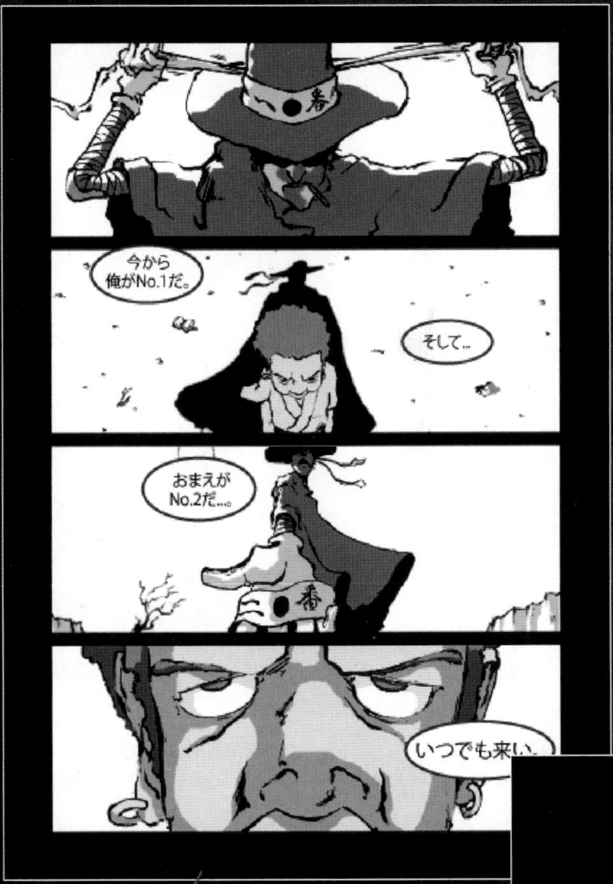
今から
俺がNo.1だ。
そして…
おまえが
No.2だ…。
いつでも来い

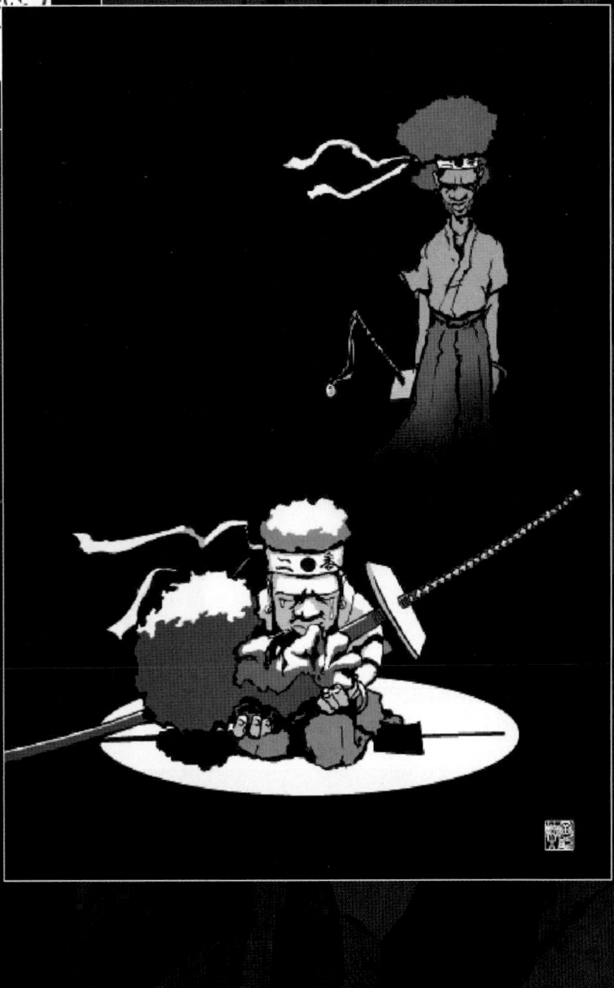

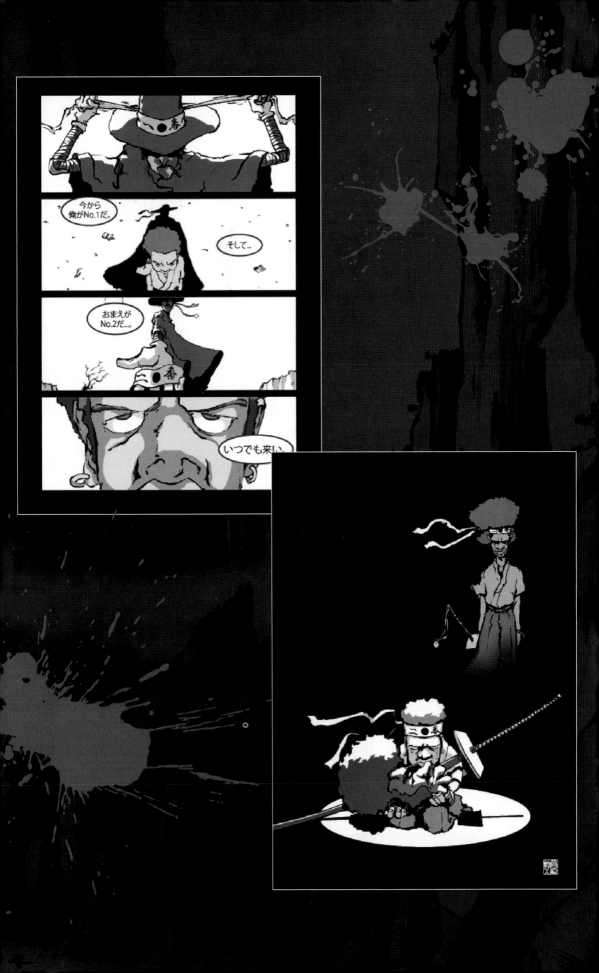

MORE FROM OUR NEW MANGA IMPRINT!

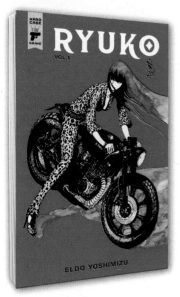

HARD CASE CRIME
RYUKO
VOL.1
ELDO YOSHIMIZU

RYUKO VOL 1

HARD CASE CRIME
RYUKO
VOL.2
ELDO YOSHIMIZU

RYUKO VOL 2

HARD CASE CRIME
GAMMA DRACONIS
Benoist Simmat
Eldo Yoshimizu
"Fast-moving and action-packed... makes for a compelling read."
BARNES & NOBLE SCI-FI BLOG (ON RYUKO)

GAMMA DRACONIS

ORIGINAL STORY: Ubisoft
SCRIPT: Takashi YANO
ART: Kenji OIWA
ASSASSIN'S CREED AWAKENING
VOLUME ONE

ASSASSIN'S CREED: AWAKENING VOL 1

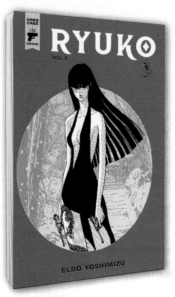

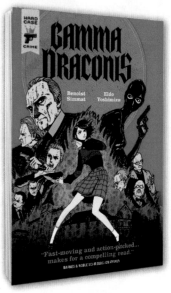

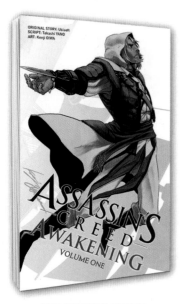

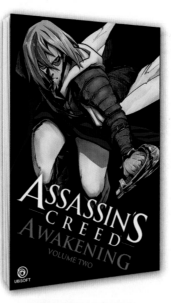

ASSASSIN'S CREED AWAKENING
VOLUME TWO
UBISOFT

ASSASSIN'S CREED: AWAKENING VOL 2

HEN KAI PAN
ELDO YOSHIMIZU

HEN KAI PAN

TITAN MANGA

ALSO AVAILABLE DIGITALLY

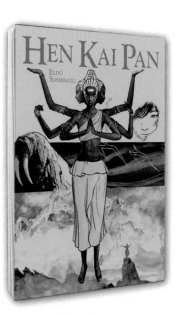

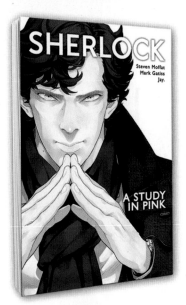

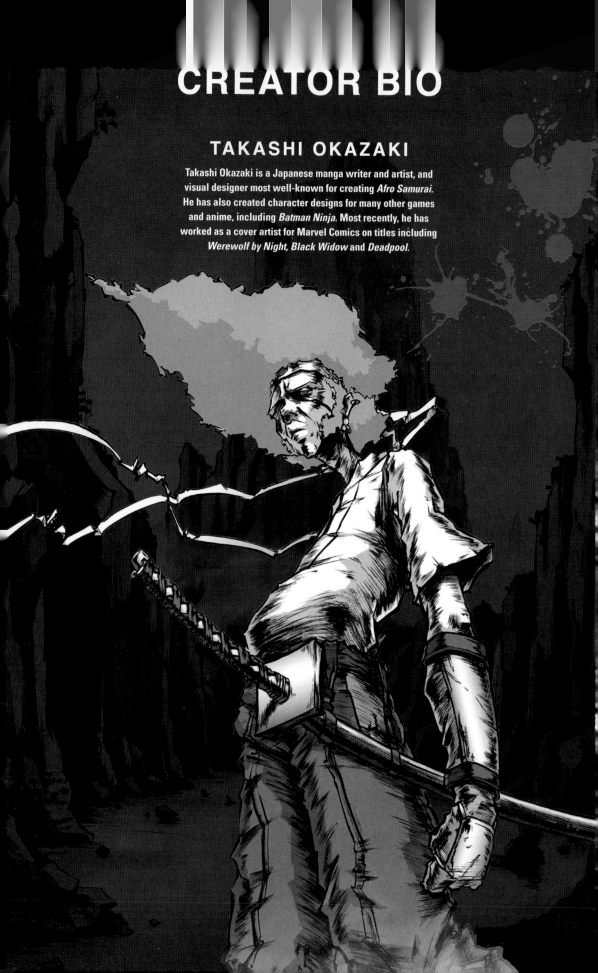

CREATOR BIO

TAKASHI OKAZAKI

Takashi Okazaki is a Japanese manga writer and artist, and visual designer most well-known for creating *Afro Samurai*. He has also created character designs for many other games and anime, including *Batman Ninja*. Most recently, he has worked as a cover artist for Marvel Comics on titles including *Werewolf by Night*, *Black Widow* and *Deadpool*.